ENERGY
TRANSITIONS IN
THE MIDDLE EAST

Middle East Institute Policy Series

The MEI Policy Series aims to inform policy debates on the most pressing issues that will shape the future of the Middle East. The series publishes manuscripts that provide cutting-edge analysis and recommendations to policymakers in the Middle East and to international actors as they work toward solutions to some of the most searing problems facing the region.

Seeking to contribute to policy debates that will influence the Middle East in the future, the MEI Policy Series promotes innovative and incisive work that focuses on issues that cut across the various countries of the region and span the areas of politics, culture, economics, society, the state, climate, health, gender and any other issue that meets the above policy impact criteria.

ENERGY TRANSITIONS IN THE MIDDLE EAST

Challenges and Opportunities

Edited by Karen Young and Katherine Wolff

I.B. TAURIS

LONDON • NEW YORK • OXFORD • NEW DELHI • SYDNEY

I.B. TAURIS
Bloomsbury Publishing Plc
50 Bedford Square, London, WC1B 3DP, UK
1385 Broadway, New York, NY 10018, USA

BLOOMSBURY, I.B. TAURIS and the I.B. Tauris logo are trademarks of
Bloomsbury Publishing Plc

First published in Great Britain 2024

Series design by Charlotte Daniels
Cover image © Getty Images

A catalogue record for this book is available from the British Library.

A catalog record for this book is available from the Library of Congress.

ISBN: HB: 978-0-7556-5038-5
        PB: 978-0-7556-5037-8
        ePDF: 978-0-7556-5039-2
        eBook: 978-0-7556-5040-8

Typeset by RefineCatch Limited, Bungay, Suffolk
Printed and bound in Great Britain

To find out more about our authors and books visit www.bloomsbury.com
and sign up for our newsletters.

CONTENTS

List of figures viii

List of tables ix

Introduction 1
   *Karen E. Young, Senior Research Scholar at the
   Columbia University Center on Global Energy Policy*

**PART ONE FINANCING, REGULATION,
AND ECONOMIC DEVELOPMENT FOR
THE ENERGY TRANSITION** 5

1 A look back at 2020: GCC COVID-19 response,
    reforms, energy transition concerns and micro-
    competitiveness 7
    *Yesar Al-Maleki, Gulf Analyst at Middle East
    Economic Survey (MEES)*

2 The future of Gulf NOC–IOC partnerships 65
    *Colby Connelly, Senior Research Analyst at Energy
    Intelligence*

3 Mechanisms to finance climate investments in the
    Middle East and North Africa 87
    *Lama Kiyasseh, Risk Management Officer at the
    Multilateral Investment Guarantee Agency*

4 Political priorities and economic realities: Financing
    the renewable energy transition in Saudi Arabia and
    Oman 125
    *Piotr G. S. Schulkes, Former Non-Resident Scholar
    at the Middle East Institute*

5 The political dimensions of energy transition in MENA: A changing landscape at the national, regional and global levels 147
Younes Abouyoub, Senior Research Fellow in the Department of Political Science at the University of New England

PART TWO NEW ENERGY TECHNOLOGIES AND THEIR DEVELOPMENT IN THE MIDDLE EAST 163

6 The next big thing in MENA power – grids and energy storage 165
Jessica Obeid, Founding Partner at New Energy Consult

7 Green hydrogen production in North Africa: Challenges and opportunities 183
Michaël Tanchum, Professor at Universidad de Navarra

PART THREE CASE STUDIES IN THE ENERGY TRANSITION 207

8 Qatar's LNG industry in the age of hydrocarbon markets: Instability and energy transition 209
Nikolay Kozhanov, Research Associate Professor at Qatar University

9 Renewable energy diplomacy: The Gulf States in the Caucasus and Central Asia 237
Li-Chen Sim, Assistant Professor at Khalifa University

Conclusion 263
    *Karen E. Young, Senior Research Scholar at the
    Columbia University Center on Global Energy Policy*

Notes 269
Index 303

FIGURES

1.1	Hydrocarbon revenues share of GDP	11
1.2	Hydrocarbon revenues contribution to state revenues	12
1.3	Hydrocarbons share of total exports	12
1.4	Government spending share of GDP	13
1.5	GCC fiscal oil breakeven prices (2005–2020)	14
1.6	GCC average spending vs Brent oil price (2005–2020)	16
1.7	World oil demand forecasts in million bpd by OPEC, IEA, and BP	18
1.8	GCC current, capital and total spending growth as share of GDP (2019–2020)	23
1.9	GCC gross official reserves	23
1.10	GCC non-oil GDP projections and growth (2000–2021)	29
1.11	GCC primary bonds and Sukuk issuance	30
1.12	GCC total government gross debt as percentage of GDP (2016–2021)	30
1.13	Government revenues as percentage of GDP (2011–2020)	33
1.14	UAE trade balance with GCC neighbours (2000–2020)	38
3.1	Chapter summary	89
3.2	Climate change is a threat multiplier in the MENA region	101
3.3	Blended finance	108
3.4	Recipient countries in the Middle East and North Africa	111
3.5	Commodity prices	112
3.6	Debt-for-nature swap schematic	118
8.1	The structure of Qatar's exports, 2022	212
8.2	Natural gas production and domestic consumprion in Qatar, 2008–2018	213
8.3	Qatar's export revenues, 2013–2021	221
8.4	LNG exports by Qatar, Australia, and the USA to Asia in 2015–2020	221

TABLES

1.1	Economic and hydrocarbon indicators (2020)	9
1.2	GCC non-oil GDP actual and projected growth rates by the IMF	28
2.1	QatarEnergy's legacy LNG partners	71
3.1	MENA exporter hydrocarbon dependence	91
3.2	Sudair Solar PV plant IPP credit facility	97
3.3	Selected geen and sustainability sukuk issuances as of end 2022	98
3.4	Selected renewables projects in MENA using project finance: 2018–2022	103
3.5	Climate funds supporting the MENA region: 2003–2022	109
3.6	Clean Technology Fund interventions in MENA	110
3.7	MENA country debt profiles	114
8.1	Real GDP growth of GCC member countries 2012–2022	220
9.1	Gulf RE greenfield projects in South Caucasus and Central Asia	241
9.2	Real GDP growth in MENA: oil exporters versus oil importers	250

INTRODUCTION

Karen E. Young

The world's largest hydrocarbon producers have made ambitious announcements of net-zero emissions targets, as pressure increases to build more international consensus on climate change action. For oil and gas producers in the Middle East, they must make the case that their business is sound, necessary for stable global economic growth, and also a reliable source of energy that may not be 100 percent clean, but is cleaner and greener than other global oil products. Moreover, the Russian invasion of Ukraine in the spring of 2022 and subsequent moves to reduce consumption of Russian energy products delivered a tectonic shock to energy markets that creates a new operating environment for Gulf producers.

For example, the Gulf states, especially Saudi Arabia and the United Arab Emirates (UAE), will focus on their ability to use existing technologies in carbon capture and storage to better inform and assist in an energy transition both in the Middle East and North Africa (MENA) as well as globally. Saudi Arabia and the UAE can also compartmentalize their green economy efforts in ways that make the business case for their own energy transition within national oil companies, to be the owners and powerbrokers of a number of clean and cleaner energy products – from natural gas, to solar power, to blue and green hydrogen production. It is possible to leverage experience in the oil and gas sector into an array of energy products, and the Gulf states are especially well-placed to do so. These states may also model how to ramp up electrification in their economies, with massive solar projects and targets for domestic power production that go from about 1 percent of domestic electricity production from renewables to 50 percent in just a decade. There is no other experiment like it in the world to invest in renewable power production at this pace and scale.

There is a competition for investment within all energy products, carbon-intensive and non-carbon, and this competition is heightened in the Gulf by a drive for investment into their economies at large, as part of a diversification strategy. A commitment to a net-zero emissions target can include offsets in green initiatives (like tree planting to carbon capture) and certain zones or clean energy projects that are showcases of new technology, as the Saudi city NEOM aspires to be. And exports of hydrocarbons do not count as domestic emissions. So, the calculation of a net-zero target has some flexibility.

A net-zero target has a business case behind it. It brands a state hydrocarbon producer in a class of the solution-finders, rather than the obstructionists, even as hydrocarbon production continues ahead. And there are important distinctions in the way oil and gas is produced that gives merit to the investment case for "designer" or "preferred" lower emissions hydrocarbons in the UAE and Saudi Arabia.

But ultimately, the MENA region will need what it always needs: government capacity to reliably deliver public goods at fair prices, namely electricity and preferably electricity produced from low carbon sources. And countries across the Middle East will need access to capital, either through loans, investment partners, or concessional financing, to make that a reality. They will also need to work on the pricing side, to reduce subsidies in both oil and gas exporters and importers, and to gain the trust of citizens that government revenues and spending are in their best interests.

This edited volume is the result of a collaboration among scholars and practitioners from the Middle East Institute's Program on Economics and Energy. Formed in mid-2021, the Program has sought to gather experts on the political economy of the Middle East and North Africa with experts on economic development, sustainable finance, and diversification, as well as industry experts from the hydrocarbon sector and new energy solutions. Our early efforts suggest that the future of both development and energy in the region will be a complex negotiation on the role of state in the economy, with a particular role for national oil companies, sovereign wealth funds, and the state leadership behind them. These chapters also suggest that innovation in new energy, whether in solar or green hydrogen production, will have a healthy chance of incubation in the Gulf and wider Middle East and North Africa. Our cases lean heavily on the Gulf states, as sites of capital accumulation and energy resource development – as well as a place where the active negotiation of state and market is taking shape. We also see a widening divergence within the region in terms of access to capital, and that will have an important mark on the development opportunities ahead. These chapter analyses are meant to showcase some of the research focus of the program and to point to our work ahead. These topics and cases are not exhaustive, but rather an invitation for further work and collaboration to come. We invite our readers to join us in seeking to understand the tremendous challenge ahead for traditional hydrocarbon producers, and the shared challenge of innovation and access to clean energy for our future.

PART ONE

FINANCING, REGULATION, AND ECONOMIC DEVELOPMENT FOR THE ENERGY TRANSITION

1 A LOOK BACK AT 2020: GCC COVID-19 RESPONSE, REFORMS, ENERGY TRANSITION CONCERNS AND MICRO-COMPETITIVENESS

Yesar Al-Maleki

Introduction

The consensus is that the six Gulf Cooperation Council (GCC) economies of Kuwait, Saudi Arabia, Bahrain, Qatar, the United Arab Emirates (UAE), and Oman are rentier par excellence. Gifted with around 32 percent and 21 percent of the world's proven oil and natural gas reserves (BP Statistical Review of World Energy 2021; OPEC Annual Statistical Bulletin 2021), respectively, they sit at the center of global energy trade as the source of around 23 percent of global oil production – with Saudi Arabia alone accounting for 13 percent of oil and 10 percent of gas. Dependent on their hydrocarbon endowments, the states accrue rent from exporting these resources while honoring a historic social contract through generous welfare and lavish public sector spending. As a group, 56 percent of total GCC fiscal revenues come from hydrocarbon exports and they constitute a 17 percent share of their combined $1.4 trillion GDP.

Nevertheless, the countries are intrinsically different from one another in terms of populations, GDP, oil and gas resources, their individual revenues, and impact on public spending (Table 1.1). The impact of these revenues, therefore, differs per country. But what is common is that the externality of the rent carries inherent risk from global macroeconomic shocks that often reflect negatively on domestic economic growth given the dominance of the role of the state. Government spending contributes 39 percent of the GCC's overall GDP.

Historically, pressure for economic diversification emerged during oil price downturns, but interest dissipated as prices surged back upwards. Over the years, governments have been able to shield their populations from the impacts of fiscal volatility largely by tapping their monetary reserves and sovereign debt markets. With the advantages of having relatively smaller population sizes compared to rentier peers in the region and maintaining considerable foreign currency reserves and investments, the state had always oriented its efforts on sustaining the political status quo and the citizenry's living standards as its first priorities.

However resilient the rentier model is, it is under an unprecedented long-term threat. GCC states are highly vulnerable to declining global oil demand that is projected to become acute by the latter half of this century due to technological breakthroughs in renewable energy, gains in energy efficiency, and a unanimous agreement on climate change mitigation. These factors are accelerating the decarbonization of the global energy sector under what has been called the 'energy transition.' With the latter's eventual success leading to possibly a consequential decline in fossil fuel revenues, the GCC appears more committed today than ever to implementing transformational reforms, particularly by increasing non-oil fiscal income, liberalizing labor markets, and pivoting towards eventual taxation as the accommodating socioeconomic circumstances, mainly public uptake, emerge in the future. Taxation is often considered to be the distinctive feature of productive states that rentier ones lack.

The twin challenges of COVID-19 and oil price shock of 2020 have 'brought forward' the fiscal policy challenges for ensuring intergenerational equity in the GCC according to the International Monetary Fund (IMF) (IMF Staff 2021). However, GCC policymakers are praised for their quick utilization of available fiscal tools to manage the immediate repercussions of these shocks. In total, GCC states pledged $190 billion to relieve their non-oil sectors. Furthermore, the pandemic and ensuing months have provided some space for GCC governments to implement

Table 1.1 *Economic and hydrocarbon indicators (2020)*

Indicator	Kuwait*	Saudi Arabia	Bahrain	Qatar*	UAE*	Oman*	GCC
Population (mn)	4.3	35.0	1.7	2.9	9.9	5.1	58.9
GDP ($ bn)	106	700	35	144	359	74	1,418
Government spending (% of GDP)	66	41	29	35	28	45	39
Proven oil reserves (bn bbl)	102	262	0.125	25	107	5	501
Proven oil reserves (% of world)	6.6	16.9	0.008	1.6	6.9	0.35	32.4
Oil production (1,000 bpd)†	2,438	9,213	195	603	2,779	762	15,990
Oil production (% of world)	3.5	13.3	0.3	0.9	4.0	1.1	23.1
Proven gas reserves (tr ft^3)	60	213	2.3	871	210	23.5	1,379
Proven gas reserves (% of world)	0.9	3.2	0.03	13	3.2	0.35	20.7
Gas production (bn ft^3/d)	1.44	10.8	1.6	16.53	5.35	3.6	39.3
Gas production (% of world)	0.4	2.9	0.4	4.5	1.4	0.9	10.5
Hydrocarbon revenues ($ bn)	29	110	3.2	37	42	15	236
Non-hydrocarbon revenues ($ bn)	5.7	98.3	2.3	10.4	59	7	183

All monetary values are in nominal U.S. dollars, approximated to a full figure or a single decimal point where necessary.

* Provisional official fiscal data.

† Crude oil production only, does not include other liquids. mn = million, bn = billion, tr = trillion, bbl = barrels, bpd = barrels per day, ft^3 = cubic feet, ft^3/d = cubic feet per day. Sources: International Monetary Fund, Central Banks of Bahrain, Qatar, and Oman, Kuwaiti Ministry of Finance, UAE Federal Competitiveness and Statistics Centre, *OPEC Annual Statistical Bulletin 2021. BP Statistical Review of World Energy 2021.*

what could be considered first steps toward taxation while solidifying labor market reforms, amending immigration systems, and reducing hurdles to foreign investment. Meanwhile, the pragmatic approach toward climate change politics taken by GCC leaders Saudi Arabia and the UAE has put them in a position to promote the case for a circular carbon economy (CCE), whereby their core competitive edge in the hydrocarbon industry could be utilized for a low-emission energy transition based on technologies such as carbon capture, utilization, and storage (CCUS) and hydrogen. These efforts may help GCC countries, in addition to other oil producers, in delaying the impacts of hydrocarbon revenue losses in the years to come as they accelerate economic diversification efforts. Nevertheless, although the six nations share almost equivalent advantages and follow a common reform template, there are indications of rising micro-competition in the bloc that could adversely affect economic integration and amplify existing political tensions.

The first section of this chapter empirically showcases the pro-cyclical nature of fiscal spending in the GCC over the past decade. The policy choices and fiscal responses of GCC governments to COVID-19 are shown in the second section, with a focus on debt and a comparison of non-oil GDP forecasts. The third section examines the energy transition, projections for peak oil demand, and opportunities stemming from the CCE and its applications. Finally, the chapter considers reform opportunities that the pandemic offered, with a focus on micro-competitiveness between GCC states. The periodic scope is heavily focused on 2020, with data acquisition and analysis mainly conducted two years after to highlight immediate impacts. That said, later and prior events are also considered to showcase their association and consequences where necessary.

Hydrocarbon dependence in the GCC

The producers of natural resources that are reliant on external rents are hostage to the volatility of commodity prices determined by markets and macroeconomic dynamics lying beyond their borders and control. This leaves them vulnerable to global economic shocks, and this volatility in turn has traditionally led to pro-cyclical spending by governments. When oil prices are high, they turn into windfalls that translate into a higher proportion of government income. In turn, public spending increases in a manner that is typically inefficient (International Energy Agency 2018). In times of lower oil prices, lower rents force constrained spending, which leads to austerity. The onset of the COVID-19 pandemic and the ensuing oil price collapse of 2020 saw Brent oil fall to a yearly average of around $42 per barrel, resulting in a combined $100 billion loss in direct oil and gas revenues compared to 2019 for GCC governments.[1] As a result, hydrocarbon revenue contribution to GDP declined by 4 percent, as shown in the Annex. Kuwait and Bahrain saw the highest collapse in revenues at around 42 percent, followed by Saudi Arabia at 31 percent and 28 percent for Oman. Qatar and the UAE each suffered a 22 percent decrease. In Saudi Arabia, the fall was the highest in five years since the 51 percent collapse of revenues in 2015 with the onset of the previous oil price downturn.

When taken as a bloc, the decade preceding the 2020 crisis shows limited improvement at best in GCC hydrocarbon reliance. By the end of 2019, the group on average was still largely dependent fiscally at 70 percent, although this still represents a decline of 9 percent compared to 2008.[2] Moreover, the share of GDP from oil revenues declined from 32 percent in 2008 to 20 percent in 2019 (Figures 1.1 and 1.2). At the

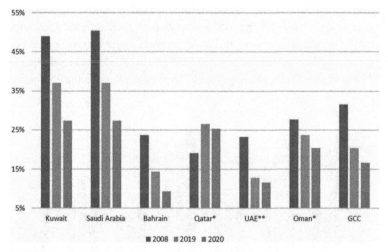

FIGURE 1.1 Hydrocarbon revenues share of GDP (%).
*Includes both oil and gas revenues and income from energy investments abroad for Qatar.
**2020 data are preliminary.
Sources: World Bank, Kuwait Ministry of Finance, Saudi General Authority for Statistics, Central Bank of Bahrain, Qatar Central Bank, UAE Federal Competitiveness and Statistics Centre, Central Bank of Oman.

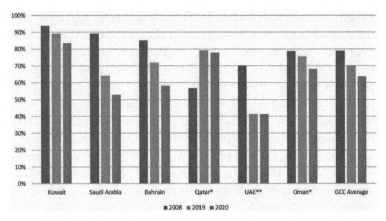

FIGURE 1.2 Hydrocarbon revenues contribution to state revenues (%).
*Includes both oil and gas revenues and income from energy investments abroad for Qatar.
**2020 data are preliminary.
Sources: Kuwait Ministry of Finance, Saudi General Authority for Statistics, Central Bank of Bahrain, Qatar Central Bank, UAE Federal Competitiveness and Statistics Centre, Central Bank of Oman.

country level, it could be assumed that members adopting and implementing income and economic diversification policies – such as Saudi Arabia, the UAE, and Bahrain – show the most progress. Qatar stands as the lone exception with both contribution to GDP and fiscal revenues increasing by 7 percent and 22 percent, respectively. This could be tied to the dominance

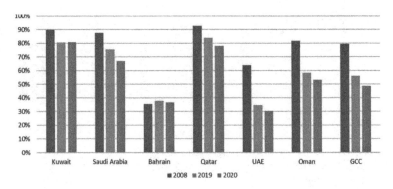

FIGURE 1.3 Hydrocarbons share of total exports (%).
*Estimates.
Sources: United Nations Conference on Trade and Development, UN Comtrade Database, accessed April 2022.

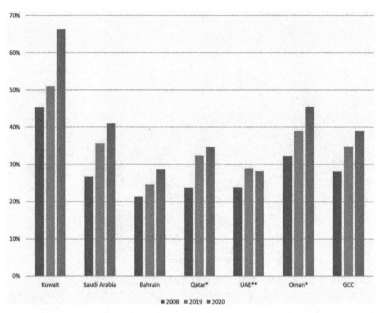

FIGURE 1.4 Government spending share of GDP (%).
*Includes both oil and gas revenues and income from energy investments abroad for Qatar.
**2020 data are preliminary.
Sources: Kuwait Ministry of Finance, Saudi General Authority for Statistics, Central Bank of Bahrain, Qatar Central Bank, UAE Federal Competitiveness and Statistics Centre, Central Bank of Oman.

of liquefied natural gas (LNG) exports and the expansion of its export capacity during these years in face of increasing global demand. Hydrocarbons still constitute a significant portion of exports (Figure 1.3) with minimal penetration of other products. Meanwhile, government spending is still dominant within the economy, even increasing between 2008 and 2019 as share of GDP (Figure 1.4). Although the contribution of oil revenues to GDP shrank by 13 percent in Kuwait, the government's reliance on oil income only improved by a modest 5 percent from 2008 to 2019 (Figure 1.2). Kuwait remains the GCC's most oil-reliant country at 89 percent and 84 percent of fiscal revenues in 2019 and 2020, respectively. On the other hand, Oman only decreased the share of oil and gas income in total revenues by 3 percent and 4 percent of GDP.

Comparing these indicators over a decade misses global developments, policy reactions, and their impact on oil and gas prices. Given the

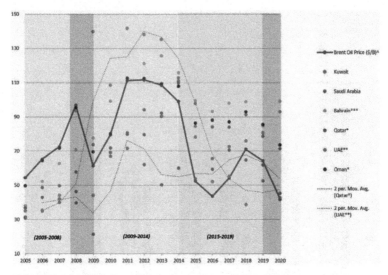

FIGURE 1.5 GCC fiscal oil breakeven prices (2005–2020).
*Includes both oil and gas revenues and income from energy investments abroad for Qatar.
**2020 data are preliminary.
Sources: Kuwait Ministry of Finance, Saudi General Authority for Statistics, Central Bank of Bahrain, Qatar Central Bank, UAE Federal Competitiveness and Statistics Centre, Central Bank of Oman.

dominance of government spending and high oil income, fiscal oil breakeven prices are usually applied as an indicator to comprehend the effect of externalities on government spending.[3] From 2005 (before oil consumption fell due to the 2009 global financial crisis), fiscal breakeven prices had been rising steadily (Figure 1.5), averaging $50.6 per barrel but kept below Brent by a hefty $21.6 margin. In response to the crisis, the Organization of Petroleum Exporting Countries (OPEC) sought to stabilize prices by cutting production, with Saudi Arabia alone reducing its output from 10 million barrels per day (bpd) to 8 million bpd (Mouawad 2009). From 2009 to 2014, fiscal breakeven prices moved upward erratically as oil prices soared. While Brent averaged $95.3 per barrel over this period, the average GCC fiscal breakeven price rose to $93.1 per barrel, eroding the pre-crisis buffer to $2.2 per barrel. Average yearly government spending during this period rose to around $83 billion with a compound annual growth rate of 11 percent for the entire group, which nevertheless was lower than the 24 percent rate for 2005–2008. Saudi Arabia and Kuwait were able to increase yearly spending by a rate of 14 percent each while maintaining five-year average fiscal breakeven prices below Brent. Spending in Qatar and Oman grew by 15 percent. For Qatar, the 2009–2014 buffer below Brent grew to a massive $37.6 per barrel. Oman's average breakeven price was $3.4 per barrel over Brent. Nevertheless, the Sultanate only suffered small budgetary deficits that averaged $900 million. Hence, this period before the 2014 oil price downturn was marked by either large surpluses or small deficits, with some exceptions.

Bahrain and the UAE present special cases. Economic growth in the region was already increasing steadily, from a combined GDP of $682 billion in 2005 to $1.65 trillion in 2014; increased spending by large exporters may have induced a similar trend in a small producer such as Bahrain, where oil revenues are relatively slight but still contribute significantly to state revenues. Bahrain received more than $36 billion in oil revenues from 2009 to 2014. The last time Bahrain had a balanced budget was in 2008. Adding to the complexity, the country is also habitually reliant on economic aid, mainly from Saudi Arabia and other GCC states (Embassy Staff 2011) with the assistance geared to ensuring political stability.[4]

The UAE – and particularly the economy of Dubai – has often been singled out as a model for non-hydrocarbon growth, given its reliance on services, tourism, trade, and logistics, which have prompted the small city-state to become a financial hub in the region. However, integration with global markets meant that the advent of the 2009 financial crisis sent a shockwave that resulted in a debt crisis. This necessitated a $20 billion rescue package, shouldered by the oil-wealthy sister emirate of Abu Dhabi (Barbuscia, Azhar, and Barbaglia 2020), inclusive of $10 billion in bonds issued by Dubai's government to the UAE Central Bank.[5] The impact of this intervention, in addition to that of oil price instability between 2008 and mid-2009, is clearly seen on the UAE's federal spending. In 2008, spending rose by $31.6 billion, followed by another $31.3 billion the next year. Although it dipped by $12.73 billion in 2010, spending climbed over the next five years, though moderately in comparison to other GCC members (see Annex). Government spending as a share of GDP decreased from 42 percent in 2009 to 35 percent and 30 percent in 2012 and 2014, respectively. Nevertheless, fiscal breakeven prices were $34.22 per barrel above Brent. At $129.48 per barrel, fiscal breakeven prices for the UAE were even higher than Saudi Arabia's $84.07 per barrel.

The onset of the oil price collapse of 2014 saw GCC governments incur large deficits and run high fiscal breakeven oil prices. Average spending was constrained in the aftermath from $101.53 billion to $88.5

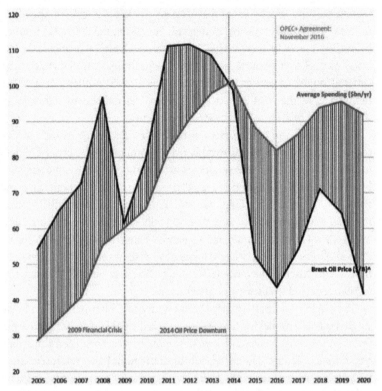

FIGURE 1.6 GCC average spending versus Brent oil price (2005–2020). *Sources:* Kuwait Ministry of Finance, Saudi General Authority for Statistics, Central Bank of Bahrain, Qatar Central Bank, UAE Federal Competitiveness and Statistics Centre, Central Bank of Oman.

billion by 2015, only to rebound above $90 billion in 2018 after the OPEC+ agreement was signed in late 2016 (OPEC Press Office n.d.). Charting average spending by all GCC states against Brent clearly shows a correlation; more importantly, however, an inability to curb expenses after low oil price events is clearly demonstrated (Figure 1.6).

With oil prices having rebounded in late-2021 and exceeding $100 per barrel in early 2022 by a large margin, even Oman and Bahrain are on track to record their first fiscal surpluses since 2008 (Magdy, Martin, and Abu Omar 2022). The IMF expects oil producers in the Middle East and Central Asia region to earn 'more than $1–1.4 trillion' by 2026 (Khan 2022), while Bloomberg sees $500 billion entering GCC coffers in 2022 alone (Bloomberg 2022). The risk for governments is to abandon fiscal discipline measures employed during the pandemic as these revenues enter their coffers. However, positive indications by mid-2022 show that this is not happening. Gulf states are not expected to reduce their dependence overnight as economic diversification is long and costly; hence, they are becoming more sophisticated and measured in their spending strategy. Saudi Arabia wants to rebuild reserves (Abu Omar and Martin 2022) while boosting the non-oil sector (el Wardany 2022). Fiscal discipline and flexibility, if successful, may help GCC states beat the historical trend of limited ability to constrain spending after periods of windfall.

Energy transition and the GCC

A long transition to peak demand

Historically, the oil market has been dominated by concerns for supply adequacy and security by both consumers and producers. For the former, the threat came from the need to maintain economic growth (Murphy and Hall 2011), while the latter sought to preserve a higher value for oil and to sustain rents through rationing production. As a result, lower-cost producers, such as those in the GCC, followed a strategy of preserving oil resources by viewing them as a store of value and expecting their price to be relatively higher in the future. Politically, this thinking contributed to nationalistic oil tendencies in GCC and Arab oil-producing states where oil reserves and their returns were understood to be an inter-generational gift that should be protected for years to come.[6] Concern over scarcity, however, was replaced with prospects of oil abundance, beginning in 2015. Through the Paris Agreement, countries pledged to reduce their greenhouse gas (GHGs) emissions and reliance on fossil fuels as part of their long-term response to climate change (UNFCCC 2015). Therefore, attention turned to the demand side of the market. Technology advances in renewable energy and its role in replacing fossil fuels in power generation, rising electric mobility, and gains in energy efficiency were aided by policy measures intended to reduce hydrocarbon reliance more quickly.

Climate security concerns have led to changing social preferences toward crude oil and natural gas consumption as well. The emerging consensus is that oil demand will continue to grow, reaching a plateau consumption level before slowing down and reducing. This is the opposite

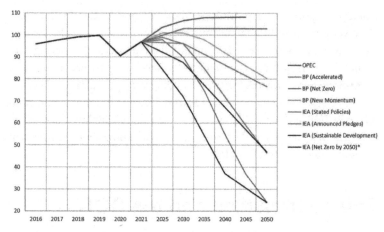

FIGURE 1.7 World oil demand forecasts in million bpd by OPEC, IEA, and BP. 2019–2020 historical data based on 2021 OPEC Annual Statistical Bulletin. 2021 Figures from May 2022 OPEC Monthly Oil Market Report.
*2030 and 2050 inferred from report text and 2040 converted from EJ (exajoules) consumption figures to mn b/d.
Sources: 2021 OPEC Annual Statistical Bulletin and World Energy Outlook 2045, 2021 IEA World Oil Outlook, IEA Net Zero by 2050, 2022 BP Energy Outlook.

of peak supply that Dale and Fattouh call a 'paradigm shift' in the oil market (Fattouh and Dale 2018). Projections for long-term oil demand prior to the Ukraine conflict varied.[7] On the high end, OPEC expected demand to peak at around 108 million bpd between 2040 and 2045, while BP's new momentum and accelerated scenarios predict a demand peak as early as 2025 at 101 million bpd and 99 million bpd, respectively (Figure 1.7). However, the IEA's controversial Net Zero by 2050 scenario sees demand peaking at 72 million bpd in 2030 to be followed by a gradual decline to 24 million bpd by 2050 – around 80 million bpd below OPEC's expectations. The report, published in 2021, was not well received by oil producers, with Saudi Energy Minister Prince Abdulaziz bin Salman Al Saud calling it a 'La La Land' fantasy (Smith 2021).

Naturally, GCC states are concerned by calls to divest from oil and gas, given their dependence on hydrocarbon revenues to cover their social expenses and development goals. Nevertheless, these projections carry many unknowns, including economic growth prospects, commercialization of technologies, and the penetration of renewable energy (Fattouh and Dale 2018), in addition to more recent concerns pertaining lowering global oil and gas supply capacities (IEA Staff 2022b). Demand growth will be affected by post-COVID recovery, the extent of an expected recession (Franklin 2022), and the policy of central banks on interest rates and inflation (Bouvet, Schroeder, and Garvey 2022). These factors could either delay peak demand, if economic recovery takes longer, or accelerate it, if pressures prove interim over the next two years while energy transition policies continue to attract interest and finances.

The politics of the energy transition have been divisive. GCC oil exporters are seen as sitting on a vanishing sunset commodity in the West, which understandably frustrates them despite their collaborative position on climate change (Mansouri and Al-Sarihi 2021). This thinking ignores the fact that even if oil and gas demand was to eventually decrease in the future, there would still be significant volumes consumed, which will require continued investment and maintenance of capacity by oil and gas exporters. The COVID-19 crisis in 2020 precipitated a huge, 20 million bpd reduction of oil demand – falling from a level of 100 million bpd in the fourth quarter of 2019 to 83 million bpd in the second quarter of 2020 (IMF Staff 2021). While this abrupt slump shares similarities with the common misconception that oil demand will see a sharp decline under the energy transition, a recurrence of such an unpredictable event is unlikely. Furthermore, as mentioned previously, demand at the peak level is both sizeable and expected to stay for a long period of time.

Nevertheless, the conflict in Ukraine may strengthen Europe's attempts to reduce fossil fuel consumption even sooner (IEA Staff 2022a). In May 2022, the European Commission announced the $225 billion REPowerEU strategy, which aims at reducing dependence on Russian fossil fuels while fast-tracking the green transition (EU Staff 2022b). Europe's energy vulnerability became acutely visible during the Ukraine conflict, as the continent relies on Moscow for 45 percent of its overall gas imports and more than 29 percent of its oil. Germany and the United Kingdom approached Qatar for LNG imports (Ingram 2022d), and a research briefing prepared for the UK's House of Commons identified Saudi Arabia and the UAE as the countries 'best able' to replace Russian oil, going on to recommend that British diplomacy focus on these two countries (Stewart, Curtis, and Loft 2022). On the same day that the REPowerEU plan was announced, the European Union entered a strategic partnership with the GCC (EU Staff 2022a) that aims to increase reliance on the bloc as an energy replacement source. While these developments may signal a change of attitude toward the GCC and its promotion of a low-carbon energy transition, it also carries the opportunity for the bloc to further develop clean hydrocarbon technologies and projects helping further delay peak oil demand.

The circular carbon economy

At the heart of the low-emission energy transition being promoted by Saudi Arabia is the circular carbon economy (CCE), which is an approach based on the four Rs: Reduce, Reuse, Recycle, and Remove (Shehri et al. 2023). This entails the reduction of the amount of GHG emissions to be produced in the first place by employing energy-efficiency measures and deploying non-bio-renewable and nuclear energy technologies through fuel switching. In addition, the approach involves reusing captured carbon in applications such as building materials, polymers, and injecting carbon dioxide (CO_2) into maturing oil and gas fields via enhanced oil recovery (EOR). Carbon could also be recycled through its natural cycle in sinks or by converting it into bioenergy, while removal entails underground storage of captured carbon by using carbon capture, utilization, and storage (CCUS). The latter is an enabler for removing carbon emissions when natural gas or other fossil fuel sources are consumed in the energy-intensive process of producing hydrogen.

Many of the advanced economies of the world see hydrogen as the fuel source of the future, as it burns emissions-free when generating power and only produces water vapor at stack. These countries, therefore, are basing their 'net zero' plans on the viability of hydrogen. CCE and its technologies would allow today's oil- and gas-exporting countries to turn their hydrocarbons to hydrogen while capturing emitted carbon, thus sustaining economic growth and revenues in the long term. The G20, under the presidency of Riyadh, endorsed CCE as a concept in 2020 (Schroder, Bradley, and Lahn 2020), and Saudi Arabia envisions itself becoming one of the largest exporters of hydrogen in the future, as it is of oil today (Al-Atrush 2022). In September 2020, Saudi Aramco shipped the first blue ammonia cargo to Japan to be used in power generation (Aramco Staff 2020).[8] The process included converting hydrocarbons to hydrogen and then to ammonia with 50 tons of CO_2 (tCO_2) being captured. Thirty tCO_2 were utilized at Saudi chemicals giant Sabic's Ibn-Sina facility for methanol production while the remaining 20 tCO_2 were injected for EOR at Aramco's Uthamaniyah field. UAE's Abu Dhabi National Oil Company (ADNOC), in partnership with fertilizer producer Fertiglobe, sold three blue ammonia shipments to Japanese trading firm Itochu in September 2021 (Mirza 2021). Saudi Arabia is planning the world's largest green hydrogen project in NEOM at a production capacity of 1.2 million tons per year of green ammonia, where the process is expected to utilize 4 gigawatts (GW) of renewables as a source of energy (Ingram 2022c). Sabic is also planning the world's largest CCUS project, capturing 500 thousand tCO_2 annually (Sabic Staff 2022). Oman has its own plans for hydrogen as well (Byrne 2022). Adnoc is planning a major hydrogen hub in Ruwais (Ingram 2022b).

Most GCC states, especially Saudi Arabia, have oil and gas production that is among the lowest in costs and emissions in the world (Aramco Staff 2018). In addition, the GCC states have decades of expertise in the oil and gas sector, existing infrastructure and investments, and depleted oil and gas reservoirs geologically suitable for storing carbon. Moreover, by investing in research and development early, Saudi Arabia is positioning itself as a potential exporter of clean hydrocarbon technology know-how and services in the future (Fattouh, Heidug, and Zakkour 2021). The IEA expects that CCUS will continue gaining momentum under net zero plans as a cornerstone technology for reducing and fully removing carbon emissions on the consumption side (Farajardy 2021). Fattouh and co-authors also argue that developing clean hydrocarbon technologies could be more successful in oil-producing states as a means of economic diversification, utilizing hydrocarbon competitiveness rather than the traditional diversification to petrochemicals (Fattouh, Heidug, and Zakkour 2021). Indeed, with the long-term consideration of carbon taxes on imported goods (depending on the carbon intensity of their manufacturing), these technologies could also help decarbonize other strategic industries such as cement, steel, and manufacturing that are key to economic diversification targets in the GCC.

GCC fiscal response to COVID-19

Increased fiscal and monetary spending

GCC nations reacted quickly and effectively to curb increases in COVID-19 cases in 2020, adopting a strategy that is based on early detection (Our World in Data 2022), prevention, employment of tracking technologies, and strict control measures (OECD Staff 2020). By September 2020, these efforts helped in bringing the average COVID recovery rate in the GCC to 81.4 percent, which is 24.45 percent above the global average of 57 percent (Malek 2020). More crucially, GCC governments made available significant financial and material resources to alleviate the adverse health, societal, and economic impacts of the pandemic on their populations. This is in addition to the historical investment in healthcare infrastructure, which made the World Health Organization (WHO) rank GCC members highly on COVID preparedness, with the exception of Qatar (WHO Staff 2020).

The pandemic also required a run at reserves, increasing debt, and providing fiscal stimulus measures by the six nations (El-Saharty et al. 2020). These measures aimed to ease the burden on households, banks, and contact-intensive sectors where small and medium enterprises (SMEs) are active, such as retail, hospitality, tourism, real estate, and others. Curfews and long closures of economic sectors saw the GCC's total GDP contract by $231 billion in 2020 to $1.4 trillion, as shown in the Annex. With this burden thrust on governments, their combined spending as a percentage of GDP grew at 4.2 percent by the end of 2020 to 39 percent, a significant 3.4 percent increase over its 0.8 percent growth rate in 2019 (Figure 1.8). In total, GCC states and their monetary organizations pledged to spend at least $190 billion immediately after or in the aftermath of the pandemic. Overall GCC gross financial reserves, not including sovereign wealth funds (SWFs) assets, fell by over $41 billion from around $706 billion in 2019 to $664.5 billion in 2020 (Figure 1.9), according to IMF data. This decline was mainly due to Saudi Arabia tapping its reserves. For the rest of the GCC, monetary reserve withdrawals were either mild or saw increases, as in the cases of Kuwait and Qatar. Current fiscal spending increased by $8 billion, $2 billion, and $1 billion, respectively, for Saudi Arabia, Kuwait, and Bahrain with the exceptions in the UAE, Qatar, and Oman. Although total GCC government spending on capital projects declined by $12 billion from $101 billion in 2019 to $89 billion in 2020, its contribution to GDP matched the 2019 rate at 6 percent with individual nations showing no change year on year.

Despite reducing current spending by a massive $18 billion, which took the growth rate of government spending as a share of GDP from a positive 3.8 percent in 2019 to a negative 0.6 percent in 2020, the UAE

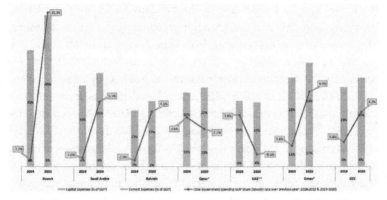

FIGURE 1.8 GCC current, capital, and total spending growth as share of GDP (2019–2020).

*Includes both oil and gas revenues and income from energy investments abroad for Qatar.

**2020 data are preliminary.

Sources: Kuwait Ministry of Finance, Saudi General Authority for Statistics, Central Bank of Bahrain, Qatar Central Bank, UAE Federal Competitiveness and Statistics Centre, Central Bank of Oman.

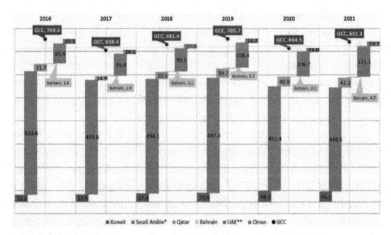

FIGURE 1.9 GCC gross official reserves ($ billion).

*SAMA (Central Bank) gross assets only.

**UAECB assets, does not include SWF assets.

Sources: 2000–2017 data from October 2019 *IMF Middle East & Central Asia (MECA) Regional Economic Outlook,* 2018 data from October 2020 *IMF MECA Regional Outlook* & 2019–2021 data from April 2022 *IMF MECA Regional Outlook.*

took the lead in responding to the pandemic with its central bank boosting liquidity and implementing capital preservation measures. These measures halved domestic banks' reserve requirements in addition to offering collateralized zero-interest rate loans, limiting SME fees, and extending the duration of principal loan and interest payments to the end of 2020 (KPMG Staff 2020e). The central bank's package increased from an initial $27 billion to $70 billion (Reuters Staff 2020c). Nevertheless, the country's central bank assets only saw a $1.7 billion decline by the end of 2020, according to IMF data (Figure 1.9). The federal government in Abu Dhabi also offered $7.2 billion in fee reductions, increased water and electricity subsidies, and commercial rebates in addition to guarantees and further liquidity support.

Bahrain announced an $11.4 billion package that guaranteed payment for three months of wages in the private sector through the Unemployment Fund, in addition to payment of water and electricity bills for a similar period (Gearon and Reichert 2020). The government's current expenses as a share of GDP increased from 23 percent to 27 percent with overall government spending growing at a rate of 4.2 percent by the end of 2020 compared to 2019. Manama also provided exemptions from municipal, industrial, tourism, and land rental fees while increasing available funds at the Liquidity Support Fund (LSF) to over $500 million. The Central Bank of Bahrain increased its loan facilities to $9.8 billion, allowing deferment of debt installments, extending further credit, and restructuring. Tamkeen, Bahrain's dedicated fund for supporting SMEs, established a $106 million Business Continuity Support Program that offered grants to most affected businesses due to the pandemic (BCI Staff 2021). Gross official reserves decreased by $1.5 billion by the end of the year.

In Qatar, the Emir issued a directive to spend $23.35 billion, most of which ($20.6 billion) was earmarked for incentives to the private sector (Khalid 2020). As a result, the National Response Guarantee Program (NRGP) (QDB Staff 2020) was established, offering a 100 percent payment guarantee for critical short-term payments such as payroll and rental fees, which the United Nation's Department of Economic and Social Affairs credits with saving 67 percent of private sector companies from bankruptcy (Department of Economic and Social Affairs 2020). Although the Qatari government's current spending increased by 2 percent over the year prior to reach 22 percent of GDP, overall government contribution to GDP grew by a rate of 2.2 percent in 2020, which was slower by 1.4 percent compared to 2019's 3.6 percent. Qatar's Central Bank took measures to postpone loan payments by six months, as did the Qatar Development Bank. Still, by the end of 2020, the Central Bank's assets grew by $1.2 billion. The government also injected $2.75 billion into the stock exchange and raised limits of salaries and wages (Gulf Times Staff 2021).

In Saudi Arabia, the support package amounted to almost $61 billion (KPMG Staff 2020a), including $13.3 billion to supporting banking and SME entities with an equivalent amount to ensure payment of government dues to contractors. The Saudi government's total spending impact on GDP was slowing in 2019 at a negative 1 percent (Figure 1.8), but these requirements saw it reverse back to growth at 5.3 percent. The current spending share of GDP grew by 5 percent from 30 percent in 2019 as well (Figure 1.8). King Salman bin Abdulaziz Al Saud ordered the subsidizing of private sector employee wages by almost 60 percent.[9] Similarly, the Saudi Arabian Monetary Authority (SAMA) injected a further $13.3 billion to enhance liquidity and support the issuance of credit facilities by financial institutions while adopting an accommodative monetary policy that allows extending working capital, flexibility of repayments, and waiver of fees and charges.[10] SAMA saw extensive withdrawal compared to other GCC nations, with Saudi gross official reserves falling by a considerable $46 billion. Another $1.6 billion by the government was geared toward a loan guarantee program for SMEs, while a 30 percent two-month discount was issued for utilities consumed by industrial, commercial, and agricultural concerns.

The Kuwaiti government eased access to the retirement pension, supported salaries, and boosted operational budgets of key ministries by $1.6 billion (KPMG Staff 2020b). The government's current spending grew at the highest rate in the region, rising from a 45 percent share of GDP in 2019 to 60 percent in 2020. With sustained COVID-19 curfews impacting the economy, the government's total spending contribution to GDP shifted from a deceleration at a negative 1.2 percent in 2019 to a massive 15.3 percent growth in 2020. Kuwait's Central Bank issued a $16.5 billion additional lending facility to support vital sectors suffering from the fallout of the pandemic while increasing its maximum lending limit to 100 percent (Market Research Kuwait 2020). Banks were ordered to reduce their credit risk weightage for SMEs from 75 percent to 25 percent, relaxing barriers to further loans with the Kuwait National Fund for SMEs also contributing. The central bank also took interest rates to a historic low of 1.5 percent; but Kuwaiti gross official reserves saw the GCC's highest addition in 2020 at $8.4 billion by the end of 2020.

For Oman, the initial impact of COVID-19 was felt almost immediately with the closure of its largest free zone in Duqm due to rising infections (Al-Khaleej Today Staff 2020). By the end of the year, current government spending as a contribution to GDP had increased by 5 percent to 33 percent while overall government spending share of GDP grew by 6.4 percent from a minor 0.4 percent growth rate a year earlier. The country's Central Bank ordered banks to maintain minimal functions to ensure that trade transactions, treasury operations, loans, and online services continued uninterrupted (KPMG Staff 2020c). The Central Bank's foreign assets lost $1.7 billion by the end of the year. The government ordered postponement of instalments for SMEs payable to the Al Raffd Fund[11] for six months as well as those owed to the Oman Development Bank. Emergency interest-free loans were offered to business owners who suffered most during the pandemic (Abu Omar and al Balushi 2020). Furthermore, factories and establishments at industrial cities were exempted from rent for three months, and payments on car mortgages were frozen for a similar period. In addition to Bahrain, Oman is considered a vulnerable economy within the GCC, and by June 2020, Omani diplomats, and the new Sultan[12] were reported to have approached wealthier neighbors for economic aid (MacDonald, al Balushi, and Westall 2020). Oman's foreign policy has often placed it as a neutral party in the region; it has pursued relations with the GCC's historic arch nemesis Iran and has been able to facilitate talks with Yemen's Houthi rebels (Coates Ulrichsen and Cafaiero 2021); hence, it has always been feared that the extension of aid would come with political pressure to change stance (Owtram and Hayek 2020). Doha also donated $1 billion in economic aid to Muscat during the pandemic (Gonçalves 2020). Oman and Kuwait had chosen a neutral and consolatory position on the 2017 Gulf rift when Riyadh, Manama, and Abu Dhabi severed diplomatic relations with Doha.

The IMF estimates that GCC fiscal measures to mitigate the impact of COVID-19 by the end of 2020 had ranged from as high as 6.7 percent and 5.5 percent of 2020 GDP in Bahrain and Saudi Arabia, to as low as 0.6 percent and 1 percent in Oman and Qatar, all respectively. The estimate is 4.9 percent for Kuwait and 2.8 percent for the UAE (IMF Staff 2021). Despite being initially protracted, non-oil activity recovery slowly rebounded by the end of 2020 and beginning of 2021. If it is of any consolation to GCC governments, their early measures had proved somewhat beneficial as 2020's non-oil GDP retracted lower than IMF projections or even slightly higher (Table 1.2). Even the rebound in 2021 shows higher non-oil GDP growth rates compared to 2019 except for a slight 0.56 percent reduction in the UAE. Furthermore, these figures are close to the October 2019 IMF projections for 2020 non-oil GDP growth before the pandemic. For the GCC as a group, the 2021 increase in non-oil GDP at 5.20 percent is close to the average from 2000 to 2015 at 6.71 percent (Figure 1.10).

More debt

Despite these large fiscal packages, GCC states reduced their reserves only by a small proportion, except for Saudi Arabia, as previously mentioned. Total reserves saw a $27 billion recovery in 2021 with higher oil prices and the revival of non-oil economic activity. The majority of this was in the UAE at $24.4 billion, with Oman second at $4.7 billion; Bahrain and Qatar added $2.5 and $1.3 billion, respectively. Kuwait and Saudi Arabia saw further withdrawals at $3.2 and $1.9 billion each in 2021. Instead of extensively tapping either reserves or SWFs to overcome their soaring deficits, 2020 saw the fevered issuance of sovereign and corporate bonds in the GCC, which continued into the first half of 2021, benefiting from a strong global bond market (Fahy 2020), low interest rates, and relatively high sovereign credit ratings compared to other emerging countries. By 2022, however, issuance decreased due to high oil prices (Mogielnicki 2021b) and interest rates hikes to accommodate rising inflation (Bhat and Ghosh 2022). According to a market survey by the Kuwait Financial Centre, GCC primary bonds and Sukuk[13] issuance had grown by $18.5 billion in 2020 (Markaz 2021), rising to $132.7 billion from $114.2 billion in 2019 (Figure 1.11). That record was broken by the end of financial year 2021, reaching $143.2 billion (Markaz 2022). Of the 2020 total, $66.3 billion were issued by governments, amounting to 50 percent, while in 2021 this amount fell marginally to $65.2 billion or 46 percent. As a result, total government gross debt in the GCC grew by 10.7 percent from 30.6 percent as a share of GDP in 2019 to 41.3 percent in 2020, before retreating to 37.4 percent in 2021 (Figure 1.12), according to IMF data.

In both years, the greatest amount was for Saudi Arabia[14] which increased its governmental debt share of GDP by 9.9 percent in 2020; the

Table 1.2 GCC non-oil GDP actual and projected growth rates by the IMF (%)

	Year	Kuwait	Saudi Arabia	Bahrain	Qatar	UAE	Oman	GCC
	2000-15*	6.15	6.25	7.13	12.31	6.20	6.86	6.71
	2016	1.45	0.23	4.35	5.30	3.16	6.24	1.86
	2017	2.06	1.26	4.88	3.84	1.95	2.45	1.88
	2018	2.89	2.20	2.39	2.25	0.68	-1.63	1.74
	2019	-1.11	2.80	2.20	2.20	3.76	-2.75	3.10
Pre-pandemic projections	Oct-19	3.00	2.53	2.50	3.56	3.00	2.52	2.77
Projections during 2020	Apr-20	-2.50	-4.00	-2.30	-5.90	-5.00	-5.00	-4.30
	Jul-20							-7.60
	Oct-20	-7.00	-4.99	-5.98	-5.67	-6.70	-7.98	-5.73
Post-pandemic actuals	2020	-7.54	-2.50	-6.00	-4.50	-6.20	-3.86	-5.70
	2021	3.40	4.90	2.80	2.70	3.20	1.80	5.20
Change	2020 vs Oct-19(P)	-0.54	+2.49	-0.02	+1.17	+0.50	+4.12	+0.03
	2021 vs 2019	+4.51	+2.10	+0.60	+0.50	-0.56	+4.55	+2.10

* Average non-oil GDP growth rate.

Sources: 2000–2017 data from October 2019 IMF Middle East and Central Asia (MECA) Regional Economic Outlook, 2018 data from October 2020 IMF MECA Regional Outlook and 2019–2021 data from April 2022 IMF MECA Regional Outlook.

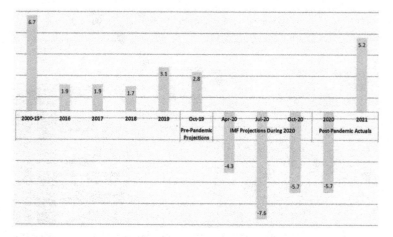

FIGURE 1.10 GCC non-oil GDP projections and growth (2000–2021).
*Average non-oil GDP growth rate.
Sources: 2000-2017 data from October 2019 *IMF Middle East & Central Asia (MECA) Regional Economic Outlook,* 2018 data from October 2020 *IMF MECA Regional Outlook* & 2019-2021 data from April 2022 *IMF MECA Regional Outlook.*

number for Qatar was 10.5 percent and 13.3 percent for the UAE. Kuwait was the only GCC state unable to tap bond markets due to a longstanding political dispute between parliament and the executive branch, which still stands as a hurdle to passing a new debt law needed for borrowing (Ingram 2022a). The previous law's validity ended in October 2017 and, as of April 2022, Kuwait has withdrawn $65 billion from its General Reserve Fund (GRF) to cover government expenses, thus nearly exhausting it (Al-Maleki 2022). Bahrain and Oman have a comparatively high stock of government public debt as high-income oil exporters. In 2019, total government gross debt as a percentage of GDP stood at 101.6 percent and 60.5 percent, respectively, even before the pandemic hit. These substantial debt levels rose in 2020 by 10.9 percent for Oman and 28.1 percent in the case of Bahrain, making Manama the GCC's highest borrower during the pandemic. With the intensified pressure on Oman's finances and the collapse in oil revenues in the first quarter of 2020, the country's sovereign credit rating was downgraded by the three major rating agencies (Fitch Ratings 2020; Reuters Staff 2020b; Saba 2020). By June 2020, the country decided to merge its General Reserve Fund and

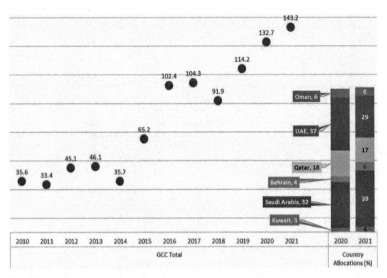

FIGURE 1.11 GCC primary bonds and Sukuk issuance in billion dollars. *Source:* Kuwait Financial Centre (Markaz).

the Oman Investment Fund into a single $17 billion entity called the Oman Investment Authority. Despite these weak fundamentals, investors continued to take issued bonds from Bahrain and Oman with the

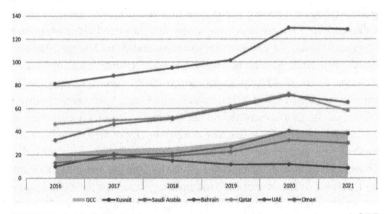

FIGURE 1.12 GCC total government gross debt as percentage of GDP (2016–2021). *Sources:* 2000–2017 data from October 2019 *IMF Middle East & Central Asia (MECA) Regional Economic Outlook*, 2018 data from October 2020 *IMF MECA Regional Outlook* & 2019–2021 data from April 2022 *IMF MECA Regional Outlook*.

expectation of a rescue package by larger GCC states in a worst-case scenario. However, any serious credit crisis at a single GCC nation may spur uncertainty and risk to others (Mogielnicki 2021b).

Adding debt is a politically accommodative option during oil price downturns, which allows GCC governments to avoid implementing deep fiscal tightening measures, increasing fees, or implementing taxation that can be considered socially unpopular. In 2015, a year after the 2014 oil price downturn, bonds and Sukuk grew by almost 83 percent from $35.7 billion to $65.2 billion before reaching $104.3 billion in 2017. The argument is that GCC nations can always reduce their debt issuance by leveraging high oil prices and their revenues. High oil prices in 2022 will deter increased bond issuance and prevent GCC states from borrowing at high interest rates. However, this approach carries the long-term risk that they will reach unmanageable levels due to an unexpected and sustained downturn; however, that is unlikely for the short- to mid-term today. Despite oil wealth being the underlying guarantee for these bonds, they are also still impacted by the fiscal, economic, and political behaviors of GCC governments. Meanwhile, withdrawing from SWFs is still considered an unattractive option as it potentially risks safeguarding the inter-generational equity for which these entities were established. Post-pandemic, listing stakes of state-controlled energy enterprises on domestic stock markets to draw funds from local and foreign investors is being increasingly adopted as a lucrative option.[15] Although this is often considered to be one-off wealth creation (Mogielnicki 2021b), it allows bypassing the controversy of privatization and helps raise finances for state capital expenditure in addition to projects planned by these companies.[16] In Saudi Arabia, funds from the Aramco initial public offering (IPO) are geared to finance ambitious economic diversification projects spearheaded by the Public Investment Fund (PIF). Following its 2019 listing of 1.5 percent of shares in the Saudi stock market (Cockayne and Ingram 2019) and the subsequent offering of 'over-allotment options,' which raised traded shares to 1.7 percent of Aramco's ownership structure (Ingram 2020), the Saudi government moved an additional 4 percent of Aramco to the PIF (Ingram 2022e). The transfer was worth $80 billion, and with the $29.4 billion collected from the IPO, raised the funds given to the PIF from Aramco to $109.4 billion. In 2021, Saudi Crown Prince Mohammed bin Salman Al Saud set a goal for the PIF to double its assets to $1 trillion by 2025 (Rashed and Azhar 2021).

Reform opportunities and micro-competitiveness

Taxation and labor reforms

The crisis in 2020 also prompted GCC nations to fast-track reform steps that would have been socially difficult to implement in normal times. The pace of these measures has been accelerating since the end of the pandemic. Starting in July 2020, Saudi Arabia raised the value added tax (VAT) from 5 percent to 15 percent in an attempt to substitute in part for lost government finances due to lower oil prices (BBC News 2020). The move also empowered Oman to introduce its VAT law in October 2020 (Oman Observer 2020), which became applicable at 5 percent by April 2021 (Moossdroff 2021). With the dominance of oil revenues, the GCC had historically positioned itself as a zero-to-low tax heaven. This was a deliberate policy intended to attract foreign direct investment and expatriates who would contribute to building infrastructure and contribute to economic growth (Alshahrani 2016) in addition to maintaining the social contract with the citizenry.

The absence of personal income taxes and property taxes in most GCC countries, as well as a generous system of exemptions and tax holidays (IMF Staff 2015), meant that non-oil fiscal revenues missed crucial enablers for their growth. In the wake of the 2014 oil price downturn, GCC nations agreed on a common VAT framework in June 2016 (GCC-SG 2017) for a 5 percent tax. This was implemented in stages, first in the UAE as early as 2017, then in Saudi Arabia in 2018 and Bahrain in 2019 (Vertex 2021). Qatar and Kuwait remain the only laggards in implementing the framework agreement for different reasons. For Qatar, government non-oil revenues are bolstered by income derived from foreign investments by the Qatar Investment Authority (QIA); hence, there is little incentive to introduce VATs. As for Kuwait, its contentious politics, and the increasingly populist stances by members of parliament, continue to stand as a hurdle to implementing VAT (Arabian Business 2022), not to mention economic reforms at large. In addition to the excise duties applied in the region (except for Kuwait), the introduction of VAT in Saudi Arabia, UAE, and Bahrain saw government tax contribution to GDP increase noticeably (Figure 1.13). In Saudi Arabia, the contribution almost tripled immediately from 3.38 percent in 2017 to 8.93 percent in

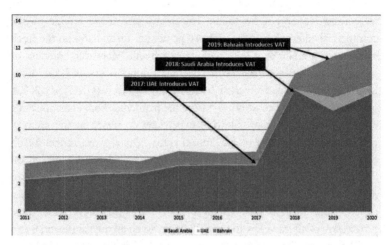

FIGURE 1.13 Government revenues as percentage of GDP (2011–2020). *Source:* International Monetary Fund (IMF) Government Finances Statistics.

2018. However, VATs are consumption taxes, and they directly impact the population; consequently, they have been met with muted social discontent in the kingdom (Al-Araby 2020) despite initial promises to revert back to 5 percent once the pandemic is over. Finance Minister Mohammed Al-Jadaan said in May 2022 (Al-Eqtisadiya 2022) that such a move was 'under study' and will 'eventually' happen. However, he changed the timeline to after the kingdom 'substitutes lost reserves.' Realistically, a reversal is unlikely to take place in the short to medium term; one of the GCC's reform objectives is complying with international norms, and boosting taxation is a measure of both income diversification and creating a business-friendly environment for investors (Schofield 2021). Nevertheless, Crown Prince Mohammed bin Salman Al Saud strongly reassured citizens in April 2021 by saying that the government has no plans to introduce personal income taxes (Reuters Staff 2021b).

The UAE managed to take important steps in late 2020 and early 2021 to increase its business attractiveness to investors and expat workers in a bid to maintain its role as a regional trade hub. In November 2020, the government revamped corporate ownership laws, allowing foreigners to own 100 percent of companies formed outside free zones but at certain sectors that excluded those with strategic impact[17] (UAE Government 2022). Previously, non-UAE citizens were only allowed to own 49 percent, and both the expense and hassle (Gibson Dunn 2020) of including a 51 percent local shareholder were a major source of hesitation. The change also allows foreign-owned commercial enterprises to list up to 70 percent of their shares on the stock market, an upgrade over the previous 30 percent. Moreover, branches of foreign companies were allowed to become Emirati firms, and conditions for requiring nationals on their boards were removed (UNCTAD 2022). With the rise of remote working during the pandemic, Dubai introduced a virtual working program, allowing expatriates to reside in the country without being employed by an Emirati entity (Dubai Government 2020). Moreover, the emirate expected 0.25–1 percent growth in its economy on the back of the 'Golden Visa' scheme, which was extended in November 2020. The scheme offers flexible and longer residency to investors, students, experts, and professionals (Reuters Staff 2020a). However, the most progressive of all moves by the end of 2020 was changing the personal and civil law codes, allowing non-Emiratis to settle disputes using their home countries' laws. Furthermore, the country relaxed regulations regarding the co-habitation of unmarried couples and restrictions on the consumption of alcohol (Nammour 2020). By the end of 2021, the government even drafted a law attempting to break monopolies of influential business families on import licenses (Kerr 2021), which may risk breaking a historic social contract between the merchant class and ruling families (Kamrava et al. 2016). In 2022, the country's Ministry of Finance announced that for the first time the UAE would impose a 9 percent corporate income tax starting in June 2023 (Fitch Ratings 2022) – stopping short of introducing personal taxation. While honoring the 50-year tax exemption granted to free zone companies, the move may still tax profits to be generated from operations within the Emirates (Fidinam 2022). The UAE has been a leader in the region in utilizing tax-free zones for encouraging economic and financial activity, but their contribution to economic diversification and growing non-oil income is still largely under-studied (Mogielnicki 2021a).

The UAE new rules still do not clarify whether they are implemented equally on citizens and foreigners alike. Corporate tax rules in the GCC are lax on citizen owners. This could be considered supportive of SMEs, women, and young entrepreneurs (IMF Staff 2021), but it also denies the state considerable non-oil revenues from large local business concerns. In Saudi Arabia, for non-Saudi or GCC-owned companies, taxes are at 20 percent, while for locally or GCC-owned corporates, only Zakat[18] is applicable at 2.5 percent (PwC 2022e). For mixed ownership, the Saudi or GCC owners are only charged the Zakat rate. In Qatar, the flat rate of 10 percent only applies to an entity that derives its income from Qatar and is wholly or partially owned by non-Qataris or GCC citizens. For the latter two, no tax is applicable (PwC 2022d). This is not the case in Oman where firms are taxed at 15 percent regardless of ownership (Fitch Ratings 2022), while SMEs that fulfil certain conditions enjoy a lower rate of 3 percent (PwC 2022c). Bahrain does not apply any corporate taxes (PwC 2022a), while Kuwait only charges foreign owners to the extent of their profits generated in the country (as Qatar does) but at a higher 15 percent rate (PwC 2022b). Hence, the UAE's decision to introduce a 9 percent tax, while being a downgrade to a tax-free status, is still attractive for foreigners compared to other GCC states, especially when combined with the new quasi-liberal lifestyle regulations enacted.

The labor market in the GCC is often seen as non-integrated, as the public sector is utilized as a large employment sink for locals while expatriates dominate the private sector (International Energy Agency 2018). According to the IMF, many foreigners left during the pandemic while the employment of nationals has either been maintained or increased (IMF Staff 2021). One of the much-promoted socioeconomic targets of diversification plans is referred to as *Gulfization*, which entails increasing the numbers of locals working in the private sector. However, an enduring structural problem is the pay gap between the public and private sectors (Hertog 2014). Another limitation to migrant workers flexibility is the Kafala system, which is criticized for its subpar protections and tendency to render workers victim to exploitation (Bandak 2021). However, GCC countries are increasingly announcing policies to depart from the system and dismantle it. In August 2020, Qatar lifted the requirement for a 'No Objection Certificate' to be obtained prior to foreigners changing employers; this followed an earlier decision to remove exit approvals when leaving the country. In June, Oman followed suit with easing sponsorship transfer rules (Migrant Rights 2020), as did Saudi Arabia in November (Batrawy 2020). However, the Omani government also introduced tighter 'Omanization' quotas and prohibited work permit renewals for foreigners at sectors where work could easily be conducted by locals, such as delivery services (Zawya 2020). In May 2021, just a month after the introduction of VAT, protests erupted in several parts of the country with young people demanding jobs. In response, the Sultan ordered the creation of 32,000 full- and part-time jobs and the introduction of subsidies (el Yaakoubi and Barbuscia 2021). By the end of 2020, Muscat was considering the introduction of income taxes on high earners (Gonçalves 2020); if implemented, Oman would be the first GCC state to impose income taxes on individuals. Even so, the plan would not go into effect in the immediate term (Castelier 2022).

Historically, GCC governments have introduced local content quotas, especially in oil and gas projects (Soupa and Mexis 2018), both to support the private sector and induce employment. In April 2020, Abu Dhabi launched a program geared at increasing local content in procurement for 1,244 government tenders (Abu Dhabi Government 2020). In September 2021, UAE Prime Minister and Ruler of Dubai Mohammed Bin Rashid Al Maktoum publicly directed the government to give local conglomerate Majid Al Futtaim Group preference in contracting after it announced offering 3,000 jobs to Emiratis. He tweeted 'there are companies that behave as partners in the country and others that want to use the country only to meet their own interests.' (Gulf Today Staff 2021). The drive to frame local content programs as a patriotic duty is not new, but this approach has increased in the region with the announcement of Saudi Arabia's Vision 2030. Crown Prince Mohammed Bin Salman Al Saud announced the Shareek programme as the vision's public–private partnerships pillar immediately after easing the pandemic restrictions in 2021. The idea is for large Saudi private sector concerns to inject $1.33 trillion of investment into the local economy, generating hundreds of thousands of jobs by 2030 (SPA 2021). In return, these firms get preferential treatment in government contracting and inclusion in PIF projects. The PIF itself will support the program with $800 billion (Forbes 2021). While these figures may sound astronomical, giant Saudi chemicals manufacturer Sabic already began a local content initiative that aimed at adding more than $3 billion to GDP and create some 10,316 jobs (Arab News 2021).

The penetration of remote working technologies was also an opportunity during the pandemic for GCC states to address partially some of their labor inequalities and vulnerabilities such as learning gaps, structural mismatches, access to knowledge, and financing. An assessment of distance learning capabilities at Dubai and Abu Dhabi schools found that 67 percent and 84 percent of the schools, respectively, had developed e-learning programs (KPMG Staff 2020e). An initiative by the Qatar Finance and Business Academy offered to train entrepreneurs in adopting best financial and management strategies during the pandemic (KPMG Staff 2020d) while the Qatar Communications Regulatory Authority launched a programme providing resources to ease work from home (QCRA 2020). In Saudi Arabia, SAMA developed a product to allow SMEs to manage their expenses, and the Human Resource Development

Fund allocated $270 million for training and skilling programs for Saudi employees (Saudi Ministry of Investment 2020).

Similar template?

Despite existing political disagreements following the 2017 diplomatic crisis[19] with Qatar, GCC nations saw the opportunity to work together during the pandemic in 2020. This was evident in several virtual meetings on the ministerial level held by the GCC Secretariat General regarding the economic, trade, logistical, and even food security responses to the pandemic (Alden and Dunst 2020; GCC-SG 2020a, 2020b, 2020c). By March 2021, disputes with Qatar were put aside after the Al-Ula summit (Khalid 2021), thereby bringing the GCC's first major public rift to an end. The reform trajectory for the six nations shares common goals, such as an emphasis on utilizing their core competitive hydrocarbon edge for economic diversification, plans to build a world-class logistics infrastructure based on their geographical location, a focus on technology and digital growth, and increasingly the liberalization of social and business environments. Of course, there are exceptions, especially in the cases of Kuwait and Oman where reform is stalled or delayed; moreover, this race to reinvent the economy and make it attractive to foreign investment is primarily noticeable in Saudi Arabia and the UAE. Even here, both nations to some extent are taking a similar path to subduing the past and fostering the future. Abu Dhabi has a distinctly pragmatic approach that is contemporary, secular, and modern; and Riyadh continues to champion unprecedented social changes (The Editorial Board 2020). These overlapping approaches prompt competition that outsiders could mistake as a threat to future GCC unity (Gardner 2021).

The UAE's growth as a major trade hub and its attractive lifestyle accommodations to expatriates have positioned it to take advantage not just of its neighboring GCC markets but also those of the region, especially with Iran struggling under sanctions (Ahmad 2021). Within the GCC, the UAE became the access point for international businesses aiming to operate within the large and rewarding Saudi market. Riyadh's second largest import partner is the UAE at 12.6 percent of its $143 billion 2020 imports – just after China's 22.1 percent (OEC 2022a). The UAE is also Saudi's fifth export partner after China, India, Japan, and South Korea. Similarly, Saudi Arabia is Abu Dhabi's third largest export market at 8.36 percent of its $216 billion in 2020 exports, just after India at 10.2 percent and China at 8.9 percent (OEC 2022b). If these figures were to exclude oil and gas trade, then both countries are each other's top import and export partners, an indication of the deeply intertwined links between them. The UAE's successful utilization of the GCC common market and economic integration mechanisms (UAE Ministry of Finance 2013), in addition to its role as a trade re-routing centre, has resulted in a growing trade surplus with its neighbors over the years (Figure 1.14). In 2000, Abu Dhabi enjoyed a small surplus of $278 million with the rest of the GCC; but with the region enjoying huge economic growth over the next twenty years with high oil prices and expanding non-oil sectors, exports grew from around $2.4 billion to a staggering $33.9 billion while imports rose from $2.1 billion to $14.8 billion. By 2020, the UAE had a surplus of $19 billion with its GCC neighbors. The trade balance with Saudi Arabia stands as the highest at $8.8 billion in 2020, which is still lower due to the pandemic than the 19-year-high $13 billion trade surplus with the Kingdom in 2019.

The UAE did not always have the upper trade hand with Saudi Arabia. In the first decade from 2000 to 2010, the trade imbalance was to Saudi's advantage, averaging at around $1.1 billion – but this changed starting 2011. With Saudi Arabia determined to transform its economy and bring in foreign investment, the government announced in February 2021 that foreign firms must move their Middle East headquarters to Riyadh by

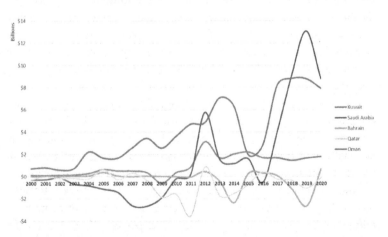

FIGURE 1.14 UAE trade balance with GCC neighbors (2000–2020). *Source*: The Observatory of Economic Complexity (OEC).

2024 for them to be considered for the multi-billion contracts expected under Vision 2030 (Martin, Nereim, and Fattah 2021). The decision was seen as a direct challenge to Dubai's position as a hub for regional and international firms. For these plans to work, another $800 billion was allocated to double the size of the capital Riyadh and turn it into a major economic, social, and cultural hub (Kane 2020). While Saudi Arabia has a blanket ban on alcohol consumption under strict Islamic rules, officials floated the idea of not ruling out allowing it at NEOM, the ambitious high-tech futuristic city at the heart of Vision 2030 (France 24 2021). The flurry of measures grew by July 2021, when the Saudi government excluded goods imported via GCC free zones (Abu Omar, el Wardany, and al Othman 2021). The decision breaks a major pillar in the GCC Customs Union Treaty (EIU 2015), which combines the states under a single port of entry and abolishes tariffs on goods manufactured domestically and imposes a unified 5 percent levy on those imported from outside the GCC.

Abu Dhabi and Riyadh also found themselves on opposite directions in terms of extending production cuts under the OPEC+ agreement to 2022 (el Wardany et al. 2021). Public disputes between OPEC's GCC group are unprecedented, especially since they have traditionally followed Saudi's lead. However, muted rifts in the GCC are not new. In 2006, Riyadh tried to block the Dolphin pipeline that carries gas from Qatar to the UAE after blocking a similar project with Kuwait in the past. Moreover, Abu Dhabi and other GCC states stood against a common currency for the bloc as it would have led to a greater Saudi role (Ingram 2021).

As these differences became a source of counterproductive outsider attention for both countries' reform plans, they were quickly amended by late 2021 (Khariche 2021). Clearly, as both sides forge their transformative agendas, they risk standing on competing sides, both economically and politically. The fact that GCC states are employing a similar reform template comes with its hurdles but also presents opportunities for increased integration and closing existing gaps. Economic development in Saudi Arabia will be key for growing the economies of the rest of the region, and its superior position within the group is hard to challenge. The UAE's existing position and international financial interlinkages will play an important factor in driving needed investment pools, not only to Riyadh but also to other GCC members. The GCC already has long-established strategic collaboration mechanisms on security, infrastructure, energy, agriculture, trade, transportation, and other areas. SMEs in all six states stand the chance of wider access to combined private financing under the current rules. These policies should be maintained, activated, and expanded with a broad GCC strategy to help promote job growth, productivity, and non-oil economic integration. Moreover, existing differences could be resolved with innovative solutions and technologies. A good example is project Aber (Central Bank of The UAE and Saudi Central Bank 2020) which aims to establish a single-issued digital currency between the UAE and Saudi Arabia for settling transactions and could thus become an alternative to a common currency.

Conclusion

The COVID-19 crisis and its ensuing oil price collapse in 2020 saw GCC states lose a combined $100 billion of hydrocarbon revenues. History shows that oil dependence in the region has produced pro-cyclical fiscal spending behavior that is hard to adjust when oil prices collapse. Oil continues to fuel state finances by a considerable share of the GCC as a group with government spending contributing significantly as a share of GDP. However, on both indicators, progress differs by country, with the UAE and Saudi Arabia leading reforms. Thus far, governments have proven prudent and fiscally disciplined with the windfall coming from higher oil prices in 2021 and 2022 and plan to re-build monetary reserves while supporting the growth of the non-oil economy. Moreover, the energy transition has played a role in fostering and fast-tracking plans for economic diversification in the region. The oil revenues of today will prove most impactful on long-term economic growth in the GCC if utilized to finance these plans efficiently while also rectifying the effects of unexpected crises. The quick and effective reaction by GCC governments to mitigate the impacts of the COVID-19 crisis on their non-oil sectors has exceeded expectations; however, it came at a high cost of more than $190 billion in pledged support. The energy transition continues to pose a long-term risk to the hydrocarbon dependence model in the GCC. However, the recent Ukraine conflict also brings opportunities for promoting and adopting the CCE. The development of clean hydrocarbon technologies, especially by Saudi Arabia and the UAE, may become an important factor in delaying peak oil demand as well as successfully diversifying the economy based on the existing core competitive hydrocarbon advantages. The good news is that the GCC have overcome the Qatar diplomatic crisis, which should help advancing economic integration plans.

Bibliography

Abdulla, Abdulkhaleq, 2022. 'Arabic: For the Emirates and Kuwait… the Story of Two Gulf Models.' CNN Arabic. https://arabic.cnn.com/middle-east/article/2022/04/14/united-arab-emirates-kuwait-story-of-two-gulf-models-oped (May 31, 2022).

Abu Dhabi Government, 2020. 'Abu Dhabi Local Content Program.' Abu Dhabi Government. https://idb.added.gov.ae/en/incentives/ADLC (May 30, 2022).

Abu Omar, Abeer, and Turki al Balushi, 2020. 'COVID-19 Recovery: Oman Offers Interest Free Loans to Businesses.' Bloomberg. https://www.bloomberg.com/news/articles/2020-06-23/oman-offers-emergency-interest-free-loans-for-firms-hit-by-virus?utm_medium=social&utm_campaign=socialflow-organic&utm_source=twitter&utm_content=middleeast (May 30, 2022).

Abu Omar, Abeer, and Matthew Martin, 2022. 'Saudi Arabia Tucks Away Billions in Oil Money For Next Year.' Bloomberg. https://www.bloomberg.com/news/articles/2022-05-26/saudi-arabia-tucks-away-billions-in-oil-money-for-next-year (May 30, 2022).

Abu Omar, Abeer, Salma el Wardany, and Reema al Othman, 2021. 'Saudi Arabia Excludes Imports From Gulf's Free Zones and Israel.' Bloomberg. https://www.bloomberg.com/news/articles/2021-07-05/saudi-arabia-excludes-imports-from-gulf-s-free-zones-and-israel (May 30, 2022).

Ahmad, Amjad, 2021. 'Saudi Arabia and the UAE Are Economic Frenemies. And That's a Good Thing.' Atlantic Council. https://www.atlanticcouncil.org/blogs/menasource/saudi-arabia-and-the-uae-are-economic-frenemies-and-thats-a-good-thing/ (May 30, 2022).

Al-Araby, 2020. 'Arabic: Saudis Starting Today Suffer under 15 percent VAT.' *Al-Araby.* https://www.alaraby.co.uk/%D8%A7%D9%84%D8%B3%D8%B9%D9%88%D8%AF%D9%8A%D9%88%D9%86-%D9%8A%D8%B1%D8%B2%D8%AD%D9%88%D9%86-%D8%AA%D8%AD%D8%AA-%D8%B6%D8%B1%D9%8A%D8%A8%D8%A9-15-%D9%84%D9%84%D9%82%D9%8A%D9%85%D8%A9-%D8%A7%D9%84%D9%85%D8%B6%D8%A7%D9%81%D8%A9 (May 30, 2022).

Al-Atrush, Samer, 2022. 'Can Saudi Arabia Become the World's Biggest Hydrogen Producer?' *The Financial Times.* https://www.ft.com/content/6dce7e6b-0cce-49f4-a9f8-f80597d1653a (May 30, 2022).

Alden, Chris, and Charles Dunst, 2020. 'COVID-19: Gulf States and the Gulf Cooperation Council (GCC).' LSE Department of International Relations. https://www.lse.ac.uk/international-relations/centres-and-units/global-south-unit/COVID-19-regional-responses/Gulf-States-and-COVID-19 (May 30, 2022).

Al-Eqtisadiya, 2022. 'Arabic: We Will Discuss Reducing the Value-Added Tax. At the Moment, We Are Still Trying to Compensate for the Lack of Reserves.' *Al-Eqtisadiya.* https://www.aleqt.com/2022/05/24/article_2322651.html (May 30, 2022).

Al-Khaleej Today Staff, 2020. 'Coronavirus: Oman Closes off Largest Free Zone after a Spate of New Infections.' Al-Khaleej Today. https://alkhaleejtoday.co/international/5005348/Coronavirus-Oman-closes-off-largest-free-zone-after-a-spate-of-new-infections.html (May 30, 2022).

Al-Maleki, Yesar, 2022. 'Kuwait Cabinet Resigns, Again.' MEES. https://www.mees.com/2022/4/8/news-in-brief/kuwait-cabinet-resigns-again/d84a3000-b737-11ec-9f8f-afa04b48f1a1 (May 30, 2022).

Alshahrani, Saad, 2016. 'Value Added Tax: Its Implementation and Implications.' 2016 quarterly workshop presentation by the Saudi Arabian Monetary Agency (SAMA). https//www.sama.gov.sa/ar-sa/EconomicResearch/Quarterly%20Workshops/%D8%A7%D9%84%D8%B1%D8%A8%D8%B9%20%D8%A7%D9%84%D8%A3%D9%88%D9%84_2016_%D8%A7%D9%84%D8%B9%D8%B1%D8%B6%20%D8%A7%D9%84%D8%AB%D8%A7%D9%86%D9%8A.pdf

Alsudairi, Mohammed A. T., and Gopikrishna Tatapudi, 2014. 'Social Innovation: Can It Be a Strategy for Influencing GCC Public Welfare?' Innovation 16(2): 273–82. https://doi.org/10.1080/14479338.2014.11081988.

Arab News, 2021. 'Investors under SABIC's Local Initiative, NUSANED, to Add $3bn to Saudi GDP.' Arab News. https://www.arabnews.com/node/1994751/business-economy (May 30, 2022).

Arabian Business, 2022. 'Kuwait's MPs "Strongly Refuse" Imposing Taxes to Address Budget Deficit.' Arabian Business. https://www.arabianbusiness.com/gcc/kuwait/kuwaits-mps-strongly-refuse-imposing-taxes-to-address-budget-deficit (May 30, 2022).

Arabian Business Staff, 2020. 'Saudi Government to Cover 60% of Private Sector Salaries Hit by COVID-19.' Arabian Business. https://www.arabianbusiness.com/industries/banking-finance/444303-saudi-government-to-cover-60-of-private-sector-salaries-hit-by-COVID-19 (May 30, 2022).

Aramco Staff, 2018. 'Study Shows Record Low Carbon Intensity of Saudi Crude Oil.' Aramco. https://www.aramco.com/en/news-media/news/2018/study-shows-record-low-carbon-intensity-of-saudi-crude-oil (May 30, 2022).

Aramco Staff, 2020. 'World's First Blue Ammonia Shipment Opens New Route to a Sustainable Future.' Aramco. https://www.aramco.com/en/news-media/news/2020/first-blue-ammonia-shipment (May 30, 2022).

Bandak, Derya, 2021. 'Saudi-Arabia: Reform of the Kafala System Comes into Force.' Rödl & Partner. https://www.roedl.com/insights/saudi-arabia-reform-of-kafala-system-comes-into-force (May 30, 2022).

Barbuscia, Davide, Saeed Azhar, and Pamela Barbaglia, 2020. 'Abu Dhabi in Talks with Dubai for Support through State Fund Mubadala.' Reuters. https://www.reuters.com/article/us-emirates-economy-mubadala-exclusive-idUSKBN22R1UL (May 30, 2022).

Batrawy, Aya, 2020. 'Saudi Arabia to Remove Key Restrictions on Migrant Laborers.' Associated Press. https://apnews.com/article/international-news-dubai-migrant-workers-saudi-arabia-united-arab-emirates-6cb5e681b00893e200fec707d92dba06 (May 30, 2022).

BBC News, 2020. 'Saudi Arabia Triples VAT to Support Coronavirus-Hit Economy.' BBC News. https://www.bbc.co.uk/news/business-52612785 (May 30, 2022).

BCI Staff, 2021. 'Bahrain Extends Business Continuity Support for SME's.' BCI. https://www.thebci.org/news/bahrain-extends-business-continuity-support-for-sme-s.html (May 30, 2022).

Beblawi, Hazem, 1987. *The Rentier State in the Arab World*. Routledge. https://www.taylorfrancis.com/chapters/edit/10.4324/9781315684864-11/rentier-state-arab-world-hazem-beblawi (November 5, 2021).

Beblawi, Hazem, and Giacomo Luciani, 1987. *The Rentier State*, ed. Giacomo Luciani. Routledge. https://www.taylorfrancis.com/books/edit/10.4324/9781315684864/rentier-state-hazem-beblawi-giacomo-luciani (November 5, 2021).

Bhat, Prerana, and Indradip Ghosh, 2022. 'Year-End View for Fed Policy Rate Rises Again as Recession Risks Remain.' Reuters. https://www.reuters.com/markets/europe/year-end-view-fed-policy-rate-rises-again-recession-risks-remain-2022-05-20/ (May 30, 2022).

Bloomberg, 2022. 'Mideast Insight: $500 Billion Natural Resource Blessing for the Gulf.' Bloomberg. https://www.bloomberg.com/news/terminal/RC42XWT0AFB6 (May 30, 2022).

Bouvet, Antoine, Benjamin Schroeder, and Padhraic Garvey, 2022. 'Rates Spark: Toppish Yields, but Central Banks Are Not Done.' ING Bank. https://think.ing.com/articles/rates-spark-toppish-yields-but-central-banks-are-not-done (May 30, 2022).

BP Statistical Review of World Energy, 2021.

Byrne, Megan, 2022. 'Oman Pushes Green Hydrogen Ambitions With Wave Of Planned Projects.' *MEES* 65(15). https://www.mees.com/2022/4/15/refining-petrochemicals/oman-pushes-green-hydrogen-ambitions-with-wave-of-planned-projects/9a7a53a0-bcae-11ec-a696-09c6bb03b77b (May 30, 2022).

Castelier, Sebastian, 2022. 'Oman on Cusp of Introducing Personal Income Tax.' Al-Monitor. https://www.al-monitor.com/originals/2022/04/oman-cusp-introducing-personal-income-tax (May 30, 2022).

Central Bank of The U.A.E. and Saudi Central Bank. 2020. 'Project Aber.' https://www.sama.gov.sa/en-US/News/Documents/Project_Aber_report-EN.pdf.

Coates Ulrichsen, Kristian, and Giorgio Cafaiero, 2021. 'Yemen War: How Oman and the US Are Finding Common Ground.' Middle East Eye. https://www.middleeasteye.net/opinion/yemen-war-how-us-and-oman-are-finding-common-ground (May 30, 2022).

Cockayne, James, and Jamie Ingram, 2019. 'Aramco Prices IPO.' *MEES* 62(49). https://www.mees.com/2019/12/6/refining-petrochemicals/aramco-prices-ipo/5004d8d0-1859-11ea-8f0d-916cf4d455e5 (May 30, 2022).

Department of Economic and Social Affairs, 2020. 'National Response Guarantee Program (NRGP).' United Nations. https://sdgs.un.org/partnerships/national-response-guarantee-program-nrgp (May 30, 2022).

Dubai Government, 2020. 'Dubai Launches Unique Virtual Working Programme for Overseas Professionals.' Dubai Government Media Office. https://mediaoffice.ae/en/news/2020/October/14-10/Dubai-launches-unique-virtual-working-programme-for-overseas-professionals (May 30, 2022).

EIU, 2015. 'GCC Customs Union up and Running.' The Economist Intelligence Unit. http://country.eiu.com/article.aspx?articleid=1522653936 (May 30, 2022).

El-Saharty, Sameh, Igor Kheyfets, Christopher H. Herbst, and Mohamed Ihsan Ajwad, 2020. *Fostering Human Capital in the Gulf Cooperation Council Countries*. 1st ed. Washington, D.C.: World Bank.

Embassy Staff, 2011. 'GCC Provides $20 Billion in Support for Bahrain and Oman.' The Embassy of The Kingdom of Saudi Arabia, Washington, D.C. https://www.saudiembassy.net/press-release/gcc-provides-20-billion-support-bahrain-and-oman (May 29, 2022).

EU Staff, 2022a. 'GCC: EU Unveils Strategic Partnership with the Gulf.' European Commission. https://ec.europa.eu/commission/presscorner/detail/en/IP_22_3165 (May 30, 2022).

EU Staff, 2022b. 'REPowerEU: A Plan to Rapidly Reduce Dependence on Russian Fossil Fuels and Fast Forward the Green Transition.' European Commission. https://ec.europa.eu/commission/presscorner/detail/en/IP_22_3131 (May 30, 2022).

Fahy, Michael, 2020. 'GCC Debt Markets Set for Slower Year Ahead after Bumper 2020.' *The National*. https://www.thenationalnews.com/business/banking/gcc-debt-markets-set-for-slower-year-ahead-after-bumper-2020-1.1138293 (May 30, 2022).

Farajardy, Mathilde, 2021. 'CCUS in Industry and Transformation.' International Energy Agency. https://www.iea.org/reports/ccus-in-industry-and-transformation (May 30, 2022).

Fattouh, Bassam, and Spencer Dale, 2018. *Peak Oil Demand and Long-Run Oil Prices*. Oxford Institute for Energy Studies (OIES). https://www.oxfordenergy.org/publications/peak-oil-demand-long-run-oil-prices/.

Fattouh, Bassam, Wolf Heidug, and Paul Zakkour, 2021. OIES Energy Insights, *Transitioning to Net-Zero: CCUS and the Role of Oil and Gas Producing Countries*. https://doi.org/10.1039/c7ee02342a (May 30, 2022).

Federico'Murchú, Sean, 2020. 'Full US-UAE-Israel Statement on Normalizing Relations.' CNN. https://edition.cnn.com/2020/08/13/middleeast/mideast-trump-full-statement-uae-israel-intl/index.html (May 30, 2022).

Fidinam, 2022. 'UAE Announce the Introduction of a 9% Corporate Tax Rate.' Fidinam. https://www.fidinam.com/en/blog/uae-announce-corporate-tax-rate (May 30, 2022).

Fioretti, Julia, and Anthony di Paola, 2022. 'Adnoc, Borealis Will Sell 10% of Chemical JV Borouge in IPO.' Bloomberg. https://www.bloomberg.com/news/articles/2022-05-17/adnoc-borealis-to-sell-10-stake-in-ipo-of-borouge-chemical-jv (May 30, 2022).

Fitch Ratings, 2020. 'Fitch Downgrades Oman to "BB"; Outlook Negative.' Fitch Ratings. https://www.fitchratings.com/research/structured-finance/fitch-downgrades-oman-to-bb-outlook-negative-12-03-2020 (May 30, 2022).

Fitch Ratings, 2022. 'UAE Income Tax Could Affect Private Corporates and Some GREs.' Fitch Ratings. https://www.fitchratings.com/research/corporate-finance/uae-income-tax-could-affect-private-corporates-some-gres-03-02-2022 (May 30, 2022).

Forbes, 2021. 'Saudi Arabia Launches Shareek Program To Garner $1.33T Private Sector Investments By 2030.' Forbes Middle East. https://www.forbesmiddleeast.com/industry/economy/new-saudi-initiative-to-enable-%24133t-private-sector-investments-by-2030 (May 30, 2022).

France 24, 2021. 'Saudi Arabia Megacity Project Flirts with Major Taboo: Alcohol.' France 24. https://www.france24.com/en/live-news/20211027-saudi-arabia-megacity-project-flirts-with-major-taboo-alcohol (May 30, 2022).

Franklin, Joshua, 2022. 'Lloyd Blankfein Warns of "Very, Very High Risk" of US Recession.' The Financial Times. https://www.ft.com/content/ce305e83-fd33-4ed2-9662-8e04764d83a2 (May 30, 2022).

Ganti, Akhilesh, 2022. 'Sukuk.' Investopedia. https://www.investopedia.com/terms/s/sukuk.asp (May 30, 2022).

Gardner, David, 2021. 'Saudi-UAE Competition Threatens to Upend the GCC.' The Financial Times. https://www.ft.com/content/054f0788-e5f4-4b59-80c6-2e9cfd7b0a5a (May 30, 2022).

GCC-SG, 2017. 'The Unified VAT Agreement for The Cooperation Council for the Arab States of the Gulf.' http://gcc-sg.org/en-us/MediaCenter/NewsCooperation/News/Pages/news2020-4-16-1.aspx

GCC-SG, 2020a. 'Arabic: An Extraordinary Meeting of the Executive Committee of Civil Aviation in the Gulf Cooperation Council Countries to Discuss the Repercussions of Corona.' Secretariat General of The Gulf Cooperation Council. https://gcc-sg.org/ar-sa/MediaCenter/NewsCooperation/NewsArchive/Pages/2020/%D8%A3%D8%A8%D8%B1%D9%8A%D9%84/news2020-4-30-2.aspx (May 30, 2022).

GCC-SG, 2020b. 'Arabic: The Finance Ministers of the Gulf Cooperation Council Hold the 111th Meeting of the Financial and Economic Cooperation Committee.' Secretariat General of The Gulf Cooperation Council. https://gcc-sg.org/ar-sa/MediaCenter/NewsCooperation/NewsArchive/Pages/2020/%D8%A3%D8%A8%D8%B1%D9%8A%D9%84/news2020-4-21-2.aspx (May 30, 2022).

GCC-SG, 2020c. 'Arabic: The GCC Commercial Cooperation Committee Holds Its Second Extraordinary Meeting on the Impact of the Corona Pandemic.' Secretariat General of The Gulf Cooperation Council. https://gcc-sg.org/ar-sa/MediaCenter/NewsCooperation/NewsArchive/Pages/2020/%D8%A3%D8%A8%D8%B1%D9%8A%D9%84/news2020-4-16-1.aspx (May 30, 2022).

Gearon, Patrick, and William Reichert, 2020. 'The Kingdom of Bahrain and COVID-19: Bahrain's Reaction to the Global Pandemic.' Charles Russell Speechlys. https://www.charlesrussellspeechlys.com/en/news-and-insights/insights/corporate/2020/the-kingdom-of-bahrain-and-COVID-19-bahrains-reaction-to-the-global-pandemic/ (May 30, 2022).

Gibson Dunn, 2020. 'UAE to Allow 100% Foreign Ownership of Businesses.' Gibson Dunn. https://www.gibsondunn.com/uae-to-allow-100-percent-foreign-ownership-of-businesses/ (May 30, 2022).

Gonçalves, Pedro, 2020. 'Oman to Introduce Income-Tax on Wealthy Individuals.' International Investment. https://www.internationalinvestment.net/news/4022586/oman-introduce-income-tax-wealthy-individuals (May 30, 2022).

Gray, Matthew, 2011. *A Theory of 'Late Rentierism' in the Arab States of the Gulf.* http://papers.ssrn.com/sol3/papers.cfm?abstract_id=2825905. Originally published: https://repository.library.georgetown.edu/bitstream/handle/10822/558291/CIRSOccasionalPaper7MatthewGray2011.pdf.

Gulf Times Staff, 2021. 'Qatar Economy Remains Resilient amid COVID-19 Pandemic.' *Gulf Times.* https://www.gulf-times.com/story/696570/Qatar-economy-remains-resilient-amid-COVID-19-pandemic (May 30, 2022).

Gulf Today Staff, 2021. 'Majid Al Futtaim to Get Priority in Government Contracts, Says Sheikh Mohammed.' Gulf Today. https://www.gulftoday.ae/news/2021/09/18/majid-al-futtaim-to-get-priority-in-government-contracts-says-sheikh-mohammed (May 30, 2022).

Herb, Michael, 2009. 'A Nation of Bureaucrats: Political Participation and Economic Diversification in Kuwait and the United Arab Emirates.' *International Journal of Middle East Studies* 41(3): 375–95. https://www.cambridge.org/core/product/identifier/S0020743809091119/type/journal_article (May 31, 2022).

Hertog, Steffen, 2014. 'Arab Gulf States: An Assessment of Nationalisation Policies.' *Gulf Labor Markets and Migration.* http://eprints.lse.ac.uk/57578/1/_lse.ac.uk_storage_LIBRARY_Secondary_libfile_shared_repository_Content_Hertog%2C%20S_Hertog_Arab_Gulf_States_Hertog_Arab_Gulf_States_2014.pdf

Huntington, Hillard G., 2015. 'Crude Oil Trade and Current Account Deficits.' *Energy Economics* 50: 70–79.

Hvidt, Martin, 2009. 'The Dubai Model: An Outline of Key Development-Process Elements in Dubai.' *International Journal of Middle East Studies* 41(3): 397–418.

IEA Staff, 2022a. *A 10-Point Plan to Cut Oil Use.* Paris. https://www.iea.org/reports/a-10-point-plan-to-cut-oil-use (May 30, 2022).

IEA Staff, 2022b. *Oil Market Report – May 2022.* Paris. https://www.iea.org/reports/oil-market-report-may-2022 (May 31, 2022).

IMF Staff, 2015. *Tax Policy Reforms in the GCC Countries: Now and How?* Doha. Annual meeting report. Tax Policy Reforms in the GCC Countries: Now and How? https://www.imf.org/external/np/pp/eng/2015/111015.pdf.

IMF Staff, 2021. *Economic Prospects and Policy Challenges for the GCC Countries.* Washington D.C.

Ingram, Jamie, 2020. 'Aramco IPO Rises To $29.4bn.' *MEES* 63(3). https://www.mees.com/2020/1/17/news-in-brief/aramco-ipo-rises-to-294bn/86f19680-3934-11ea-b1a2-bde6dda18fc9 (May 30, 2022).

Ingram, Jamie, 2021. 'Sparks Fly As Saudi-Emirati Economic Competition Intensifies.' *MEES* 64(27). https://www.mees.com/2021/7/9/geopolitical-risk/sparks-fly-as-saudi-emirati-economic-competition-intensifies/8591af80-e0cd-11eb-8c0d-15b22a2dd2d7 (May 30, 2022).

Ingram, Jamie, 2022a. 'Kuwait Set For 2022-23 Budget Surplus?' *MEES* 65(4). https://www.mees.com/2022/1/28/economics-finance/kuwait-set-for-2022-23-budget-surplus/deb5a9b0-804d-11ec-ae31-b1c978571d34 (May 30, 2022).

Ingram, Jamie, 2022b. 'Masdar, Engie To Develop Abu Dhabi Green Hydrogen.' *MEES* 65(3). https://www.mees.com/2022/1/21/refining-petrochemicals/masdar-engie-to-develop-abu-dhabi-green-hydrogen/b7eaeb30-7ac5-11ec-9384-e1e9b89bbf3d (May 30, 2022).

Ingram, Jamie, 2022c. 'Neom Hydrogen Project Advances.' *MEES* 65(14). https://www.mees.com/2022/4/8/news-in-brief/neom-hydrogen-project-advances/9f07f5e0-b737-11ec-9266-ef44bf7323eb (May 30, 2022).

Ingram, Jamie, 2022d. 'Qatar & Germany Sign Energy Partnership Roadmap.' *MEES* 65(21). https://www.mees.com/2022/5/27/geopolitical-risk/qatar-germany-sign-energy-partnership-roadmap/8a145d80-ddb9-11ec-8d7e-0f8c567bf424 (May 30, 2022).

Ingram, Jamie,. 2022e. 'Saudi Arabia Bolsters PIF With $80bn Aramco Transfer.' *MEES* 65(7). https://www.mees.com/2022/2/18/economics-finance/saudi-arabia-bolsters-pif-with-80bn-aramco-transfer/52e7da80-90ba-11ec-976d-278ecf76e179 (May 30, 2022).

International Energy Agency, 2018. *Outlook for Producer Economies.* Paris. October 2018 special report of the World Energy Outlook. https://www.iea.org/reports/outlook-for-producer-economies.

Kamrava, Mehran, Gerd Nonneman, Anastasia Nosova, and Marc Valeri, 2016. 'Ruling Families and Business Elites in the Gulf Monarchies: Ever Closer?' Research Paper by Chatham House, London. https://www.chathamhouse.org/sites/default/files/publications/research/2016-11-03-ruling-families-business-gulf-kamrava-nonneman-nosova-valeri.pdf.

Kane, Frank, 2020. '$800bn Plan to Turn Riyadh into Cultural Hub for the Middle East.' Arab News. https://www.arabnews.com/node/1700591/saudi-arabia (May 30, 2022).

Kerr, Simeon, 2021. 'UAE Pushes Merchant Families to Open up to Competition.' *The Financial Times.* https://www.ft.com/content/116b083a-1811-4501-ad9b-2f6a3183db3e (May 30, 2022).

Khalid, Tuqa, 2020. 'Coronavirus: Qatar Emir Bans Non-Citizen Entry, Reveals $23 Bln Stimulus Package.' Al Arabiya English. https://english.alarabiya.net/News/gulf/2020/03/15/Coronavirus-Qatar-suspends-all-incoming-flights-halts-public-transport (May 30, 2022).

Khalid, Tuqa, 2021. 'Full Transcript of Al-Ula GCC Summit Declaration: Bolstering Gulf Unity.' Al Arabiya English. https://english.alarabiya.net/News/gulf/2021/01/06/Full-transcript-of-AlUla-GCC-Summit-Declaration-Bolstering-Gulf-unity (May 30, 2022).

Khan, Sarmad, 2022. 'GCC Economies Set to Reap $1.4tn in Additional Oil Windfall in 5 Years, IMF Says.' *The National.* https://www.thenationalnews.com/business/economy/2022/05/24/gcc-economies-set-to-reap-14tn-in-additional-oil-windfall-in-5-years-imf-says/ (May 30, 2022).

Khariche, Dana, 2021. 'UAE Prince Sheikh Mohammed Bin Zayed Meets Saudi Arabia's Mohammed Bin Salman.' Bloomberg. https://www.bloomberg.com/news/articles/2021-07-19/uae-prince-travels-to-saudi-arabia-after-opec-dispute (May 30, 2022).

KPMG Staff, 2020a. 'Kingdom of Saudi Arabia – Measures in Response to COVID-19.' KPMG Global. https://home.kpmg/xx/en/home/insights/2020/04/saudi-arabia-government-and-institution-measures-in-response-to-COVID.html (May 30, 2022).

KPMG Staff, 2020b. 'Kuwait – Measures in Response to COVID-19.' KPMG Global. https://home.kpmg/xx/en/home/insights/2020/04/kuwait-government-and-institution-measures-in-response-to-COVID.html (May 30, 2022).

KPMG Staff, 2020c. 'Oman – Measures in Response to COVID-19.' KPMG Global. https://home.kpmg/xx/en/home/insights/2020/04/oman-government-and-institution-measures-in-response-to-COVID.html (May 30, 2022).

KPMG Staff, 2020d. 'Qatar – Measures in Response to COVID-19.' KPMG Global. https://home.kpmg/xx/en/home/insights/2020/04/qatar-government- and-institution-measures-in-response-to-COVID.html (May 30, 2022).

KPMG Staff, 2020e. 'United Arab Emirates – Measures in Response to COVID-19.' KPMG Global. https://home.kpmg/xx/en/home/insights/2020/04/united-arab-emirates-government-and-institution-measures-in-response-to-COVID.html (May 30, 2022).

Liberto, Daniel, 2021. 'Zakat.' Investopedia. https://www.investopedia.com/terms/z/zakat.asp (May 30, 2022).

Losman, Donald L., 2010a. 'The Rentier State And National Oil Companies: An Economic And Political Perspective.' Middle East Journal 64(3): 427–45. https://www.jstor.org/stable/40783108 (November 5, 2021).

Losman, Donald L., 2010b. 'The Rentier State and National Oil Companies: An Economic and Political Perspective.' *Middle East Journal* 64(3).

Luciani, Giacomo, 2015. 'Allocation vs. Production States: A Theoretical Framework.' *The Rentier State*: 63–82. https://www.taylorfrancis.com/chapters/edit/10.4324/9781315684864-4/allocation-vs-production-states-theoretical-framework-giacomo-luciani

MacDonald, Fiona, Turki al Balushi, and Sylvia Westall, 2020. 'Oman Weighs Financial Aid Request From Gulf.' Bloomberg. https://www.bloomberg.com/news/articles/2020-06-11/oman-said-to-test-waters-for-aid-from-gulf-neighbors-amid-crisis (May 30, 2022).

Magdy, Mirette, Matthew Martin, and Abeer Abu Omar, 2022. 'Surging Oil Price Is Budget Boon for the Middle East's Exporters.' Bloomberg. https://www.bloomberg.com/news/articles/2022-02-25/surging-oil-is-budget-boon-for-the-middle-east-s-exporters (May 30, 2022).

Mahdavy, H., 2015. 'The Patterns and Problems of Economic Development in Rentier States: The Case of Iran.' In M. A. Cook (ed.), *Studies in the Economic History of the Middle East*. Routledge. https://www.taylorfrancis.com/chapters/edit/10.4324/9781315000312-36/patterns-problems-economic-development-rentier-states-case-iran-hossein-mahdavy-harvard

Malek, Caline, 2020. 'High COVID-19 Recovery Rates Put GCC Region in the Limelight.' Arab News. https://www.arabnews.com/node/1733941/middle-east (May 30, 2022).

Maloney, Suzanne, 2008. 'The Gulf's Renewed Oil Wealth: Getting It Right This Time?' *Survival* 50(6): 129–50.

Mansouri, Noura, and Aisha Al-Sarihi, 2021. 'A Saudi Perspective on COP26 and Current Initiatives.' *Oxford Energy Forum* (129): 58–63. https://www.oxford energy.org/wpcms/wp-content/uploads/2021/09/OEF-129.pdf (May 30, 2022).

Markaz, 2021. Marmore MENA Intelligence *GCC Bonds and Sukuk Market Survey 2020* . https://www.marmoremena.com/reports/gcc-bonds-and-sukuk-market-survey-2020/ (May 30, 2022).

Markaz, 2022. *GCC Bonds and Sukuk Market Survey 2021*. https://www.marmoremena.com/reports/gcc-bonds-and-sukuk-market-survey-2021/ (May 30, 2022).

Market Research Kuwait, 2020. 'The Central Bank of Kuwait Launches KD 5 Billion Stimulus Package.' Market Research Kuwait. https://www.marketresearchkuwait.com/insight/the-cbk-launches-kd-5-billion-stimulus-package (May 30, 2022).

Martin, Matthew, Vivian Nereim, and Zainab Fattah, 2021. 'Saudi Arabia Adds Pressure on Global Firms to Move to Riyadh.' Bloomberg. https://www.bloomberg.com/news/articles/2021-02-15/saudi-arabia-aims-to-sideline-firms-without-base-in-the-kingdom (May 30, 2022).

Migrant Rights, 2020. 'Oman Eases Restrictions on Sponsorship Transfer.' Migrant Rights. https://www.migrant-rights.org/2020/06/oman-eases-restrictions-on-sponsorship-transfer/ (May 30, 2022).

Mirza, Adel, 2021. 'Adnoc Makes New Blue Ammonia Shipment to Japan.' Argus Media. https://www.argusmedia.com/en/news/2252286-adnoc-makes-new-blue-ammonia-shipment-to-japan (May 30, 2022).

Mogielnicki, Robert, 2021a. 'A Political Economy of Free Zones in Gulf Arab States.' https://link.springer.com/10.1007/978-3-030-71274-7 (May 30, 2022).

Mogielnicki, Robert, 2021b. 'The Politics of Leverage: Bond Issuances, Debt Dynamics, and State Finances in the Gulf.' https://agsiw.org/the-politics-of-leverage-bond-issuances-debt-dynamics-and-state-finances-in-the-gulf/ (May 31, 2022).

Moossdroff, Bastiaan, 2021. 'The Impact of VAT on the Omani Economy.' Gulf Business. https://gulfbusiness.com/the-impact-of-vat-on-the-omani-economy/ (May 30, 2022).

Moritz, Jessie Alethea, 2016. 'Slick Operators: Revising Rentier State Theory for the Modern Arab States of the Gulf.' Australian National University. https://openresearch-repository.anu.edu.au/handle/1885/112895 (May 31, 2022).

Mouawad, Jad, 2009. 'OPEC Achieves Cuts in Output, Halting Price Slide.' *The New York Times*. https://www.nytimes.com/2009/01/26/business/worldbusiness/26opec.html (May 29, 2022).

Murphy, David J., and Charles A. S. Hall, 2011. 'Energy Return on Investment, Peak Oil, and the End of Economic Growth.' *Annals of the New York Academy of Sciences* 1219(1): 52–72. https://onlinelibrary.wiley.com/doi/full/10.1111/j.1749-6632.2010.05940.x (May 30, 2022).

Nammour, Marie, 2020. 'UAE Issues Landmark Reforms to Civil, Criminal Law.' *Khaleej Times*. https://www.khaleejtimes.com/uae/uae-issues-landmark-reforms-to-civil-criminal-law (May 30, 2022).

OEC, 2022a. 'Saudi Arabia (SAU) Exports, Imports, and Trade Partners.' The Observatory of Economic Complexity. https://oec.world/en/profile/country/sau?yearlyTradeFlowSelector=flow1 (May 30, 2022).

OEC, 2022b. 'United Arab Emirates (ARE) Exports, Imports, and Trade Partners.' The Observatory of Economic Complexity. https://oec.world/en/profile/country/are (May 30, 2022).

OECD Staff, 2020. 'COVID-19 Crisis Response in MENA Countries.' OECD Policy Responses to Coronavirus (COVID-19). https://www.oecd.org/coronavirus/policy-responses/COVID-19-crisis-response-in-mena-countries-4b366396/ (May 30, 2022).

Oman Observer, 2020. '5% VAT to Come into Force Soon.' *Oman Observer*. https://www.omanobserver.om/article/9130/1/5-vat-to-come-into-force-soon (May 30, 2022).

OPEC Annual Statistical Bulletin. 2021. OPEC Secretariat General in Vienna. https://www.opec.org/opec_web/static_files_project/media/downloads/publications/OPEC_ASB_2021.pdf.

OPEC Press Office. 'OPEC : Declaration of Cooperation.' OPEC. https://www.opec.org/opec_web/en/publications/4580.htm (May 30, 2022).

Our World in Data, 2022. 'Daily COVID-19 Tests per Thousand People.' *Our World in Data*. https://ourworldindata.org/grapher/daily-tests-per-thousand-people-smoothed-7-day?tab=table&time=latest (May 30, 2022).

Oweiss, Ibrahim M., 1984. 'Petrodollar Surpluses: Trends & Economic Impact.' *Journal of Energy and Development* 9(2): 177–202. https://www.jstor.org/stable/24807042 (November 5, 2021).

Owtram, Francis, and Malak Hayek. 2020. 'Oman in the COVID-19 Pandemic: People, Policy and Economic Impact.' LSE Middle East Centre. https://blogs.lse.ac.uk/mec/2020/07/23/oman-in-the-COVID-19-pandemic-people-policy-and-economic-impact/ (May 30, 2022).

di Paola, Anthony, and Tracy Alloway, 2018. 'Heading Downstream: Abu Dhabi's Big Plans for Business Beyond Oil.' Bloomberg. https://www.bloomberg.com/news/articles/2018-05-10/as-saudis-pursue-aramco-ipo-abu-dhabi-hedges-to-stay-relevant (May 30, 2022).

Puscaciu, Viorica, and Florin-Dan Puscaciu, 2015. 'Paradox of Plenty or Resource Curse?' *Knowledge Horizons. Economics* 7(3): 239–43. http://search.proquest.com/docview/1696658064?accountid=28103.

PwC, 2022a. 'Bahrain – Corporate – Taxes on Corporate Income.' *PwC Worldwide Tax Summaries*. https://taxsummaries.pwc.com/bahrain/corporate/taxes-on-corporate-income (May 30, 2022).

PwC, 2022b. 'Kuwait – Corporate – Taxes on Corporate Income.' *PwC Worldwide Tax Summaries*. https://taxsummaries.pwc.com/kuwait/corporate/taxes-on-corporate-income (May 30, 2022).

PwC, 2022c. 'Oman – Corporate – Taxes on Corporate Income.' *PwC Worldwide Tax Summaries*. https://taxsummaries.pwc.com/oman/corporate/taxes-on-corporate-income (May 30, 2022).

PwC, 2022d. 'Qatar – Corporate – Taxes on Corporate Income.' *PwC Worldwide Tax Summaries*. https://taxsummaries.pwc.com/qatar/corporate/taxes-on-corporate-income (May 30, 2022).

PwC, 2022e. 'Saudi Arabia – Corporate – Taxes on Corporate Income.' *PwC Worldwide Tax Summaries.* https://taxsummaries.pwc.com/saudi-arabia/corporate/taxes-on-corporate-income (May 30, 2022).

Qasem, I.Y., 2010. 'Neo-Rentier Theory: The Case of Saudi Arabia (1950–2000).' https://hdl.handle.net/1887/14746 (November 5, 2021).

QCRA, 2020. 'Cisco Joins CRA Initiative to Make Remote Work Easy.' Qatar Communications Regulatory Authority. https://www.cra.gov.qa/en/press-releases/cisco-joins-cra-initiative-to-make-remote-work-easy (May 30, 2022).

QDB Staff, 2020. 'National Guarantee Program.' Qatar Development Bank. https://www.qdb.qa/en/Pages/national-guarantee-program.aspx (May 30, 2022).

Rashed, Marwa, and Saeed Azhar, 2021. 'Saudi Sovereign Fund to Double Assets in next Five Years to $1.07 Trillion: Crown Prince.' Reuters. https://www.reuters.com/article/us-saudi-pif-assets-idUSKBN29T0MC (May 30, 2022).

Raval, Anjli, David Sheppard, and Derek Brower, 2020. 'Saudi Arabia Launches Oil Price War after Russia Deal Collapse.' *The Financial Times.* https://www.ft.com/content/d700b71a-6122-11ea-b3f3-fe4680ea68b5 (May 30, 2022).

Reuters Staff,. 2014. 'UAE, Abu Dhabi Roll over $20 Billion of Dubai's Debt.' Reuters. https://www.reuters.com/article/us-emirates-dubai-debt-idUSBREA2F0EQ20140316 (May 30, 2022).

Reuters Staff, 2020a. 'Dubai Expects Economic Boost from UAE Golden Visa Extension.' Reuters. https://www.reuters.com/article/emirates-economy-dubai-int-idUSKBN2831EN (May 30, 2022).

Reuters Staff, 2020b. 'Moody's Cuts Oman's Rating by a Notch to "Ba2".' Reuters. https://www.reuters.com/article/oman-ratings-moodys-idUSL4N2AY423 (May 30, 2022).

Reuters Staff, 2020c. 'UAE Central Bank Boosts Anti-Coronavirus Stimulus to $70 Billion.' Reuters. https://www.reuters.com/article/us-health-coronavirus-emirates-cenbank-idUSKBN21N069 (May 30, 2022).

Reuters Staff, 2021a. 'Qatar's New Electoral Law Stirs up Tribal Sensitivities.' Reuters. https://www.reuters.com/world/middle-east/qatars-new-electoral-law-stirs-up-tribal-sensitivities-2021-08-12/ (May 30, 2022).

Reuters Staff, 2021b. 'Saudi Crown Prince Says Kingdom Has No Plans to Introduce Income Tax.' *Reuters.* https://www.reuters.com/world/middle-east/saudi-crown-prince-says-kingdom-has-no-plans-introduce-income-tax-2021-04-27/ (May 30, 2022).

Rosser, Andrew, 2006. *The Political Economy of the Resource Curse?: A Literature Survey.* https://opendocs.ids.ac.uk/opendocs/handle/20.500.12413/4061 (May 31, 2022).

Saba, Yousef, 2020. 'Oman Bonds Weaken Following S&P Rating Downgrade.' Nasdaq. https://www.nasdaq.com/articles/oman-bonds-weaken-following-sp-rating-downgrade-2020-03-30 (May 30, 2022).

Sabic Staff, 2022. 'Creating the World's Largest Carbon Capture and Utilization Plant.' Sabic. https://www.sabic.com/en/newsandmedia/stories/our-world/creating-the-worlds-largest-carbon-capture-and-utilization-plant (May 30, 2022).

Sampson, Anthony, 1988. *The Seven Sisters: The Great Oil Companies and the World They Made*. 1st ed. New York: Hodder and Stoughton. https://archive.org/details/sevensistersgrea00samp_0/page/n5/mode/2up

Saudi Ministry of Investment, 2020. 'Initiatives and Services Introduced by Saudi Arabian Government Authorities to Support Businesses during the Emerging COVID-19 Pandemic.' Saudi Ministry of Investment. https://misa.gov.sa/en/COVID-19-gov-initiatives/ (May 30, 2022).

Schofield, Mark, 2021. 'From No Tax to Low Tax: As the GCC Relies More on Tax, Getting It Right Is Critical for Diversification.' PwC Middle East Economy Watch. https://www.pwc.com/m1/en/publications/middle-east-economy-watch/april-2021/no-tax-to-low-tax-gcc-relies-more-getting-right-critical-diversification.html (May 30, 2022).

Schroder, Patrick, Sian Bradley, and Glada Lahn. 2020. 'G20 Endorses a Circular Carbon Economy: But Do We Need It?.' Chatham House. https://www.chathamhouse.org/2020/11/g20-endorses-circular-carbon-economy-do-we-need-it (May 30, 2022).

Shehri Thamir Al, Jan Frederick Braun, Nicholas Howarth, Alessandro Lanza and Mari Luomi, 2023. 'Saudi Arabia's Climate Change Policy and the Circular Carbon Economy Approach.' *Climate Policy*, 23(2): 151–167. DOI: 10.1080/14693062.2022.2070118. https://www.tandfonline.com/doi/full/10.1080/14693062.2022.2070118

Sievers, Marc J., 2020. 'Sultan Haitham Makes a Strong Start by Addressing Economic Challenges.' Atlantic Council. https://www.atlanticcouncil.org/blogs/menasource/sultan-haitham-makes-a-strong-start-by-addressing-economic-challenges/ (May 30, 2022).

Smith, Grant, 2021. 'Saudis Dismiss Call to End Oil Spending as "La La Land" Fantasy.' Bloomberg. https://www.bloomberg.com/news/articles/2021-06-01/saudis-dismiss-call-to-end-oil-spending-as-la-la-land-fantasy (May 30, 2022).

Soupa, Olivier, and Georgios Mexis, 2018. *Local Content after a Booming Oil & Gas Cycle*. Dubai. https://www.adlittle.com/sites/default/files/viewpoints/adl_local_content_after_a_booming_oil_gas_cycle.compressed.pdf.

SPA, 2021. '"Shareek" Program Aims to Strengthen Cooperation between Public and Private Sectors.' Saudi Press Agency. https://www.spa.gov.sa/viewfullstory.php?lang=en&newsid=2209666 (May 30, 2022).

Stewart, Iona, John Curtis, and Philip Loft, 2022. 'Alternatives to Russian Oil: Saudi Arabia, the Gulf and Venezuela?' UK House of Commons Library. https://commonslibrary.parliament.uk/research-briefings/cbp-9518/ (May 30, 2022).

Stiglitz, Joseph, 2015. 'Overcoming the Copenhagen Failure with Flexible Commitments.' *Economics of Energy & Environmental Policy* 4(2). http://dx.doi.Org/10.5547/2160-5890.4.2.jsti (May 30, 2022).

SWFI Staff, 2022. 'Al Raffd Fund.' Sovereign Wealth Fund Institute. https://www.swfinstitute.org/profile/5d2b99effc63494bebed3005 (May 30, 2022).

The Editorial Board, 2020. 'Gulf Social Changes Are in the Global Spotlight.' *The Financial Times*. https://www.ft.com/content/b0fa3fdf-94ea-4b4c-a96e-80d24c33e667 (May 30, 2022).

Thomas, George, and George Parks, 2006. *Potential Roles of Ammonia in a Hydrogen Economy*. February 2006 US Department of Energy report. https://www.energy.gov/eere/fuelcells/articles/potential-roles-ammonia-hydrogen-economy

Trade Arabia, 2020. 'Saudi Arabia's SAMA Renamed Saudi Central Bank.' Trade Arabia. http://www.tradearabia.com/news/BANK_375709.html (May 30, 2022).

UAE Government, 2022. 'Full Foreign Ownership of Commercial Companies.' The Official Portal of the UAE Government. https://u.ae/en/information-and-services/business/full-foreign-ownership-of-commercial-companies (May 30, 2022).

UAE Ministry of Finance, 2013. 'GCC Economic Integration.' UAE Ministry of Finance. https://www.mof.gov.ae/en/StrategicPartnerships/Pages/GCCEconomicIntegration.aspx (May 30, 2022).

UN ESCWA, 2022. 'Al Raffd Fund: SME Digital Enabling Portal for the Arab Region.' UN ESCWA. https://smeportal.unescwa.org/financing/al-raffdoc.tab=0 (May 30, 2022).

UN Staff, 2022. *Global Impact of War in Ukraine on Food, Energy and Finance Systems*. Global Crisis Response Group (GCRG). https://unctad.org/system/files/official-document/un-gcrg-ukraine-brief-no-1_en.pdf.

UNCTAD, 2022. 'United Arab Emirates – Opens to 100 per Cent Foreign Ownership in Most Sectors.' UNCTAD Investment Policy Hub. https://investmentpolicy.unctad.org/investment-policy-monitor/measures/3786/united-arab-emirates-opens-to-100-per-cent-foreign-ownership-in-most-sectors (May 30, 2022).

UNFCCC, 2015. 'Paris Agreement.' United Nations. https://unfccc.int/sites/default/files/english_paris_agreement.pdf

Vertex, 2021. 'VAT in the Gulf: Oman Becomes 4th State to Introduce a VAT System.' Vertex. https://www.vertexinc.com/resources/resource-library/vat-gulf-oman-becomes-4th-state-introduce-vat-system (May 30, 2022).

el Wardany, Salma, 2022. 'Saudi Arabia to Use Windfall From Oil Prices to Boost Private Sector.' Bloomberg. https://www.bloomberg.com/news/articles/2022-05-23/saudi-arabia-to-use-oil-windfall-to-boost-private-sector (May 30, 2022).

el Wardany, Salma, Grant Smith, Javier Blas, and Dina Khernnikova, 2021. 'OPEC+ Shows No Sign of Healing Rift Hours Before Talks Restart.' Bloomberg. https://www.bloomberg.com/news/articles/2021-07-05/opec-shows-no-sign-of-healing-rift-hours-before-talks-restart (May 30, 2022).

WHO Staff, 2020. 'Updated Country Preparedness and Status for COVID-19.' World Health Organization. https://www.who.int/who-documents-detail/updated-country-preparedness-and-response-status-for-COVID-19-as-of-16-march-2020 (May 30, 2022).

el Yaakoubi, Aziz, and Davide Barbuscia, 2021. 'Oman Orders Speedier Job Creation amid Protests over Unemployment.' Reuters. https://www.reuters.com/world/middle-east/job-seeking-omanis-protest-again-press-cash-strapped-government-2021-05-25/ (May 30, 2022).

Zawya, 2020. 'Omanisation: Ministry of Transport to Take Regulatory Measures in Delivery Profession.' Zawya. https://www.zawya.com/en/economy/omanisation-ministry-of-transport-to-take-regulatory-measures-in-delivery-profession-schp82b6 (May 30, 2022).

Annex: GCC fiscal and economic data

Year	2005	2006	2007	2008	2009	2010	2011	2012	2013	2014	2015	2016	2017	2018	2019	2020
Brent oil price ($/b)*	54.4	65.1	72.5	96.8	61.5	79.5	111.3	111.7	108.6	99.0	52.4	43.5	54.2	71.1	64.4	41.8
						Indicators (US billion or percentage where applicable)										
Kuwait																
Hydrocarbon revenues	44.4	50.2	61.3	72.2	57.7	71.5	103.5	106.6	103.2	78.1	40.0	38.5	47.2	60.8	50.5	29.0
Non-hydrocarbon revenues	2.6	3.5	4.5	4.7	3.8	5.6	6.0	7.2	8.9	8.4	5.2	4.7	5.7	7.0	6.1	5.7
Total revenues	**47.0**	**53.6**	**65.8**	**77.0**	**61.5**	**77.1**	**109.5**	**113.8**	**112.1**	**86.5**	**45.1**	**43.2**	**52.9**	**67.8**	**56.6**	**34.7**
Hydrocarbon share (%)	94	94	93	94	94	93	94	94	92	90	89	89	89	90	89	84
Non-hydrocarbon share (%)	6	6	7	6	6	7	6	6	8	10	11	11	11	10	11	16
Total spending	**23.5**	**35.6**	**33.5**	**66.9**	**39.1**	**58.2**	**61.6**	**68.7**	**66.6**	**74.3**	**60.4**	**58.4**	**63.7**	**72.1**	**69.4**	**70.3**
Budget balance	23.5	18.0	32.2	10.1	22.4	18.9	47.9	45.1	45.5	12.2	-15.3	-15.2	-10.8	-4.3	-12.9	-35.5

(continued)

Annex: Continued

Year	2005	2006	2007	2008	2009	2010	2011	2012	2013	2014	2015	2016	2017	2018	2019	2020
Balance post RFFG deduction**	**18.8**	**12.6**	**25.7**	**2.4**	**16.2**	**11.2**	**37.0**	**16.7**	**17.5**	**-9.4**	**-19.8**	**-19.5**	**-16.0**	**-4.3**	**-12.9**	**-35.5**
Fiscal breakeven price	**31.3**	**48.8**	**42.1**	**93.7**	**44.2**	**67.0**	**71.5**	**94.2**	**90.2**	**111.0**	**78.3**	**65.6**	**72.7**	**76.0**	**80.8**	**92.9**
vs Brent	-23.1	-16.4	-30.4	-3.2	-17.3	-12.5	-39.7	-17.5	-18.4	12.0	25.9	22.0	18.4	5.0	16.4	51.2
GDP	**80.8**	**101.5**	**114.6**	**147.4**	**106.0**	**115.4**	**154.1**	**174.1**	**174.2**	**162.6**	**114.6**	**109.4**	**120.7**	**138.2**	**136.2**	**106.0**
Oil contribution (%)	55	49	53	49	54	62	67	61	59	48	35	35	39	44	37	27
Government spending (%)	29	35	29	45	37	50	40	39	38	46	53	53	53	52	51	66
Saudi Arabia																
Hydrocarbon revenues	134.5	161.2	149.9	262.2	115.8	178.7	275.8	305.3	276.0	243.6	119.0	89.0	116.2	163.0	158.5	110.1
Non-hydrocarbon revenues	15.9	18.5	21.5	31.4	20.1	18.8	22.2	27.1	31.4	33.8	44.3	49.5	68.2	78.5	88.6	98.3

Total revenues	150.5	179.6	171.4	293.6	135.9	197.6	298.0	332.4	307.4	277.4	163.4	138.5	184.4	241.5	247.2	208.5
Hydrocarbon share (%)	89	90	87	89	85	90	93	92	90	88	73	64	63	67	64	53
Non-hydrocarbon share	11	10	13	11	15	10	7	8	10	12	27	36	37	33	36	47
Total spending (%)	**92.4**	**104.9**	**124.3**	**138.7**	**159.0**	**174.4**	**220.5**	**244.6**	**265.3**	**304.2**	**267.0**	**221.5**	**248.0**	**287.9**	**282.5**	**286.9**
Budget balance	**58.1**	**74.8**	**47.1**	**154.9**	**−23.1**	**23.2**	**77.6**	**87.8**	**42.1**	**−26.8**	**−103.6**	**−82.9**	**−63.6**	**−46.4**	**−35.4**	**−78.4**
Fiscal Breakeven Price	**30.9**	**34.9**	**49.7**	**39.6**	**73.8**	**69.2**	**80.0**	**79.5**	**92.1**	**109.9**	**97.9**	**84.1**	**83.9**	**91.3**	**78.7**	**71.5**
vs Brent	−23.5	−30.2	−22.8	−57.2	12.3	−10.3	−31.3	−32.1	−16.6	10.9	45.6	40.6	29.7	20.2	14.4	29.7
GDP	**328.5**	**376.9**	**416.0**	**519.8**	**429.1**	**528.2**	**671.2**	**736.0**	**746.6**	**756.4**	**654.3**	**644.9**	**688.6**	**786.5**	**793.0**	**700.1**
Oil contribution (%)	41	43	36	50	27	34	41	41	37	32	18	14	17	21	20	16
Government spending (%)	28	28	30	27	37	33	33	33	36	40	41	34	36	37	36	41
Bahrain§																
Hydrocarbon revenues	3.4	3.8	4.3	6.1	3.8	4.9	6.6	7.0	6.9	7.1	4.2	3.8	4.4	6.1	5.6	3.2

(continued)

Annex: Continued

Year	2005	2006	2007	2008	2009	2010	2011	2012	2013	2014	2015	2016	2017	2018	2019	2020
Non-hydrocarbon revenues	1.1	1.1	1.1	1.0	0.8	0.9	0.9	1.0	0.9	1.1	1.2	1.2	1.5	1.3	2.2	2.3
Total revenues	**4.4**	**4.9**	**5.4**	**7.1**	**4.5**	**5.8**	**7.5**	**8.1**	**7.8**	**8.2**	**5.4**	**5.0**	**5.9**	**7.4**	**7.7**	**5.5**
Hydrocarbon share (%)	76	77	80	85	83	85	88	87	88	86	78	76	75	82	72	58
Non-hydrocarbon share (%)	24	23	20	15	17	15	12	13	12	14	22	24	25	18	28	42
Total spending	**3.4**	**4.1**	**4.8**	**5.5**	**5.5**	**7.0**	**7.6**	**8.7**	**8.9**	**9.4**	**9.2**	**9.4**	**9.4**	**9.8**	**9.5**	**10.0**
Budget balance	**1.0**	**0.7**	**0.6**	**1.6**	**-1.0**	**-1.2**	**-0.1**	**-0.6**	**-1.1**	**-1.2**	**-3.8**	**-4.3**	**-3.6**	**-2.4**	**-1.8**	**-4.4**
Fiscal breakeven price	**38.0**	**52.2**	**62.7**	**70.7**	**77.7**	**99.3**	**112.7**	**121.2**	**125.8**	**116.0**	**99.4**	**93.1**	**98.1**	**98.9**	**84.8**	**99.3**
vs Brent	-16.4	-12.9	-9.7	-26.2	16.2	19.7	1.4	9.6	17.1	16.9	47.0	49.6	43.8	27.8	20.5	57.6
GDP	**16.0**	**18.5**	**21.7**	**25.7**	**22.9**	**25.7**	**28.8**	**30.7**	**32.5**	**33.4**	**31.1**	**32.2**	**35.5**	**37.8**	**38.7**	**34.7**
Oil contribution (%)	21	20	20	24	16	19	23	23	21	21	14	12	12	16	14	9

Government spending (%)	21	22	22	21	24	27	26	28	27	28	30	29	27	26	25	29
Qatar*																
Hydrocarbon revenues	12.0	15.2	19.4	22.0	22.7	26.6	42.7	48.8	53.7	75.8	42.1	38.7	36.5	47.6	46.7	36.6
Non-hydrocarbon revenues	5.9	8.4	12.9	16.8	23.7	16.2	18.5	29.3	40.5	16.4	9.3	8.3	8.3	9.6	12.3	10.4
Total revenues	**17.9**	**23.6**	**32.4**	**38.7**	**46.5**	**42.9**	**61.2**	**78.1**	**94.2**	**92.2**	**51.4**	**46.9**	**44.9**	**57.1**	**59.0**	**47.0**
Hydrocarbon share (%)	67	64	60	57	49	62	70	62	57	82	82	82	81	83	79	78
Non-hydrocarbon share (%)	33	36	40	43	51	38	30	38	43	18	18	18	19	17	21	22
Total spending	**14.0**	**18.4**	**23.7**	**27.3**	**31.6**	**40.3**	**49.4**	**56.5**	**65.3**	**62.4**	**52.6**	**60.9**	**55.9**	**53.0**	**57.3**	**50.1**
Budget balance	**3.9**	**5.2**	**8.7**	**11.5**	**14.9**	**2.6**	**11.7**	**21.6**	**28.9**	**29.9**	**-1.2**	**-14.0**	**-11.0**	**4.1**	**1.7**	**-3.1**
Fiscal breakeven price	**36.8**	**42.9**	**40.1**	**46.2**	**21.3**	**71.7**	**80.6**	**62.2**	**50.1**	**60.0**	**53.8**	**59.3**	**70.6**	**64.9**	**62.0**	**45.3**
vs Brent	-17.6	-22.2	-32.4	-50.6	-40.2	-7.8	-30.6	-49.5	-58.5	-39.0	1.4	15.8	16.3	-6.2	-2.4	3.5

(continued)

Annex: Continued

Year	2005	2006	2007	2008	2009	2010	2011	2012	2013	2014	2015	2016	2017	2018	2019	2020
GDP	**44.5**	**60.9**	**79.7**	**115.3**	**97.8**	**125.1**	**167.8**	**186.8**	**198.7**	**206.2**	**161.7**	**151.7**	**161.1**	**183.3**	**176.4**	**144.4**
Oil contribution (%)	27	25	24	19	23	21	25	26	27	37	26	25	23	26	26	25
Government spending (%)	31	30	30	24	32	32	29	30	33	30	33	40	35	29	32	35
UAE**																
Hydrocarbon revenues	30.3	44.9	48.0	73.3	33.3	46.2	71.5	76.0	79.8	69.1	37.6	23.6	39.5	53.6	53.7	41.6
Non-hydrocarbon revenues	8.9	9.9	14.3	31.2	30.5	30.6	32.0	36.3	45.6	40.7	45.4	80.2	70.0	76.5	76.6	59.0
Total revenues	**39.2**	**54.8**	**62.3**	**104.5**	**63.8**	**76.8**	**103.4**	**112.4**	**125.5**	**109.8**	**83.0**	**103.8**	**109.4**	**130.1**	**130.2**	**100.6**
Hydrocarbon share (%)	77	82	77	70	52	60	69	68	64	63	45	23	36	41	41	41
Non-hydrocarbon share (%)	23	18	23	30	48	40	31	32	36	37	55	77	64	59	59	59

Total spending	28.4	34.3	43.5	75.1	106.4	93.7	123.0	130.5	145.2	119.5	106.0	108.4	110.2	105.7	120.5	101.5
Budget balance	**10.7**	**20.5**	**18.8**	**29.5**	**−42.6**	**−16.9**	**−19.6**	**−18.1**	**−19.7**	**−9.6**	**−23.0**	**−4.6**	**−0.8**	**24.4**	**9.8**	**−0.8**
Fiscal breakeven price	**35.1**	**35.4**	**44.1**	**57.9**	**140.0**	**108.6**	**141.8**	**138.3**	**135.4**	**112.8**	**84.4**	**52.0**	**55.3**	**38.7**	**52.6**	**42.6**
vs Brent	−19.3	−29.7	−28.4	−38.9	78.5	29.0	30.5	26.6	26.8	13.8	32.1	8.5	1.0	−32.3	−11.7	0.8
GDP	**180.6**	**222.1**	**257.9**	**315.5**	**253.5**	**289.8**	**350.7**	**374.6**	**390.1**	**403.1**	**358.1**	**357.0**	**385.6**	**422.2**	**417.2**	**358.9**
Oil contribution (%)	17	20	19	23	13	16	20	20	20	17	10	7	10	13	13	12
Government spending (%)	16	15	17	24	42	32	35	35	37	30	30	30	29	25	29	28
Oman*																
Hydrocarbon revenues	9.2	10.0	11.7	15.6	13.6	16.6	23.3	29.7	31.0	30.9	18.6	13.5	16.1	22.3	20.8	15.1
Non-hydrocarbon revenues	2.5	3.0	3.7	4.3	4.0	3.9	4.3	5.4	5.2	5.8	5.0	6.3	6.0	6.2	6.7	7.0
Total revenues	**11.7**	**12.9**	**15.4**	**19.9**	**17.5**	**20.6**	**27.6**	**35.0**	**36.2**	**36.7**	**23.6**	**19.8**	**22.1**	**28.5**	**27.5**	**22.1**
Hydrocarbon share (%)	79	77	76	79	77	81	84	85	86	84	79	68	73	78	76	68

(continued)

Annex: Continued

Year	2005	2006	2007	2008	2009	2010	2011	2012	2013	2014	2015	2016	2017	2018	2019	2020
Non-hydrocarbon share (%)	21	23	24	21	23	19	16	15	14	16	21	32	27	22	24	32
Total spending	10.9	12.8	15.3	19.7	19.3	20.7	27.9	35.2	36.4	39.4	35.6	33.6	31.9	35.4	34.3	33.6
Budget balance	0.8	0.1	0.1	0.2	−1.8	−0.1	−0.3	−0.2	−0.2	−2.8	−12.0	−13.8	−9.8	−6.9	−6.8	−11.5
Fiscal breakeven price	49.8	64.4	71.8	95.6	69.5	80.1	112.7	112.4	109.4	107.9	86.3	88.0	87.1	93.0	85.5	73.6
vs Brent	−4.6	−0.7	−0.6	−1.3	8.0	0.6	1.4	0.8	0.8	8.9	34.0	44.5	32.9	22.0	21.1	31.9
GDP	31.1	37.2	42.1	60.9	48.4	65.0	77.5	87.4	89.9	92.7	78.7	75.1	80.9	91.5	88.1	74.0
Oil contribution (%)	30	27	28	26	28	26	30	34	34	33	24	18	20	24	24	20
Government spending (%)	35	34	36	32	40	32	36	40	40	43	45	45	39	39	39	45
GCC																
Hydrocarbon revenues	233.8	285.2	294.6	451.5	246.9	344.7	523.3	573.4	550.7	504.5	261.5	207.1	260.0	353.3	335.7	235.7

Non-hydrocarbon revenues	36.9	44.3	58.0	89.4	82.9	76.0	83.9	106.4	132.4	106.3	110.4	150.2	159.6	179.1	192.5	182.8
Total revenues	**270.7**	**329.5**	**352.7**	**540.8**	**329.9**	**420.7**	**607.3**	**679.8**	**683.1**	**610.8**	**371.9**	**357.3**	**419.6**	**532.4**	**528.2**	**418.5**
Hydrocarbon share (%)	86	87	84	83	75	82	86	84	81	83	70	58	62	66	64	56
Non-hydrocarbon share (%)	14	13	16	17	25	18	14	16	19	17	30	42	38	34	36	44
Total spending	**172.7**	**210.3**	**245.2**	**333.1**	**361.0**	**394.2**	**490.0**	**544.2**	**587.6**	**609.2**	**530.8**	**492.2**	**519.0**	**563.7**	**573.5**	**552.3**
Average annual spending	28.8	35.0	40.9	55.5	60.2	65.7	81.7	90.7	97.9	101.5	88.5	82.0	86.5	94.0	95.6	92.0
Spending growth rate (%)		21.8	16.6	35.8	8.4	9.2	24.3	11.0	8.0	3.7	-12.9	-7.3	5.5	8.6	1.7	-3.7
Average breakeven price	**37.0**	**46.4**	**51.8**	**67.3**	**71.1**	**82.6**	**99.9**	**101.3**	**100.5**	**102.9**	**83.3**	**73.7**	**77.9**	**77.1**	**74.1**	**70.9**
vs Brent	17.4	18.7	20.7	29.6	-9.6	-3.1	11.4	10.3	8.1	-3.9	-31.0	-30.2	-23.7	-6.1	-9.7	-29.1
GDP	**681.5**	**817.2**	**932.0**	**1,184.6**	**957.7**	**1,149.2**	**1,450.0**	**1,589.6**	**1,632.1**	**1,654.4**	**1,398.5**	**1,370.5**	**1,472.3**	**1,659.6**	**1,649.5**	**1,418.1**
Oil contribution (%)	34	35	32	38	26	30	36	36	34	30	19	15	18	21	20	17

(continued)

Annex: Continued

Year	2005	2006	2007	2008	2009	2010	2011	2012	2013	2014	2015	2016	2017	2018	2019	2020
Government spending (%)	25	26	26	28	38	34	34	34	36	37	38	36	35	34	35	39

* Based on U.S. Energy Information Administration monthly Brent FOB data

** Kuwait's Future Generations Fund (RFFG) deductions are 10% in 2011, 25% from 2012-15, 10% from 2016-18 and 0% from 2019 onwards

† Includes both oil and gas revenues

‡ 2020 data are preliminary

§ Actual Bahrain budget balance before rollover

Sources: World Bank, MEES, KAPSARC, Kuwait Ministry of Finance, Saudi General Authority for Statistics, Central Bank of Bahrain, Qatar Central Bank, UAE Federal Competitiveness and Statistics Centre, Central Bank of Oman.

2 THE FUTURE OF GULF NOC–IOC PARTNERSHIPS

Colby Connelly

Introduction

International oil companies (IOCs), mostly from the United States and Europe, have been critical partners of the Gulf region's national oil companies (NOCs) since the discovery of the region's oil and gas reserves in the 1930s. These partnerships have evolved enormously over time, and they continue to transform the way Gulf NOCs develop their resources and expand into new business segments. The pandemic-induced demand shock of 2020 led many of the region's major NOCs to rethink their long-term corporate strategies, profoundly impacting the nature of NOC–IOC partnerships across the region.

The three leading NOCs of the Gulf – the Saudi Arabian Oil Company (Saudi Aramco), the Abu Dhabi National Oil Company (ADNOC), and the recently rebranded QatarEnergy (QE, formerly Qatar Petroleum) – maintain partnerships with a range of IOCs. Many of these firms played key roles in the early development of NOC capacity.[1] An enormous amount of Saudi Aramco's upstream capabilities were developed through IOC partnerships, which resulted in the company's massive refining and petrochemical capacity. QE's world-scale LNG operation at Ras Laffan has been developed with a range of foreign firms, as have most of its other capabilities. For its part, ADNOC has thoroughly transformed the nature of Abu Dhabi's oil sector, and IOCs have played an important role in the NOC's ability to develop not only the emirate's oil and gas reserves, but also its growing downstream sector. While these companies have all relied on IOCs to varying extents in order to expand their capacity across the hydrocarbon value chain, the nature of these partnerships is evolving, with each NOC taking an increasingly different approach. Gulf NOCs are not as reliant on IOCs as they once were, and their work with international oil firms is likely to become increasingly more limited in scope – although it may be more targeted in areas that are new to traditional oil and gas firms, such as the development of low-carbon hydrogen capacity. Securing a long-term share of key markets remains a common feature of IOC–NOC cooperation, but IOCs are increasingly challenged in this role by Asian NOCs and other firms that allow NOCs to both grow their market share and diversify their portfolios into downstream production or other business units.

The first section of this chapter will first provide a breakdown of key existing partnerships between the region's three major NOCs, examining how these relationships have developed, and why they are critical to the day-to-day operations of regional NOCs. While not exhaustive, these cases will demonstrate that, for the Gulf NOCs, there are likely few alternatives to the major IOCs that could have offered the same type of critical partnership. In the case of QE and ADNOC, the chapter will explore the ways in which IOC partnerships have been essential to expanding upstream capacity and capturing additional market share. For Aramco and ADNOC, the chapter will explore how these relationships enabled a large-scale downstream expansion – which is expected to continue growing – expanding the global footprint of each firm.

The second section of the chapter will explore the ongoing changes to NOC strategy at a critical juncture, and how these changes have begun to influence each company's interaction with its IOC counterparts. It will also explore the relationships that are gradually displacing – but not replacing – those between Gulf NOCs and their IOC counterparts. In the case of QE, the chapter will delineate the strategies that have seen the company assume full ownership of its legacy assets (particularly in the upstream oil sector) as well as those that look likely to influence the ongoing North Field Expansion (NFE), which will drastically expand QE's liquefaction capacity. It will also examine evolving relationships such as that between QE and TotalEnergies, which is playing an active role in decarbonizing QE's upstream operations as the last IOC present in Qatar's upstream oil sector. QE has also partnered with Chevron to develop a methodology accounting for the emissions associated with producing each LNG cargo.[2]

For ADNOC, the chapter will look closely at IOC partnerships that are more geared towards the energy transition, such as the company's recently announced hydrogen venture with BP. However, considerable attention will also be devoted to upstream partnerships that are critical to expanding oil production capacity to 5 million bpd by 2027, as well as helping the UAE achieve gas self-sufficiency by 2030. Finally, potential or likely partnerships between IOCs and Saudi Aramco will also be explored, as Saudi Arabia is typically more averse to opening its oil sector to any large degree of foreign investment. The chapter will conclude by speculating as to how this range of partnerships will likely evolve further as the energy transition progresses.

State of play

Abu Dhabi National Oil Company (ADNOC)

The framework of ADNOC's partnerships with IOCs is rooted in a multi-year restructuring of Abu Dhabi's energy industry, which in earnest began in 2016. The restructuring initially began with ADNOC's oil and gas concessions, which allowed IOCs to make equity investments in the country's upstream sector; a policy that has not been replicated by every Gulf country.[3] Its three critical concessions, the Abu Dhabi Company for Onshore Oil Operations (ADCO), its offshore arm the Abu Dhabi Marine Operating Company (ADMA-OPCO), and the Zakum Development Company (ZADCO), formed the backbone of the emirate's oil industry for decades. Of equal importance, these structures laid the groundwork for decades of cooperation between ADNOC and what would become many of its strongest IOC partnerships. The ADMA-OPCO consortium initially consisted of BP (14.67 percent), Total (now TotalEnergies, 13.33 percent), and the Japan Oil Development Company (JODCO), a subsidiary of Inpex (12 percent).[4] The ZADCO consortium contained a more limited range of partners, with ExxonMobil (28 percent) and JODCO (12 percent) accounting for both international partners.[5] Total, BP, and ExxonMobil were also part of the ADCO consortium, and along with Shell each held a 9.5 percent stake in the concession, in addition to Partex with 2 percent.[6] ADNOC held a

60 percent interest in each concession, and this is one feature of its previous concession structure that has endured up to the present day; ADNOC will traditionally award firms a 100 percent stake in a concession during the exploration phase, with the option of taking up to a 60 percent stake during the production phase.

ADNOC has since traveled some distance from its origins. Across the range of business units that it has either restructured or established since oil production began in Abu Dhabi, IOCs have been present nearly every step of the way, and it would not be controversial to suggest that such a transformation would have been impossible without this set of partnerships. In fact, IOC participation still appears preferential for many of the firm's newer ventures, in particular the establishment of the Murban futures contract, which represents a significant departure from the official selling price formula system that is preferred by regional peers like Saudi Aramco. Additionally, ADNOC's strategy of awarding concessions to a consortium of partners was specifically designed to prevent any one firm from developing too much influence in Abu Dhabi's upstream sector, and ADNOC has a growing list of non-IOC partners that may represent another iteration of such a strategy.

Yet, as the restructuring of the energy sector continues, it is also important to note the ways in which IOCs have seen their influence wane in favor of partnerships that Abu Dhabi looks to prioritize for the purposes of both oil market share and geopolitics. In this regard, ADNOC's two most recent bid rounds are highly revealing. While the company has largely continued its traditional preference of awarding assets to a consortium of operators to avoid one single firm developing too much influence in its upstream, ADNOC has increasingly displayed a tendency to award acreage to consortia that represent key markets, in addition to important geopolitical partners for Abu Dhabi. Japanese IOCs have remained an important part of this picture, but firms from India, Pakistan, Thailand, and to a lesser extent China have expanded their presence in recent years.

QatarEnergy

QatarEnergy (QE), formerly known as Qatar Petroleum, is most well-known for the fact that it is the largest single holder of equity liquefaction capacity in the world. From the port of Ras Laffan, Qatari volumes of liquefied natural gas (LNG) make their way to buyers around the world. While Asian consumers represent QE's largest market by far, the firm is considering how it can replace Russian gas supplies as European countries seek to phase out Russian imports following Moscow's early 2022 invasion of Ukraine. This may hold the potential to change the way QE views its IOC partnerships; in recent years it has appeared that marketing offtake volumes from its upcoming LNG expansion is a necessity for QE, especially as the long-term demand prospects for natural gas are anything but certain. The suggestion that Asian firms may be granted minority stakes in QE's new LNG trains is supportive of this, as the company has a well-established record of preferring buyers that favor long-term supply agreements without the need for much flexibility.

QE is no stranger to cooperation with IOC partners, which played an indispensable role in the development of Doha's massive offshore gas reserves. IOC partnerships have formed the bulk of the equity stakeholders in QE's liquefaction trains. The early involvement of ExxonMobil was a critical factor in developing Qatar's offshore gas resources and establishing it as a major LNG player. Exxon was one of the first IOCs present in Qatar through the establishment of Mobil Oil of Qatar in 1955, and was present at the beginning of QE's LNG journey with its 10 percent stake in the Qatargas-1 venture.[7] Qatar's lucrative success as an LNG exporter has enabled Doha to pursue one of the more unique foreign policy pathways of any of the Gulf states and punch well above its weight in the geopolitical arena.

QE's ongoing upstream expansion at the North Field East and North Field South was widely expected to see the NOC form new partnerships with familiar names, as IOCs have sought to ingratiate themselves with QE in hopes of securing an equity stake in one of the four new LNG mega-trains being built as a part of the expansion, as well as securing access to what some speculate will be among the last major upstream hydrocarbon projects in the Gulf region. While it was viewed as likely that Asian buyers might receive minority stakes in QE's new capacity, none were a part of the initial cohort of awardees for either the NFE or NFS expansions. This may change in the near-term, as QE is expected to hold at least 70 percent of each project and currently still holds 75 percent, in addition to late 2022 reports that Chinese NOCs were still in talks to receive a small stake.

QE has slowly reduced the number of IOC partnerships in its portfolio in recent years, suggesting that the technical and financial aspects of IOC involvement in Qatar are less essential than they once were. This trend first took shape in QE's domestic upstream oil operations, where it has steadily terminated production-sharing contracts with IOCs to assume 100 percent ownership of its oil operations.[8] The exceptions to this rule can be found at two specific fields where Total remains partnered with QE through its joint ventures at the Al Shaheen and Al Khaleej fields. While oil exports are not QE's primary concern, the NOC likely views these assets as an important source of cash flow in addition to a critical piece of QE's mandate to safeguard Qatar's energy security. The Al Shaheen field is crucial to this as it represents 45 percent of Qatar's oil production and is the largest of Qatar's predominately offshore oilfields.[9] As such, QE likely views Total's involvement in each case as critical to maintain oil production levels.

To the surprise of some, QE extended the practice of taking full ownership of its domestic assets to Qatargas-1, the first of its 14 LNG trains, announcing that its partnership agreement with a consortium of ExxonMobil, TotalEnergies (each with a 10 percent stake), Marubeni, and Mitsui (each with 7.5 percent stakes) would conclude on January 1, 2022.[10] While this does reflect a change in the nature of QE's selection of partners, it does not necessarily signal that they will be any less essential to the firm going forward. QE's 100 percent stake in Qatargas-1 will translate into an increased cash flow for the company, and the timing of the announcement comes in advance of partnership selection for its upstream expansion, making it less likely that IOCs involved in Qatargas-1 would object to the decision not to renew the partnership, with firms presumably much more interested in their prospects for a stake in new capacity.

However, its LNG stakeholders are not the only set of partners that make QE unique as a Gulf-based NOC. QE is also the only regional NOC to acquire non-operated equity stakes in a massive amount of offshore exploration acreage around the world, which at the time of writing added up to over seventy blocks.[11] While most assets are currently not producing, QE now has a target of reaching 500,000 barrels of oil equivalent per day (boe/d) in overseas production by 2030. Yet they have indisputably served to bolster its partnerships with IOCs, as the nature of its position in each block sees it partner with either Exxon, Total, Shell, or Italian major Eni. There are several cases in which exploration activity at these overseas assets has resulted in discoveries, and the most compelling of these is likely to be its offshore assets in Cyprus, which places QE at the heart of maritime boundary disputes in the eastern Mediterranean region. In March 2022, the Exxon–QE partnership (Exxon 60 percent, QE 40 percent) saw the successful completion of an appraisal well at its Glaucus discovery, which was previously believed to contain 5 to 8 trillion cubic feet (Tcf) of gas. The award of the adjacent Block 5 to the same consortium could have strong implications for QE's overseas gas portfolio, which is currently limited.[12]

However, it is impossible to discuss QE's overseas operations without mentioning its Golden Pass LNG (QE 70 percent, ExxonMobil 30 percent) venture. Upon its expected completion in 2024, the project will add 16 million tons per year to QE's gross liquefaction capacity, and will enable the company to market volumes from the U.S. Gulf of Mexico in addition to its main operations at Ras Laffan. This is significant not only because of its status as QE's first LNG project outside of Qatar, but for the fact that it expands the firm's cooperation with ExxonMobil into a new sphere and may serve as a springboard for further energy investments into the United States.[13] It is not possible to state whether this will lead to more IOC partnerships, since the nature of any future ventures is what will determine what sort of partners are needed. Yet the development ties Exxon

Table 2.1 *QatarEnergy's legacy LNG partners*

Qatargas I	QE 100%
Qatargas II T1	QE 70%, ExxonMobil 30%
Qatargas II T2	QE 65%, ExxonMobil 18.3%, Total 16.7%
Qatargas III	QE 68.5%, ConocoPhillips 30%, Mistui 1.5%
Qatargas IV	QE 70%, Shell 30%
Rasgas I	QE 63%, ExxonMobil 25%, KOGAS 5%, Itochu 4%, LNG Japan 3%
Rasgas II T1	QE 70%, ExxonMobil 30%
Rasgas II T2	QE 70%, ExxonMobil 30%
Rasgas II T3	QE 70%, ExxonMobil 30%
Rasgas III T1	QE 70%, ExxonMobil 30%
Rasgas III T2	QE 70%, ExxonMobil 30%

Source: International Group of Liquefied Natural Gas Importers.

and QE ever closer together, likely enhancing the lifespan of the partnership and expanding areas where future cooperation will be feasible.

Saudi Aramco

Saudi Aramco is nothing short of an industry juggernaut. While the company originally developed through Saudi partnerships with Western firms, the eventual 'nationalization' of the firm (which Saudi officials prefer to describe as a commercial acquisition) largely closed Saudi Arabia's upstream to international investors.[14] However, there has been one key exception of upstream operations that also helps establish a clear trend governing IOC partnerships across Aramco's value chain, which is the desire to access more complex oil and gas technologies and processes. An early example of this was Aramco's desire to learn enhanced oil recovery techniques from Chevron at its operations in the Saudi-Kuwaiti Neutral Zone.[15]

Currently, most of Aramco's partnerships with IOCs are limited to its downstream segment, where Aramco's capacity dwarfs that of its aforementioned peers. Aramco's downstream unit was the largest single consumer of its upstream crude production in 2021, with the company's annual report claiming a figure of 43 percent in a year when production averaged 9.2 million barrels per day (b/d).[16] This would mean that crude consumption in Aramco's downstream accounted for almost all of its net refining capacity of 4 million b/d. By comparison, ADNOC's distillation capacity stands at just over 1 million b/d, while QE's capacity is slightly below 450,000 b/d, with 70 percent of this figure represented by its two condensate refineries.[17]

The tendency to pursue technology-seeking strategies is also clear throughout Aramco's downstream operations, and accounts for most current IOC involvement with Aramco. The NOC also uses partnerships and strategic purchases in its downstream segment to secure long-term buyers for its crude in key downstream markets, but this is a strategy that has not required a strong degree of IOC participation in order to bear fruit. IOC involvement in Aramco's downstream operations has enabled the NOC to grow its refining and petrochemical production capacity significantly, but it is unlikely that the company is pursuing the development of new refining capacity with IOCs.

Total and ExxonMobil are the only IOCs that retain significant downstream partnerships with Aramco. Since 2014, Total has operated the Saudi Aramco Total Refining and Petrochemical Company (SATORP), which consists of 440,000 b/d in refining capacity and significant capacity to produce paraxylene, benzene, and propylene.[18] The SAMREF joint venture between Saudi Aramco and ExxonMobil has seen its operations grow from what was initially a 263,000 b/d refinery to a facility that processes over 400,000 b/d. Shell had also been involved in a large scale joint venture with Aramco before the NOC acquired its stake in the operation of the 305,000 b/d Saudi Aramco Shell Refinery Company (SASREF) facility in 2019.[19] While SASREF now operates without its IOC parent, the life cycle of the partnership is actually illustrative of one of the long-term goals that Aramco had likely baked into the partnership, which is the acquisition of knowledge and experience handling more complex oil and gas operations alongside the industry's leading firms before assuming full ownership over high-capacity assets.

Aramco's other downstream ventures have brought in NOCs like China Petroleum & Chemical Corporation (Sinopec), with which it partnered to build the 400,000 b/d Yanbu Aramco Sinopec Refinery (YASREF), in addition to securing a partnership with a key player in one of its largest export markets. In a rare example of cooperation between Saudi, Chinese, and US firms, Aramco also partnered with Sinopec and ExxonMobil in developing the Fujian Refining and Petrochemical Company, in which Aramco and Exxon each retain a 25 percent stake.[20]

Yet this may represent the limits of Aramco's use for IOC partnerships in its long-term journey to secure an ever-greater share of Asian fuel and petrochemicals markets. The company has long sought to expand its downstream footprint in Asia, where major IOCs arguably represent competitors more than potential collaborators, with some exceptions as noted in the case of Aramco's partnership with Exxon in Fujian. However, Aramco does have a history of using IOC partnerships to gain market share, as evidenced by the end of its partnership with Shell after acquiring the Motiva brand along with a 600,000 b/d refinery on the U.S. Gulf of Mexico.[21] This partnership ended with a division of assets rather than Aramco's absorption of its former partner's interest, as Shell assumed 100 percent ownership of other refineries elsewhere in the United States, though its gross capacity fell short of Motiva at just 427,700 b/d. Yet perhaps equally as important to Aramco as the acquisition of the Motiva refinery was another component of the deal which gave Motiva 'the right to exclusively sell Shell-branded gasoline and diesel in Georgia, North

Carolina, South Carolina, Virginia, Maryland, and Washington, D.C., as well as the majority of Florida and the Eastern half of Texas.'[22] This agreement secured a substantial share of retail fuel markets in the United States for Aramco's now wholly-owned subsidiary. The deal has since helped Aramco expand its downstream footprint in the United States, with Motiva acquiring 100 percent of the Flint Hills Resources Chemical Plant, which is adjacent to the Motiva facility in the US state of Louisiana and now operates under the Motiva Chemicals brand.[23]

As previously stated, IOC partnerships are of limited use to Aramco in gaining a greater share of Asian markets, and it is more likely that the NOC will look to cooperate with other NOCs like Sinopec or Malaysia's Petronas, with which it established the PRefChem refining and petrochemicals project in Malaysia. The site contains a 300,000 b/d refinery along with a 3.3 million tons per year in petrochemicals production capacity, with Aramco contractually guaranteed rights to supply 50 percent of the site's feedstock.[24]

Emerging trends

The 'energy transition,' the meaning of which is often debated, is a primary factor influencing many of the new partnerships that Gulf NOCs have pursued in recent years. This is likely to continue weighing on the selection of partners for new ventures, as each company will pursue a different long-term strategy in preparing for a world that is expected to gradually consume less oil and gas in favor of low-carbon energy systems. As such, there will be some areas in which IOC partnerships are more beneficial, but Gulf NOCs may be less likely to prioritize these partnerships for the sake of preserving legacy relationships that may be less relevant in the years to come. Gaining access to key growth markets and new technologies, for example, may be supported through new fields of cooperation with IOC partners. Yet the nature of the transition means that IOCs may not always be the most beneficial partners for state oil firms, who have already displayed a tendency to build ties with new energy firms outside of their conventional partnerships.

IOCs are likely to remain important players in efforts to maximize the value of each country's resource base by minimizing long-term stranded asset risks, but there is evidence to suggest that Asian NOCs and other firms are already playing an increasingly prominent role in this space.

However, the capacity of major IOCs will likely remain an attractive feature for ongoing and new upstream expansions.

Using energy sector partnerships to support geopolitical goals is a strategy that draws on a long history of NOC–IOC cooperation, but with many Gulf states placing increased weight on the importance of bilateral ties with major Asian economies, there is a limit to the usefulness of IOC partnerships in this regard. The previously mentioned examples of ADNOC awarding concessions to consortia of partners from strategically important countries is the most cogent example of this, while QE made seemingly less of an effort to leverage this strategy through its NFE and NFS expansion awards. For its part, Saudi Aramco has used downstream ventures both in the kingdom and abroad as an opportunity to partner with Chinese NOCs and secure access to key downstream markets. This strategy is likely to persist, especially as the firm places a greater emphasis on crude-to-chemicals businesses.

Abu Dhabi National Oil Company

The results of ADNOC's latest bid round indicate that the firm will continue to rely on IOC partnerships to carry out its 1 million b/d expansion, which will bring ADNOC's maximum crude production capacity to 5 million b/d and easily secure a position for Abu Dhabi as OPEC's second largest producer. The NOC's decision to award a second concession to U.S.-based Occidental Petroleum in 2020 is a clear indicator of this trend, as Occidental (Oxy) has been an important partner for ADNOC through its stake in ADNOC Sour Gas (ADNOC 60 percent, Oxy 40 percent).[25] A significant driver of ADNOC's upstream expansion is its role in supporting the UAE's ambitions for gas self-sufficiency by 2030 and ending dependence on pipeline imports from Qatar, as well as seasonal LNG imports to Dubai. Somewhat ironically, Oxy also holds a 24.5 percent stake in the Dolphin Pipeline project, which satisfies approximately 25 percent of the UAE's total gas demand. However, Oxy's participation in ADNOC Sour Gas and the Al Hosn gas project have also secured a critical role for the U.S. independent of supporting ADNOC's gas ambitions, and Al Hosn output accounted for a wide majority of Oxy's non-U.S. gas production in 2021.[26]

Looking ahead, Oxy's relationship with ADNOC has strong potential to evolve into more energy transition-related fields. Oxy made headlines in 2020 when it became the first U.S. operator to announce a goal of net-zero Scope 1 and 2 emissions by 2040, while aiming to achieve net-zero Scope 3 emissions by 2050. Although ADNOC has not set a net-zero target for itself, the UAE has pledged net-zero emissions on a national level by 2050, and the nature of ADNOC's businesses will require it to play a substantial role in supporting this target. Critically, ADNOC is targeting 5 million tons per year in carbon capture and storage (CCS) capacity by 2030, and Oxy's experience developing CCS facilities in the U.S. as well as its complex carbon handling infrastructure may position the firm as a strong candidate for future partnerships. One item of potential interest is its experience using CCS for enhanced oil recovery (EOR) techniques, as ADNOC seeks to prolong the life of its mature fields. With all three of the major Gulf NOCs looking to maximize the value of their resource bases, the role of EOR is only likely to grow. Oxy's experience in this regard may also prove vital for ADNOC's blue hydrogen ambitions, as well as those of the broader UAE, to capture 25 percent of the global hydrogen market by 2030.

Another prominent area of interest, though one whose prospects are less certain, is Oxy's plan to deploy commercial-scale direct air capture (DAC) facilities. Though DAC remains an unproven technology at scale, Oxy CEO Vicki Hollub has already singled out Abu Dhabi as a strong candidate for international DAC deployment.[27] Should the technology prove effective, ADNOC may develop a strong interest in using DAC to support the UAE's national net-zero target. Oxy's January 2021 announcement that it delivered the world's first shipment of what it claimed to be 'carbon-neutral' crude oil may also pique ADNOC's interest.[28]

In its downstream segment, ADNOC had previously been more reliant on IOCs, and while they may play a role moving forward, this will likely be an area in which the necessity of IOCs continues to decline. In 2021, ADNOC became the first regional NOC to announce that it would pursue the development of a framework for the decarbonization of its downstream businesses, mostly focused on power used in downstream operations. The focus on power is likely what motivated it to partner with General Electric, as a key area of exploration will be the potential for using ammonia, likely produced by ADNOC or another local entity, in the GE-built turbines used to power downstream processes. This serves to illustrate the point that energy transition-related partnerships are much more likely to be partnerships of necessity than ventures that built on existing NOC–IOC ties; as both types of oil and gas firms prepare for a future that will impact their primary business model, firms will seek to gain a competitive edge – which will be best pursued, in many cases, by partnering with firms that traditionally sit outside the scope of the oil and gas industry.

It is also important to consider that the UAE's gradual moves to liberalize greater portions of its economy may envision a continued, albeit limited role for IOCs as strategic investors. In January 2019, Italian IOC Eni, along with Austrian OMV (which is 25 percent owned by Abu Dhabi sovereign wealth fund Mubadala) acquired 35 percent in ADNOC Refining for $5.8 billion. Both firms were also involved in the creation of ADNOC's trading arm, which began operating in 2020.[29] While ADNOC's partial privatizations and strategic asset sales are likely to continue, new initiatives that favor a more commercial approach to the energy sector, such as the launch of a futures contract for ADNOC's flagship Murban crude, will likely draw on a range of partners that include but are not limited to IOCs. Though the involvement of TotalEnergies and Shell likely supported the view that another crude benchmark in the Middle East would be sustainable, these firms were far from the only partners involved in the launch of the ICE Futures Abu Dhabi exchange, which also involved Inpex and ENEOS of Japan, in addition to PetroChina, PTT of Thailand, and trading giant Vitol.[30]

With respect to the energy transition, ADNOC is expanding its partnerships to include IOCs as well as a range of non-traditional partners as the company expands the breadth of its work into areas that are traditionally untouched by NOCs in the Gulf. An emerging area that provides significant examples for this dynamic is the region's effort to develop commercial-scale production of blue and green hydrogen. The UAE goal of capturing 25 percent of the global hydrogen market by 2030 is unlikely to be achieved without IOC partners, especially given the fact that use of blue or green hydrogen in refining and other downstream operations is likely to represent a significant portion of global demand.

To this end, ADNOC has already partnered with BP, signing an initial agreement to develop hydrogen capacity in both the UAE and the UK.[31] Crucially, this partnership also involves Masdar, the UAE's state-owned renewable energy champion. Though Masdar had previously been 100 percent owned by Mubadala, the company has since been restructured. ADNOC now owns 43 percent of Masdar's green hydrogen business unit, in addition to 24 percent of its renewable power unit. This also illustrates a dynamic in which Gulf states are marshalling a greater number of state resources to develop renewable energy and hydrogen production capacity, and while a high degree of potential for IOC involvement in this arrangement is still present, closer cooperation between state-owned enterprises may also serve to displace the role of IOC partnerships in developing hydrogen production capacity in the UAE.

However, in the long term it is highly likely that business units that focus specifically on oil production and marketing will require IOC partnerships for some time. This may be especially relevant to natural gas production, especially if the UAE is to achieve its goal of self-sufficiency and sustain it for years to come. There is little to suggest that the IOC appetite for Gulf oil and gas assets is waning, and, in the long-term, it is highly likely that Abu Dhabi will look to preserve the status of its legacy IOC partners as significant sources of foreign investment.

QatarEnergy

QE's partnerships are currently in a state of flux. The NOC has made a series of announcements pertaining to its sustainability strategy in recent years, but, subsequent to its final investment decision on the NFE expansion, the announcement that industry observers were most keenly awaiting in 2022 was QE's selection of equity partners for the four new liquefaction trains it intends to build.[32] This process became ever more intriguing as it was delayed several times, and while delays are not an unusual feature of oil and gas projects in the Gulf region, Europe's newfound push to replace its imports of Russian gas after Moscow's invasion of Ukraine reinvigorated European interest in Qatari volumes. Germany plans to construct at least two LNG import terminals and has inked preliminary agreements to secure long-term supply agreements with QE.[33]

With Asia as a strong growth market, it is still likely that Chinese NOCs or other Asian firms will receive minority stakes in the expansion, which would remain a clear indication that QE's partnership strategy is closely linked to securing market share. However, it was also widely believed that there would be a chance that European IOCs such as Total, Shell, and Eni, which had previously been viewed as some of the most likely candidates for larger stakes, would play an increasingly important role as European nations push to diversify gas imports away from Russian supply. Though the final selection of firms for participation did include legacy European partners in addition to newcomer Eni, it is also strongly possible that this decision came as a result of QE's preference for maintaining its strongest ties with those firms with which it is most familiar.

TotalEnergies has been a critical partner of QE for some time through its presence in the NOC's upstream oil and gas operations in Qatar and overseas, where the two partner at multiple exploration blocks. The significant discovery recently made at the offshore Venus prospect in Namibia may tie the two even more closely together. Of the dozens of assets QE has accumulated overseas, a select few contain commercial discoveries, while even fewer are currently producing. This raises the prospect that QE may choose to divest from a significant number of these assets in the medium- to long-term, but assets that do yield commercial discoveries will likely bring QE closer to whichever IOC maintains operatorship of the asset, thus potentially yielding new avenues of cooperation between the firms.

One core component of QE's strategy that may attract the interest of IOCs is its effort to build out its low-carbon LNG credentials, which it sees as critical to maintaining European market share, as well as a share of Asian markets that become increasingly carbon-conscious. A prime example of this type of activity is QE's development of a methodology that accounts for the carbon intensity of each LNG cargo from wellhead to point of delivery. To accomplish this, QE partnered with Pavilion Energy of Singapore in addition to US major Chevron. The methodology will eventually be used to provide a statement of greenhouse gas emissions (SGE) with each of QE's cargoes, laying the groundwork for potential carbon offset strategies on the part of buyers.

Should this become a more significant avenue for QE's cooperation with IOCs, TotalEnergies is the firm that is best positioned to capitalize on this dynamic. Total is a partner in the Siraj Energy joint venture, which along with QE includes Marubeni of Japan.[34] The project represents Qatar's first utility-scale solar project and marks one of the first instances of a Gulf NOC stepping into power generation, which had previously been a space dominated by national renewables champions such as ACWA Power and Masdar. More importantly, however, the involvement of Total and QE sets a potential framework for decarbonization of QE's upstream operations in Qatar (and by extension Total's Qatar operations as well). Although this may not become a highly-frequented area of

NOC–IOC cooperation, both peer groups have an interest in building out this capacity, and it is likely that QE and Total will further build on their cooperation in this segment.

Geopolitical dynamics were also likely to have played a role in QE's decision to pursue the USGC II petrochemical project with CP Chem, a joint venture between U.S. firms Chevron and Conoco Phillips. The agreement for the two firms to pursue this project, which would be an $8 billion, US-based facility, was signed during a visit of Qatari Emir Tamim bin Hamad Al Thani to the United States in 2019, notably in the presence of former U.S. President Donald Trump.[35] At the outset of the 2017 boycott of Qatar by Saudi Arabia, Bahrain, the UAE, and Egypt, Trump appeared to support assertions that Qatar had engaged in support for terrorist organizations, an allegation that Doha did not take lightly from the country that has long served as its security guarantor.[36] Qatar responded by making a concerted effort to 'buy American' for several years, unsurprisingly viewed by many as a way to stay in the Trump administration's good graces, with there likely being few better ways to do so than a commitment to invest billions of dollars in an American industry and ostensibly create hundreds, if not thousands, of new jobs. Qatar has established a pattern in making such investments or other large-scale purchases at earlier dates, and QE's fortress balance sheet was a vital asset in enabling it to maximize its investment, or the perception thereof, in the United States.[37]

A final investment decision was taken in late 2022, and the project's announcement arguably contributed to achieving Doha's geopolitical goals, as Qatar never again found itself drawing the same level of unwanted attention from the White House for the remainder of Trump's time in office. Additionally, QE's existing partnership with CP Chem to develop another petrochemical facility in Qatar's Ras Laffan Industrial City likely set a precedent for the USGC II partnership that enabled Doha to sign a multi-billion dollar agreement directly in front of a US president who arguably attached significant political weight to such sizeable investments.

Saudi Aramco

As discussed in the previous section, IOC investment has been critical to Saudi Aramco reaching its 6.8 million b/d gross refining capacity. However, greenfield refinery projects have become somewhat anachronistic for Gulf NOCs. ADNOC's recent cancelation of a new refinery project, combined with QE CEO Saad Al Kaabi's statement ruling out new refining capacity, may indicate that leading Gulf NOCs have relegated refining projects to history. Much of Aramco's strategy to face the energy transition involves safeguarding the value and viability of its crude exports as far into the future as possible, and while IOCs are still likely to be major players in this space, Aramco's strategy has not prioritized them for this purpose.

Downstream partnerships are expanding overseas, continuing the strategy of securing long-term markets for crude exports. Aramco's latest announcement of a 300,000 b/d greenfield refinery and petrochemicals complex through its participation in the Huajin Aramco Petrochemical Company joint venture, through which it partners with two Chinese firms, is further evidence that it does intend to continue growing its downstream businesses in Asia, as well as furthering the trend of seeking local partnerships rather than IOC cooperation.[38] However, a possible avenue for Aramco to cooperate with IOCs may lie in Europe, which at the time of writing is engaged in a monumental shift of its energy policy with the ultimate goal of eliminating or at least marginalizing of Russian energy imports. Even prior to the war that triggered this generational policy shift, Saudi Aramco took the unusual decision of purchasing a 30 percent stake in a 210,000 b/d refinery located in Gdansk, Poland. Critically, the refinery's owner, PKN Orlen, also signed an agreement that would see the facility purchase 200,000 to 337,000 b/d of crude from Saudi Aramco, in addition to stating that it saw further opportunities with Aramco in its petrochemicals businesses.[39]

It is highly probable that Aramco will continue to seek opportunities to partner with or purchase stakes in key downstream players across regional markets. This may increasingly take the shape of smaller purchases and partnerships, such as those mentioned above, over large-scale greenfield refining or petrochemicals capacity. This is evidenced in Aramco's repeated attempts to penetrate downstream markets in India, which it initially did through its planned involvement in the now-suspended Ratnagiri refinery project, as well as its aborted attempt to purchase a $15 billion stake in Reliance Industries, India's largest refiner.[40] However, the appointment of Saudi Aramco chair and Public Investment Fund governor Yasser Al Rumayyan to Reliance's board indicates that Aramco's long-term interest in India remains strong and that new pursuits in the coming years are likely.[41]

Conclusion

While the above is not an exhaustive list of Gulf NOC partnerships with IOCs or the efforts of these firms to prepare for a low-carbon future, it illustrates the nature of shifting industry trends for both peer groups. A significant factor in the trend of Gulf NOCs becoming gradually less reliant on IOC cooperation is the fact that both peer groups will need to develop new capacities in similar business segments. This may require IOCs to pursue partnerships with firms that traditionally operate outside the scope of the wider oil and gas industry. To put it more simply, the effort to develop competitive advantages in preparation for the energy transition is a competitive practice in and of itself, and the long-term strategy of Gulf NOCs being the 'last producers standing' will require these firms to develop strategies that outlast those of IOCs. In order to accomplish this, much of the behavior previously exhibited in favor of IOCs, such as the acquisition of new technologies and practices, will gradually shift in favor of non-IOC partners that continue to expand the overall capabilities of Gulf NOCs. There is no reason to expect that the corporate strategies of regional NOCs will be decoupled from the policy priorities of their national governments. Yet the role of IOC partners for Gulf NOCs looking to bolster their capabilities and prepare for a low-carbon future is likely to grow smaller in the coming years, with legacy partnerships coming to a close as new agreements are developed.

Bibliography

'About Golden Pass | Golden Pass LNG.' Accessed April 5, 2022. https://www. goldenpasslng.com/about/about-golden-pass.

'ADNOC and GE to Develop Decarbonization Roadmap for Power Generation in ADNOC's Downstream and Industry Operations.' Accessed April 2, 2022. https://www.adnoc.ae:443/en/news-and-media/press-releases/2021/ adnoc-and-ge-to-develop-decarbonization-roadmap-for-power-generation.

'ADNOC Announces Plans to Consolidate ADMA-OPCO and ZADCO.' Accessed April 7, 2022. https://www.adnoc.ae:443/en/news-and-media/ press-releases/2016/adnoc-announces-plans-to-consolidate-adma-opco-and-zadco.

'ADNOC Refining.' Accessed April 6, 2022. https://www.adnoc.ae:443/en/ adnoc-refining.

'ADNOC, Bp and Masdar Agree to Expand UAE-UK New Energy Partnership.' Accessed April 3, 2022. https://www.adnoc.ae:443/en/news-and-media/

press-releases/2021/adnoc-bp-and-masdar-agree-to-expand-uae-uk-new-energy-partnership.

Arab Gulf States Institute in Washington. 'Aramco and ADNOC: Playing the Long Game,' June 12, 2019. https://agsiw.org/aramco-and-adnoc-playing-the-long-game/.

'Aramco JV to Develop Major Refinery and Petrochemical Complex in China.' Accessed March 29, 2022. https://www.aramco.com/en/news-media/news/2022/aramco-jv-to-develop-major-refinery-and-petrochemical-complex-in-china.

Arab Gulf States Institute in Washington. 'Everything at Once: Transformation of Abu Dhabi's Oil Policy,' April 15, 2021. https://agsiw.org/everything-at-once-transformation-of-abu-dhabis-oil-policy/.

ArgaamPlus. 'Saudi Aramco's Motiva Takes over Flint Hills' Texas Chemical Plant.' ArgaamPlus. Accessed March 29, 2022. https://www.argaam.com/en/article/articledetail/id/1328338.

Chevron Phillips Chemical. 'Chevron Phillips Chemical and Qatar Petroleum Announce Plans to Jointly Develop U.S. Gulf Coast Petrochemical Project.' Accessed March 31, 2022. https://www.cpchem.com/media-events/news/news-release/chevron-phillips-chemical-and-qatar-petroleum-announce-plans-jointly.

Energy Intelligence. 'Aramco Starts to Pivot From Focus on Defense,' January 14, 2022. https://www.energyintel.com/0000017e-5867-dd1c-ab7f-fe6777420000.

Energy Intelligence. 'Exxon Wraps Up Glaucus Appraisal Well,' March 23, 2022. https://www.energyintel.com/0000017f-b2fb-ddab-a1ff-bfffb3340000.

Energy Intelligence. 'Germany in Talks With Qatar for LNG Supplies,' March 21, 2022. https://www.energyintel.com/0000017f-ae77-de65-afff-efff8bc60002.

Energy Intelligence. 'Oxy Expands CCS Ambitions Abroad,' October 7, 2021. https://www.energyintel.com/0000017c-5be5-d779-ad7e-dfed0d260000.

Energy Intelligence. 'Pavilion Unveils GHG Methodology for LNG with Qatar, Chevron,' November 17, 2021. https://www.energyintel.com/0000017d-2cf8-dd20-af7f-2dfdf6160000.

Energy Intelligence. 'Qatar LNG Partner Selection Slips,' February 4, 2022. https://www.energyintel.com/0000017e-c69d-d21f-a3fe-cedf78750000.

Energy Intelligence. 'QP Doubles Down on Expansion,' July 6, 2021. https://www.energyintel.com/0000017b-a7dd-de4c-a17b-e7df9e460000.

Energy Intelligence. 'Total Strike Elevates Namibia's Offshore Oil Prospects,' February 24, 2022. https://www.energyintel.com/0000017f-2b41-d94d-a97f-7f795ec60000.

ExxonMobil. 'Our History in Qatar | ExxonMobil Qatar.' Accessed April 7, 2022. https://www.exxonmobil.com.qa:443/en-QA/Company/Who-we-are/Our-history-in-Qatar.

'Fujian Refining and Petrochemical Company Ltd.' Accessed March 29, 2022. https://china.aramco.com/en/creating-value/products/refining-and-chemicals/fujian-refining-and-petrochemical-company-ltd.

'Historic Milestone for ADNOC as New Trading Arm Begins Derivatives Trading.' Accessed April 6, 2022. https://www.adnoc.ae:443/en/news-and-media/press-releases/2020/historic-milestone-for-adnoc-as-new-trading-arm-begins-derivatives-trading.

Landler, Mark. 'Trump Takes Credit for Saudi Move Against Qatar, a U.S. Military Partner.' *The New York Times*, June 6, 2017, sec. World. https://www.nytimes.com/2017/06/06/world/middleeast/trump-qatar-saudi-arabia.html.

Marcel, Valérie, and John V. Mitchell. *Oil Titans: National Oil Companies in the Middle East*. London: Chatham House [u.a.], 2006.

McQue, Katie. 'Qatar to Takeover Qatargas 1 LNG Trains as IOCs Exit,' March 30, 2021. https://www.spglobal.com/commodity-insights/en/market-insights/latest-news/natural-gas/033021-qatar-to-takeover-qatargas-1-lng-trains-as-iocs-exit.

Motiva. '3-06-17 Affiliates of Saudi Aramco and Shell Achieve Significant Milestone.' Accessed March 29, 2022. https://motiva.com/media/in-the-news/3-06-17-affiliates-of-saudi-aramco-and-shell-achieve-significant-milestone.

North Oil Company. 'Al-Shaheen.' Accessed March 31, 2022. https://noc.qa/al-shaheen.html.

Offshore Energy. 'ADNOC Looking for Partners for ADMA-OPCO Offshore Oil Concession,' August 7, 2017. https://www.offshore-energy.biz/adnoc-looking-for-partners-for-adma-opco-offshore-oil-concession/.

Offshore Energy. 'Qatar Petroleum Taking over Offshore Oil Field from Oxy,' October 15, 2018. https://www.offshore-energy.biz/qatar-petroleum-taking-over-offshore-oil-field-from-oxy/.

'Oxy Low Carbon Ventures, Together with Macquarie, Deliver World's First Shipment of Carbon-Neutral Oil.' Accessed April 3, 2022. https://www.oxy.com/news/news-releases/oxy-low-carbon-ventures-together-with-macquarie-deliver-worlds-first-shipment-of-carbon-neutral-oil/.

'PRefChem At a Glance | PRefChem.' Accessed April 6, 2022. https://prefchem.com/prefchem-at-a-glance.

'Qatar Buys U.S. F-15s Days After Trump Says Country Funds Terrorism.' Accessed March 31, 2022. https://www.nbcnews.com/news/world/qatar-buys-12b-u-s-jets-days-after-trump-says-n772691.

'Qatargas – Operations.' Accessed April 6, 2022. https://www.qatargas.com/english/operations/laffan-refinery.

'Refining.' Accessed April 6, 2022. https://www.qatarenergy.qa/en/WhatWeDo/Pages/Refining.aspx.

'Reliance Backs Saudi Aramco Chairman as Independent Director | Reuters.' Accessed April 8, 2022. https://www.reuters.com/business/energy/reliance-backs-saudi-aramco-chairman-independent-director-2021-09-29/.

'Reliance, Aramco Call off $15 Billion Deal Amid Valuation Differences, Sources Say | Investing News | US News.' Accessed April 8, 2022. https://money.usnews.com/investing/news/articles/2021-11-25/reliance-aramco-call-off-15-billion-deal-amid-valuation-differences-sources-say.

Reuters. 'Motiva Enterprises' Co-Owners to Split U.S. Refineries on May 1: Sources,' March 7, 2017, sec. Commodities. https://www.reuters.com/article/us-refineries-motiva-split-idUSKBN16E05B.

Reuters. 'UPDATE 1-BP Strikes Deal for 10 Percent Stake in Abu Dhabi's ADCO Concession,' December 17, 2016, sec. Oil Report. https://www.reuters.com/article/energy-emirates-adnoc-bp-idUSL5N1EC0AB.

Saadi, Dania. 'ADNOC Awards Occidental Concession amid Plans to Hit 5 Mil b/d Output,' December 9, 2020. https://www.spglobal.com/commodity-insights/en/market-insights/latest-news/natural-gas/120920-adnoc-awards-occidental-concession-amid-plans-to-hit-5-mil-bd-output.

Saadi, Dania. 'Murban Futures Contract Opens at $63.43/b as Trading of ADNOC's Flagship Crude Begins,' March 28, 2021. https://www.spglobal.com/commodity-insights/en/market-insights/latest-news/oil/032821-murban-futures-contract-opens-at-6343b-as-trading-of-adnocs-flagship-crude-begins.

'Saudi Aramco Annual Report 2020.' Annual Report. Saudi Aramco, March 23, 2021. https://www.aramco.com/-/media/publications/corporate-reports/saudi-aramco-ara-2020-english.pdf?la=en&hash=FA2C1E6CFBA897EC4F64E3A0DBEA7739DA193826.

'Saudi Aramco Completes Acquisition of Shell's Share of the SASREF Refining Joint Venture.' Accessed March 28, 2022. https://www.shell.com/media/news-and-media-releases/2019/saudi-aramco-completes-acquisition-of-shells-share-of-the-sasref-refining-joint-venture.html.

TotalEnergies.com. 'Al Kharsaah, a Pioneering Solar Power Plant in Qatar.' Accessed April 8, 2022. https://totalenergies.com/projects/renewables-electricity/al-kharsaah-pioneering-solar-power-plant-qatar.

TotalEnergies.com. 'SATORP: An Exceptional Partnership.' Accessed March 28, 2022. https://totalenergies.com/energy-expertise/projects/refining-petrochemical-platform/satorp.

Wald, Ellen R. *Saudi, Inc: The Arabian Kingdom's Pursuit of Profit and Power.* First Pegasus Books edition. New York: Pegasus Books, 2018.

'Who We Are.' Accessed April 2, 2022. https://www.adnoc.ae:443/en/adnoc-sour-gas/about-us/who-we-are.

3 MECHANISMS TO FINANCE CLIMATE INVESTMENTS IN THE MIDDLE EAST AND NORTH AFRICA

Lama Kiyasseh

Introduction

The acceleration of the global energy transition poses critical challenges for the Middle East and North Africa (MENA), with the transformation evolving into an all-encompassing economic, social, and political project for the region. In an effort to embrace and secure their positioning within the global energy transition, countries in the MENA region, and especially those in the Gulf Cooperation Council (GCC), have adopted multi-pronged strategies. Directed by policy, these strategies have included building a portfolio of clean and renewables assets and committing to sustainable practices in otherwise hard-to-abate sectors.

In the last decade, energy and climate investments in the region have been: (i) large projects financed by corporate or project finance loans, often from a consortium of banks and/or development finance institutions (DFIs); (ii) funded and backed by governments (including state-owned enterprises); and (iii) supported by multilateral climate funds, as well as concessional finance in the form of grants from donors. Today, a portion of these investments has taken on a 'sustainable' characteristic, in the form of green and sustainability-linked debt issuances from both sovereigns and corporates. The importance of this type of financing was central to climate conversations at COP27 in helping to scale investment needs in the region and beyond.

This chapter has a twofold purpose (Figure 3.1). First, it provides an analytical overview of existing and upcoming transition finance mechanisms in the region, highlighting relevant country examples. Second, it speculates where the region is headed and what this means in terms of interventions that can optimize the mobilization of necessary capital. The first section seeks to highlight the diverse funding provided from the public and private sectors, and important metrics for investors, such as Environmental, Social, and Governance (ESG) considerations, especially as ESG continues to matter for shareholders over greenwashing concerns and capital markets become more sophisticated with assessing ESG risk. The chapter begins by providing an assessment of the current status of the market, followed by defining the different sources of finance. This includes showcasing that blended finance – the combination of concessional finance from donors with commercial finance – can play an important role in de-risking investments in projects, thereby catalyzing investment in, and potentially scaling, new technologies necessary for the transition. The chapter also examines what is being financed and explores how these projects and technologies are accessing finance today, including the policies and institutional frameworks that support such access. Of significance is the evolution of types of investors, particularly private sector participants, and the types of instruments used.

The second section presents future considerations that will shape access to finance. This involves identifying macroeconomic drivers and challenges to the existing financial ecosystem, followed by potential mitigants. It suggests tools to strengthen the region's value proposition vis-à-vis sustainable finance. In that vein, and building on current 'green' finance, it introduces innovative governance approaches and financing tools, including the more recent introduction of blue finance, and debt-for-nature solutions (e.g., swaps or DNS) that combine synergies between public and private sectors. As DNS tools are inherently a sovereign issue, this approach can explore how the state can potentially manage its fiscal obligations such as debt and how the private sector can support initiatives that help the sovereign achieve its obligations in the swap. Financing projects that deliver on the commitments or can apply additionality of carbon credits in the servicing of the debt can also be explored. Moreover, this section of the chapter posits that transition finance is still at a

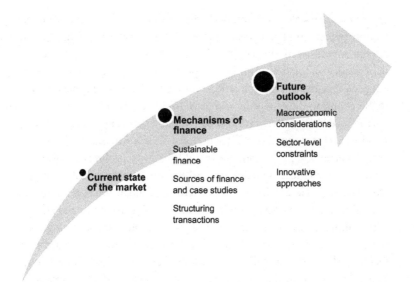

FIGURE 3.1 Chapter Summary.

formative stage and must be strengthened as an asset class in response to growing transition risks, requiring new standards. Broader uptake of decarbonization strategies will add to efficiency and industrial competitiveness, reduce the risk of stranded assets, and have a positive longer-term impact in the region. Given that climate events are a threat globally and continue to be a catastrophic risk, with substantial impacts on the financial system, the outlook will highlight the need for climate resilience regulation from central banks and financial regulators that support liquidity facilities, which can help buffer bank capital and enable banks to continue to lend to the market. Ultimately, sustainable finance is providing an opportunity to 'green' an energy-intensive group of economies.

Current state of the market

Hydrocarbons form the backbone of economies in the Middle East. For a majority of the region, fossil fuels continue to be a major source of (i) exports, ranging from 67 percent to over 95 percent as a share of merchandise exports for some of the region's largest players; (ii) government (fiscal) revenues; and (iii) income, with oil rents ranging from 16 percent to 44 percent as a share of GDP (Table 3.1). For importers, energy inputs form the engines behind their economies. This over-dependence on fossil fuels for both exporters and importers in the region suggests that the energy transition will be challenging and have major implications on the economic and fiscal health in MENA.

The region's exporters must proactively diversify their energy sources, despite the cost competitiveness of their fossil fuels, while also contending with expected falling demand. Demand is likely to decline as a result of increasingly rigorous policies on carbon and climate, greater energy efficiencies (such as those derived from product improvements or switching to cleaner energy sources), and a growing decoupling of energy consumption from income in some advanced economies, as highlighted by International Monetary Fund (IMF) research.[1] These demand-side factors will cause the shift to be more costly for those undertaking 'transition' investments. This is especially true for MENA's exporter economies, many of which already face high fiscal breakeven prices (see Table 3.1) and need to embark on diversification drives, often spearheaded by the public sector, while they simultaneously lose oil and gas revenue.

The dramatic drop in petroleum prices in the third quarter of 2014 was pivotal in driving MENA oil and gas producers to launch ambitious reform programs aimed at widening their economic base, notably by developing their non-hydrocarbon and private sectors, thereby delinking economic growth from their natural resources. Since then, these plans to develop and strengthen the private sector have taken on varied forms, although they typically rely heavily on government-funded projects, and sometimes they have taken a back seat when energy prices recover.

Mechanisms of finance

What is sustainable finance and what is it used for?

Sustainable finance is the process of driving capital toward investments that encompass environmental, social, and governance (ESG) factors to address and mitigate related challenges, such as climate/biodiversity, the use of sustainable resources, labor standards, and more, and which

Table 3.1 *MENA exporter hydrocarbon dependence*

	Fiscal breakeven oil price[1]				Oil rents[2]	Fuel exports[3]
	(US dollars per barrel)				*(% GDP)*	*(% Merchandise exports)*
APSP[4]	61.4	41.8	69.2	96.4		
				Projections		
	2019	2020	2021	2022	2019	2020
Algeria	106.3	89.7	111.7	169.2	14.4	96.1
Bahrain	98.9	120.7	131.9	127.6	2.2	42.1
Iran	166.6	548.1	263.6	291.5	20.4	68.7
Iraq	52.3	55.2	54.2	60.7	39.6	99.9
Kuwait	57.6	80.1	67.7	56.7	42.1	92.9
Libya	36.0	141.7	52.2	69.7	43.9	95.4
Oman	64.7	86.4	76.7	70.9	24.9	75.2
Qatar	50.5	50.5	49.0	48.1	16.9	81.8
Saudi Arabia	81.8	76.3	84.6	73.3	24.2	67.6
United Arab Emirates	62.5	61.4	61.3	63.9	16.2	71.5

Sources: International Monetary Fund (IMF), October 2022; World Development Indicators (WDI), World Bank.

[1]The oil price at which the fiscal balance is zero; Kuwait's fiscal breakeven oil price is before the compulsory 10 percent revenue transfer to the Future Generations Fund including investment income.
[2]Iran's data is based on 2018.
[3]2020 or based on latest available data.
[4]APSP is Average Petroleum Spot Price, a simple average of three spot prices: Dated Brent, West Texas Intermediate, and Dubai Fateh based on the IMF Primary Commodity Price System (PCPS). APSP unit is U.S. dollars/barrel.

go beyond only financial considerations. Sustainable finance can take on multiple forms, such as loans, and bonds, which delineate the use of proceeds, i.e. specifying where the borrowing goes.[2] These instruments may also be designed to ensure their beneficiaries meet certain Key Performance Indicators (KPIs), and/or if they are aligned with the Sustainable Development Goals (SDGs).[3] Sustainable finance can also refer to structuring innovative products that meet global standards and market practices.

Since 2013, the universe of sustainable debt has grown from $28.7 billion, primarily in green bonds and loans, to incorporate several sub-categories, reaching an estimated $1,644 billion in 2021 before witnessing this asset class's first decline to $1,455 billion in 2022 since its introduction.[4] Despite green bonds' continued dominance over this period, macroeconomic conditions marked by higher interest rates and increased skepticism about the label impacted borrower appetite in 2022. During the last several years, sustainable bond issuances had been primarily led by corporates; however, sovereign issuers' share of the market has grown to account for $406 billion in 2021 from a modest $17 billion in 2015[5] highlighting the increasing trend of sovereigns engaging in capital markets.

When assessing the current state of the market, understanding the drivers that have fueled the rise of sustainable finance in MENA is key. First is the continued need for these economies to diversify into productive and value-added sectors, coupled with the region experiencing rapid population growth – a scenario with critical implications for increased domestic energy demand and electricity consumption growth over the coming decades. The unintended consequences of rapid urbanization, including water stress and degradation and depletion of natural resources, have prompted a shift toward sustainable finance.

Second, given renewed international fervor toward meeting climate goals (and emissions reductions), regulatory reform and the role of the government and the public sector is significant. The fact that hydrocarbons still form the lion's share of economies means these countries need to rethink how best to rebalance transition risk to ensure long-term economic viability moving forward. This speaks to the country-specific transition roadmaps, including green agendas set forth by the different MENA governments, which act as enablers and incentivize varied stakeholders, including the private sector and financial institutions, to engage in this market and offer more sustainable products.

Recently, the role of the government has extended beyond regulatory and legal support to encompass active participation in capital markets. Starting in 2020, there have been several examples of government-owned-entity issuances that have emanated from MENA markets. These issuances have taken place in Egypt, the United Arab Emirates (UAE), and Saudi Arabia, as outlined in Box A.[6]

BOX A. SELECTED CAPITAL MARKETS TRANSACTIONS IN MENA

In September 2020, in an emblematic transaction, Egypt issued its first-ever green sovereign bond in the region, valued at $750 million and with a tenor of five years and a 5.25 percent interest rate. Proceeds were earmarked for financing clean transportation, renewable energy, pollution prevention and control, sustainable water and wastewater management, energy efficiency, and climate change adaptation. On the heels of this investment, preliminary data in 2022 suggests that Egypt is on track to achieving its Vision 2030 goal of increasing the proportion of green projects in its investment budget from 14 percent in 2020 to 30 percent in 2022.

In the GCC, Etihad Airways, the national carrier of Abu Dhabi in the UAE, launched the world's first Transition Sukuk – raising $600 million in October 2020 – and the first sustainability-linked bond in aviation – raising $1.2 billion in November 2021 – under their Transition Finance Framework. The sustainability-linked bond (SLB) is tied to one KPI: a 17.8 percent reduction in emission intensity in Etihad's passenger fleet by 2024, from their 2017 baseline of 682 CO_2 per revenue tonnes kilometers (gCO_2/RTK), to reach 574 gCO_2/RTK for the total fleet. The decision behind this KPI appears to be motivated by its use by the International Energy Agency (IEA) and the Transition

Pathway Initiative (TPI). Failure to meet such a target means that Etihad will have to buy offsetting carbon credits and abide by its commitment under the Carbon Offset and Reduction Scheme for International Aviation, which could include local reforestation, biodiversity, and natural carbon sink projects.

In Saudi Arabia, in September 2020, the Saudi Electricity Company raised $1.3 billion in International Green Sukuk in line with the company's Green Sukuk Framework to finance green capital projects such as the smart meter rollout. It also represented several 'firsts' in this space: the first Green Islamic Bond from the kingdom, the largest in terms of value for MENA that year, and the first Saudi USD denominated Green Sukuk issuance. In support of the country's green agenda, in October 2022, Saudi Arabia's sovereign wealth fund, the Public Investment Fund (PIF), raised $3 billion from its debut green bond sale.

While these issuances represent selected examples, they have had an important signaling effect on the broader market. Corporates and the private sector are now actively engaging in this space, including the largest commercial banks in the region. In the UAE, for example, First Abu Dhabi Bank has total green issuances amounting to $1.36 billion across multiple currencies and is currently the only bank from the MENA region to issue green bonds in the Swiss Francs market as of end 2021; in Saudi Arabia, the Saudi National Bank established a Sustainable Finance Framework in December 2021; and in Egypt, Commercial International Bank issued a $100 million Green bond in June 2021 with the International Financial Corporation (IFC) subscribing to the full value of the issue. This momentum, together with the growing trend of investors demanding more transparency and accountability and eco-friendly or ESG-aligned deals, will ultimately dictate where capital goes, impacting financial flows and growth within these economies.

Sources of finance and selected case studies from the region

Energy projects in MENA are typically financed by a diverse group of local, regional, and international financiers, and include those from the public, private, and multilateral sectors.

Public sector

Government support, including soft loans and loan guarantees Soft loans are loans with below market interest rates that have favorable conditions, including extended grace repayment periods, if any. Bringing a project to financial close requires all risks that the project bears to be allocated, mitigated, or transferred to the stakeholder best able to manage them. A sovereign guarantee is a government's guarantee that an obligation will be satisfied if the primary obligor defaults. Usually, sovereign guarantees relate to payment defaults, but they can cover all kinds of obligations and commitments. This carries with it implications for the sovereign and can be considered as contingent liabilities that may have to be added to the national debt in the assessment of the level of indebtedness of a country (as percentage of GDP).[7] This ratio, in turn, defines the capacity of a country to take on additional debt. While many governments in MENA, particularly the GCC, have supported their infrastructure and renewables sectors using these tools, incentives need to be strengthened to create an enabling environment that encourages private sector capital mobilization and ensures project sustainability moving forward beyond the reliance on the public sector.

Export Credit Agencies (ECAs) Governments provide officially supported export credits through ECAs in support of national exporters competing for overseas sales. Such support can take the form either of 'official financing support,' such as direct credits to foreign buyers, refinancing, or interest-rate support, or 'pure cover support,' such as export credits insurance or guarantee cover for credits provided by private financial institutions. ECAs can be government institutions or private companies operating on behalf of governments.[8] A recent example of this is in Saudi Arabia, where, having reached financial close in mid-2021, solar photovoltaic (PV) Independent Power Producer

(IPP) Rabigh, at 300MW, became one of the first renewables projects to draw on financing from an ECA: Japan's Bank of International Cooperation (JBIC) provided a soft mini-perm structure amounting to approximately $78 million, which has been combined with an Islamic facility tranche.

Private sector and capital markets

Commercial bank loans These are typically syndicated, in which a group of banks works together to provide funding for a project to mitigate concentration risk for any one bank to undertake, and to address legal lending limits that constrain extending up to a certain percentage of any one individual bank's capital to a single borrower. In August 2021, ACWA Power, a leading Saudi-based developer, investor, and operator of power generations and desalinated water plants, announced the financial close for the 1500MW Sudair Solar plant – one of the key projects under PIF's renewable energy program, drawing on credit facilities from five banks (Table 3.2).

Sukuk (Islamic-/Shari'a-compliant-bond) A Sukuk is a capital markets instrument that is an Islamic financial certificate representing a portion of ownership in a portfolio of eligible existing or future assets.[9] Global outstanding Sukuk reached $765.3 billion in 2022, growing 7.6% year on year, of which outstanding ESG Sukuk reached $24.5 billion, growing 62.9% over the same period.[10] Although sovereign Sukuk issuances have taken place regionally by several governments over the past few years (Bahrain, Oman, Saudi Arabia, Sharjah), quasi-sovereign and corporate issuances have been at the fore of green Sukuk (Table 3.3), in which issuers exclusively use the proceeds to finance investments in environmental and renewable assets. Standards such as the Green Bond Principles and the ASEAN Green Bond Standards serve to guide the issuance to meet key qualifying criteria.[11] Despite how young this market is, with the first green Sukuk issuance having taken place in July 2017, the adoption of green Sukuk is growing.

Green and blue asset classes in response to climate change Since the first green bond issuance in 2007 by the European Investment Bank (EIB), under the label Climate Awareness Bond, various assets have been identified to qualify for green. EIB's structure funnelled proceeds towards

Table 3.2 *Sudair solar PV plant IPP credit facility*

Name	Value (USD millions)	Role
Mizuho Bank	92.87	MLA
Al Rajhi Bank	92.87	MLA
Riyad Bank	92.87	MLA
Saudi National Bank	92.87	MLA
Standard Chartered Bank	92.87	MLA
Korea Development Bank	92.87	Development Bank
Arab Petroleum Investments Corporation	92.87	Multilateral

Source: IJGlobal.

Note: The project's credit facility amounts to USD 650.12 million. MLA = Mandated Lead Arranger.

renewable energy and energy efficiency projects, a trend that has since taken hold globally and regionally. Initially, only multilateral development banks were issuing green bonds, until 2012 when the first private transaction was completed. The growth of the international green bond market serves to showcase how capital markets can channel private capital to address climate change.

A fairly nascent market, the notion of blue capital, blue finance, and the blue economy emerged in 2014. In the same way the green space developed in response to increased carbon emissions, the premise of blue is centered on contributing to ocean protection and improved water management – an ever-growing challenge in water-poor MENA. In January 2022, the IFC released its Guidelines for Blue Finance, which delineated how to structure, evaluate, and monitor blue bonds and loans. This framework is supported by the International Capital Market Association (ICMA), which acts as a repository for promoting internationally accepted standards of practice.

For both green and blue assets, external second party opinion providers and third-party verification are becoming increasingly important, especially in bonds and capital markets, to address risks of 'greenwashing' – that is, portraying an asset, investment, or initiative as ESG-aligned where no real sustainability impacts exist – and similar

Table 3.3 Selected green and sustainability Sukuk issuances in MENA as of end 2022

Issue date	Issuer	Country	Sector	Issue Size (USD million)§	Coupon rate (% per annum unless stated otherwise)	Issue tenor (Years)
2022 (Mar)	Infracorp – Green Sukuk*	Bahrain	To develop projects and assets promoting the transition toward low-carbon, climate change-resilient and environmentally sustainable economies	900	7.5 (semi-annual basis)	Perpetual
2021 (Mar)	Islamic Development Bank (IsDB) – Sustainability Sukuk	Saudi Arabia	Finance and refinance green (10%) and social development projects (90%)	2,500	1.262 (semi-annual basis)	5
2020 (Sep)	Saudi Electricity Company (SEC) – Green Sukuk‡	Saudi Arabia	Energy efficiency and renewable energy	1,300	1.74 and 2.413	5 and 10 year tranches
2020 (Oct)	Etihad Airways – Transition Green Sukuk†	United Arab Emirates	Climate reduction projects to reduce carbon emissions	600	2.394	5

2019 (Nov)	Islamic Development Bank (IsDB) – Green Sukuk*	Saudi Arabia	Renewable energy, clean transportation, energy efficiency, pollution prevention and control, environmentally sustainable management of natural living resources and land use and sustainable water and wastewater management.	1,000	0.037	5
2019 (Oct)	Majid Al Futtaim – Green Sukuk	United Arab Emirates	Finance and refinance green projects (renewable energy, energy efficiency, sustainable water management, green buildings)	600	3.933	10
2019 (May)	Majid Al Futtaim – Green Sukuk*	United Arab Emirates	Finance and refinance green projects (renewable energy, energy efficiency, sustainable water management, green buildings)	600	4.637	10

Source: International Islamic Financial Market Sukuk Report, 2021; Islamic Development Bank; company and bank news sources

Notes: * debut green sukuk issuances; † first-ever aviation, and transition, sukuk issuance; ‡ in addition to this being the company's debut green sukuk issuance, it was also Saudi Arabia's first green issuance with SEC being the first utility company in MENA to issue green sukuk; § IsDB's Nov 2019 issuance was EUR 1,000 million

risks that can result from ascertaining what qualifies as blue to ensure the use of proceeds are being directed appropriately.

MENA is one of the most climate-vulnerable regions facing extreme high temperatures (up to 56°C becoming the norm), worsening droughts and floods, and sea-level rise (Figure 3.2). This, together with the region's level of water stress, means blue finance may provide an innovative financing solution in the region to address not only more sustainable practices in wastewater and sanitation services, but also coastal resilience and interventions in countries like Algeria, Egypt, Morocco, and Tunisia where erosion, increased flooding, and overfishing in the Mediterranean present challenges. The World Bank is currently engaged in the region through MENA Blue, whose program is designed to strengthen physical, social, and economic resilience, through technical assistance and the mobilization of climate finance.

Structuring transactions with corporate and project finance The capital structure of any project is a combination of debt and equity. In theory, the optimal capital structure is defined as the proportion of debt and equity that results in the lowest weighted average cost of capital, or otherwise the average rate a company expects to pay to finance its assets. There are different reasons for opting for debt or equity: debt investors have the first claim on the assets of a business in the event of bankruptcy and so take on less risk than equity holders. However, the cost of debt financing is contingent on various factors, including capital market breadth and depth, the sophistication of the financial ecosystem, levels of liquidity, bank concentration, and the type of funding needed (local currency or USD), amongst several others

Within this context, there are two ways the development of a (renewable) energy asset can be financed: corporate or project finance. In the former, the sponsors (or borrowers) use their balance sheet for leverage, and debt capacity and borrowing costs are determined based on the assets and risk of the entire sponsor company (or group of companies). Under corporate finance, lenders can generally lay claim to the assets of the sponsors beyond the project under development. By contrast, the amount of debt that can be raised in project finance is based on the project's ability to repay debt through the cashflows generated of that project alone. Project finance transactions cover a spectrum from non-recourse to full recourse such that any default will entitle

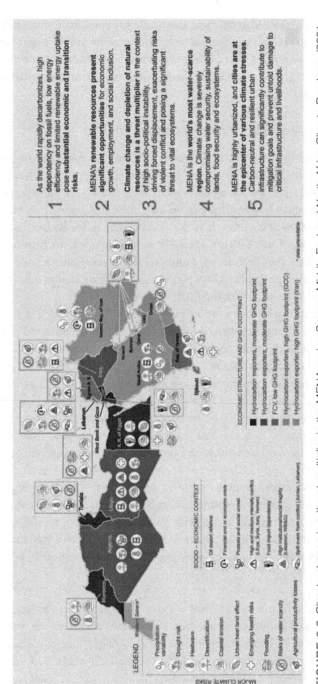

FIGURE 3.2 Climate change is a threat multiplier in the MENA region *Source:* Middle East and North Africa Climate Roadmap (2021–2025), World Bank Group.

the debt provider to repayment from only the asset being financed to that which is being financed in addition to other assets and financial accounts. Over the last ten years, a portfolio of renewables assets in MENA has been completed using project finance structures (Table 3.4).

Bilateral/multilateral finance

Donor/grant funding/concessional finance Within climate and environment, key donors to MENA include European countries, with France and Germany taking the lead on individual country and regional programs, and a host of other peer nations, including Japan, contributing through other channels such as the European Bank for Reconstruction and Development (EBRD), the EIB, and multilateral climate funds, notably, the Clean Technology Fund and the Green Climate Fund. The Islamic Development Bank also plays a role in climate change initiatives, co-financing projects with the EBRD and others.

Concessional finance is below market rate finance provided by major financial institutions, such as development banks and multilateral funds, to developing countries to accelerate development objectives. The term concessional finance does not represent a single mechanism or type of financial support but comprises a range of below market rate products used to accelerate a climate or development objective. The most common financial products used to deliver concessional finance come in the form of loans, grants, and, to some extent, equity investments. How these products are delivered must remain flexible to the unique needs of each development challenge. For example, concessional finance can be applied as grants, funding technical assistance to prepare a region's policies for industry decarbonization. Concessional finance can also come in the form of a first loss guarantee, whereby a third party compensates lenders if the borrower defaults; having such a guarantee in place can help a renewable power plant, for example, crowd in private sector investors.[12]

Other Beyond the World Bank's tools, which, can include technical advisory and assistance in addition to the above, development finance institutions' (DFI) investments come in the form of senior or mezzanine debt or equity and can take on hybrid forms such as blended finance (BF). BF is when a DFIs' normal own (balance sheet) account finance

Table 3.4 Selected renewables projects in MENA using project finance: 2018–2022

Transaction Name	Transaction Value (USD m)	Transaction Debt (USD m)	Transaction Equity (USD m)	Debt/Equity Ratio	Sponsors	Debt Providers	Financial Close Date	Transaction Country/Region	PPP	Contract
Sidi Solar PV Plant (60MW) IPP	52.25	38.01	14.24	73:27	Scatec Solar	European Bank for Reconstruction and Development, Proparco	3/24/2022	Tunisia	No	BOO
Tozeur Solar PV Plant (60MW) IPP	52.4	38.12	14.28	73:27	Scatec Solar	European Bank for Reconstruction and Development, Proparco	3/24/2022	Tunisia	No	BOO
Red Sea Tourism Megaproject Renewable Energy & Water Infrastructure PPP	1,500.00	1,446.70	53.3	96:4	ACWA Power, PowerChina	Al Rajhi Bank, Banque Saudi Fransi, Riyad Bank, Standard Chartered Bank, SABB, Arab Petroleum Investments Corporation, Bank Albilad, Bank AL-Jazira, Arab National Bank	1/7/2022	Saudi Arabia	Yes	BOT

(continued)

Table 3.4 *Continued*

Transaction Name	Transaction Value (USD m)	Transaction Debt (USD m)	Transaction Equity (USD m)	Debt/ Equity Ratio	Sponsors	Debt Providers	Financial Close Date	Transaction Country/ Region	PPP	Contract
King Salman Energy Park Phase I PPP	119.98	N/A	N/A		Alfouzan Alsabiq, Almutlaq Real Estate Investment Company		9/15/2021	Saudi Arabia	Yes	BOOT
Kom Ombo Solar PV Plant (200MW)	154.1	116.6	37.5	76:24	ACWA Power, European Bank for Reconstruction and Development, Arab Petroleum Investments Corporation	European Bank for Reconstruction and Development, OPEC Fund for International Development, African Development Bank, Arab Bank Group, Green Climate Fund	4/21/2021	Egypt	No	BOO

Project					Sponsors	Lenders	Date	Country		Structure
Jeddah Solar PV Plant (300MW) IPP	227.21	160.44	66.77	71:29	Masdar, EDF, Nesma Holding	Natixis, Sumitomo Mitsui Banking Corporation, Norinchukin Bank, First Abu Dhabi Bank, Commercial Bank of Dubai, Riyad Bank	4/12/2021	Saudi Arabia	No	DBFMO
Rabigh Solar PV Plant (300MW) IPP	207	157	50	76:24	Aljomaih Energy & Water, Marubeni	Mizuho Bank, Japan International Cooperation Agency, Al Rajhi Bank	4/12/2021	Saudi Arabia	No	DBFMO
Mohammed bin Rashid Al Maktoum Solar PV Plant Phase V (900MW) IPP	646	532	114	82:18	Dubai Electricity & Water Authority, ACWA Power, Gulf Investment Corporation, Commercial Bank International, Emirates NBD, Mashreq Bank	Standard Chartered Bank, Abu Dhabi Islamic Bank, Arab Petroleum Investments Corporation, Natixis, Saudi National Bank, Warba Bank, ICBC, Commercial Bank International, Emirates NBD, Mashreq Bank	9/3/2020	United Arab Emirates	No	BOOT

(continued)

Table 3.4 *Continued*

Transaction Name	Transaction Value (USD m)	Transaction Debt (USD m)	Transaction Equity (USD m)	Debt/Equity Ratio	Sponsors	Debt Providers	Financial Close Date	Transaction Country/Region	PPP	Contract
Boujdour Wind Farm (300MW) IPP	0	N/A	N/A		Enel Green Power, Nareva Holding, Siemens		8/3/2020	Morocco	No	DBFMO
Kahramaa Solar PV Plant Phase I (350MW) IPP	467	330	137	71:29	Total, Marubeni, Qatar Petroleum, Qatar Electricity & Water Company (QEWC), Sumitomo Mitsui Banking Corporation	Japan Bank for International Cooperation, Mizuho Bank	7/22/2020	Qatar	No	BOOT

Project					Sponsors	Lenders	Date	Country	PPP	Contract
Dumat Al Jandal Wind Farm (400MW) IPP	428.31	266.91	161.4	62:38	EDF, Masdar	Korea Development Bank, Natixis, National Commercial Bank, Norinchukin Bank, Sumitomo Mitsui Banking Corporation, Societe Generale	7/9/2019	Saudi Arabia	No	BOO
Daehan Wind Farm (51.75MW)	103	71.4	31.6	69:31	Korea Southern Power, Daelim, Shinhan Bank	International Finance Corporation, Standard Chartered Bank, Shinhan Bank	9/16/2018	Jordan	No	BOO

Source: IJGlobal.

Note: Table presents selected projects that have reached financial close, and whose sector is classified as renewables. PPP = Public Private Partnership. Contract refers to the project delivery model; BOO = Build, Own and Operate; BOT = Build, Operate and Transfer; BOOT = Build, Own, Operate and Transfer; DBFMO = Design, Build, Finance, Maintain and Operate.

and/or commercial finance from other investors is 'blended' with concessional finance from donors or third parties to develop private sector markets – in essence, the project is not fully commercial on a standalone basis and needs a temporary subsidy to enable its high-impact, without which it would not otherwise materialize (Figure 3.3). In the energy transition story, many projects still carry risks in terms of their commercial viability, credit risk, or the success of technologies deployed (e.g. green hydrogen), among many others.

Climate funds There are twelve climate funds active in the MENA region (Table 3.5).[13] The largest contributions are from the Clean Technology Fund (CTF), which is one of two multi-donor trust funds under the Climate Investment Funds framework, with an estimated pool of $5.4 billion in funds. As at the end of 2021, CTF, through concessional finance, has approved a total of $825 million for four projects in Morocco and Egypt and five regional projects (Table 3.6).[14]

More broadly among the various climate funds, between 2003 and 2021 an estimated $1.6 billion of financing was approved for over 139 projects, whose scopes were centered largely on mitigation efforts – despite pressing adaptation needs in the region, especially for water conservation and food security measures. Of the total funding approved for the region, $560 million has taken the form of grants. $964 million has

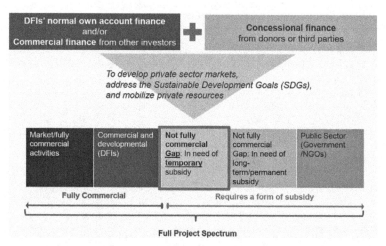

FIGURE 3.3 Blended finance *Source:* Development Finance Institution Blended Concessional Finance Working Group for Private Sector Projects (2017).

Table 3.5 *Climate funds supporting the MENA region: 2003–2022*

Fund	Amount approved USD millions (as of Jan 2022)	Projects approved (through end 2020)
Clean Technology Fund (CTF)	825.1	9
Green Climate Fund (GCF-IRM, GCF-1)	362.4	7
Global Environmental Facility (GEF-4, 5, 6, 7)	152.1	53
Adaptation Fund (AF)	91.2	13
Least Developed Countries Fund (LDCF)	44.1	9
Special Climate Change Fund (SCCF)	37.3	7
Adaptation for Smallholder Agriculture Programme (ASAP)	22.1	4
Global Energy Efficiency and Renewable Energy Fund (GEEREF)	16.6	1
Global Climate Change Alliance (GCCA)	11.6	2
Partnership for Market Readiness (PMR)	10.2	6
Millenium Development Goals Achievement Fund (MDG-F)	7.6	2
Pilot Program for Climate Resilience (PPCR)	2.6	1

Source: Climate Finance Regional Briefing: Middle East and North Africa, February 2021, Overseas Development Institute and Heinrich Böll Stiftung.

Note: The climate finance fundamentals are based on climate funds update data (www.climatefundsupdate.org).

Table 3.6 *Clean Technology Fund interventions in MENA*

Name	Fund	Country	Funding (USD millions)	Cofinancing (USD millions)	MDB
Egypt Kom Ombo CSP	Clean Technology Fund	Egypt			AFDB
Morocco – Noor Midelt I	Clean Technology Fund	Morocco	25	240	IBRD
Noor II and III Concentrated Solar Power Project	Clean Technology Fund	Morocco	119	2,304	IBRD
Noor II and III Concentrated Solar Power Project	Clean Technology Fund	Morocco	119	4,054.57	AFDB
Noor-Midelt Phase 1 Concentrated Solar Power Project	Clean Technology Fund	Morocco	25		AFDB
Ouarzazate I Concentrated Solar Power Project	Clean Technology Fund	Morocco	100	1,389.88	AFDB
Ouarzazate I Concentrated Solar Power Project	Clean Technology Fund	Morocco	97	584.65	IBRD
Technical Assistance Program	Clean Technology Fund	Algeria, Egypt, Libya, Morocco, Tunisia	9.5		IBRD

Source: Climate Investment Funds.

Note: MDB = Multilateral Development Bank; AFDB = African Development Bank; IBRD = International Bank for Reconstruction and Development (part of the World Bank Group).

been provided in the form of loans or concessional loans for just a few large-scale energy infrastructure projects approved by the CTF and GCF. The top two recipients – Egypt and Morocco – respectively have received 29 percent and 19 percent of total approved climate finance in the region (Figure 3.4).

Future outlook

As MENA countries continue to draw on public and private sector participants to carve out their energy transition roadmaps, the opportunity to optimize this transformation necessitates a brief examination of macroeconomic considerations and potential challenges within the financial ecosystem, as well as innovative ways to access capital.

Macroeconomic conditions and role of the public sector

As macroeconomic conditions in the medium term reflect higher inflation, and commodity prices indicate increasing inflationary pressures, various governments in the region will be impacted depending on whether they are commodity exporters or importers. Higher commodity prices have been driven by various factors including the impact of COVID, tighter investments in oil and gas over the last several years, as well as global conflict, including the war in Ukraine. For energy,

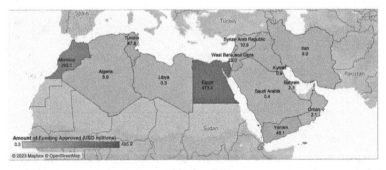

FIGURE 3.4 Recipient countries in the Middle East and North Africa *Source:* Climate Funds Update (http://climatefundsupdate.org/data-dashboard/regions/).

during the pandemic, upstream oil and gas investments declined by approximately 30 percent as energy companies reduced their capital expenditures to shore up their balance sheets – a trend which, in 2022, saw a reversal with upstream oil and gas spending expected to rise 16 percent (or $142 billion) from 2021.[15]

These dynamics will affect fiscal budgets, placing additional burdens for governments that have commodity-related subsidies in place (e.g. the net effect on fossil fuel exporters, or importers such as Egypt, Jordan, and Morocco for wheat) thereby impacting their fiscal space to channel funds efficiently toward the transition. Importing economies may attempt to keep end prices for consumers the same as before and would thus be forced to increase the amount of spending on such initiatives. For exporters, higher commodity prices are a welcome change to the volatility experienced since 2020. Figure 3.5 represents the two core commodities impacting MENA from an exporter and/or importer perspective.

For importers especially, current account deficits will remain large due to higher imports (in value terms) of fuel and agricultural commodities. Global inflation is also pushing input prices upwards, including material and labor costs, and key metals within renewables for battery and solar PV like copper, lithium, and nickel have already pushed renewable project costs upwards. Consequently, diverse sources of funding are key to help buoy the transition momentum, as well as to support the development of the private sector.

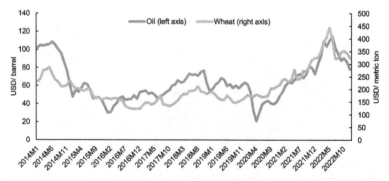

FIGURE 3.5 Commodity prices *Source:* Primary Commodity Price System, IMF. *Note:* Oil Price is represented by APSP = Average Petroleum Spot Price, a simple average of three spot prices: Dated Brent, West Texas Intermediate, and Dubai Fateh. Wheat = No.1 Hard Red Winter, ordinary protein, Kansas City.

Growth in the private sector has lagged, and labor productivity in MENA has seen relative declines. Many MENA economies are still characterized by the concentration of labor in the public sector, evidenced by large public wage bills. Ultimately, the inflow of hydrocarbon revenues, on the back of periods of elevated prices, has fostered a bloated public sector that absorbs national labor. This factor, along with structural challenges resulting from labor market rigidities, has helped prevent the development of internationally competitive domestic private sectors. This dynamic necessitates wide-ranging reforms in how governments transfer hydrocarbon wealth to their citizens. Countries need to rapidly address misaligned incentives in the old social contract that have conventionally relied on the rentier state model. Such incentives perpetuate challenges, including in labor dynamics, that could thwart states' ability to generate high-value-added jobs and products, and ultimately their need to industrialize. There are no 'quick wins' to bypass manufacturing, unfortunately, so enabling an export-oriented private sector supported by a skilled workforce is key.

Challenges in the financial ecosystem

The role of central banks and the mechanisms within the financial ecosystem are of paramount importance to the transition toward a decarbonized economy. Financiers can channel funds away from fossil fuels and polluting types of activities and toward investing in greener activities.

Strengthening the private sector in these countries will require obtaining diverse sources of funding and tapping domestic, regional, and international financial markets, especially given the limited availability of public funds and high debt levels (Table 3.7).

Inadequate access to finance remains a constraint in some areas. While banking systems in the Gulf are well-capitalized, those in other energy exporters, such as Algeria and Iraq, and more fragile countries remain weak. Financial institutions in the region are characterized by concentrated lending to the sovereign or government-led projects, which reflects the outsized role of the state, including exposure to national oil companies through syndicated bank loan financing. This presents several challenges, including the crowding out of small and medium-size enterprises. In addition, the impending impact on bank portfolios and balance sheets of re-evaluation based on stranded assets and the effects of

Table 3.7 *MENA country debt profiles*

| | Total government gross debt (% GDP) | | | | |
	2019	2020	2021	Projections 2022	2023
Oil exporters					
Algeria	46.0	52.3	63.0	62.7	70.3
Bahrain	101.6	129.7	128.5	119.5	121.7
Iran	42.7	44.1	42.4	34.2	31.9
Iraq	45.2	84.2	59.1	36.7	34.8
Kuwait	11.6	11.7	8.7	7.1	6.9
Oman	52.5	69.7	62.9	45.4	41.1
Qatar	62.1	72.6	58.4	46.9	43.4
Saudi Arabia	22.5	32.4	30.0	24.8	25.1
United Arab Emirates	27.1	39.7	34.7	30.7	29.5
Oil importers					
Egypt	80.1	85.3	89.2	89.2	85.6
Jordan	78.0	88.0	91.9	91.0	89.8
Lebanon	172.3	150.6			
Morocco	60.3	72.2	68.9	70.3	70.1
Tunisia	69.0	82.8	81.8	88.8	89.2
West Bank and Gaza	34.5	47.1	50.4	44.7	40.2

Sources: International Monetary Fund (IMF).

climate change may also create a liquidity squeeze, limiting private credit provision. Stranded assets are fossil fuel reserves that cannot be recovered due to changes in regulations, technology, and market direction, including pressures to prioritize spending on cleaner energy, but which banks have already taken into consideration when determining their provisions and capital requirements. Nearly 60 percent of both oil and fossil methane gas and almost 90 percent of coal must remain in the ground by 2050 to keep global warming below 1.5°C. In addition to these unutilized reserves, the capital invested in the value chain (extraction, refining, transportation, etc.) and ancillary services can also become stranded. This point is increasingly important as stranded assets could form a systemic risk to financial stability – but so can climate change, whether it is related to hydrocarbon reserves or not. For example, MENA faces elevated water and environmental stress more broadly, but access to existing reserves in the region is also under threat from extreme heat and dust storms.

Given these increasing vulnerabilities, it is imperative for policymakers and financial regulators to put in place prudent frameworks that mitigate the negative impact of physical and transition risks on the financial sector.[16] This is the only way to ensure a more resilient and sustainable path forward for MENA.

Innovative interventions

Governance structures

Governance is critical for a sustainable and just energy transition. This includes careful management, coordination, and inclusion of relevant stakeholders beyond the public's sector management of natural resources. This will help drive capital into the region and into these projects that are backed by experienced sponsors.

BOX B

In December 2022, three of the UAE's energy giants – ADNOC, TAQA and Mubadala – successfully completed the Masdar transaction to form the Emirate's flagship clean energy powerhouse with the aim to grow to 100 GW of renewable energy capacity globally by 2030 (through mainly wind and solar), and an ambition to reach over 200 GW. The company's new green hydrogen business will target an annual production capacity of up to 1 million tonnes over the same period, equivalent to saving more than 6 million tonnes of CO_2 emissions.

Financial arrangements

ESG-based repo

A repurchase agreement ('repo') is a form of short-term secured borrowing between parties where one party sells securities to another and agrees to repurchase those securities at a higher price – essentially bonds for cash.[17] Repo transactions facilitate the flow of cash and securities in the financial system. In November 2021, Standard Chartered Bank executed a $250 million repo with Saudi National Bank (SNB) based on ESG principles. The transaction was the first of its kind in MENA, and SNB will allocate the financial proceeds to several large renewable energy projects and green initiatives in the kingdom and beyond. It is likely that the region will continue to innovate on financial tools within capital markets.

Debt for nature (climate) swaps (DNS)

DNS are capital market tools in which a portion of a developing nation's foreign debt is restructured in exchange for local investments that drive forward the climate agenda (environmental conservation, adaptation, mitigation, resilience, etc.) (Figure 3.6). DNS transactions were first introduced in 1987 by Conservation International in Bolivia. Their resurgence as of late has followed the escalating debt burdens globally and ways through which potential innovative solutions can be operationalized to capture a green recovery that would alleviate debt and tackle climate.

Given the emergence of carbon markets, there is also the possibility of linking debt markets with them to create incentives for private sector debt holders to engage in transformative climate finance where the payout to investors is in the form of carbon credits, whose value can then be recouped by investors in international markets.

While climate change is a global crisis, the solutions are local. Local projects that generate carbon credits need to be supported through investment and monetization of additionalities for they provide the carbon offsets and mitigation mechanisms across the globe that, combined, will get the world to net zero. For these markets to scale and have the level of impact necessary to shift the carbon balance, a global, market-driven trading ecosystem is needed to create an additional asset class that generates a new equity or investment base to finance those projects and create means for securitization through blockchain. Such a system would resolve these limitations and simultaneously democratize the widespread purchasing and impact of credits of standardized assets.

By enabling a sustainable long-term carbon credit trading market, additional projects that support the goal of a net-zero economy will gain access to additional financial instruments and incentives. Blockchain not only delivers an inviolable accounting system. The verified reduction of carbon dioxide emissions or sequestration of one metric ton of emissions by a registered program represents a value that can be tokenized on that blockchain as part of a trading system. Doing so involves the validation of reduction and the issuance of a digital certificate by a well-accepted international standards agency, which in turn authorizes the issuance of tradeable carbon credits in the form of tokens. The token is held on a blockchain network and features transparent value substantiation with a public record of the underlying collateral. It can then be purchased and held or traded as an investment at prevailing rates, or, to offset one's carbon footprint, retired.

The issuance of tokenized carbon credits can create a new investable asset class that results in a tradeable market whose global clearing price is set by its buyers and sellers, which can facilitate and mobilize financial resources directly toward environmental project. Through blockchain, tokens will be fully accounted for and permanently retired upon offsetting, enabling tracing back to the original project through the retiree's own balance sheet. The integration of blockchain technology into the carbon credit creation, verification, registration, transfer, and accounting process can have a strong impact on creating a transparent, robust, and efficient trading and post trade infrastructure that has not been available before and which is a key objective of the UN Task Force on Scaling Voluntary Carbon Markets (VCM).

BOX C. CARBON MARKETS IN MENA

In March 2022, Saudi Arabia's PIF announced a VCM initiative to be supported by five local players: Saudi Aramco, Saudi, ACWA Power, Ma'aden, and ENOWA (a subsidiary of NEOM). These partners will support the PIF in the development of a VCM through the supply, purchase, and trading of carbon credits, as the market is expected to be established in 2023. Saudi Arabia continues to take a leading role in pioneering ways of furthering the mandate of sustainability in MENA.

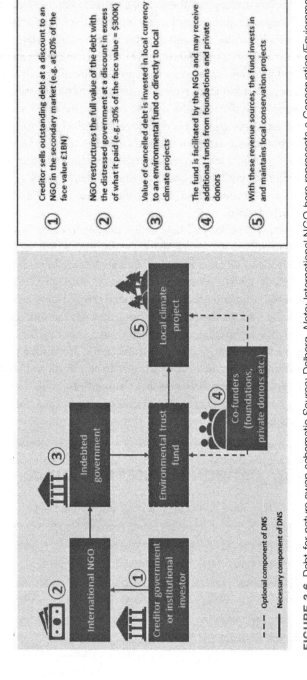

FIGURE 3.6 Debt-for-nature swap schematic *Source:* Dalberg. *Note:* International NGO here represents a Conservation/Enviornmental NGO.

① Creditor sells outstanding debt at a discount to an NGO in the secondary market (e.g. at 20% of the face value £1BN)

② NGO restructures the full value of the debt with the distressed government at a discount in excess of what it paid (e.g. 30% of the face value = $300K)

③ Value of cancelled debt is invested in local currency to an environmental fund or directly to local climate projects

④ The fund is facilitated by the NGO and may receive additional funds from foundations and private donors

⑤ With these revenue sources, the fund invests in and maintains local conservation projects

Creditor government or institutional investor

International NGO

Indebted government

Environmental trust fund

Co-funders (foundations, private donors etc.)

Local climate project

– – – Optional component of DNS

——— Necessary component of DNS

Targeted funds

Targeted funds are another instrument that MENA economies can use to mobilize private capital into priority sectors, often designed alongside existing sovereign wealth funds as part of natural resource management. They are no new feat, especially for resource-rich economies, having previously been set up by several countries to play active roles in facilitating financing in key markets. They are often funded through the country budget, or in partnership with MDBs and the private sector, which can determine their ownership structure. Targeted funds are often characterized by policy objectives that align with the overall investment strategy and determine the profile of investments, including risk tolerance.

In October 2021, Saudi Arabia announced the establishment of a National Infrastructure Fund (NIF), enlisting US asset manager BlackRock to help advise on it. This fund – backed by Saudi's National Development Fund which was set up in 2017 – has an investment target of $53 billion spanning various sectors, including power and water, and is likely to further propel renewables investment forward. It is set to participate through debt and equity, and offer credit guarantees to mobilize domestic and foreign capital.

BOX D. GLOBAL EXAMPLES OF TARGETED FUNDS

Corporación de Fomento de la Producción (CORFO) was one of the first national development banks in Latin America and played a decisive role in Chile's national development strategy. Through many instruments, it played a key role in the process of Chilean economic development, including the creation of many crucial enterprises that it also helped to run. Its support for strategic sectors has been decisive to incentivize innovative, value-added activities, such as the Start-Up programme or renewable energy projects.

The Nigeria Infrastructure Fund, established by the Nigeria Sovereign Investment Authority in 2013 and allocated $600 million, has an investment mandate focused on five core sectors, including healthcare, motorways, and power, to stimulate the growth and diversification of the economy and attract foreign investment. It is worth noting that one of its main KPIs is additionality – the financing of projects which would not have otherwise happened without their involvement.

In September 2021, the Islamic Development Bank (IsDB) and the Government of Uzbekistan (GoU) announced the launch of Uzbekistan's first impact investment fund, Economic Empowerment Fund for Uzbekistan (EEFU), with start-up capital of $100 million. Capital was provided by GoU (35 percent), IsDB (20 percent), and private sector investors from Saudi Arabia (45 percent). EEFU is envisioned to target small and medium enterprises and to benefit women and youth-led initiatives.

Conclusion

The MENA region is facing a tremendous opportunity to benefit from, and contribute to, the global energy transition. Despite the country-specific idiosyncrasies, the region has been able to innovate and experiment with new technologies and financial approaches, supported by the state, and new regulatory frameworks. Nonetheless, the region's over-dependence on hydrocarbons will spell greater inequities between exporters and importers as the pace of the energy transition accelerates. For those with fiscal space and stronger financial systems, the transformation will mean better access to diverse sources of funding, driving optimal capital allocation and resulting in more sustainable growth.

Irrespective of where they sit in the region, and due to compounding challenges brought on by massive change, the economics of the energy transition will surface difficult decisions regarding the social contracts countries have established with their citizens and will exert pressure on their development plans. Economic diversification remains a key priority, and so balancing the needs of growth and of a rising young population, together with meeting climate goals, necessitates both a dynamic private sector and a strong financial ecosystem.

Despite this, the region's net zero ambitions and ensuing new solutions are fueling excitement from participants, given that MENA is compelled to find interventions that will help it meet its sustainability goals while simultaneously providing the world with the energy it needs.

Bibliography

ACWA Power, 'ACWA Power Announces Financial Close for 1500 MW Sudair
    Solar Plant and Aramco Joining the Consortium under PIF Renewables
    Program.' ACWA Power, August 15, 2021. https://www.acwapower.com/
    news/acwa-power-announces-financial-close-for-1500-mw-sudair-solar-
    plant-and-aramco-joining-the-consortium-under-pif-renewables-program/.
Baklanova, Viktoria, Isaac Kuznits, and Trevor Tatum, 'Money Market Funds and
    the Repo Market – SEC.' Primer: Money Market Funds and the Repo Market,
    February 18, 2021. https://www.sec.gov/files/mmfs-and-the-repo-
    market-021721.pdf.
Bassetti, Victoria, Norman Eisen, Michael Jarvis, Suneeta Kaimal, Daniel
    Kaufmann, Kelsey Landau, Robin Lewis, Allison Merkel, Mario Picon, and
    Erica Westenberg, 'Time to Pivot: The Role of the Energy Transition and
    Investors in Forging Resilient Resource-Rich Country Outcomes.' Brookings.
    February 9, 2022. https://www.brookings.edu/blog/up-front/2021/01/15/
    time-to-pivot-the-role-of-the-energy-transition-and-investors-in-forging-
    resilient-resource-rich-country-outcomes/.
Beyene, Winta, Kathrin De Greiff, Manthos D. Delis, and Steven R. G. Ongena.
    'Too-Big-To Strand? Bond Versus Bank Financing in the Transition to a
    Low-Carbon Economy (November 1, 2021).' CEPR Discussion Paper No.
    DP16692. Available at SSRN: https://ssrn.com/abstract=3960296.
Bogmans, Christian, Lama Kiyasseh, Akito Matsumoto, and Andreas Pescatori.
    'Energy, Efficiency Gains and Economic Development: When Will Global
    Energy Demand Saturate?' (November 1, 2020). IMF Working Paper No.
    20/253. Available at SSRN: https://ssrn.com/abstract=3758087.
Browning, Noah. 'Climate Change Imperils World's Oil and Gas Reserves:
    Research.' Reuters. Thomson Reuters, December 16, 2021. https://www.
    reuters.com/article/global-oil-risks-idAFL8N2T02HI.
Cheng, Jeffrey, and David Wessel. 'What Is the Repo Market, and Why Does It
    Matter?' Brookings. March 9, 2022. https://www.brookings.edu/blog/
    up-front/2020/01/28/what-is-the-repo-market-and-why-does-it-matter/.
'Climate Finance in West Asia: Big Pockets, Empty Hands.' Youth4Nature.
    February 26, 2022. https://www.youth4nature.org/blog/climate-finance-in-
    west-asia-big-pockets-empty-hands.
'DFI Working Group on Enhanced Blended Concessional Finance for Private
    Sector Projects.' ifc.org. Accessed April 18, 2022. https://www.ifc.org/wps/wcm/
    connect/topics_ext_content/ifc_external_corporate_site/bf/bf-details/bf-dfi.
Dibley, Arjuna, Thom Wetzer, and Cameron Hepburn. 'National Covid Debts:
    Climate Change Imperils Countries' Ability to Repay.' *Nature News*. Nature
    Publishing Group, April 6, 2021. https://www.nature.com/articles/d41586-
    021-00871-w.
Elgendy, Karim. 'Competition Hots up for Climate Leadership in Mena.'
    Chatham House – International Affairs Think Tank, July 7, 2021. https://
    www.chathamhouse.org/2021/05/competition-hots-climate-leadership-mena.

'ESG Sukuk: A next Step in the Evolution of the Global Sukuk Market.' Akin
    Gump Strauss Hauer & Feld LLP, October 12, 2021. https://www.akingump.
    com/en/news-insights/esg-and-sukuk-in-the-middle-east.
    html#:~:text=Likewise%2C%20a%20green%20Sukuk%20is,as%20energy%20
    and%20infrastructure%20projects).
Grippa, Pierpaolo. 'Climate Change, Central Banks and Financial Risk – IMF
    F&D: December 2019.' Accessed 8. https://www.imf.org/external/pubs/ft/
    fandd/2019/12/climate-change-central-banks-and-financial-risk-grippa.htm.
Group, African Development Bank. 'Potential for Green Banks & National
    Climate Change Funds in Africa – Scoping Report.' African Development
    Bank Group – Building today, a better Africa tomorrow. February 3, 2022.
    https://www.afdb.org/en/documents/potential-green-banks-national-
    climate-change-funds-africa-scoping-report.
Hall, Max. 'Masdar Wants 200GW of Renewables Capacity.' pv magazine
    International, March 21, 2022. https://www.pv-magazine.com/2022/03/21/
    masdar-wants-200gw-of-renewables-capacity/#:~:text=Masdar%20was%20
    launched%20by%20UAE,24%25%20stakeholder%2C%20and%20
    Mubadala%20retaining.
'ISDB, Uzbekistan Launch $100M Impact Investment Fund.' IsDB, Uzbekistan
    Launch $100m Impact Investment Fund | News, September 2, 2021. https://
    www.isdb.org/news/isdb-uzbekistan-launch-100m-impact-investment-fund.
'Islamic Sustainable Investing Thought Leadership Report.' Accessed April 18,
    2022. https://iifm.net/frontend/media/ifn-islamic-sustainable-investing-
    thought-leadership-report-ijlal-alvi-article-1638366115.pdf.
Kiyasseh, Lama, Lina Osman, and Karen Young. 'Sustainable Finance in MENA.'
    Washington, D.C.: Middle East Institute, February 11, 2022.
Kiyasseh, Lama. 'Financing MENA's Energy Transition: Risks and Implications.'
    Middle East Institute, February 2022. https://www.mei.edu/sites/default/files/
    mei_library/pdf/20542.pdf.
Kiyasseh, Lama. 'Strong Momentum in Saudi Arabia's Drive toward Renewables
    and Infrastructure.' Middle East Institute, January 4, 2022. https://www.mei.
    edu/publications/strong-momentum-saudi-arabias-drive-toward-
    renewables-and-infrastructure.
Mahdi, Shatha Almasoudi and Wael. 'ACWA Power Won't Start Other Hydrogen
    Projects before NEOM Venture Advanced: CEO.' Arab News. September 12,
    2021. https://www.arabnews.com/node/1926881/business-economy.
Meeddubai. 'A New Road for Project Finance.' *Middle East Economic Digest*, June
    12, 2020. https://www.meed.com/a-new-road-for-project-finance.
Person. 'Etihad Raises $1.2 Bln in Sustainability-Linked Debt.' Reuters. Thomson
    Reuters, October 13, 2021. https://www.reuters.com/business/aerospace-
    defense/etihad-raises-12-bln-first-sustainability-linked-esg-loan-
    aviation-2021-10-13/.
Ravindirane, Jordan. 'Etihad's $600 Million Sustainability-Linked Sukuk: The
    First of Many Things.' Our Center of Expertise. gsh-cib-natixis, November
    30, 2020. https://gsh.cib.natixis.com/our-center-of-expertise/articles/
    etihad-s-600-million-sustainability-linked-sukuk-the-first-of-many-things.

'Regional Economic Outlook for the Middle East and Central Asia.' IMF. Accessed April 18, 2022. https://www.imf.org/en/Publications/REO/MECA/ Issues/2021/10/14/regional-economic-outlook-october.

Romero, Santiago. 'What Is Sustainable Financing?' NEWS BBVA. BBVA, September 23, 2021. https://www.bbva.com/en/sustainability/what-is-sustainable-financing/.

'SEC Record US$1.3bn Green Sukuk Marks Saudi Arabia's Entry into the Green Finance Agenda Amidst Huge Diverse Investor Uptake.' DDCAP, March 27, 2022. https://www.ddcap.com/sec-record-us1-3billion-green-sukuk-marks-saudi-arabias-entry-into-the-green-finance-agenda-amidst-huge-diverse-investor-uptake/.

Singh, Sunil. 'ESG: How Middle East's Net Zero Ambition Is Shifting the Future of Investing in the Region.' Wealth Manager. Citywire, November 8, 2021. https://citywiremiddleeast.com/news/esg-how-middle-east-s-net-zero-ambition-is-shifting-the-future-of-investing-in-the-region/a1578813.

'Sovereign Sukuk: Current Status, Opportunities & Challenges.' Marmore MENA Intelligence, March 15, 2022. https://www.marmoremena.com/ sovereign-sukuk-current-status-opportunities-challenges/.

'Sukuk Report: A Comprehensive Study of the Global Sukuk Market,' July 2021. https://www.iifm.net/frontend/general-documents/ bcd691cfb4233fb37d78355021010392163525 1580.pdf.

'Sustainability Bond Guidelines (SBG).' ICMA – International Capital Market Association. Accessed April 18, 2022. https://www.icmagroup.org/ sustainable-finance/the-principles-guidelines-and-handbooks/sustainability-bond-guidelines-sbg/.

'Sustainable Bonds Insight 2022 Published.' Environmental Finance, February 16, 2022. https://www.environmental-finance.com/content/news/sustainable-bonds-insight-2022-published.html.

'Sustainable Debt Issuance Breezed Past $1.6 Trillion in 2021.' BloombergNEF, January 12, 2022. https://about.bnef.com/blog/sustainable-debt-issuance-breezed-past-1-6-trillion-in-2021/#:~:text=Green%20bonds%2C%20raised%20 for%20environmentally,sustainable%20debt%20issued%20through%202021.

Takouleu, Jean Marie. 'Libya: Government Launches Construction of a Solar Power Plant in Kufra.' Afrik 21, April 16, 2020. https://www.afrik21.africa/en/ libya-government-launches-construction-of-a-solar-power-plant-in-kufra/.

'Taqa, Mubadala and ADNOC Become Shareholders in Masdar.' Energy Connects, December 5, 2021. https://www.energyconnects.com/news/renewables/2021/ december/taqa-mubadala-and-adnoc-become-shareholders-in-masdar/.

Vigotti, Roberto. 'The Mena Region: A Key Scenario for the Energy Transition.' Energy Capital & Power, November 24, 2021. https://energycapitalpower. com/the-mena-region-a-key-scenario-for-the-energy-transition/.

Walsh, Tessa, and Sudip Roy. 'Etihad Airways Pushes Boundaries with 'Transition Sukuk''. IFRe, October 30, 2020. https://www.ifre.com/ story/2597802/etihad-airways-5fw6gt9ygn.

Watson, Charlene, Liane Schalatek, and Aurélien Evéquoz. n.d. 'Climate Finance Regional Briefing: Middle East and North Africa.' Accessed January 25, 2023.

https://climatefundsupdate.org/wp-content/uploads/2022/03/CFF9-MENA_2021.pdf.

World Bank Group. 'Climate Explainer: Concessional Finance.' World Bank Group, September 27, 2021. https://www.worldbank.org/en/news/feature/2021/09/16/what-you-need-to-know-about-concessional-finance-for-climate-action#:~:text=Put%20simply%2C%20concessional%20finance%20is,countries%20to%20accelerate%20development%20objectives.

World Bank Group. 'Middle East & North Africa Climate Roadmap.' World Bank Group, January 25, 2022. https://www.worldbank.org/en/region/mena/publication/middle-east-north-africa-climate-roadmap#:~:text=The%20World%20Bank%20Group's%20Roadmap,green%20recovery%20in%20the%20region.

World Bank Group. 'Pioneering the Green Sukuk : Three Years On.' World Bank Group, October 6, 2020. https://www.worldbank.org/en/country/malaysia/publication/pioneering-the-green-sukuk-three-years-on.

World Bank Group. 'Supporting Egypt's Inaugural Green Bond Issuance.' World Bank Group, March 15, 2022. https://www.worldbank.org/en/news/feature/2022/03/02/supporting-egypt-s-inaugural-green-bond-issuance#:~:text=Egypt%20Vision%202030%20aims%20to,to%2030%20percent%20in%202022.

Vigeo Eiris. 'Second Party Opinion on Etihad Airways' Sustainability-Linked Financing Framework', October 2020. https://www.etihadaviationgroup.com/content/dam/eag/corporate/etihadaviation/en-ae/desktop2/sustainability/20201020_SLB_SPO_Etihad_VF.pdf. Accessed 15 April 2022.

4 POLITICAL PRIORITIES AND ECONOMIC REALITIES: FINANCING THE RENEWABLE ENERGY TRANSITION IN SAUDI ARABIA AND OMAN

Piotr G. S. Schulkes

Introduction

Succeeding in the energy transition is of vital importance to the Arab states of the Persian Gulf. Across the six Gulf Cooperation Council (GCC) member states, gas on average accounts for 75 percent of electricity generating capacity with most of the remaining 25 percent comprising of oil.[1] Three of the states are in the top five largest global carbon emitters per capita, with Qatar on top, and all six are among the top fifteen.[2] The Middle East is warming at twice the global average, with several cities expected to become uninhabitable by the end of the century if current trends continue.[3] At present, GCC states also have strong economic and political incentives to diversify their energy mix. Saudi Arabia, for example, spent around $80 billion on subsidies in 2015, which equates to around 25 percent of total expenditures that year.[4] The precipitous drop in oil prices in 2014, continued price instability, and growing global initiatives to decarbonize economies and value chains has meant that a fundamental reorganization of economic priorities has become necessary. To fund these reorganizations, encapsulated in programs like Saudi Vision 2030 and Oman Vision 2040, the countries must cut costs, limit waste, and diversify their economies away from a near-total reliance on fossil fuels for both energy production and exports earnings.

With 41 percent of MENA power demand coming from the residential sector (compared to, for example, 22 percent in Norway and the Netherlands), countries cannot afford to keep building fossil fuel power stations to keep up with demand.[5] Oman has announced that 30 percent of its energy mix will be non-gas by 2030, focusing on reducing the role of fossil fuels in generating electricity for households.[6] This would free up gas for the more energy-intensive diversification target sectors such as manufacturing and mining. Saudi Arabia has been even more ambitious, aiming renewables to be 50 percent of the country's energy mix by 2030.[7] Thankfully for MENA countries, they are well-situated to capitalize on renewable energy (RE) investments. The Arab Peninsula has some of the highest levels of solar insolation in the world, two to three times higher than most of Europe.[8] Oman's capacity of solar energy is so high that the country's entire electricity consumption could theoretically be supplied by placing solar collectors on just 0.1 percent of its land area.

This chapter will focus on the energy transition in two GCC countries, Oman and Saudi Arabia, concentrating on funding mechanisms. The first section looks at how expensive energy subsidies are cut to free up capital, and how renewable energy projects and investments are incentivized through tax exemptions and government aid. The next section covers how funding is implemented, looking at project funding and ownership, and comparing the role of the government to that of the private sector in the two countries. The third and final section discusses the political economy behind the trends seen in section two.

What this will show is that the first driver of different approaches is the health of the economies. Oman has for several years had enormous budget deficits which have led to a rapidly growing debt burden. The country's sovereign credit rating has tumbled, as have those of all domestic Omani banks. As a result, the country and its financial institutions do not have the reserves to pour capital into the renewable energy sector to the same extent as Saudi Arabia, leading to a slower energy transition and the necessity to open the sector up to foreign actors.

The acute necessity of cost-cutting in Oman has also led to faster privatization in the electricity sector. The second cause relates to the countries' individual political economy. Saudi Arabia wants to become a global hub for renewable energy production and research. For that reason, Saudi Arabia has kept a much tighter rein on renewable energy projects in the kingdom, with only 30 percent being open tenders and the remaining 70 percent being given to the Public Investment Fund (PIF). This allows the PIF to guarantee business for Saudi Arabia's national power generation company ACWA Power, facilitating the company's growth into a national champion that can expand its reach throughout the region and compete with Qatari and Emirati renewable energy companies.

Facilitating the energy transition

Oman

Oman has two primary objectives to successfully fund its renewable energy transition: cut costs and attract foreign direct investment (FDI). Oman's debt ballooned to 80 percent of GDP in 2020, up from 5 percent in 2014, cratering the country's sovereign credit rating and the credit rating of domestic banks. In 2020, the country also saw a 16 percent budget deficit. To reverse this trend, Oman has had to liberalize its domestic energy market faster than other GCC countries, introducing more permissive investment laws, selling off a stake in a transmission network, and introducing the GCC's first electricity spot market. In an effort to achieve these two objectives, Oman has followed a three-pronged approach: finding ways to reduce subsidies and cut costs, introducing laws to encourage FDI, and improving its energy-related infrastructure.

Ongoing Omani legal changes aim to encourage the uptake of renewable energy and reduce the reliance on fossil fuel, while also reducing subsidies and reinvesting these funds in diversification sectors. Oman has struggled with the uptake of renewables because its Electricity Sector Law required the Omani Water and Power Procurement Company (OPWP), the sole buyer of power in the country, to use the least costly and most technically feasible technologies.[9] Subsidized gas and oil meant that these options have historically been cheaper and easier to implement than renewables, though the continually decreasing costs of solar cells has changed that calculation. There is, however, still no law specifically regulating renewable energy. Instead, the Authority for Public Services Regulation (APSR), a government branch that regulates energy, issues guidelines to steer Omani energy policy. In 2020, the APSR launched the Sahim initiative, which encourages residential customers to put solar panels on their houses. Residential customers consume 45 percent of total electricity in Oman and receive 80 percent of subsidies provided to the electricity sector.[10] The Sahim initiative will reduce subsidy costs, a major drain on government coffers, and free up gas to be used for energy-intensive industries targeted by the government's diversification program. That same thinking drives the country's fuel diversification policy, which aims to have 10 percent of electricity generation to come from renewable sources by 2025.

To further cut costs, the Omani government is privatizing state-owned enterprises (SOEs). The most eye-catching privatization initiative was the sale of a 49 percent stake in the Oman Electricity Transmission Company (OETC), the owner of Oman's main transmission networks, to the Chinese-owned State Grid International Development for $1 billion in late 2019. Nama Holding, a government entity and the other shareholder of OETC, stated that 'the deal was concluded at a price substantially higher than the book value of the shares of OETC.'[11] The reason behind the high price is unclear. The APSR has stated that a partial privatization of the country's electricity companies is next, with a portion to be offered on the Muscat Stock Exchange and the remainder to private investors. The proceeds would go to the country's sovereign wealth fund, the Oman Investment Authority (OIA), which is the ultimate shareholder of these entities. In August 2022 the privatization of the Muscat Electricity Distribution Company, which was slated to be the first regional electricity distributor to be privatized, was put on hold by the APSR due to a desire to bundle several of the country's local electricity distribution companies – which will be discussed later – together and sell them off as a single unit. This would raise the value of the entity sold, while also leading to cost savings through higher efficiency thanks to a single entity developing policy for the whole country's increasingly integrated electricity grid.[12] The OPWP is also a target for privatization down the line.[13] The Omani government intends that the money earned from these initiatives will both reduce the country's fiscal deficit, budgeted to be at 3 percent of GDP in 2023, down from 5 percent in 2020, and be invested in upgrading the country's power infrastructure.

To facilitate these (and many more) privatization initiatives and encourage FDI, the Omani government has also promulgated several laws to ease investment. The first is the Public Private Partnership Law, whose primary innovation is allowing 100 percent foreign ownership of companies.[14] While power companies will still be regulated under the older Electricity Sector Law, increased FDI will accelerate diversification initiatives, encourage foreign-owned power generation ventures, and create room for more private capital to enter the Omani economy. The Privatization Law, promulgated in late 2019, expands upon this, regulating how government-owned entities are to be privatized, such as the aforementioned case of OETC. The third and final impactful law is the Foreign Capital Investment Law (FCIL), whose article 18 states that the council of ministers may grant 'collection of additional benefits to foreign investment projects that are established in the least developed areas in the Sultanate.'[15] Considering that renewable energy projects will overwhelmingly be in rural areas, often in the south, they are likely to be recipients of these 'additional benefits.' This can mean reduced or non-existent land rental fees, a reduction on import tariffs and certain tax exemptions, thus drastically reducing operating costs for RE projects. Next to these legal incentives, Oman has introduced several financial incentives as well. Companies registered under the FCIL will have reduced registration fees, in line with Omani companies, and companies that started operations between January 2021 and December 2022 in diversification sectors received a five-year exemption from income taxes.[16]

Oman's infrastructure, both physical and economic, also needs investment before renewable energy can make a substantial impact. On the physical side, Oman's electricity infrastructure is highly disjointed, with the northern areas around Muscat being one system (MIS), the south around Dhofar another (DPS), two more systems in Eastern and Central Oman, and finally the Rural Areas Electricity Company (RAECO) supplies areas outside major population centers. The Rabt Project, also known as the North–South Interconnect Project, will connect the MIS system around Muscat with the other systems through the country.[17] In the short term, the North–South interconnect will allow Duqm to supply energy to the MIS, where consumption is rising faster than capacity can be built. In the medium term, this will help the government save costs, allowing RAECO to burn less diesel for electricity and instead get electricity from gas-burning facilities, and lead to better reserve sharing between the electricity grids. In the longer term, it facilitates the transmission of electricity from Oman's south, where several large renewable energy projects are planned, to the north, where most of the population lives. Phase one of the Rabt project is slated to be completed in 2023, connecting Al Wusta, which is considered an area with enormous solar power potential, with northern population centers. The second and last phase is expected to be completed in 2026, and tenders for that were opened in August 2022.[18]

On the economic side, Oman is the first country in the Middle East to introduce an electricity spot market, which became active January 1, 2022.[19] The electricity spot market is a department within OPWP and has two main goals: increasing competition and therefore efficiency, and make available additional capacity that is currently unavailable due to long-term power procurement contracts.[20] With several power purchase agreements (PPAs) ending in the early 2020s, the OPWP hopes to steer some generation toward the spot market by not awarding certain plants new PPAs. OPWP will still be the sole buyer of electricity, but the spot market will allow generating companies, including those with active PPAs, to sell their spare capacity. This allows more revenue streams for companies, rewards efficiency, and allows a gradual move towards a more liberalized market as more PPAs expire. Since the spot market is currently only available for generating companies in the MIS, the North–South Interconnector will spread those opportunities to the other electricity systems.

Saudi Arabia

Saudi Arabia is making similar changes to Oman, but on a smaller scale, partially because Saudi Arabia has not been under comparable financial pressure, and partially due to a stronger tendency in Saudi to retain control over strategic sectors.

On the legal front, Saudi Arabi also introduced a Public–Private Partnership (PPP) Law, sometimes called the Privatization Law, with comparable goals to the one introduced in Oman.[21] Article 3 wants to increase citizen ownership in government assets, hinting at a more active stock market and potentially a preference to only sell shares on Saudi Arabia's Tadawul exchange. Similar to article 18 of the Omani FCIL, article 33 of the PPP Law states that any project can be excluded 'from some of the applicable provisions regulating personnel affairs,' like

Saudization requirements. A strong indication of where ultimate power lies within the Saudi political system is article 9. The Council of Economic and Development Affairs (CEDA), led by Crown Prince Mohammed bin Salman, has total latitude to classify any project as 'subject to the provisions of the Law, or classify it as a project that is not subject to the provisions of the Law, irrespective of whether the definition of PPP or the definition of Divestment contained in the Law applies or not.' The equivalent Omani law has no such provision, which allows CEDA to give and remove benefits with little oversight.

Unlike in Oman, where foreign ownership is allowed with the exception of certain sectors, foreign ownership in Saudi Arabia is *only* allowed in certain excepted sectors. Renewable energy projects are one of these exceptions, however, and 100 percent foreign ownership is permitted. To further encourage investment in renewables and industry, the Human Resource Development Fund pays between 30 percent and 50 percent of wages for men and women in the private sector at the start of their employment, in addition to paying for on-the-job training.[22] Additionally, the National Industrial Development Center (NIDC) offers a 50 percent tax credit on Saudi workers' payroll and training costs.[23] With a stronger economy and healthier balance sheets, Saudi has substantial room to absorb costs associated with an accelerated renewables program, whereas Oman does not.

That does not mean that the Saudi power sector is not ripe for transformation. The social contract requires the state to ensure cheap fuel and low living costs to its citizens, an arrangement that has become untenably expensive due to Saudi's growing population and energy usage. Industry has been subsidized through cheap feedstock and minimal taxes, again increasing financial strain on the state, which came to a head after the 2014 oil price crash. In 2015, for example, the Saudi government spent around SAR 300 billion (approximately $80 billion) on subsidies, out of a total budget of SAR 975 billion (approximately $259 billion).[24] Echoing what is happening in Oman, Saudi Arabia aims to free up cash to reinvest into its Vision 2030 diversification program by cutting subsidies, rationalizing spending, and reducing public sector bloat. The two countries will also face a challenging balancing act when subsidizing industry enough to engender growth without causing systemic inefficiencies. Growing energy demand has emphasized this precariousness. Saudi Arabia's power PPAs are longer than in Oman (20 or 25 years compared to 15) and have an agreed-upon price for the duration of the contract. Furthermore, to reduce uncertainty and insulate independent power producers (IPPs) from price fluctuations, the government also signed fuel agreements with them. With a subsidized fuel supply and an assured buyer, IPPs could guarantee a steady income for decades, while the government bore the financial risk. To keep up with the growing electricity demand, Saudi Electricity Company (SEC) has had to borrow heavily: $3.7 billion in 2014 and 2015, $5.1 billion in 2016, $4 billion in 2019, and $2.6 billion in 2021.[25] To rescue SEC from ballooning debt payments, the government reformed SEC's debt, but this will be discussed in depth later. It does, however, highlight that it has become financially unsustainable for Saudi Arabia's power generation sector to continue as-is, and sectoral reforms are required to alter both funding sources and power generation methods.

Funding and ownership

Oman

The implementation of Oman's renewable energy agenda follows three trajectories. First is the reorganization of funding mechanisms and several institutions into the Oman Investment Authority (OIA), after a 2020 merger of the State General Reserve Fund (SGRF) and Oman Investment Fund (OIF). The OIA will have a similar purpose to Saudi Arabia's PIF: investment into strategically important sectors and entities, with renewable energy projects featuring prominently. Second is tariff changes. This is a minor step and a continuation of the subsidy reforms mentioned earlier. Higher tariffs and better targeting of subsidies, especially in the household sector, leave more capital free for investment, some of it focused on renewables. The third and final trajectory involves the funding and ownership of renewable energy projects in Oman. As will become clearer in the following pages, a notable difference between Oman's and Saudi Arabia's renewable energy projects is that the latter are operated and often owned by domestic actors. This is less the case in Oman. Furthermore, the funding for these projects is, in Oman's case, overwhelmingly from outside the country.

The OIA was created in 2020 by Royal Decree 61/2020, transferring to it all assets and investments owned by the SGRF, the OIF, the investments of the Ministry of Finance, and all government companies and investments. The only notable exception is Petroleum Development

Oman (PDO), the Omani national oil company. The proceeds of the aforementioned partial privatization of the OETC therefore went to an OIA subsidiary, Nama Holding (also known as the Electricity Holding Company). Through Nama, the OIA owns 99.99 percent of OPWP, the single buyer of all power and water in Oman.

While the OIA has a long way to go before its role compares to the PIF's position in Saudi Arabia, the OIA and its subsidiaries are heavily involved in the country's burgeoning hydrogen industry. The OQ Group, an OIA subsidiary, owns 90 percent of Salalah Methanol Company, which started building an ammonia plant in 2017 with a target capacity of 1,000 metric tons per day in the Salalah Free Zone.[26] Production at the plant started in September 2022 and it was officially opened in January 2023.[27]

OQ, together with the Japanese Marubeni Corporation, Germany's Line plc, and Dutco Group from the UAE, has announced plans to create a 400 megawatt (MW) green hydrogen project in the same area, powered by as yet to be built solar and wind farms, but hydrogen production is planned to start in early 2028.[28,29] Saudi Arabia's ACWA Power, America's Air Products, and OQ have announced a $7 billion deal to produce green hydrogen as feedstock for an annual production target of around one million tons of ammonia, though the timeline of this project remains unclear.[30]

Duqm, another Free Zone, is seeing as much if not more investment, also with consistent OQ involvement. OQ and Uniper, a German company, in a consortium led by the Belgian DEME Concessions, will be building the Duqm Hyport.[31] Its starting capacity will be between 250MW and 500MW, but already upscaling is planned to increase capacity from 330,000 tons per annum of green ammonia in phase one starting in 2026, to up to a million tons per annum when phase three is concluded.[32] InterContinental Energy, the world's largest renewable hydrogen developer, has also launched a project in Oman with OQ and the Kuwaiti EnerTech that will be powered by 25GW of renewable energy, making it by far the largest green hydrogen and ammonia project in the Middle East.[33] For comparison, the enormous hydrogen plant in NEOM, Saudi Arabia's futuristic city, is powered by 4GW. No production numbers have been announced, but the press release of this project promises to 'produce millions of tons per annum of truly zero-carbon fuels.'[34] These projects are still in relatively early stages, but it is unlikely that there will be major financial obstacles considering the torrent of green financing going into the Middle East, with 2020 alone seeing $3.3 billion in green bonds. The project also benefits from substantial political support. The head of renewables at OQ stated 'OQ and our shareholders Oman Investment Authority continue to support this project,' in an effort to make Oman and Duqm a global green energy hub.[35]

The breakneck pace of the hydrogen and ammonia enterprises, the variety of actors, and the level of government involvement in them stands in contrast to Oman's non-hydrogen renewable energy projects, whose purpose is to generate power for the domestic market. Whereas the government, through the OIA and the OQ Group, is an important actor in all hydrogen and ammonia projects, Omani companies play only a trivial role in solar and wind power projects. The primary exception here is the Amin Solar Power project. The Marubeni Corporation has a 50.1 percent stake, two Omani companies own a combined 40 percent, while Qatar's Nebras Power has 9.9 percent. Ibri 2, in northern Oman close to the UAE, has zero Omani companies. Instead, Saudi Arabia's ACWA power has a 50 percent stake, the Kuwaiti Gulf Investment Corporation's stake is 40 percent, and AEPCO, also from Kuwait, has the final 10 percent.[36] The Dhofar Wind Project, the first large-scale wind farm in the GCC, has Masdar from the UAE as its only shareholder.

When it comes to funding, renewable energy projects serve as a potent reminder of the limitations placed on Oman's government and financial sector due to its deep financial troubles between 2015 and the early 2020s. Again, the Amin Solar project is the exception, with its $94 million cost funded solely by Bank Muscat.[37] The Dhofar wind project's $105 million capital cost was financed exclusively by the Abu Dhabi Fund for Development. Ibri 2 is an interesting case: of its $400 million price tag, six lenders including Muscat Bank, Riyadh Bank, and the Kuwaiti Warba Bank fund $215 million, while the Beijing-based Asian Infrastructure Investment Bank (AIIB) approved $60 million, making it the AIIB's first renewable energy investment in the Middle East.[38] The final $125 million is financed through an equity investment. The large role of the AIIB in this project, together with the 49 percent stake of State Grid in the OETC, highlights the important position China already has in Omani infrastructure and renewable energy projects.[39] China's role will only increase: the Special Economic Zone at Duqm is one of the four key Middle Eastern economic zones identified by China's Belt and Road Initiative (BRI), while the port in the same economic zone is one of the four regional ports targeted by the BRI-associated Maritime Silk Road Initiative.[40]

Compared to Saudi banks, which will be discussed later, Omani banks are scarcely present in the renewable energy sector. The APSR launched its Sahim program in 2017, allowing large households and businesses to install PV systems connected to the grid. Potential returns were earned by selling excess energy to the OPWP. Sahim II is an ongoing initiative that hopes to deploy small-scale PV systems to between 10 percent and 30 percent of residential housing in Oman (APSR, 2021). Private developers, not houseowners, would compete to install and operate the systems at pre-designated premises, mainly in Muscat. The goal of both stages of Sahim is to introduce solar cells without having the government bear the large upfront costs.[41] Omani banks have been slow to capitalize on this opportunity, with only a few offering limited financing. Bank Muscat, together with the International Finance Corporation, offers green loans ranging from RO1,000 to RO25,000 to individuals wanting to install solar panels on their houses. HSBC Oman, as part of a global HSBC program, allows up to 100 percent financing on green personal loans with a discounted interest rate for solar panels or solar-powered water heaters.[42] The National Bank of Oman is the only other private financial institution to imply spending money on renewable energy, though it is no more specific than saying that $1 billion was spent on a variety of sectors, including tourism, infrastructure, and renewable energy.[43] In Oman, foreign players are overwhelmingly the main actors in renewable energy investment, and while this is not a major surprise considering the pressure the Omani financial sector has been under, it is an important area for improvement.

Saudi Arabia

Saudi Arabia's implementation of their renewable energy initiatives and funding is broadly similar to that of Oman, but there is substantial divergence in the details. While there has been institutional restructuring, the institutions and markets are not seeing transformations on the same scale as in Oman. Saudi ownership – through either ACWA Power exclusively or a joint venture (JV) structure involving the PIF, Saudi Aramco, or ACWA – is found across the renewable energy spectrum, instead of being limited to the hydrogen projects only, as is the case in Oman. Government funding initiatives are more developed, and the private banking sector has mobilized effectively to create funding mechanisms targeting renewable energy projects.

To attract investment, Saudi has allowed foreign ownership of companies in certain sectors, and under Saudi Arabia's National Renewable Energy Program (NREP), renewable energy projects can be 100 percent foreign owned. Under NREP, monthly salaries are subsidized by the Human Resources Development Fund, raw materials and manufacturing equipment may be exempted from customs, and subsidized leases for land are also possible.[44] Invest Saudi, a program launched by the Ministry of Investment, organizes the incentives available to companies. PPPs are, for example, given loans with reduced interest rates and extended borrowing periods. The Saudi Exim Bank, founded in 2020, was set up specifically to ease imports and exports beyond the oil sector and reduce barriers for domestic Saudi companies.[45] The King Abdullah City for Science and Technology offers investment in R&D projects with the 'potential to boost the country's economic growth and self-reliance,' among them renewable energy projects.[46]

Saudi Arabia also explicitly calls upon the private sector to play a larger role. The Saudi Electricity Company (SEC), the owner of the offtaker of all Saudi electricity generation, runs a private sector participation program, which in 2020 aimed for 8.2GW in additional generating capacity to meet future loads.[47] While only approximately 1.5GW of that capacity is comprised of renewable energy, it shows a willingness to bring in the private sector when it is on the terms of the Saudi state. It is also notable that while the SEC has a substantial stake in several regional power procurement companies, 100 percent of the investment capital in renewable energy projects is from the private sector. A motivating factor for this is that IPPs reduce the fiscal pressure on the SEC, freeing it from having to provide all the substantial upfront capital required. Considering the enormous debts the SEC has racked up while growing capacity to keep up with demand, this is a necessary development.[48]

How the Saudi government has handled SEC debts is another difference between Oman and Saudi Arabia, and it highlights how the latter's stronger financial situation helps to accelerate the implementation of renewable energy while still maintaining control over the process. Before the debt conversion, SEC had a debt-to-equity ratio of well above two to one, with repayment fees growing to such an extent that they could start hindering SEC investments.[49] SAR167 billion ($45 billion) of SEC debt to the government was transformed into 'an equity-like non-dilutive perpetual Mudaraba instrument,' delaying and deprioritizing repayments for so long the debt is functionally no longer relevant.[50] The government also removed fees imposed on the company, allowing it to retain all the revenues it generates from selling electricity, which, in the words of the SEC Chairman, will help the 'SEC overcome several financial and structural challenges' it has recently faced.[51] The chairman also mentioned that these reforms will 'enable the SEC to distribute dividends to all of its shareholders,' where the most important actor is the PIF with a 75 percent stake.

While OQ is prominent in some of Oman's renewable energy projects, the PIF is directly or indirectly nearly omnipresent in Saudi Arabia. Saudi Arabia's NREP is divided in two. The Renewable Energy Project Development Office (REPDO) is a part of the Ministry of Energy and will deliver 30 percent of planned renewable energy capacity, doing so through open tenders. The remaining 70 percent is under the control of the PIF, giving the Fund free rein to negotiate closed deals with developers. ACWA Power is the prime beneficiary of this policy. ACWA and the PIF entered a strategic agreement in 2020, ensuring the former will lead the development of all the projects under the purview of the PIF. Furthermore, ACWA is also allowed to bid on REPDO tenders.[52] Unsurprisingly, ACWA is present in most renewable energy projects in Saudi Arabia, a trend that will likely accelerate once the PIF finalizes more deals.

The Sakaka solar power plant, a JV between ACWA (70 percent) and alGihaz (30 percent) was the first REPDO IPP and came online in late 2019. Other REPDO projects include the Dumat al-Jandal Wind Project, developed by the American EDF Renewables and the Emirati Masdar, the former having a 51 percent majority stake; the same consortium also does the 300MW Jeddah solar project; two Saudi companies, al-Blagha and Al-Fanar, will do the Rafha and Medina solar power projects.[53] ACWA Power won the REPDO tenders for the 200MW Qurayyat and the 600MW al-Faisaliah Solar PV projects. Next to the REPDO projects, the PIF-controlled initiatives include the 700MW al-Rass, where ACWA holds a 40.1 percent stake, the Water and Electricity Holding Company (Badeel) 20 percent, and the Chinese State Power Investment Corporation a 39.9 percent stake.[54] Another non-REPDO project, the leviathan 1500MW Sudair solar power plant, is an excellent example of how some of the PIF-controlled projects will be structured. ACWA Power, where the PIF is a 75 percent shareholder, has a 35 percent stake in Sudair; Badeel has a 35 percent stake and is fully owned by the PIF; the remaining 30 percent is owned by Saudi Aramco Power Company, a fully owned subsidiary of Saudi Aramco which in turn is majority owned by the government, with the PIF holding a small number of shares.[55] In November 2022, ACWA announced another NREP project under the aegis of the PIF: Shauibah II. Badeel and ACWA are equal shareholders in the project, estimated to cost $1.75 billion and will be the Middle East's largest solar power plant when it is completed in late 2025.[56] Badeel will invest in power generation projects in Saudi Arabia, though its close relationship via PIF with ACWA Power raises questions about impartiality, especially considering the PIF's opaque decision-making process.[57]

A major difference between Oman and Saudi Arabia is the latter's capacity to effectively leverage domestic capital to implement its renewable energy goals. The Saudi Industrial Development Fund (SIDF) has since 2017 become an important tool to drive the Saudi diversification effort. SIDF's Mutajadeda (literally, 'renewable') program aims to finance the domestic production of renewable energy components and renewable energy projects.[58] Mutajadeda has three types of loan, all given at below-market interest rates. The first type finances the manufacture of RE components with a longer repayment period of 15 years and a 36-month grace period, with up to 75 percent of project costs being financed. This loan is aligned with REPDO projects to ensure faster assessments and more targeted investments. The second loan type is targeted at RE IPPs, giving them a 20-year repayment period. The third type targets project developers in commercial and agricultural sectors for distributed electrical generation, meaning RE produced by owners for their own use.

The SIDF loans are the only state-funded lending initiative, but in October 2022 the PIF became the world's first sovereign wealth fund to issue green bonds, raising $3 billion to finance renewable energy projects, clean transport, and sustainable water management. However, Saudi Arabia's private sector is also positioning itself to play a large role in financing green energy. Natixis, a French investment bank, entered a strategic agreement with ACWA Power in late 2021, aiming to finance around $2 billion in renewable energy projects in 2022 and 2023. Natixis has already financed several ACWA Projects outside of Saudi Arabia, including the DEWA 5 project in the UAE, and financed 75 percent (equaling $240 million) of the Sakaka solar power plant and is one of six banks financing the Dumat al-Jandal wind project. Domestic Saudi banks are also prominent actors. Sudair is funded by a group of banks that include Riyad Bank and Al-Rajhi as senior lenders, while Bank al-Bilad and Saudi British Bank (SABB) provide the equity bridge.[59] NCB was one of the banks financing Dumat al-Jandal.

Saudi banks have also taken steps to create green financing instruments. Four Saudi banks, among them Saudi National Bank (SNB) and SABB, made the first Saudi Riyal-denominated green loan in April 2021.[60] SNB has also worked with HSBC to create a sustainable finance framework which aims to increase financing for the 'development, construction, and installation' of RE projects and transmission systems.[61] SABB has developed a green deposit account, where short- and medium-term returns are higher and the money will be invested in green projects, among them renewable energy.[62] The Saudi Investment Bank (SAIB) stated it 'proactively supports' public and private sector environmental initiatives, including energy, but does not say what specific policies.[63] It has however said it has set a target that at least 10 percent of its financing portfolio will go to green and low-emission activities. Finally, al-Rajhi was in 2020 the Kingdom's largest lender to renewable energy projects, financing parts of the Rabigh and Sudair solar power plants.[64]

The political economy of the renewable energy transition

The economic necessities of the energy transition are often emphasized in the discourse, pointing out the unsustainably high fuel subsidies and the need for fossil fuel-based rentier economies need to diversify. For countries in the GCC, and especially Saudi Arabia, whose global clout is based on their control over enormous hydrocarbon reserves, the energy transition is concurrent with fundamental policy reorientations.

Oman, as was shown earlier, is an important node in China's Belt and Road Initiative, and in a Sino-Emirati meeting in early 2022 the participants said that a 'China-GCC Free Trade Area (FTA) should be established as soon as possible.'[65] Five GCC states, including Oman and Saudi Arabia, were among the 53 states that voted in support of China's National Security Law in Hong Kong at the United Nations. Their historical allies – the UK and the United States – both voted against the measure. Close Omani and Saudi relations with China are not surprising. Beijing will not ask embarrassing questions about the countries' human rights policies and is the largest trading partner of both countries. In the renewable energy sector, China is especially important. Eight of the largest ten solar companies are Chinese, and China produces more than 64 percent of the world's polysilicon material (necessary for wafer production) and holds an 80 percent global market share in solar cell manufacturing.[66] The energy transition is an existential question for these countries, more so for Oman due to its weaker financial situation, and alienating China is therefore not an option. For Saudi Arabia, there is a second important factor that is driving its renewable energy policy. Saudi Aramco has for 70 years been Saudi Arabia's economic crown jewel. With the slow but inexorable transition away from oil, Saudi Arabia is positioning ACWA Power to capitalize on that transition and make the kingdom a renewable energy powerhouse as well. The PIF's control over 70 percent of RE projects in Saudi Arabia guarantees business and capacity building for ACWA, as agreements made by the PIF with foreign companies contain technology transfer clauses. There are also local production requirements, currently at 16–18 percent but planned to be increased for successive bidding rounds, for components for renewable energy systems.[67] The NIDLP, one of Vision 2030's sub-programs, states that there is a 'need to train and develop national competencies to qualify them to occupy the created job opportunities based on the objectives of the localization of renewable energy.'[68] The ACWA Power annual report states that the PIF took a greater stake in the company to expand its 'operations domestically and internationally, [reflecting] the strategic importance the [Government] places on the group and its role as a leading private sector investor in the power' infrastructure and energy transition agenda.[69] Saudi Arabia is aggressively pursuing its objective to become a global center for renewable energy research and production and is tailoring its domestic energy policy and regional outreach to attain that goal.

The Saudi Green Initiative (SGI) and the related Middle East Green Initiative must be seen in this context. As stated in its communique, the SGI aims to make Saudi Arabia a hub for climate change and carbon extraction research and will seed a regional investment fund for circular carbon economy solutions.[70] According to its website, the SGI 'aims to make KSA both a moral and economic leader in green energy and environmentalism in the Middle East.'[71] The primary competition in this sphere come from the UAE and Qatar. Masdar, the Abu Dhabi-based renewable energy company that has invested in several regional RE projects, is owned by the Emirati sovereign wealth fund Mubadala. Nebras Power is a joint venture between two entities, Qatar Electricity &

Water Company and Qatar Holding, that have 55 percent and 100 percent Qatari sovereign wealth fund shareholding, respectively. PIF's decision to reserve a substantial portion of renewable energy projects in Saudi Arabia, by far the region's biggest market, gives ACWA Power a substantial advantage over its two regional competitors.

Conclusion

While this chapter has focused on the developments in Oman and Saudi Arabia, similar laws have been implemented in most other GCC countries, though they are generally not as generous regarding foreign ownership as the Omani ones. Oman and Saudi Arabia have the highest renewable energy targets in the GCC at 30 percent and 50 percent by 2030, respectively. Considering these two countries are by far the largest and therefore have the most room to build renewable energy projects, this is not entirely a surprise. However, this chapter has shown by comparing these two countries that there is substantial divergence within GCC countries on how they achieve these goals: while legal reforms to attract FDI and cost-cutting to free up cash for investments follow similar trends in both countries, the actual implementation of renewable energy projects is different. Oman, restricted by a tight fiscal context, poor credit ratings, and enormous debts, has more aggressively privatized its energy sector, put fewer restrictions on foreign investment, and has shown little capability to develop domestic renewable energy-related manufacturing. Since it was not facing equally deep financial problems, Saudi Arabia has been able to selectively privatize and liberalize its energy sector. Unlike Oman, Saudi Arabia also has the financial clout and domestic productive capacity to limit foreign entry into its renewable energy sector, reserving large parts of it for domestic actors like ACWA Power. Not only does this create a captive market for these companies, but it also limits the entry of competing companies – Masdar and Nebras among them – into Saudi Arabia. The threats to the successful implementation of these projects are exogenous rather than domestic. Global competition for raw materials and increasingly politicized supply chains may increase the costs, both political and financial, of these projects. However, the presence of substantial political initiative, the absence of meaningful regulatory barriers, and a prime geographic location means that Oman and Saudi Arabia, with their staggering renewable energy potential and strategic location at the crossroads between Asia, Africa, and Europe, will be well-situated to weather potential future political realignments and economic upheavals. If executed well, the countries will be able to reap the rewards of an economic and energy policy that is both uniquely appealing and singularly future-proof.

Bibliography

Abdel-Baky, Mahmoud and Mahairi Main Garcia, 2021. *Renewable Energy Laws and Regulations Saudi Arabia 2022.* International Comparative Legal Guides International Business Reports. https://iclg.com/practice-areas/renewable-energy-laws-and-regulations/saudi-arabia. Accessed April 5, 2022.

Acwapower.com. 2020. *ACWA POWER | Ibri 2 PV IPP.* https://www.acwapower.com/en/projects/ibri-2-pv-ipp/. Accessed April 5, 2022.

ACWA Power, 2021. *Annual Report 2020.* Riyadh, Saudi Arabia: ACWA Power. Available at: https://acwapower.com/media/341298/acwa-annual-report-2020-en-single-pages.pdf. Accessed April 6, 2022.

ACWA Power, 2021. 'ACWA Power announces financial close for 1500 MW Sudair Solar plant and Aramco joining the consortium under PIF renewables program.' https://www.acwapower.com/news/acwa-power-announces-financial-close-for-1500-mw-sudair-solar-plant-and-aramco-joining-the-consortium-under-pif-renewables-program/. Accessed April 5, 2022.

ACWA Power, 2022. 'PIF subsidiary Badeel and ACWA Power to develop the MENA region's largest solar energy plant in Saudi Arabia: ACWA Power.' https://www.acwapower.com/news/pif-subsidiary-badeel-and-acwa-power-to-develop-the-mena-regions-largest-solar-energy-plant-in-saudi-arabia/. Accessed January 25, 2023.

Al-Badi, Abdullah and Imtenan Al-Mubarak, 2019. 'Growing energy demand in the GCC countries.' *Arab Journal of Basic and Applied Sciences*, 26(1): 488–496.

Al-Badi, Hammam. 'Oman's OETC Invests $166mln in New Power Networks,' Zawya, July 25, 2022. https://www.zawya.com/en/projects/utilities/omans-oetc-invests-166mln-in-new-power-networks-bpckp7gl.

Almeenaprojects.com, 2020. 'Oman have commissioned 100MW Amin Solar PV Plant.' https://almeenaprojects.com/oman-have-commissioned-100mw-amin-solar-pv-plant/. Accessed April 5, 2022.

Al-Rajhi Bank, 2021. *Al-Rajhi Bank ESG Report 2020.* Riyadh, Saudi Arabia: Al-Rajhi Bank. https://www.alrajhibank.com.sa/ir/esg_report/esg_report.html. Accessed April 5, 2022.

AIIB, 2020. *Ibri II 500MW Solar PV Independent Power Plant Project.* Available at: https://www.aiib.org/en/projects/details/2020/approved/_download/Oman/PSI-Oman-Ibri-II-500MW-Solar-PV-Independent-Power-Plant-Project_March-16-2020.pdf. Accessed April 5, 2022.

APICORP Energy Research, 2018. *Saudi Energy Price Reform Getting Serious*. APICORP Energy Research. Dammam, Saudi Arabia: Arab Petroleum Investments Corporation.

APSR, 2021. *Annual Report 2020*. Muscat, Oman: Authority for Public Services Regulation. https://www.apsr.om/downloadsdocs/annual-reports/2020Englis hAnnualReportFinal.pdf. Accessed April 5, 2022.

APSR, 2021. 'Product Application for Sahim 2.' Muscat, Oman: Authority for Public Services Regulation. https://apsr.om/en/product-application-for-sahim2. Accessed April 5, 2022.

Azhar, Saeed, 2020. 'Saudi Electricity to convert $45 billion in government liabilities into perpetual instrument.' Reuters. https://www.reuters.com/article/saudi-electrcity-debt-int-idUSKBN27W0V0. Accessed April 5, 2022.

Benali, Leila R., Ramy Al-Ashmawy, and Shatila Suhail, 2021. *MENA Energy Investment Outlook 2021–2025*. Dammam, Saudi Arabia: Arab Petroleum Investment Corporation, p. 38.

DEME Group, 2020. 'Kick-off of the Hyport Duqm Green Hydrogen Project.' https://www.deme-group.com/news/kick-hyportr-duqnm-green-hydrogen-project. Accessed April 5, 2022.

Embassy of the People's Republic of China in the United States of America, 2022. 'Wang Yi Holds Telephone Talks with Minister of Foreign Affairs and International Cooperation Sheikh Abdullah bin Zayed Al Nahyan of the UAE.' http://www.china-embassy.org/eng/zgyw/202201/t20220114_10495618.htm. Accessed April 5, 2022.

Fulton, Jonathan, 2019. *China's Gulf Investments Reveal Regional Strategy*. Arab Gulf States Institute in Washington. https://agsiw.org/chinas-gulf-investments-reveal-regional-strategy/. Accessed April 5, 2022.

HSBC Oman, 2021. 'HSBC Green Loan.' https://www.hsbc.co.om/loans/products/green/. Accessed April 5, 2022.

Implementation Support and Follow-up Unit, 2020. *Annual Report 2019: Towards a Diversified and Sustainable Economy*. Muscat, Oman: Implementation Support and Follow-up Unit, p. 176. https://isfu.gov.om/ISFU-ANNUALREPORT(2019)-Eng.pdf. Accessed April 5, 2022.

International Trade Administration, 2020. *Oman's Renewable Energy Projects*. https://www.trade.gov/market-intelligence/omans-renewable-energy-projects. Accessed April 5, 2022.

InterContinental Energy, 2021. 'Green fuels mega project set to make Oman world leader in green hydrogen and green ammonia.' https://intercontinentalenergy.com/documents/ICE-Announcement-20210511.pdf. Accessed April 5, 2022.

Invest Saudi. 2021. *Incentives for Investors*. https://www.investsaudi.sa/en/investor/incentives. Accessed April 5, 2022.

Invest Saudi, 2020. *Wadi Aldawasir Solar PV 120 MW*. Riyadh, Saudi Arabia: Invest Saudi. https://investsaudi.sa/medias/ew-e-inv-opp-scorecard-wadi-aldawasir-solar-pv-120-mw.pdf?context=bWFzdGVyfHBvcnRhbC1tZWRp YXwzNDI5ODV8YXBwbGljYXRpb24vcGRmfHBvcnRhbC1tZWRp YS9oNGUvaDk1Lzg4NTUyMjA4NzkkzOTAucGRmfGEzYTExZDQ1

ZjMwZGY5OTNmZDc2YmE0MDkxMjc2NGZjNDdiYjQ5MDFjOTTdl
MDUzMWU3YTJjZGFmYzQxMmYxZTU. Accessed April 5, 2022.

IRENA, 2016. *Renewable Energy in the Arab Region. Overview of Developments.* Abu Dhabi: International Renewable Energy Agency.

Joint Research Centre (European Commission), 2019. *Fossil CO2 and GHG emissions of all world countries: 2019 report.* Luxembourg: Publications Office of the European Union. https://op.europa.eu/en/publication-detail/-/publication/9d09ccd1-e0dd-11e9-9c4e-01aa75ed71a1/language-en. Accessed April 5, 2022.

KACST Impact, 2019. *KACST Impact – Smart Energy.* https://kacstimpact. kacst.edu.sa/perspective/45/smart-energy. Accessed April 5, 2022.

Marubeni, 2021. 'Marubeni Signs Joint Development Agreement for Green Hydrogen & Green Ammonia Production Infrastructure in Oman.' https://www.marubeni.com/en/news/2021/info/00016.html. Accessed April 5, 2022.

'Marubeni-led consortium's Green Ammonia project in Oman launch likely in Q1 2028,' 2022: Zawya: https://www.zawya.com/en/projects/industry/marubeni-led-consortiums-green-ammonia-project-in-oman-launch-likely-in-q1-2028-report-siqoiz1a. Accessed January 25, 2023.

Mygov.sa. 2021. *Labor and Employment.* https://www.my.gov.sa/wps/portal/snp/aboutksa/employment#header2_2. Accessed April 5, 2022.

Nama Group, 2021. *Annual Report 2020.* Muscat Oman: Nama Group. https://www.nama.om/media/1443/ng-annual-report-2020-english-opt-11.pdf. Accessed April 5, 2022.

National Bank of Oman, 2021. *Sustainability Report 2020.* Muscat, Oman: National Bank of Oman. https://www.nbo.om/en/Documents/Annual%20Reports/NBO_Sustainability%20report_English_for%20web.pdf. Accessed April 5, 2022.

National Industrial Development and Logistics Program. Saudi Arabia. https://www.vision2030.gov.sa/v2030/vrps/nidlp// Accessed April 6, 2022

Nsenergybusiness.com. 2021. 'Sudair PV Solar Power Plant.' https://www.nsenergybusiness.com/projects/sudair-solar-power-plant/. Accessed April 5, 2022.

PricewaterhouseCoopers, 2021. *Oman: Incentives announced by the Government as part of Oman Vision 2040.* Muscat, Oman: PricewaterhouseCoopers. https://www.pwc.com/m1/en/tax/documents/2021/oman-incentives-announced-by-the-government-as-part-of-oman-vision-2040.pdf. Accessed April 5, 2022.

Oman Investment Authority, 2021. 'As Saudi Crown Prince Visits Oman OIA Companies sign MOUs with their Saudi Counterparts.' https://www.oia.gov.om/Index.php?r=en%2Fsite%2Fnewsview&nid=as-saudi-crown-prince-visits-oman-oia-companies-sign-mous-with-their-saudi-counterparts&cs rt=5608872309545054218. Accessed April 5, 2022.

Oman News Agency, 'OQ celebrates opening of $463 million ammonia plant in Salalah,' https://timesofoman.com/article/125541-oq-celebrates-opening-of-463-million-ammonia-plant-in-salalah. Accessed January 25, 2023.

Oman Observer. 2021. 'Privatisation of Muscat utility planned by year-end.' https://www.omanobserver.om/article/1100736/business/privatisation-of-muscat-utility-planned-by-year-end. Accessed April 5, 2022.

Oomen, Anup, 2022. 'Saudi's SPPC, ACWA Power ink power purchase agreement for $450mn Ar Rass solar PV project in Saudi Arabia.' Arabian Business. https://www.arabianbusiness.com/industries/energy/saudis-sppc-acwa-power-ink-power-purchase-agreement-for-450mn-ar-rass-solar-pv-project-in-saudi-arabia. Accessed April 5, 2022.

OPWP, 2019. *7-Year Statement: 2019–2025.* Muscat, Oman: Oman Power and Water Procurement Co. (SAOC). https://omanpwp.om/PDF/7%20Year%20Statement%202019-2025%20New.pdf. Accessed April 5, 2022.

Oq.com. 2022. *Methanol | OQ.* https://oq.com/en/products/intermediates/methanol. Accessed April 5, 2022.

Power Technology. 2019. *Dumat Al Jandal Wind Farm.* https://www.power-technology.com/projects/dumat-al-jandal-wind-farm/. Accessed April 5, 2022.

Prabhu, Conrad, 2021. 'Hyport Duqm project eyes 1m mtpa of green ammonia at full capacity.' *Oman Observer.* https://www.omanobserver.om/article/1111712/business/energy/hyport-duqm-project-eyes-1m-mtpa-of-green-ammonia-at-full-capacity. Accessed April 5, 2022.

Prabhu, Conrad, 'Oman Puts MEDC Privatisation on Hold Pending Review of New Options,' *Oman Observer.* https://www.omanobserver.om/article/1124085/business/energy/oman-puts-medc-privatisation-on-hold-pending-review-of-new-options. Accessed January 23, 2023.

Private Sector Participation Law. Saudi Arabia.

Rapoza, Kenneth, 2021. 'How China's Solar Industry Is Set Up To Be The New Green OPEC.' Forbes. https://www.forbes.com/sites/kenrapoza/2021/03/14/how-chinas-solar-industry-is-set-up-to-be-the-new-green-opec/?sh=688bd3c31446. Accessed April 5, 2022.

Reuters. 2022. 'Oman launches first Middle East electricity spot market.' https://www.reuters.com/world/middle-east/oman-launches-first-electricity-spot-market-middle-east-2022-01-26/. Accessed April 5, 2022.

Royal Decree 50/2019 Promulgating the Foreign Capital Investment Law, Oman.

Royal Decree 52/2019 Promulgating the Public Private Partnership Law, Oman.

Saadi, Dania, 2021. 'Saudi Arabia's ACWA Power, Oman's OQ to study hydrogen project in Dhofar.' Spglobal.com. https://www.spglobal.com/commodity-insights/en/market-insights/latest-news/energy-transition/120821-saudi-arabias-acwa-power-omans-oq-to-study-hydrogen-project-in-dhofar. Accessed April 5, 2022.

Saba, Yousef and Saeed Azhar, 2021. 'Saudi Red Sea project secures $3.8 billion "green" loan for new hotels.' Reuters. https://www.reuters.com/article/saudi-redsea-loans-idUSL4N2MK1MM. Accessed April 5, 2022.

SABB, 2021. 'SABB Green deposit account.' https://www.sabb.com/en/everyday-banking/accounts/green-deposits/. Accessed April 5, 2022.

Saudi Exim Bank, 2021. *Vision and Mission.* https://saudiexim.gov.sa/en/About/Pages/Vision.aspx. Accessed April 5, 2022.

Saudi Green Initiative, 2021. 'The Saudi Green Initiative aims to improve quality of life.' https://www.saudigreeninitiative.org/about-saudi-green-initiative/. Accessed April 5, 2022.

Saudi Green Initiative/Middle East Green Initiative, 2021. 'Middle East Green Initiative Summit Communiqué.' https://www.saudigreeninitiative.org/pr/MGI_Communique_26Oct_EN.pdf. Accessed April 5, 2022.

Saudi Investment Bank, 2019. *Credit Policy Guide – Lending Policy*. Riyadh, Saudi Arabia: Saudi Investment Bank. https://www.saib.com.sa/sites/default/files/2019-09/cpg-en.pdf. Accessed April 5, 2022.

SEC, 2021. *SEC Annual Report 2020*. Riyadh, Saudi Arabia: Saudi Electricity Company. https://www.se.com.sa/en-us/Lists/AnnualReports/Attachments/22/Annual%20Report-EN-2020.pdf. Accessed April 5, 2022.

SEC, 2021. '"Saudi Electricity" announces its financial results for Q2 and first half of 2021.' https://www.se.com.sa/en-us/Pages/newsdetails.aspx?NId=1070. Accessed April 5, 2022.

SEC, 2020. 'Saudi Electricity Company Signs an Agreement with the Government, represented by the Ministry of Finance, to Reclassify its Net Government Liabilities.' Riyadh, Saudi Arabi: Saudi Electricity Company. https://www.se.com.sa/en-us/invshareholder/Pages/Financial_Agreement.aspx. Accessed April 5, 2022.

SIDF, 2021. *Annual Report 2020*. Riyadh, Saudi Arabia: Saudi Industrial Development Fund. https://www.sidf.gov.sa/en/AboutSIDF/Pages/AnnualReport.aspx. Accessed April 5, 2022.

SNB, 2021. *SNB Sustainable Finance Framework*. Riyadh, Saudi Arabia: Saudi National Bank. https://www.alahli.com/en-us/Investor_Relation/Documents/SNB-Sustainable-Finance-Framework-15-11-2021-v2.pdf. Accessed April 5, 2022.

Special Economic Zone at Duqm, 2021. 'Duqm, a global centre for green hydrogen production.' https://www.duqm.gov.om/upload/files/Duqm_Magazine25_Greenhydrogen_EN.pdf. Accessed April 5, 2022.

The Law for the Regulation and Privatisation of the Electricity and Related Water Sector. Oman.

Vohra, Anchal, 2021. 'The Middle East Is Becoming Literally Uninhabitable.' Foreign Policy. https://foreignpolicy.com/2021/08/24/the-middle-east-is-becoming-literally-uninhabitable/. Accessed April 5, 2022.

5 THE POLITICAL DIMENSIONS OF ENERGY TRANSITION IN MENA: A CHANGING LANDSCAPE AT THE NATIONAL, REGIONAL, AND GLOBAL LEVELS

Younes Abouyoub

Introduction

In a fast-changing world, energy is playing – even more so today than before – a major defining role, both at the national and international levels. Fossil fuel producing countries in the Middle East and North Africa (MENA) have been concerned, for some time now, about the sustainability of their economic model, which is heavily dependent on hydrocarbon revenues. A plethora of studies have predicted that oil and gas reserves will eventually be depleted and certain countries are more concerned in the short- and medium-term than others. Bahrain and Oman, for example, find themselves in a more precarious situation in this regard, with reserves expected to run out within the next decade for Bahrain and within twenty-five years for Oman.[1] To mitigate the economic consequences of this expected depletion, several MENA countries, particularly in the Gulf Cooperation Council (GCC), have devised economic diversification as a solution to the consequences of energy transition. Yet, this shift in the economic paradigm will have to address the political exigencies of the governing social contract, based on wealth transfer derived exclusively from hydrocarbon to the populations. But old habits die hard. The rent-based power channels have so far been a staunch obstacle in the way of economic reforms, especially that structural changes required by economic diversification may end up empowering emerging constituencies that could potentially challenge the ruling elites. At the global level, the geopolitical changes, the increasing role of emerging economies, and the rise of new powers are already shaking the global order. This new reality presents both risks and opportunities for the oil and gas producing countries in the MENA region.

Energy remains at the heart of the geopolitical chessboard. Despite recent advances in the development of renewable energy sources, and the advent of electric vehicles, their share in the energy mix remains limited as oil still meets most of the transportation sector's needs. The development of renewable energies – wind, solar, and geothermal – is not yet able to drastically change this reality, as fossil fuels still predominate in the global energy mix. Oil accounts for 34 percent of global energy consumption, gas for 23 percent, and coal for 28 percent.[2] The Middle East, including the Gulf region, contains almost half of the oil that is easily accessible. Russia, the Middle East, and now the United States are the main sources of gas. Until after the second half of the twentieth century, the world economy benefited from relatively cheap oil, and this critical commodity shaped the era's geopolitics. In the aftermath of World War II, oil became the main source of energy at the global level. Developed economies realized their strong dependence on this energy source, the main proven reserves of which are in the countries of the Global South and more particularly in the Middle East. This reality has had a strong impact on international relations and the geopolitics of the region. Oil has become a source of wealth and prosperity, but also conflict and misery.

Energy policies underwent a systemic shock beginning in 1973. These policies had been based on the logic of the quest for energy since World War I, and over time this became a major component of diplomacy and international relations, with oil companies playing a substantial role. The first oil crisis, by destabilizing the main world market, constituted a real break, leading to a rethinking of pricing methods. A change in market logic took place, with a transition from a stable price relationship to a volatile one that is increasingly becoming prevalent on the various markets, concomitant with the rise in power of international finance. There are at least three main actors in the oil industry that have unequal bargaining power: oil-producing countries, consumer countries, and transnational oil companies. More often than not, the interests of these three actors do not converge. Conflicts of interest are often first played out at the economic and financial level, with ideological considerations a factor as well (e.g., liberalization, privatization, state control, and deregulation). These conflictual interests lead at times to geopolitical confrontations.

At the national level, for the oil-producing countries of the Middle East and North Africa region, hydrocarbon-based economies and oil rents have long been seen as a blessing. However, the role that oil rent has played in most of the region's economic systems has been detrimental to the polities of the region. Because of oil rent, economic dysfunction and authoritarian modes of governance have prevailed. It fundamentally altered the relationship between the political and economic spheres, and undermined prospects for democratic social contracts and rule-of-law-based governance systems. Rentierism, insofar as it has provided significant budgetary revenues to the state apparatus, blocked political and economic reforms and, most of all, the establishment of a real fiscal system capable of bringing about a compromise with various social groups. What is more, the rentier mode of governance has been able to co-opt elites and redistribute part of the rent in order to silence social and political demands. This contributed to the development of political clientelism as political logic takes precedence over sound economic policies.

This situation makes it difficult to put in place a real economic policy based on a revision of the tax and banking system. The strong dependence of the region's oil-producing countries on their exports regularly leads to macroeconomic instability due to fluctuations in the international oil market. The development of a real national entrepreneurial class is difficult because the economy is so protected, and rent-seeking behaviors are so prevalent. In parallel with the development of unsustainable consumption patterns, this rentier system is incapable of creating employment opportunities in line with demographic growth. Moving away from rentier forms of governance implies effective economic diversification, which needs to address the political-economic realities of the governing social contract, in which governments rely on specific economic channels to transfer hydrocarbon wealth to their citizens. These channels often stand in the way of necessary reforms. A process of economic diversification has serious implications in terms of the power structure for ruling elites, who realize this reality only too well. Structural changes demanded by economic diversification would undoubtedly empower business constituencies that could be tempted to challenge the ruling elite. Establishing a new social contract will not be easy even as oil revenues decline.

Toward an alternative development paradigm?

Economic diversification is a process which goes beyond the economic realm, as it encompasses a wider societal process, which entails shifting the national revenue paradigm away from a single source of income, namely oil and gas in the case of MENA countries, to a one where multiple sources of income are generated across the primary, secondary, and tertiary sectors of the national economy, and where large sections of population, including public and private enterprises, partake in the development process. In other words, economic diversification requires the enactment of policies that reduce the dependence on a single industry or sector such as oil in terms of its contribution to GDP, export earnings, and government revenues. Decreasing dependence on oil occurs by developing non-hydrocarbon economic sectors such as services, manufacturing, tourism, and agriculture in order to become new sources of national income.

A diversified economy strategy is intended to reduce or minimize economic and financial risks associated with fossil fuel demand and price fluctuation. In such unstable and unpredictable markets as energy, diversification strategies can offer policy options to compensate for the decline in international oil prices and hence the associated export revenues. In the current economic conditions, diversification has become a necessity, as the economic structure is increasingly unsustainable, and all MENA oil-producing countries have suffered from the negative effects of the fluctuation in international oil prices and increasingly declining demand on fossil fuel in light of technological advancement in renewable energy and growing concerns over the environment, more specifically climate change.[3] In fact, MENA oil-producing countries are increasingly facing huge political, economic, demographic, social and environmental challenges, which affect directly and indirectly the sustainability of their socioeconomic development model.

A strategic economic transformation can mobilize efficiently national resources to serve long-term sustainable development, as MENA countries are aware of the infinite nature of fossil fuels resource, but the options to diversify their economies have not been sufficiently explored. An assessment of the current national visions, and development strategies in MENA countries, particularly in the GCC, though ambitious in theory, indicates that little has been achieved in economic diversification because local economic cycles are still largely dependent on oil and gas revenues. While GCC states achieved relative progress during the past decade, fossil fuel production continues to dominate national revenues by over 40 percent of GDP in most GCC countries, except for the United Arab Emirates (30 percent) and Bahrain (18 percent).[4]

The first phase of diversification began in the 1970s by expanding the oil sector in the upstream and downstream industries, as well as the creation of oil-related industries such as petrochemicals and aluminum. This implied an investment shift from the extractive industries to capital-intensive and energy-intensive industries such as petrochemicals, fertilizers, steel, and aluminum, with comparative advantage in the energy sector, as well as expanding in industries that could benefit from low-cost energy such as cement and construction materials. More recently, a new phase of diversification was initiated with investment in physical and human capital development, notably in infrastructure, education, and health sectors. Diversification has gone beyond the energy sector and its related industries, with the intention of working toward the creation of knowledge-based economies.

In fact, several MENA countries, particularly in the GCC, have been developing economic vision documents and national development strategies focusing on export diversification and development of service industries, including finance, tourism, aviation, media, education, healthcare, and real estate. These national visions target key pillars of development – human, social, economic, and environmental – as building blocks for a sustainable development paradigm, along the lines of the internationally agreed Development Agenda 2030. Yet, several challenges obstruct the development of a knowledge economy in MENA countries, given the current condition of the education systems. In GCC countries, states offer access for their nationals to public sector jobs at high wages and benefits as a distribution channel of citizens' share of the economic rents. This rent-based system affects the education and career choices of nationals, who generally are content with the minimum credentials needed to access public sector jobs, giving little attention to developing the skills needed to access more competitive jobs in the private sector.

Furthermore, investment in research and development is still insufficient, with less than 1 percent of the GDP compared to the global average of 3 percent, not to mention restricted civil liberty and political space which obstruct private sector development.[5] However, and in the case of GCC, where large amounts of financial capital are available coupled with a scarcity in non-energy resources, a shift toward a knowledge-based economy is a sound strategic choice, as it can help create a viable economy that sustains the livelihood of society in a post-oil era.

GCC countries have resorted to three main drivers in attempting to diversify their economies. They created a profitable state-owned enterprise in the manufacturing and services sectors. They also enacted policies to create a vibrant private sector, even though this sector remains weaker than the public sector when it comes to economic activities, because of the nature of the current allocation state model. Most GCC citizens still prefer to work for the government and the public sector, a phenomenon which undermined the base of a skillful and qualified workforce. This led private enterprises to depend on expatriates who are not permanent residents. In reality, the private sector has the potential to play a catalyst role, largely because the energy sector does not provide many jobs, while the public sector is overcrowded and is unable to absorb new candidates. Finally, GCC countries increasingly rely on sovereign wealth funds to invest in key economic sectors such as infrastructure, finance, banking, Islamic finance, technology, transportation, telecommunications, education, construction, and real estate.

Yet, and despite innovative national visions and economic development strategies, GCC economies remain heavily dependent on hydrocarbons as driver of their economic growth. Non-hydrocarbon sectors remain weak and continue to be dependent on oil revenues and, in turn, on the price of oil. For example, private enterprises are heavily dependent on the public sector and government expenditures. To ensure their competitiveness, industries such as manufacturing, petrochemicals, water desalination, and aviation depend on low energy costs and effective government subsidies. The banking and financial services still rely on financial flows which originate from oil revenues and any change in oil-enabled government spending policies will have serious impacts on all sectors of the economy. Much of the region's other economic activities, such as construction and infrastructure development, are also supported by revenues from oil and gas.

Channeling economic rents through expanded public services, government employment, and exclusive business contracts has weakened efforts to develop a competitive, dynamic private sector that can generate sustainable economic growth in a post-hydrocarbon future. Any policy effort to reduce rent-seeking behavior requires addressing the constraints of the governing social contract. Once fossil fuel rents are depleted, GCC countries will be in a precarious position, if no effective replacement strategies are put in place. This transition will require policy changes that increase private citizen activity both at the economic and political levels. This will not be easy in countries that subscribe to a rentier development paradigm.

Geopolitical power and influence at the international level

At the global level, in addition to the economic and socio-political aspects internal to the exporting countries, with oil as the foundation of political and economic structures of several MENA polities, hydrocarbon resources are also a factor of power and influence at the international level. The region, as the largest net crude exporter in the world, home to half of global proven oil reserves and more than a third of gas reserves, has relied heavily on energy in shaping its geopolitical status.[6] The clearest example of this is the enduring political and security alliance between Saudi Arabia and the United States since the 1930s around the export of its oil. This strategic alliance, known as the 'Quincy Pact,' became an essential pillar of American foreign policy in the following decades. It has also allowed oil-producing countries to exert relative political pressure for political gains at times. Yet, the gradual decrease in imports since the beginning of the 2010s and the prospect of the United States becoming a net oil exporter well before 2030, thanks to the exploitation of unconventional resources, are sources of economic and political concern for the Gulf countries, particularly Saudi Arabia, which may fear a weakening of their alliance with Washington.[7] Qatar is another example: its liquefaction and regasification capacity has provided the country with a substantial portfolio of international oil company partners and therefore strong political leverage in terms of foreign policy. This has allowed Doha to pursue ambitious foreign policy goals regionally – and at times globally – while shielding itself from major geopolitical shocks, the most recent of which was the Gulf blockade.

The gradual U.S. strategic disengagement from the MENA region, as well as its confrontation with states such as Russia, Iran, and Venezuela, among others, allowed for the deepening of relations between Moscow and a number of oil and gas-producing MENA countries, thus introducing both a diversification and expansion of energy diplomacy in the region. While several MENA states are traditionally aligned with American positions, they are not ready to alienate Russia. The UAE's abstention from the UN Security Council vote condemning Russia's invasion of Ukraine in February 2022 demonstrates a certain desire for independence, despite its later support for the (legally non-binding) March 2, 2022 General Assembly resolution entitled 'Aggression against Ukraine.'[8] With the exception of Kuwait, victim of an invasion by Iraq in 1990, which distinguished itself by explicitly denouncing Moscow, a majority of MENA countries have chosen to be more nuanced in their respective positions.[9] After 2011, with the upheavals in the Middle East and their tense relations with the Obama administration, as well as the sudden withdrawal by the United States from Afghanistan in 2021, certain MENA countries seem to follow geopolitical developments closely and wish to diversify their diplomatic relations. This is all the more important for countries like Saudi Arabia and the UAE, which are mired in the conflict in Yemen. Finally, with oil demand reaching its peak in Europe in the middle of the 2000s, MENA crude exporters accelerated their shift toward Asian markets, charting new paths with immense geopolitical implications.[10]

Against this backdrop, it is widely assumed that MENA producing countries will be negatively affected by the energy transition, and hence their energy-based strategic geopolitical clout would fade away. In fact, as the energy transitions are mostly dictated by concerns over climate change, it is expected that oil demand will decline, and the pattern will shift across geographies, with strategic geopolitical implications. Alongside a decline in fuel oil, demand for liquefied gas and ethane is expected to grow. The new energy mix will also include other types of renewable energies, as all previous energy transitions have been more of a stratification, with the addition of new sources of energy, rather than an all-out shift from old sources to new ones. The global energy transition could help reduce the political benefits that some countries derive from the export of their hydrocarbons. As with coal from the 1960s onwards, oil will continue to be consumed but its economic and geopolitical value will eventually decrease progressively.

While several energy-related factors may contribute to the erosion of the region's geopolitical status, the strategic loss remains relative and should be construed with nuance. All regions of the world will be impacted one way or another by the energy transition process. For now, in the midst of the ongoing Ukraine war, with sanctions imposed on the Russian hydrocarbon industry, the MENA region's fossil-fuel producers have become valuable partners. Furthermore, the geostrategic role of gas in the MENA region is set to grow, as this valuable commodity will become an increasingly important part of the MENA energy sector. Iraq, a major flaring country, is working on developing fields in its western region and Diyala Province, while Saudi Arabia is increasingly betting on unconventional gas development in Jafurah and South Ghawar. As for Qatar, it is probably the best example of growing – not diminishing – strategic geopolitical power, with its increasing share in the energy mix, the decarbonization of the gas value chain, and the strengthening role played by gas in the transition phase.

Thanks to unconventional hydrocarbons, U.S. energy production has increased over the past two decades, allowing the country to practically achieve energy self-sufficiency. This changes the geopolitical balance and the close relationship that the United States, given its long-standing dependence on energy imports, had developed with MENA countries since World War II. The United States is now free of this dependence and has a great deal of latitude in its foreign policy. China, by contrast, is now the world's largest net importer of oil.[11] With its reserves in the Middle East, China is developing in-depth relations by investing in oil and gas exploration and production projects in Iran, Iraq, the UAE, and Qatar. China is therefore set to play a growing role in geopolitical issues in the region. The turn of MENA energy-exporting countries toward the Asian market, with the growing economic and political power of states like China and India, has created new opportunities for exporters to impose themselves as major players as clean energy geopolitics grow in importance, thus mitigating as much as possible the potential loss in terms of geopolitical influence induced by the energy transition.

China's growing influence in the MENA region

China's growing influence in the MENA region is a result of its strategic interests and economic ambitions, as well as its ability to balance between different actors and avoid direct involvement in conflicts. China has established comprehensive strategic partnerships with many countries in the region, and has increased its trade, investment, and cooperation in various fields, especially energy, infrastructure, technology, and green development. China's Belt and Road Initiative has also provided a platform for enhancing connectivity and mutual benefit with the MENA countries.

The Middle East and North Africa region is a strategic partner for China in Its Belt and Road Initiative, a global infrastructure and economic development project that aims to connect Asia, Europe, Africa, and the Middle East through land and sea routes. The MENA region is a major source of oil and gas for China, as well as a potential market for Chinese goods and services. The initiative offers opportunities for MENA oil producing countries to diversify their economies, upgrade their infrastructure, and enhance their regional integration. According to the China Global Investment Tracker, China has invested over $100 billion in the MENA region since 2013, mainly in energy, transportation, and construction sectors.[12] Some of the major BRI projects in the region include: the Suez Canal Economic Zone (SCZone) in Egypt, a $10 billion industrial and logistics hub that aims to create 1 million jobs and attract $30 billion of foreign investment by 2030; the Trans-Anatolian Natural Gas Pipeline (TANAP) in Turkey, a $12 billion project that transports natural gas from Azerbaijan to Europe via Turkey, reducing Europe's dependence on Russian gas; the Attarat Oil Shale Power Plant in Jordan, a $2.1 billion project that will produce 470 megawatts of electricity from oil shale, meeting 15 percent of Jordan's power demand and reducing its energy imports; the Hassyan Clean Coal Power Plant in UAE, a $3.4 billion project that will generate 2,400 megawatts of electricity from clean coal technology, supporting Dubai's goal of diversifying its energy mix and increasing its renewable energy share to 75 percent by 2050.

China's growing influence in the MENA region is a result of its expanding economic, political, and security interests in the area. It has become a major trade partner and investor for many MENA countries, especially in the fields of energy, infrastructure, telecommunications, and technology. China has also established strategic partnerships and multilateral forums with various MENA actors, such as the China–Arab States Cooperation Forum (CASCF), the Forum on China–Africa Cooperation (FOCAC), and the Shanghai Cooperation Organization (SCO).[13] It has also engaged in diplomatic efforts to address regional conflicts and hot spots, such as the Israeli-Palestinian issue, the Syrian civil war, and the Iranian nuclear deal. China's engagement with the MENA region aims at pursuing its own national security and development goals and its growing presence in the MENA region offers more options and leverage for the MENA countries to diversify their economic and diplomatic relations and to seek more balanced and cooperative solutions for regional problems. China's role in the MENA region is likely to increase in the coming years as it pursues its Belt and Road Initiative and its vision of building a community of shared future for mankind.

Saudi Arabia–Iran diplomatic rapprochement brokered by China

This increasing engagement by China in the MENA region has recently achieved a major diplomatic prowess by brokering a watershed deal between the two regional foes. Iran and Saudi Arabia have long been rivals in the geopolitics of energy, competing for influence and market share in the oil-rich Middle East. Their relationship has been marked by periods of hostility and cooperation, depending on the regional and global context. However, in recent years, both countries have faced new challenges and opportunities that have reshaped their energy strategies and outlooks. One of the main drivers of change has been the rise of China as a major energy consumer and partner for both Iran and Saudi Arabia. China has become the largest importer of oil from both countries, and has also invested heavily in their energy sectors, especially in Iran's gas and renewable projects. China has also played a key role in brokering a diplomatic deal between Iran and Saudi Arabia in 2023, which ended a seven-year rift and paved the way for more cooperation on energy and other issues.

Another factor that has influenced the geopolitics of energy between Iran and Saudi Arabia is the global transition to a low-carbon economy, driven by the urgency of climate change and the development of new technologies. Both countries have realized that they need to diversify their energy sources and reduce their dependence on oil exports, which are vulnerable to price fluctuations and environmental regulations. Iran has been pursuing nuclear power as a way to meet its domestic electricity demand and assert its technological prowess, while Saudi Arabia has been investing in solar power and other renewables to capitalize on its abundant natural resources and create new industries.

The geopolitics of energy between Iran and Saudi Arabia is therefore complex and dynamic, reflecting their historical rivalry, their common interests, and their changing circumstances within a changing geopolitical landscape, especially with the Russia–Ukraine war. While there are still many sources of tension and mistrust between the two countries, such as their involvement in regional conflicts and their opposing versions of political Islam, there are also signs of pragmatism and dialogue that could lead to more stability and cooperation in the future.

It remains that Iran and Saudi Arabia are two of the most influential actors in the geopolitics of energy in the Middle East and beyond. Their rivalry has shaped the regional dynamics for decades, affecting issues such as security, trade, and diplomacy. The deal, brokered by China, has the potential to end the seven-year diplomatic rift that began in 2016 after Saudi Arabia executed a prominent Shiite cleric and Iran-backed protesters attacked Saudi embassies. The deal also seeks to revive a security cooperation pact, reopen embassies, and resume trade, investment, and cultural ties. This can be seen as a major achievement for China, which has been expanding its economic and strategic interests in the region, especially in the energy sector. The Iran–KSA deal could also affect the global energy markets and the role of other major players such as the United States, Russia, and the European Union. Iran and Saudi Arabia are both major oil and gas producers and exporters, and their policies have a significant impact on the supply and demand balance, as well as on the price and stability of energy commodities. At the geopolitical level, this diplomatic rapprochement could potentially ease some of the tensions and conflicts that have disrupted oil and gas production and transit in the region, such as the war in Yemen, the blockade of Qatar, and the attacks on oil facilities and tankers.

Conclusion

The economic development of MENA countries in the context of the current geopolitics of energy is a complex and multifaceted issue. The region faces several challenges and opportunities as it adapts to the global energy transition, which entails a shift from fossil fuels to renewable sources of energy. As argued earlier, one of the main challenges for MENA countries is to diversify their economies away from their dependence on oil and gas revenues, which are expected to decline in the long term due to lower demand and prices, as well as increased competition from other producers. This requires investing in human capital, infrastructure, innovation, and other sectors that can create jobs and growth for their populations. Some MENA countries have already taken steps to reform their fiscal and subsidy policies, promote private sector development, and enhance regional integration. Policy makers in MENA fossil-fuel producing countries must focus on developing the necessary building blocks for a dynamic and sustainable post-hydrocarbon economy. To this end, policy efforts aimed at economic diversification must find alternative solutions to the entrenched rent-seeking behavior.

Another challenge is to ensure the security and sustainability of their energy supply and demand, both domestically and internationally. This involves enhancing their energy efficiency and conservation measures, developing their renewable energy potential, and reducing their greenhouse gas emissions. It also involves maintaining their market share and influence in the global oil and gas markets, especially in Asia, where an increasing share of their customer base is located. Some MENA countries have also invested in strategic partnerships and infrastructure projects with other regions, such as Africa and Europe, to diversify their export routes and markets.

A third challenge is to manage the geopolitical implications and risks of the energy transition, which may affect their relations with other actors and regions. For instance, the energy transition may create new areas of cooperation or competition with other major energy producers or consumers, such as the United States, China, Russia, or Europe. It may also affect the stability and security of the region, which is already plagued by conflicts, fragility, and humanitarian crises. Some MENA countries have sought to play a constructive role in resolving regional disputes and supporting peace processes.

The Chinese-brokered diplomatic rapprochement between Iran and Saudi Arabia, while promising, still faces many challenges and uncertainties. Iran and Saudi Arabia have deep-rooted ideological and political differences that are not easily resolved by diplomatic engagement. They have competing interests and visions for the region, and they support opposing sides in various proxy wars and sectarian conflicts. They also have divergent views on how to address the global climate change challenge, which requires a radical transformation of the energy sector. Iran has been pursuing nuclear power as a way to diversify its energy mix and reduce its dependence on fossil fuels, while Saudi Arabia has been investing heavily in renewable energy sources such as solar power. While this is a historic step that could open new opportunities for cooperation and dialogue on energy issues, and which has the potential to change the geopolitics of the region, it is also a fragile and complex arrangement that could be undermined by internal and external factors. The geopolitics of energy in the Middle East will remain dynamic and unpredictable, requiring constant adaptation and innovation from all actors.

In conclusion, the economic development of MENA countries in the current geopolitics of energy is a fine balance between mitigating risks and exploring new opportunities. The region has a unique position and potential in the global energy landscape, but it also faces significant challenges and uncertainties. The success of its adaptation to the energy transition will depend on its ability to implement sound policies and strategies that can foster inclusive and sustainable growth for its people, while navigating cautiously the rough waters of global geopolitics.

Bibliography

Aubert Jean-Eric, and Jean-Louis Reiffers, 'Knowledge Economies in the Middle East and North Africa: Toward New Development Strategies,' World Bank Series, World Bank Group, 2003, https://digitallibrary.un.org/record/542993?ln=en.

'China Global Investment Tracker,' American Enterprise Institute, 2022, https://www.aei.org/china-global-investment-tracker/.

'China surpassed the United States as the world's largest crude oil importer in 2017,' US Energy Information Administration, December 21, 2018, https://www.eia.gov/todayinenergy/detail.php?id=37821.

'China-Arab States Cooperation Forum Holds the 17th Senior Officials' Meeting and the 6th Senior Official Level Strategic Political Dialogue,' Ministry of

Foreign Affairs of the People's Republic of China, June 23, 2021, https://www. fmprc.gov.cn/eng/wjbxw/202106/t20210624_9134414.html.

'Economic Diversification in Oil-Exporting Arab Countries,' International Monetary Fund, April 29, 2016, https://www.imf.org/en/Publications/ Policy-Papers/Issues/2016/12/31/Economic-Diversification-in-Oil- Exporting-Arab-Countries-PP5038.

'Energy mix,' Our World in Data, Accessed April 2023, https://ourworldindata. org/energy-mix.

'Europe facing peak oil,' The Greens in the European Parliament, 2012, https:// www.greens-efa.eu/legacy/fileadmin/dam/Documents/Publications/Energy/ Fossil_fuels/PIC%20petrolier_EN_lowres.pdf.

Fattah, Zainab, 'UAE Joined China, India in Abstaining on UN Ukraine Vote,' Bloomberg News, February 26, 2022, https://www.bloomberg.com/news/ articles/2022-02-26/uae-abstained-in-un-vote-on-ukraine-to-put-emphasis- on-diplomacy?leadSource=uverify%20wall.

Forum on China–Africa Cooperation, accessed April 2023, http://www.focac. org.cn/eng/.

Kabbani, Nader, and Nejla Ben Mimoun, 'Economic Diversification in the Gulf: Time to redouble efforts,' Brookings Institution, January 31, 2021, https:// www.brookings.edu/research/economic-diversification-in-the-gulf-time-to- redouble-efforts/.

'OPEC Share of World Crude Oil Reserves,' OPEC Annual Statistical Bulletin 2022, https://www.opec.org/opec_web/en/data_graphs/330.htm.

'Shanghai Cooperation Organization,' UN Political and Peacebuilding Affairs, accessed April 2023, https://dppa.un.org/en/shanghai-cooperation- organization.

Somasekhar, Arathy, 'US poised to become net exporter of crude oil in 2023,' Reuters, December 19, 2022, https://www.reuters.com/business/energy/ us-poised-become-net-exporter-crude-oil-2023-2022-12-19/.

'The UN Resolution on Ukraine: How Did the Middle East Vote?,' Washington Institute for Near East Policy, March 2, 2022, https://www. washingtoninstitute.org/policy-analysis/un-resolution-ukraine-how-did- middle-east-vote.

Vohra, Anchal, 'Xi Jinping Has Transformed China's Middle East Policy,' *Foreign Policy*, February 1, 2022, https://foreignpolicy.com/2022/02/01/xi-jinping- has-transformed-chinas-middle-east-policy/.

PART TWO

NEW ENERGY TECHNOLOGIES AND THEIR DEVELOPMENT IN THE MIDDLE EAST

6 THE NEXT BIG THING IN MENA POWER – GRIDS AND ENERGY STORAGE

Jessica Obeid

Introduction

This chapter finds that while demand for electricity is increasing in the Middle East and North Africa (MENA), along with investments in renewable energy, states have not granted enough focus to the power grid and electricity capacity. This situation may present a challenge to power quality and reliability and may delay renewable energy plans.

An unsustainable growth in electricity demand in the region is driven by fuel and electricity subsidies, growing population and economic activity, climate change impact on cooling and water needs, electrification of sectors such as transport, and digitization. This growth has been driving a race for additional power generation capacity. Despite that, some countries suffer from chronic power shortages or periodic black-outs, driven by record-high peak demands as temperatures soar in summer.

While acknowledging disparities across countries, within the region planned power sector projects top the energy sector's investments. The bulk of investments, however, targets the generation sector, and only a minor share is allocated for transmission and distribution networks. Investments in power generation are increasingly targeting renewable energy projects, mostly solar and wind, and the intermittency of these variable renewable energy resources adds challenges to the power grid.

The challenges increase with the increasing penetration of renewable energy into the mix. This is especially relevant to Jordan, where renewables have reached a 20 percent share of generation capacity in 2020, and soon will be Saudi Arabia, which is aiming for 50 percent of electricity generation from renewables by 2030. Dealing with this challenge requires expanding and modernizing the power grid, investing in efficient electricity exchange markets, and deploying energy storage systems.

This chapter covers the grid stability in the MENA region, examines the status and prospects of electricity exchange and grid interconnection, and analyzes the opportunities and challenges for energy storage systems.

Rising power consumption

Electricity consumption is on the rise in MENA, prompting electricity utilities to race for additional power generation capacity, an unsustainable strategy in the long run. Demand growth rate averages 7–8 percent annually, compared to a global average of 5 percent. The total demand is expected to grow 80 percent by 2040 compared to 2021 baseline records.[1] The residential sector is the highest electricity consumer in the region, surpassing 45 percent of the total electricity consumption.[2] The reasons behind this growth are economic and population growth, increased water and cooling demand driven by climate change, and the fuel and electricity subsidies leading to wasteful consumption. Countries across MENA are witnessing increased power consumption as temperatures soar to 125°F in some cities and the demand for cooling skyrockets.

The growth in demand is driving significant increases in installed generation capacity, mainly thermal generation, and consuming a larger share of fossil fuels. The annual growth rate of installed generation capacity in the region averages 7–10 percent,[3] compared to the global rate of 6 percent for thermal generation.[4] The race for thermal generation capacity is the highest in the Arab Gulf states, explained by their higher financing capacity compared to other countries in the region. Yet, the growth in peak demand saw a few years of retraction in the Arab Gulf states. The average annual growth in peak demand in these states dropped to 3 percent from 2016 to 2020 from 9 percent between 2005 and 2015.[5] However, it is unlikely that this retraction in annual growth will be sustained.

The future promises more electricity consumption, driven by the rising temperatures and electrification of sectors. Efforts to adapt and mitigate the impacts of climate change would not eliminate the increasing temperatures and overheating of the MENA region. Thus, cooling and water demands will maintain their increasing trajectory and require more and more electricity supply. It is estimated that by 2040, fourteen out of the thirty-three most water-stressed countries will be in the Middle East.[6] The region suffers from the highest rate of economic losses related to water scarcity, expected to range between 6 and 14 percent of the region's GDP by 2050.[7]

Additionally, albeit slowly, the energy transition is leading to an electrification of many sectors. E-mobility and digitization are starting to contribute to the electricity demand growth, and this is bound to grow drastically. Electric vehicles are currently struggling to penetrate the regional market due to low incentives, lack of infrastructure, and the weak power systems across many MENA countries. Yet, as car manufacturers adopt the electric vehicles and trucks, combustion engines will retract, and as supporting policies are increasing adopted in the region, other countries will have to catch up.

As the region overall records a race of power generation addition, several countries face growing power supply shortages resulting in chronic and lengthy power outage, including Yemen, Lebanon, and Iraq. The shortages are linked to conflicts and damage to infrastructure, vested interests in the status quo, weak governance, and structural inefficiencies. Power outages are also increasingly recorded in countries of more robust power sectors, due to rises in peak demand driven by record-high temperatures, such as in Kuwait. The current rate of growth in electricity demand in the region is unsustainable. Additional capacity must be paired with improvements in energy efficiency and a power-rationing strategy for peak periods.

Growing share of renewable energy

The race to add power generation capacity to meet the growing demand is increasingly incorporating renewable energy investments. The MENA region boasts strong natural resources of both hydrocarbon and renewable energy. The region's geography bestows it with a solid standing for the deployment of solar, wind, and geothermal energy projects. Insolation levels are high and predictable, and many countries have vast, sparsely-populated land. Many areas record commercially viable wind speeds, and although largely under-explored, geothermal is promising.[8] Geothermal exploration requires in-depth drilling, which could benefit from the large experience and cost-competitiveness of petroleum-producing economies in the region and contribute to oil companies' diversification efforts.

Achieving energy diversification in this fossil-fuel-dominated and energy intensive region is not a simple task. Yet, the deployment of renewable energy systems has been gaining traction, with varying pace and rate across countries. The total installed capacity of non-hydropower renewable energy in MENA crossed 11.8GW in 2021,[9] up from 10.6GW in 2020, and more than double the installed capacity of 5.4GW in 2010.[10] Accounting for hydropower, the installed capacity exceeded 20.3GW in 2021, yet hydropower has been witnessing only slight increases, mostly due to the retraction of these sources due to drought. Installed renewable energy capacity is bound to grow substantially and the region is expected to implement 33GW by 2026.[11] Governments have pledged hefty national renewable energy targets to showcase the political commitment toward clean power production and increase the latter's share in the power mix. These targets range from 15 to 50 percent of power generation by 2030, with some interim targets for 2022 or 2025, such as in Egypt, Oman, and Saudi Arabia.

The major drivers prompting governments' commitment to renewable energy are energy security and the reduction of fossil fuel demand for domestic power generation. Hydrocarbon-importing countries have strained their budgets and reduced their energy security through the dependence on fuel imports. Meanwhile, petroleum-producing economies are driven by the economic opportunity to free hydrocarbons for exports.

Other commonly cited drivers for energy diversification include job creation, readiness for low oil prices in the long term, cost-competitiveness of renewable energy generation, and the opportunity to save water.[12]

The Saudi Kingdom has committed to the most ambitious renewable energy target in the region, with a pledge of 10 percent of electricity generation from renewables by 2025 and 50 percent by 2030, up from a current share of 1 percent of generation. The lower bracket, 15 percent target of power generation by 2030, holds for Kuwait, which currently depends on oil for 65 percent of power generation, while the remaining share is for natural gas. The biggest gains in renewable energy integration in the region so far have been in Morocco and Jordan. Morocco recorded a 37 percent share of renewable energy in its installed capacity in 2020, compared to a target of 42 percent, and its 2030 renewables target is 52 percent of installed capacity. Jordan reached almost 20 percent of generation capacity by 2020, out of its target of 21 percent. However, several bottlenecks are currently facing Jordan's renewable energy industry and hindering the kingdom's ability to further increase the share of renewables in the mix. These include the high cost of recovery of electricity, the significant reserve margin, and grid limitations.

Expanding grids: High-capacity, smart, and flexible grids

At the core of a successful energy transition is an expanded, upgraded, and modernized grid. The grid of the future will have to be large, flexible, and bi-directional. Current grid expansions are not fast enough and grid restrictions pose major operational challenges to the integration of variable renewable energy across the globe. Renewable energy investments have been developed at a faster rate than power grids' expansion, including in China and the United States, creating bottlenecks for further renewable energy additions.[13] In MENA countries, the pace of renewable energy deployment has started slow, thus grid challenges have mostly not come out to the spotlight except in a few countries like Jordan. In early 2019, Jordan had to suspend utility-scale renewable energy auctions to invest in the electricity grid.[14]

Middle Eastern countries are beset with a set of challenges facing the integration of renewable energy into the grid, such as curtailment, low flexibility and limited capacity, non-reliability and losses, low access in rural areas, and under-investments.

The deployment of variable renewable energy (VRE), such as solar and wind, creates a new set of challenges for power grid stability. Solar and wind energy generate non-dispatchable electricity, due to their availability only when the sun is shining or when the wind is blowing, and not necessarily when there is demand. If the grid is weak and cannot withstand the generated renewable energy, or if demand is lower than power generation, then the latter will be curtailed. As governments and utilities in the region have been signing power purchase agreements from renewable energy sources with take-or-pay clauses, any curtailed electricity will not be dispatched or consumed, but must still be paid for.

However, when the generated power from renewable energy sources drops, and demand is higher than generation, then grid operators must balance supply and demand through flexible solutions and rapid ramp-up of other sources. Systems' flexibility is the ability to manage such variabilities.

Whereas some grids are more flexible than others in MENA countries, investments in system flexibility are needed across the entire region. A flexible system requires flexible power generation, fast dispatch, reserves management, demand response, and demand side flexibility. Natural gas-powered generation is considered flexible power generation due to these plants' fast ramp-up ability compared to other types of thermal power generation. Natural gas is the dominant source of power generation in the Middle East, yet many countries still rely on heavy fuel oil and diesel as their power source. Rural areas also record a heavy reliance on diesel-powered generation, even in high-income countries in the region such as the Arab Gulf states.

Additionally, there is no sufficient grid capacity across most countries. Utility-scaled solar and wind systems are typically installed far away from areas of high electricity demand, referred to as demand or load centers, as these systems require vast land availability located outside populated areas. Transporting the generated renewable power across vast geographic locations to demand centers requires high-capacity transmission systems.

The grid is most unreliable in conflict and post-conflict countries, due to the technical damages and attacks on the networks, obsolete transmission lines, and network losses. Grid status further deteriorates on these countries' financial constraints and low capacity to tap into major private financing to implement necessary reforms and rehabilitation plans. Consequently, the grid is unreliable and mostly unavailable in countries such as Yemen. Systematic, financial, and administrative corruption are also taking their toll on the grid and power supply in countries like Iraq and Lebanon, resulting in losses and unreliable supply and networks. The level of losses varies across countries and averages at 18 percent.[15] The lowest losses are recorded in Arab Gulf states, while the highest are in Lebanon and Iraq and can reach 40–50 percent.[16] These losses are of two types, technical and non-technical, and affect grid efficiency. Technical losses constitute the energy lost through the transmission network between generation and distribution and are unavoidable. These losses are the sum of losses in cables, transformers, and other network equipment. Non-technical losses are linked to administrative mismanagement and corruption, as well as the dominant social contract, and are comprised of non-billing, non-collection, and illegal connections by end-consumers to the network.

In many countries, rural electrification remains a challenge, especially in the region's least developed countries. Only 50 percent of the latter's rural population had access to electricity in 2017.[17] In Yemen, only 69 percent of the rural population has access to electricity and electricity theft in rural areas amounts to 71 percent.[18] Addressing access is necessary for any power sector reform and any future grid reinforcement.

Increasing reliance on intermittent sources of power generation causes low system inertia in cases where investments in modernizing the power grid are not sufficient.[19] Integrating renewable energy will require large-scale grid infrastructure. Yet, in the Middle East, investments in grid enhancements and modernization have been lagging. Total investments in the power sector in the region constitute the largest share of energy investments, with one third of the total of $879 billion earmarked for 2022–2026.[20] Yet only 8–12 percent of these investments target the transmission and distribution networks, and the largest share covers the generation sector. That is because grid investments in the region have been primarily dependent on public spending, as the power systems are mostly state-owned. Pressure on public budgets in many MENA countries has reduced the prospects for grid investments, leading to major under-investments.

Investments in grid infrastructure, including transmission and distribution networks, substations, and transformers, need to be significantly ramped up to address the challenges of renewable energy integration and mitigate potential power supply disruptions.[21] Significant investments in system flexibility, scalability, and energy storage systems are needed as current conventions of balancing supply and demand in power generation do not rise to the needs of the complex modern power systems that integrate significant VRE.

Connecting grids: Imagining a Pan-Arab super grid

In addition to grid expansions, power systems of the future need greater connectivity. Grid interconnections enable a smoother integration of renewable energy and enhance energy security, grid stability, and flexibility across the region. Connectivity is critical for the region's power systems, especially given that the peak demand varies from one country to another, allowing greater benefits. The MENA region has three sets of grid interconnections:

1   The Maghreb Countries Interconnection, connecting the power grids of Morocco, Algeria, and Tunisia, kickstarted in 1952 as the first interconnection in the region and synchronized with the European high-voltage transmission network. Libya's grid should have been linked to Tunisia's, but the weak grid status in the former and subsequent electricity fluctuations resulted in de-activation of the link. Morocco's grid was connected to Spain's in the late 1990s.

2   The Eight Country Interconnection (EIJLLPST), connecting the power grids of Egypt, Iraq, Jordan, Lebanon, Libya, Palestine, Syria, and Turkey, kickstarted in 1988, with the last connection completed in 2009.

3   The Gulf Cooperation Council Interconnection Authority (GCCIA), connecting the power grids of the six Arab Gulf states (Saudi Arabia, the United Arab Emirates, Oman, Kuwait, Bahrain, and Qatar) kickstarted in 2001 and completed through three phases in 2011.

The GCCIA's grid capacity varies by Arab Gulf state and its capital investment cost was distributed accordingly. Saudi Arabia and Kuwait hold the largest capacity and have invested the largest share with 31.6 percent and 26.7 percent respectively. Despite the high potential, the grid interconnection has been operating at 5 percent of its capacity due to fiscal and structural challenges such as tariff structures, subsidies, and power sector regulations.[22]

The original purpose of the grid interconnections was to increase energy security and reduce costs through cross-border electricity exchange. In practice, the Eight Country and the GCCIA interconnections have been used mostly for emergencies.

Fuel and electricity subsidies are a deterrent to an efficient electricity exchange market. Financial losses are accrued from the cross-subsidies provided by each country for every unit of electricity exported at a subsidized tariff. The electricity subsidies would be easier to compute as part of the cost of recovery, if not for the fact that most countries in the region also subsidize the fuel consumed in power generation.

Discussions and memorandums of understanding (MoUs) have been ongoing for years to connect new countries to the existing interconnections, but these have yet to materialize. Once awarded, the technical works require up to two years to be developed. Saudi Arabia and Egypt have awarded the implementation of a 3GW interconnection. Though the plans are less developed, Saudi Arabia and the GCCIA also aim to connect to Iraq. The latter is also of interest for Jordan. But these plans remain on paper. Saudi Arabia and Iraq inked a deal in June 2022 to build a 1,000MW/400KV interconnection of 435 kilometers between the north of Saudi Arabia and Yusufiya near Baghdad. This deal followed two years of discussions and could yield technical and political benefits to both countries. If implemented, the project could mitigate some of Iraq's chronic power outages and reduce Iran's influence on Iraq.

In their current, business-as-usual scenario, grid interconnections serve as an aversion mechanism for power outages, ensuring continuous supply across connected countries. Yet, there are several advantages to enhancing the interconnections utilization rate if countries can overcome the financial and structural barriers and develop a regional trading mechanism:

1 reduced reliance on thermal power and better integration and development of renewables;

2 more efficient, energy-secure power systems with less need to race for additional power generation capacity;

3 improved prospects for alternative energy integration, paving the way for green electric future; and

4 in the long-term, potential to trade across the Middle East and beyond. The highest potential resides in connecting countries with elevated reserve margins and growing demand, such as Saudi Arabia, United Arab Emirates, Egypt, and Jordan, and post-conflict countries suffering from chronic electricity supply shortages, such as Iraq and Yemen.

Interconnected grids are not only operating on low utilization rates but also missing on significant revenues that can be achieved through wider trading across the Middle East and Africa in the future. As countries seek economic diversification, activating new business models and switching to electricity exports will be key to the sustainability of MENA economies and their integration of future energy models. The highest potential is in establishing a Pan-Arab regional electricity trade platform and connecting that grid beyond the region to energy-poor African countries. A more efficient electricity exchange market will also be important for economic improvement in countries like Iraq, Lebanon, and Yemen, which suffer from chronic electricity supply shortages that can be mitigated through other countries' power generation. In general, the power exchange market could play a tremendous role in post-conflict economies, reducing the time and substantial capital costs needed to refurbish the damaged power sectors. Post-conflict economies, however, cannot afford the investment costs required to connect their power sectors to existing grids.

Future electricity exchange markets should also include a power-wheeling fee to incentivize third-party countries to permit electricity transit through their transmission lines to the destination country. Lessons from the European electricity exchange market showcase that the road ahead for establishing one is bumpy and non-homogenous and will require restructuring utilities and pricing. European electricity market liberalization was completed in the 1990s, following the unbundling of utilities into generation, transmission, and distribution companies leading the way to a competitive market. Producers were guaranteed access to the transmission network, with incentives to adopt clean energy sources. Whereas the market liberalization was harmonized and followed an EU directive, the establishment of transnational electricity markets was less homogenous, and each country followed its own guidelines and principles. The main reasons for that were the difficulties in amending regulations, strategic government decisions, and infrastructure development.[23]

The EU electricity market has changed with time, increasing both in efficiencies and challenges. The lessons learned from the EU can help to kickstart improvements in the MENA interconnection grids. One such lesson includes the day-ahead market and prices, which has led to a more efficient use of electricity across borders. But there is also competition between national trade and transnational, cross-border trade. The integration of renewable energy is adding uncertainties as grid limitations were not originally part of the challenges for connectivity. Complex forecast centers and grid integration operators would also be required.

Adding technology to the grid: The case for energy storage systems

Meeting national renewable energy targets will also require the deployment of energy storage systems (ESS), as these systems manage the intermittencies of variable renewable energy (VRE) resources and their impact on the grid.

The higher the share of VRE in the power mix, the higher the variability and prospects for imbalances in supply and demand. ESS enables mitigating these challenges and managing the need for curtailment or fast ramp-up in power generation sources. In fact, one of the functions of ESS is to ensure that electricity is available for dispatch when there is demand. But there is a multitude of grid services that ESS can perform, the most lucrative currently being capacity firming, frequency regulation, and energy arbitrage, among other ancillary services. ESS also allows for countries to defer upgrades for the transmission and distribution network, thus delaying the need for additional investments.

Historically, power systems have focused on balancing supply and demand through continuous increases of power generation capacities. New power systems have the reduction of peak demand as a key focus. This service, referred to as peak shaving, is also enabled by ESS and constitutes a major need for Middle Eastern power markets to support expected growth.

Additionally, several grid measures are required to rectify the 'duck curve,' one of which is ESS. The difference of power demand and available supply from renewables throughout a given day is described as the 'duck curve,' as the shape of the resulting curve resembles a duck. The required measures constitute additional flexibility solutions, demand-side management, and storage of electricity to use depending on demand. Moreover, accounting for storage in rural areas to mind the discrepancies in power supply in rural areas, and among rural utilities such as in Oman, would also be a key contributor to growth of the rural economy.

Various ESS technologies and applications are available on the market to deliver this multitude of storage and ancillary services. These technologies fall within several categories:

1 chemical such as hydrogen and ammonia;
2 electro-chemical, commonly known as batteries, including lithium-ion, sodium-sulfur, vanadium redox-flow;

3 thermal, such as molten salt;

4 mechanical, such as pumped hydro, compressed air, and flywheel; and

5 electrical, as in supercapacitors.

Technology and application are selected based on site and grid requirements, power market, regulations, potential revenue schemes, and cost-benefit assessments. Pumped hydro storage (PHS) is the world's oldest and remains the dominant energy storage technology with 90 percent of the globally installed ESS capacity. However, batteries are gaining traction and constitute the bulk of new ESS projects, given their ease of deployment and falling costs. Among batteries, lithium-ion holds the fastest growing share as it promises applications across many sectors, including electric vehicles, power systems, and electronic appliances.

There are two models of ESS grid-applications: front-of-meter (FTM) application which constitutes the utility scale ESS connected at the generation sources or transmission network, and behind-the-meter (BTM) applications, which refer to systems storing electricity much closer to the consumer, behind the meter.

Project finance constitutes a key challenge for the mass deployment of ESS, as the cash flow is complex, uncertain, and depends on stacked revenues. Unlike renewables, where most technologies are mature and off-take agreements are straightforward and almost standardized, various ESS technologies have varying maturity levels, applications, grid services, and corresponding value, and, therefore, revenues are not constant.

Early adopters of ESS grid-applications, such as the United Kingdom and the United States, have championed 'value stacking' of ESS services yielding 'revenues stacking' to developers. These markets are compensating energy storage developers for the provision of grid services such as frequency regulation and energy arbitrage, depending on the need and value of these services for the grid operators. Thus, the energy storage developer would stack revenues from the capacity agreement for the stored electricity and shorter-term contracts for various services provision. It is worth noting, however, that not all ESS services can be quantified and monetized, and that compensation is interlinked to power market regulation, demand, service pricing, and deployment time. Additionally, demand for ESS is directly correlated to the share of renewable energy in the generation mix. Yet, the value of ESS services is indirectly proportional to the level of deployment of such systems.

Energy storage systems in MENA: The next big market

In 2020 the MENA region had deployed 1.46GW of on-grid ESS applications, compared to a global operational capacity exceeding 10GW. MENA's total ESS capacity amounts to 10,134MW, and the bulk of that operational capacity is deployed in Morocco. FTM applications accounted for 89 percent of the capacity, while BTM applications constituted the remaining capacity.[24]

PHS holds the largest share of installed capacity in MENA with 55 percent, compared to a global share of 90 percent. This PHS capacity comes from only two projects located in Morocco of 350MW/2,800MWh and 465MW/3,720MWh. Thermal storage, mostly molten salt, constitutes 29 percent of MENA ESS capacity. Batteries constitute only 7 percent of the operational capacity but 80 percent of the total projects. Batteries are gaining traction as most of the new ESS projects are of the electrochemical/battery type. The largest share of battery capacity has been installed in the United Arab Emirates and is of sodium-sulfur type.[25] Sodium-sulfur has advantages over lithium-ion in the MENA region presented in its lower sensitivity to temperature and ability to provide power for a longer duration, up to six hours compared to up to two hours. ESS deployment in the MENA is dictated by two drivers:

1 ambitious renewable energy targets; and

2 Cost-competitiveness, driven by advancements in storage technologies and upcoming long-duration energy storage crossing the 10-hour duration, coupled with falling costs.

The pace of deployment, however, will depend on policy support, incentives, and the elimination of financial and regulatory barriers. On the financial front, the high credit risk due to negative economic outlook, high financing costs in project finance, and pressure on state budgets reduce the funding available for ESS in the MENA region. Additionally, many countries suffer organizational and management inefficiencies, leading to a high management risk and require the implementation of a thorough reform roadmap.

Heightened political risk and negative economic outlooks limit borrowing ability and hike debt servicing costs of many MENA countries, especially the ones plagued with high power outages. Whereas ESS creates an opportunity to stabilize the grid and displace some of the diesel generators' reliance in these countries, the MENA countries' typical high political and economic risks drive up the risk premiums and cost of financing.

In addition to credit and financial risk, lenders consider ESS financing to be nascent and the cash flow is volatile. All this increases the cost of financing and requires direct governmental interventions. Yet most states also face pressure on their budgets. These budgets are further strained by the fossil fuels and electricity subsidies, exceeding $50 billion annually. As electricity tariffs typically do not reflect the actual cost of recovery, the cost of ESS will have to be borne by the utilities, and consequently by the governments, given electricity utilities in MENA are mostly state-owned enterprises.

Partnerships between the public and private sectors and international financing institutes will therefore be critical in securing flexible financing for energy storage projects. Eliminating the electricity subsidies to achieve a cost-reflective tariff and a time-of-use tariff will also be essential for the viability of ESS projects. A share of the subsidies could be redirected for the establishment or funding of green financing facilities. Energy storage systems should also be established as technologies eligible for funding within green financing facilities, to further catalyze private investments. Such funds could cover renewable energy, plus small-scale storage systems or micro-grids for rural areas and municipalities in countries with elevated power shortages.

On the regulatory front, MENA countries have not yet issued any definition or laws governing ESS. The deployment targets for renewable energy focus on the generation side and do not so far account for storage. Although some auctions have focused on ESS or solar plus storage, a regulatory framework and specific targets are lacking. Some of the regulatory challenges that have risen in countries that have a higher deployment of ESS have included the absence of clear indication of whether ESS assets are considered as part of the generation, transmission, or distribution sectors, which impacts the mandates of utilities that are not vertically integrated. Although more than 60 percent of electricity utilities in the region are vertically integrated, the majority of utilities have plans to unbundle. Therefore, a comprehensive regulatory framework with a clear definition and categorization of ESS is required.

Moreover, the net-metering scheme over a flat tariff, enacted in many MENA countries, limits the deployment of ESS as consumers lack any incentive to install BTM ESS, except in countries where the grid is unreliable. Through the net-metering scheme, consumers can offset their electricity consumption from the utility by injecting any surplus of electricity generated on-site through a renewable energy system. While this scheme has encouraged the deployment of small-scale renewable energy systems across countries such as Saudi Arabia, Jordan, and Lebanon, once the share of renewable energy in the power mix is significant a revision of the scheme would be necessary. The Hawaiian model could serve as a potential model, where re-injecting up to 60–70 percent of the generated power would be approved. This would maintain the promotion of small-scale renewable energy while also encouraging the adoption of distributed energy storage.

Lastly, MENA power markets are characterized by the single-buyer model, which hinders investments in energy storage projects. This model restricts the revenue-stacking business model necessary for the economic viability of ESS. Private sector participation in the power sector has mostly been on the generation sector through independent power producers since the largest share of power investments happen in this sector. This has increased competition and presents an opportunity to drive cost-competitive ESS projects in front-of-the-meter schemes.

Conclusion

The current rate of growth in electricity demand in MENA is unsustainable and driving a race for power generation capacity. Additional capacity must, however, be paired with improvements in energy efficiency and a power-rationing strategy for peak periods. The race to add power generation capacity to meet the growing demand is increasingly incorporating renewable energy investments.

The deployment of variable renewable energy systems, such as solar and wind, creates a set of challenges for power grid stability. Curtailment, low flexibility and limited capacity, non-reliability and losses, low access in rural areas, and under-investment all pose challenges for Middle Eastern countries to integrate renewable energy into the grid on a larger scale.

Investments in grid infrastructure, including transmission and distribution networks, substations, and transformers, need to be significantly ramped up to address the challenges of renewable energy integration and mitigate potential power supply disruptions.[26] Significant investments in system flexibility, scalability, and energy storage systems are needed, as the current mechanisms to balance the supply and demand in power generation do not rise to the needs of the complex modern power systems.

In addition to grid expansions, power systems of the future will have to rely on connectivity to enable a smoother integration of renewable energy and enhance energy security, grid stability, and flexibility across the region. Connectivity is critical for the region's power systems, especially given that peak demand varies from one country to another, allowing greater benefits. The MENA region has three sets of grid interconnections. In their current business-as-usual scenario, these grid interconnections serve as an aversion mechanism for power outages, ensuring continuous supply across connected countries. Yet, there are several advantages to enhancing interconnections utilization if countries can overcome the financial and structural barriers and develop a regional trading mechanism.

Meeting the national renewable energy targets also requires the deployment of energy storage systems as these systems manage the intermittencies of variable renewable energy resources. The pace of deployment, however, will be driven by the prospects of policy support, incentives, and eliminating financial and regulatory barriers.

Bibliography

Al-Aqeel, Turki, and Shahid Hasan, 2020. 'Energy Exchanges on the GCCIA Interconnector'. King Abdullah Petroleum Studies and Research Center, Riyadh: KAPSARC.

Al-Wesabi, Ibrahim, Fang Zhijian, Chukwunonso Philip Bpsah and Hanlin Dong, 2022. 'A review of Yemen's current energy situation, challenges, strategies, and prospects for using renewable energy systems'. *Environmental Science and Pollution Research*, 29, 53907–53933.

Arab Petroleum Investments Corporation, 2021. *Leveraging Energy Storage Systems in MENA*. Dammam: APICORP.

Arab Petroleum Investments Corporation, 2022. *MENA Energy Investments 2022–2026*. Dammam: APICORP.

Bellini, Emilio. 'Jordan suspends renewables auctions, new licenses for projects over 1 MW'. *PV Magazine*, 28 January 2019. Available online: http://surl.li/blkfz.

General Electric, 2021. *Pathways to Faster Decarbonization in the GCC's Power Sector*. https://www.ge.com/content/dam/gepower-new/global/en_us/

downloads/gas-new-site/future-of-energy/whitepaper-pathways-for-decarb-
GEA35042-.pdf

Gianfranco, Chico, 2009. 'Electricity Market Evolution in Europe.' *Scientific
Bulletin of the Electrical Engineering Faculty*, 2, 13–22.

International Energy Agency, 2021. *Electricity Market Report: January 2021*.
Paris: IEA.

International Energy Agency, 2021. *World Energy Outlook 2021*. Paris: IEA.

International Renewable Energy Agency. 'Five Reasons why Countries in the
Region are Turning to Renewables.' IRENA, 20 October 2019. Available
online: https://www.irena.org/newsroom/articles/2019/Oct/Five-Reasons-
Why-Countries-in-the-Arabian-Gulf-are-Turning-to-Renewables.

International Renewable Energy Agency, 2021. *Renewable Energy Statistics 2021*.
Abu Dhabi: IRENA.

International Renewable Energy Agency, 2022. *Renewable Energy Statistics 2022*.
Abu Dhabi: IRENA.

National Academy of Engineering and National Research Council, 2010. *The
Power of Renewables: Opportunities and Challenges for China and the United
States*. Washington, D.C.: The National Academies Press.

Sedaoui, Radia, 2022. 'Energy and the Economy in the Middle East and North
Africa,' in role="initials">M. Hafner and role="initials">G. Luciani (eds),
The Palgrave Handbook of International Energy Economics, 667–691. Cham:
Palgrave Macmillan.

World Bank Group, 2018. *Beyond Scarcity: Water Security in the Middle East and
North Africa*. Washington D.C.: World Bank.

World Resources Institute, 2015. *Ranking the World's Most Water Stressed
Countries in 2040*. https://www.wri.org/insights/ranking-worlds-most-water.
stressed-countries-2040

7 GREEN HYDROGEN PRODUCTION IN NORTH AFRICA: CHALLENGES AND OPPORTUNITIES

Michaël Tanchum

Introduction

North Africa boasts the world's greatest potential to produce green hydrogen. With green hydrogen forming one of the main pillars of the European Union's (EU) strategy for a transition to a carbon-free economy, the prospect of green hydrogen exports to Europe from the nearby nations of North Africa has catalyzed initial exploration into developing green hydrogen production capacity in the region. Morocco and Egypt have emerged as regional leaders in the sector, but have done so by following a pathway that differs from the initial exploratory efforts. Distinct from the development aid framework that has typified much of Europe–North Africa relations, the success of Morocco's and Egypt's respective efforts derive from the use of foreign private sector partnerships to establish a viable, home-grown model for the commercialization of green hydrogen.

The EU formally adopted its hydrogen strategy for a climate-neutral Europe in 2020, but Europe–North Africa joint efforts to develop production capacity began several years earlier, with Germany's green hydrogen diplomacy spearheading the effort.[1] Having pledged €7 billion for domestic green hydrogen projects, Germany also invested €2 billion in hydrogen exports from abroad.[2] While providing an initial catalyst, these efforts have been conducted primarily in an outmoded development aid framework. In contrast, private sector partnerships now form the leading edge of green hydrogen development in both Morocco and Egypt, providing a pathway for each country to use green hydrogen in its own value-added manufacturing as well as selling it as an export commodity. The key to this breakthrough has been each country's robust fertilizer industry and the production of green ammonia, a green hydrogen derivative, to service the fertilizer sector. While being an input for fertilizer production and thus providing an immediate market outlet for local off-take, green ammonia also serves as a cost-effective way to store and transport green hydrogen for export for other uses.

Using green ammonia as the basis for developing a green hydrogen production sector is proving successful for Morocco, which has no domestic natural gas resources, as well as for Egypt, which is Africa's second largest natural gas producer. Egypt, in contrast to Algeria, does not possess an extensive natural gas pipeline network to Europe. From the outset, Egypt needed to develop a non-pipeline transport option and the enormous energy requirements for hydrogen liquefaction put liquified hydrogen beyond commercial feasibility. As will be shown, green ammonia has proven to be a conducive option for gas-rich Egypt. Algeria, Africa's largest natural gas producer, will likely have to adopt a modified version of Egypt's model to get its floundering green hydrogen sector off the ground. For Tunisia, which has no significant hydrocarbon reserves, Morocco's example provides a commercially viable pathway for the country to develop its embryonic green hydrogen sector with great export potential.

Why green hydrogen? Why North Africa?

Hydrogen (H_2) is an energy carrier that can be used directly as fuel, an input to industrial manufacturing process and products, or as an energy storage system. Typically, hydrogen is produced cost-effectively from natural gas through a process called steam methane reforming (SMR), in which methane reacts with pressurized high temperature steam. However, carbon dioxide (CO_2) is also produced from the process, contributing to climate change and earning hydrogen produced by SMR the label 'gray hydrogen.' When a carbon capture mechanism is employed to lower the carbon footprint of the process, the output is referred to as 'blue hydrogen.' In contrast to natural gas-derived hydrogen, green hydrogen is produced by using electricity generated from renewable sources to split water (H_2O) into its hydrogen (H_2) and oxygen (O) components, creating a versatile, carbon-free (hence, 'green') energy carrier.

In addition to its use as a green fuel for shipping and freight transportation, green hydrogen can reduce the carbon footprint of industrial manufacturing processes such as steel production by being used as a feedstock fuel. Most importantly, green hydrogen can serve as an energy storage system for renewable energy sources such as solar and wind power whose production is variable according to the hours of daylight or wind available. The electrolysis process that produces hydrogen can be reversed in a fuel cell providing electric current by recombining hydrogen and oxygen into water. Hydrogen potentially can provide an alternative technology, alongside utility-scale batteries, for storing energy produced by renewable sources and then deploying it when needed.

North Africa is awash in abundant solar energy resources to create green hydrogen. Large swathes of the region possess the world's largest photovoltaic (PV) power potential and concentrated solar power (CSP) potential,[3] boasting direct normal irradiation (DNI) levels reaching or exceeding 2,300kWh/m².[4] By comparison, the most sun-drenched parts of southern Germany reach only half that DNI level, with most of the country receiving even less solar irradiation.[5] The high DNI region of North Africa includes the Sahara Desert and comprises 3.5 million square miles (9 million square km). Just slightly smaller than the total area of the United States of America, it receives the world's highest levels of solar irradiation and has the abundant open land necessary to host the distributed infrastructure required by solar power generation. The solar energy that hits the Sahara, were it all converted into usable power, could produce 7,000 times the electricity required to power Europe over any given period.[6] In addition, North Africa has ample onshore wind power resources, as well as offshore wind resources from Morocco's Atlantic coast to Egypt's coasts along the Gulf of Suez, that could also be used for the production of green hydrogen.[7]

In the previous decade, the idea of harnessing North Africa's renewable resources for export gave birth to the ambitious Desertec project. Initiated in Germany in 2009, the visionary project sought to create solar and wind power facilities across a 6,500 square mile area of North Africa, along with the requisite trans-Mediterranean electricity interconnection to supply about 15 percent of Europe's electricity demand. The ill-fated project, however, collapsed in 2014.[8] Despite involving public–private partnerships, the project evolved out of a development aid framework and was not sufficiently attuned to the economic and political needs of the region. It also raised concerns about the emergence of a green energy neo-colonialism. Desertec's demise dampened enthusiasm for trans-regional renewable energy transmission, calling into question its commercial feasibility.

Nevertheless, Morocco and Egypt continued with their plans to construct large, utility-scale solar and wind power facilities, providing the foundation for these two countries to become the trailblazers in North Africa's emerging green hydrogen industry. Morocco, which was the first entrant into green hydrogen production, has no significant hydrocarbon energy reserves at present. Reliant on gas and coal imports, Morocco has a strong economic imperative to replace its use of fossil fuels with renewable energy and green hydrogen. Egypt, by contrast, is Africa's second largest natural gas producer, with an annual output of about 59 billion cubic meters (bcm) per year.[9] With the discovery of major offshore natural gas reserves in 2015, Egypt has devoted considerable resources to developing its natural gas sector and gas-fired power plants to ensure the country's energy security. In 2019, thanks to production from its large offshore natural gas deposits, Egypt achieved natural gas self-sufficiency and became a net energy exporter in the form of liquified natural gas (LNG).

The anticipation of natural gas self-sufficiency spurred Cairo's concurrent advances in developing renewable energy resources. During the same timeframe in which Egypt developed the Zohr offshore natural gas field and installed the gas-fired power plants, it also built the massive Benban solar park outside of Aswan.[10] One of the world's largest operational PV solar parks, the $4 billion solar complex has an installed capacity of 1.8 GW.[11] Egypt also installed its largest wind power generation complex, the 262.5MW Ras Ghareb wind farm near the Gulf of Suez.[12] The Benban solar park and the Ras Ghareb wind farm combined are equivalent to around 16 percent of Egypt's surplus power generation capacity. By developing natural gas in conjunction with renewables, Egypt had reversed its 6GW electricity generation capacity deficit and turned it into a surplus of 13GW by 2020.[13] Egypt's example demonstrates the compatibility between developing natural gas and renewable energy resources in tandem, providing a model for how a gas-rich economy can develop green hydrogen.

While Morocco and Egypt represent different pathways for the development of green energy, these distinct pathways share a common element that has proven crucial for the initiation of green hydrogen production: both nations have highly developed fertilizer manufacturing sectors. Synthetic fertilizers commonly use ammonia (NH_3) as an input, which forms the source of nitrogen in the mineral nitrogen fertilizers used to boost crop yields. Fertilizer production accounts for about 70 percent of global ammonia consumption.[14] While the nitrogen is sourced from the air, the hydrogen used for ammonia production is primarily gray hydrogen produced from natural gas. Morocco and Egypt's fertilizer industries have incentivized the development of green hydrogen production capacity through production of its derivative green ammonia. With a guaranteed domestic offtake option, green ammonia has emerged as a preferred end-product of green hydrogen production. Moreover, green ammonia is one of the most cost-effective ways to store green hydrogen. While green hydrogen can be transmitted through natural gas pipelines, trans-Mediterranean pipeline export faces formidable technological and economic challenges that renders its commercial viability questionable. Throughout the remainder of the decade, green ammonia is likely to be the dominant form of transport green hydrogen from North Africa.

Morocco's green ammonia breakthrough

Morocco's development of its green hydrogen sector is intimately connected with the production of the derivative green ammonia to supply its fertilizer industry. The enormous production capacity and international reach of Morocco's fertilizer industry has made the Kingdom the world's fourth largest fertilizer exporter, following Russia, China, and Canada.[15] Operated by the state-owned company OCP (formerly Office Chérifien des Phosphates), Morocco's fertilizer sector specializes in the production of phosphorus fertilizers, as Morocco possesses over 70 percent of the world's phosphate rock reserves from which the phosphorus used in these fertilizers is derived.[16] In 2020, OCP's total revenue amounted to $5.94 billion,[17] accounting for about 20 percent of the Kingdom's export revenues.[18]

While Morocco has ample sources of phosphorus, its lack of natural gas is a limiting factor on its fertilizer production. Natural gas is not only a manufacturing power source for fertilizer production but also a constituent component of the nitrogen-rich ammonia needed to make phosphorus fertilizers. Diammonium phosphate or DAP ($NH_4)_2(HPO_4$), the most popular type of phosphorus fertilizer worldwide, is comprised of 46 percent phosphorus and 18 percent nitrogen.[19] It is produced by causing a reaction between phosphoric acid (H_3PO_4) and ammonia (NH_3). The gray hydrogen used to make ammonia is derived from natural gas, meaning natural gas accounts for at least 80 percent of the variable cost of the fertilizer.[20] By November 2021, the spike in natural gas prices prior to the Russia–Ukraine war saw the cost of producing ammonia rise to $1,000 per ton compared to $110 earlier in the year.[21] Accordingly, the price of DAP rose to its highest level in ten years.[22]

With Morocco's scant natural gas resources, OCP imports 1.5 to 2 million tons of ammonia per year.[23] Instead of importing ammonia synthesized from gray hydrogen, Morocco could synthesize green ammonia from green hydrogen produced from its domestic renewable energy resources. The bulk of green hydrogen's production costs, about 70 percent, come from the electricity required to split water into its hydrogen and oxygen components and could be powered by Morocco's solar energy resources. In 2018, OCP signed a cooperation agreement with a German research organization, the Fraunhofer Institute, Europe's largest applied science research institute, to develop a green hydrogen manufacturing project in Benguerir in partnership with the Moroccan Institute for Research in Solar Energy and New Energies (IRESEN).[24] The project would replicate the Fraunhofer Institute's pilot plant in Germany but with the addition of a green ammonia synthesis unit. OCP has invested $200 million in the pilot plant with annual production capacity of 1,460 tons of green ammonia.[25] OCP projects that green ammonia production could be scaled up from the pilot plant to reach 600,000 tons per year and is eyeing European and other export markets in addition to satisfying its input production requirements.[26]

Upon Germany's promulgation of its 'German National Hydrogen Strategy' in June 2020, Morocco became the first country to sign a green hydrogen agreement with Berlin to create Africa's first industrial plant for green hydrogen production using Morocco's solar power infrastructure.[27] Within the framework of that agreement the Moroccan Agency for Solar Energy (Masen), Morocco's privately-owned, publicly-funded integrated renewable energy projects company, undertook the creation of a 10,000-ton-per-year green hydrogen production facility financed by the German development bank KfW.[28] Masen spearheaded the development of Morocco's massive Noor solar power complex, the world's largest solar power facility, having received €830 million (about $934 million) in German financing facilitated by KfW, which amounts to 41.5 percent of the investment total.[29]

However, both the IRASEN and Masen projects have faltered following Morocco's March 2021 suspension of diplomatic relations with Germany over Berlin's stance on the issue of the contested Sahara region, forcing both projects to come to a virtual standstill. The new government that came to power in Germany in December 2021 under Chancellor Olaf Scholz repaired the breech in February 2022, paving the way for the August 25, 2022 visit to Rabat by German Foreign Minister Annalena Baerbock, during which she highlighted cooperation in renewable energy as a primary focus.[30] Although progress on the German green hydrogen projects will likely resume, now the leading project in Morocco is an $850 million green ammonia plant being developed by the Ireland-headquartered hydrogen technology firm Fusion Fuel using its HEVO proprietary technology with the Athens-based Middle East construction firm Consolidated Contractors Company building the installation.

Morocco announced the launching of its HEVO Ammonia Morocco project in July 2021, three months after the rupture in relations with Germany. Morocco's largest green ammonia and green hydrogen project to date, the HEVO facility is slated to produce 183,000 tons of green ammonia per year by 2026, equivalent to about 10 percent of OCP's 2021 production input requirements. The global energy and commodity trading giant Vitol has signed a memorandum of understanding (MoU) to manage offtake from the HEVO project to market green ammonia in Europe and other nearby markets.[31] On August 25, 2022, Netherlands-based green ammonia company Proton Ventures secured financing from a Dutch investment firm to build a green ammonia plant in Jorf Lasfar port.[32] The Netherlands is the world's second largest food exporter and a large consumer of fertilizer. The investment was backed by a loan guarantee from the Dutch credit export agency Atradius DSB. The pilot green ammonia plant will have an annual production capacity of 1,460 tons, the same as the stalled Fraunhofer Institute project.[33]

For Morocco, as throughout water-depleted North Africa, water is potentially a limiting factor for green hydrogen production. The electrolysis process used to produce green hydrogen by splitting water into its oxygen and hydrogen constituents requires 9 kilograms of water for every kilogram of hydrogen.[34] Morocco's phosphate and fertilizer industry consumes about 1 percent of its water.[35] According to OCP, the fertilizer manufacturing giant met 31 percent of its water needs with unconventional water resources, including treated wastewater from Khouribga, Benguerir, and Youssoufia, the three cities near which 92 percent of OCP's mining operations are located, as well as desalinated seawater from the Jorf Lasfar and Laayoune desalination plants.[36]

Another significant source of competing demand pressure for water is Morocco's high-value agricultural export sector, advanced by Rabat's 2010–2020 Green Morocco Plan (Plan Maroc Vert, PMV). As a result of the PMV, Morocco's agri-food sector now accounts for 21 percent of its exports.[37] Morocco is expanding on its PMV with a new 10-year initiative called Green Generation 2020–2030, which is intended to enhance the resilience and sustainability of the country's agricultural production.[38] To attain these goals, Morocco will need to mitigate its vulnerability to the impact of climate change and the increasing prevalence of drought. Morocco's National Water Plan 2020–2050, which envisages the construction of desalination plants as well as other measures to promote sustainable agriculture and the preservation of ecosystems, is estimated to cost approximately $40 billion.[39] Morocco's growing reliance on sea water reverse osmosis (SWRO) desalination plants to satisfy industrial, agricultural and residential needs will require sizeable new investments in power generation from renewable energy sources, as SWROs require ten times the amount of energy to produce the same volume of water as conventional surface water treatment, creating another form of demand competition over renewables with green hydrogen.[40] To expand its green ammonia production, Morocco will need to increase its power generation from renewable energy sources while carefully balancing the requirements of its fertilizer agricultural export sector and the need to provide sufficient and affordable drinking water to its population.

How quickly Morocco replaces the gray ammonia in its fertilizer manufacturing with climate-friendly green ammonia will depend on the extent to which Rabat prioritizes exports of green hydrogen over domestic manufacturing use. Ultimately, the sustainability of Morocco's fertilizer industry will require considerable capital expenditures to develop its nascent green hydrogen sector and the additional power generation capacity from renewable energy sources that it requires.

Egypt's expanding green hydrogen horizons

Egypt's nascent green hydrogen industry, as in the case of Morocco, is primarily focused on green ammonia. Egypt is the world's seventh largest ammonia producer, just behind Saudi Arabia, which is the largest Middle Eastern producer.[41] Already a major gray ammonia producer, Egypt can utilize part of its existing ammonia storage and transportation infrastructure for green ammonia. As such, green ammonia is likely to form a central part of Egypt's low carbon hydrogen strategy for both domestic use and exports.

Egypt is expected to officially announce its national low-carbon hydrogen strategy sometime before the November COP 27 climate summit, which it is hosting.[42] While Cairo has already made a commitment to reducing its carbon footprint, reducing the amount of natural gas required for its domestic ammonia production will also free up more natural gas to be sold more lucratively as LNG. In early March 2022, the European Bank for Reconstruction and Development (EBRD) signed an MoU with Egypt to provide guidelines for the country's low-carbon hydrogen strategy to promote cost-effective green hydrogen production and export.[43] In 2021, Cairo had already set into motion a few initial green hydrogen projects, and the EBRD will assess these initial projects as well as potential hydrogen production in Egypt, valuating the storage and transportation of hydrogen and its derivatives.

In March 2021, Egypt signed an agreement with the Belgian conglomerate DEME, already involved in Egypt's Mediterranean port capacity expansion, to conduct feasibility studies for the production and export of green hydrogen.[44] DEME, which offers expertise in offshore oil and gas production as well as offshore wind power production, will reportedly be involved in determining the optimal locations for hydrogen production hubs.[45] Locating Egypt's green hydrogen facilities is a critical task. Although water consumption accounts for only a small share of the total cost of green hydrogen production, the supply of water as an input is a critical issue in Egypt where water is a highly scarce resource. Egypt's average annual rainfall is only 33.3 mm, about five time less than what Morocco receives.[46] Given its high evaporation rate and lack of permanent surface water across large swaths of its territory, water resource availability is a perennial challenge for Egypt. It relies on the Nile River to provide approximately 90 percent of its freshwater consumption of about 65 billion cubic meters (bcm),[47] around 80 percent of which is used in agriculture.[48]

Egypt cannot easily afford to divert significant volumes of its scant freshwater resources for green hydrogen production. Egypt's estimated 2019 'gray' hydrogen production totaled 1.82 million tons.[49] To produce this amount as green hydrogen would require approximately 16.22 million cubic meters (mcm) of water. To use seawater as an alternative would require desalination since seawater would damage the electrolyzers used for green hydrogen as well as produce chlorine as a by-product. Using desalinated seawater for green hydrogen production means that Egypt's new facilities would need to be located near the coast, requiring the expertise of a company like DEME, a world leader in dredging and coastal marine infrastructure.

One of Egypt's most promising green hydrogen projects will be constructed on the western shore of the Gulf of Suez. The Norwegian renewable energy company Scatec and Dutch-Emirati fertilizer producer Fertiglobe have partnered with the Sovereign Fund of Egypt and the Egyptian construction giant Orascom to build a green hydrogen facility in the industrial zone of the Red Sea port of Ain Sokhna, near Fertiglobe's subsidiary Egypt Basic Industries Corporation (EBIC).[50] The facility's 100MW polymer electrolyte membrane electrolyzer will be one of the world's largest upon the plant's expected inauguration of operations in November 2022.[51] As majority stakeholder, Scatec will build and operate the Ain Sokhna facility with Fertiglobe enjoying a long-term off-take agreement for the plant's green hydrogen output as a feedstock for EBIC's green ammonia production.[52]

Furthering Egypt's ambitions to become a green hydrogen hub, the Egyptian Electricity Holding Company (EEHC) signed an MoU in August 2021 with Siemens, which built the country's gas power plants, to jointly develop a hydrogen-based industry in Egypt with export capabilities, intended to maximize hydrogen production based on renewable energy sources.[53] The initial development phase will entail a pilot project with an electrolyzer capacity of 100 to 200MW, which

Siemens believes 'will help to drive early technology deployment, establish a partner landscape, establish and test regulatory environment and certification, setup off-take relations, and define logistic concepts.'[54]

However, for Egypt to replace its entire gray hydrogen production with domestically produced green hydrogen is a tall order in the near term. To do so, Egypt would need an estimated 21GW of electrolyzer capacity, or roughly 100 times the capacity currently under construction.[55] While Cairo builds up its green hydrogen capacity, it is likely to opt for a combination of green hydrogen and blue hydrogen. In July 2021, Italian energy major Eni, one of Egypt's leading natural gas partners, signed an agreement with EEHC to assess the technical and commercial feasibility to produce both green hydrogen and blue hydrogen.[56] In the case of blue hydrogen, Eni is eyeing the possibility of using Egypt's depleted natural gas fields for the storage of CO_2 produced by carbon capture. Egypt is currently the world's sixth largest producer of urea, also used in nitrogen-based fertilizers, and could relatively easily use the captured CO_2 for urea manufacture.[57]

Algeria: Green hydrogen pipedreams, blue and green ammonia realities

Despite its tremendous potential, Algeria's solar power sector is woefully underdeveloped, accounting for just 1 percent of the country's electricity generation.[58] Africa's largest natural gas exporter, Algeria's oil and gas sector accounts for 94 percent of its export revenues and dominates the economy.[59] Like other industries outside the hydrocarbon sector, the development of Algeria's solar power sector has been set back by institutional challenges that have hampered foreign private sector engagement.[60] Even if Algeria had the solar power generation capacity in place, the feasibility of its plan to ship hydrogen to nearby European markets through its existing network of undersea natural gas pipelines faces formidable technical and economic challenges.

When hydrogen is transmitted through long distance or undersea natural gas pipeline, which is composed of hard steel, the hydrogen molecules severely degrade the material and drastically reduce its useful lifetime. In contrast to larger natural gas molecules, the small hydrogen molecules can permeate the micro-fissures that develop in the pipe due to repeated changes of pressure.[61] The weld parts of the pipe are even more susceptible to the formation and expansion of micro-fissures. While natural gas pipelines typically have a methane (CH_4) emission rate of 3.5 percent,[62] the emission rate for the much smaller H_2 molecules will be significantly higher. The released hydrogen would have a global warming potential 7.9 times that of the CO_2 it is intended to replace.[63] Refurbishing the pipelines with sealants would significantly increase the cost of hydrogen shipments.

Beyond the pipeline material itself, the added compression costs to ship hydrogen through natural gas pipelines instead of the natural gas itself makes the transmission of questionable commercial feasibility. Being 8.5 less dense than natural gas, hydrogen is more difficult to move and therefore less energy efficient. For the same quantity of heat energy, hydrogen requires 200 percent more energy to compress as natural gas.[64] This means that compressors in the existing natural gas network would need to be replaced with units three times as powerful, with three times the suction displacement, and with special capabilities to prevent the smaller hydrogen molecules from leaking.[65] When combining the capital expenditures and operating costs of transportation alone, replacing Algeria's natural gas exports to Europe with green hydrogen would be over three times more expensive.

Much of Algeria's green hydrogen strategy was initiated within the framework of the German-Algerian Energy Partnership, signed in 2015, with its green hydrogen focus formally promulgated in December 2021.[66] On February 14, 2022, the German development agency Deutsche Gesellschaft für Internationale Zusammenarbeit (GIZ) published a feasibility study for a three-phased green hydrogen development program through 2050.[67] Conducted by the Algerian Ministries of Energy and Energy Transition along with the German Ministry of Economic Affairs and Energy, the study envisioned the transportation of Algerian green hydrogen to foreign markets starting between 2030 and 2040.[68] The study does not adequately address the technical and commercial challenges of pipeline shipments of green hydrogen. While the study does propose transporting a blend of 20 percent hydrogen and 80 percent natural gas, the blend would not sufficiently resolve the above-mentioned transportation problems, nor would it be entirely green. In fact, it would not be even 20 percent green. The proportion is by volume and contains only 86 percent of the energy content of the same amount of natural gas alone. With the 20–80 blend requiring 14 percent more of the blend to produce the same amount of energy as natural gas, the greenhouse gas reduction would be closer to 6 percent.[69] The actual reduction would likely be even smaller since the 20–80 blend would require 13 percent more energy to compress.[70]

Beyond its cooperation with Germany, Algeria's state-owned energy company Sonatrach has been working with Italy's Eni, its lead foreign partner in the oil and gas sector, to develop both blue and green hydrogen, with the former being of higher priority. In May 2022, Algeria's Ministry for Energy and Mines made clear the primacy of blue hydrogen in the short- and medium-term, declaring blue hydrogen as an important step toward the development of green hydrogen.[71] Amid Europe's urgent need to find new sources to replace its Russian natural gas supplies, Eni and Sonatrach signed an MoU on May 26, 2022 to accelerate the development of Algeria's natural gas fields. The MoU also included an agreement to conduct a technical and economic evaluation for a green hydrogen pilot project in the Algerian desert.[72] While a positive development, the MoU seemed also designed to deflect the criticism of green energy advocates within Europe over the expanded development of natural gas.

Even more than Egypt, Algeria has a robust oil producing sector, in addition to natural gas, which incentivizes the production of blue hydrogen, as captured CO_2 has been used for enhanced oil recovery for about fifty years. Sequestered CO_2 from blue hydrogen's carbon capture process will most likely be put to use for enhanced oil recovery, resulting in new CO_2 being vented into the atmosphere. While the CO_2 emissions are 12 percent lower than for gray hydrogen, recent research has shown that burning blue hydrogen results in 60 percent higher greenhouse gas emissions than diesel fuel.[73] Algeria's blue hydrogen production may be commercially beneficial for oil extraction, but it cannot be justified as an approach to climate change mitigation.

The revival of Algeria's fertilizer industry may be the most feasible way to advance green hydrogen production. Once a net exporter of fertilizer, Algeria is now a net importer of fertilizer, importing roughly 85 percent of its needs.[74] In 2018, fertilizer consumption for Algerian agriculture was 20.7 kilograms (kg) per hectare of arable land, compared to 44.2 kg in Tunisia and 74.9 kg in Morocco.[75] To help alleviate the problem, Sonatrach signed an agreement in 2018 with China's CITIC Construction to build a $6 billion integrated phosphate production complex, utilizing the country's own phosphate rock reserves. The mega-plant would see Algeria's annual phosphate output rise to 10 million metric tons, resulting in increased annual fertilizer output worth around $2 billion on global markets, while greater domestic use of fertilizer would lead to higher crop yields in the future.[76] Like Morocco, Algeria's phosphorous fertilizer production would benefit from green ammonia production, reducing the need for gray ammonia imports or additional gray ammonia production. Like Egypt, the natural gas not used for additional gray ammonia production could be lucratively exported as either piped gas to Europe or as LNG.

As in Egypt, water scarcity poses a challenge for green hydrogen development. Algeria has suffered from poor stewardship of its scant water resources. In 2012, its fresh groundwater withdrawal was 3 bcm, about double the annual recharge rate, and subsequently jumped to 8.1 bcm in 2017.[77] Algeria's inadequate water management has been exacerbated by faulty infrastructure that results in water transportation losses to urban areas of about 30 percent.[78] After Egypt, Algeria has the lowest annual rainfall in North Africa, registering 62 mm in 2021,[79] and Algeria's dams are heavily impacted by siltation and contamination. To increase its water supply, the government has turned to energy-intensive SWRO desalination technology and renewed its efforts to upgrade and develop seawater desalination plants. Algeria has eleven desalination plants spread over nine provinces and Algiers is in the processes of rehabilitating and upgrading four of them, with plans to build an additional three.[80] Any program to develop truly 'green' hydrogen in Algeria will need to ensure that the water produced from desalination or by some other means is also powered from renewable energy sources.

Tunisia: Modest beginnings, strong export potential

While Tunisia has a strong potential for green hydrogen production, the efforts to develop the sector have been rather limited and conducted mostly within a development aid framework. The effort is being led by TuNur, a Tunisian renewable energy developer founded in 2011. The company was created as a joint venture between Tunisian investment group Top Group and UK-based firm Nur Energie,[81] and was endorsed by the Desertec project.[82] The company is a key player in Tunisia's plan to achieve its goal of having expanding renewables make up 33 percent of its power supply mix by the year 2030, as opposed to the current 3 percent.[83] In December 2020, the Tunisian Ministry of Industry, Energy and Mines signed an MoU with the German Federal Ministry of Economic Cooperation and Development (BMZ) to help Tunisia advance its green hydrogen production capabilities.[84] Resulting in a $36 million grant for the development of a green hydrogen pilot project known as *Amun Vert*, the small scale plant is slated to produce 1,500 tons of green ammonia per year.[85]

At the end of 2021, GIZ published a study on the potential of Tunisia's hydrogen industry and found that the country displayed favorable conditions for the production and export of renewable hydrogen, but the study does not adequately address the challenges entailed with transmitting hydrogen through the undersea natural gas pipelines that connect Tunisia and Italy.[86] The economic logic for Tunisia to develop a green hydrogen industry through green ammonia and fertilizer production is more compelling. In October 2021, Tunisia could only satisfy 25 percent of its domestic fertilizer demand.[87] Replacing imported gray ammonia with locally produced green ammonia would boost Tunisia's domestic fertilizer industry. With a total population three times smaller than that of Morocco, Tunisia would be well-positioned also to develop an export industry for green ammonia.

Water scarcity poses a significant challenge for large-scale green hydrogen production in Tunisia, where about 80 percent of the nation's water resources are used for agriculture.[88] Plagued by drought, Tunisia's situation has been exacerbated by the poor stewardship of the country's scant water resources. In some areas of the country, as much as 50 percent of water is lost before reaching the tap due to poor water distribution infrastructure.[89] In September 2021, water volumes in Tunisia's dams stood at 730 mcm, down from 1.1 bcm during the same period in 2020.[90]

Tunisia's food and water problems are not insurmountable and would not preclude the development of a green hydrogen industry. However, the construction of new dams, irrigation systems, and desalination facilities, along with the additional power plants to run them, will all require significant capital investment. As elsewhere in North Africa, power from renewable energy sources for green hydrogen production will compete with the demand requirements for water desalination, upon whose output green hydrogen production would depend for sufficient water input. Beyond foreign investment partnerships, Tunisia's development of a green hydrogen industry will require expert policy planning and the good governance to implement the necessary measures. The need creates an opportunity for both Morocco and Egypt to engage Tunisia in the development of its green hydrogen sector along with their own foreign private sector partners.

A way forward for green hydrogen in North Africa

North Africa has a way forward for green hydrogen production as Morocco and Egypt are poised to see significant growth in green hydrogen production and exports throughout the decade. However, the manner in which the green hydrogen sector will grow will not mimic natural gas exports from North Africa to Europe. Large-scale, trans-Mediterranean pipeline shipments of green hydrogen to Europe are unlikely to occur in the near and medium term. The examples of green hydrogen development in Morocco and Egypt demonstrate that, regardless of whether there is an already existing natural gas sector, green hydrogen industries are catalyzed by the production of the derivative green ammonia to service local fertilizer sectors.

For North African nations, green ammonia is the most cost-effective way to store and transport green hydrogen. Replacing gray ammonia in domestic fertilizer production with green ammonia means that green hydrogen production has a guaranteed market for off-take from the outset. Additionally, green ammonia can be exported to Europe and other nearby locations for use in fertilizer production or other industrial processes in the receiving country. Exported green ammonia can also be converted back into hydrogen for use in fuel cells, as a fuel, or in industrial manufacturing. In the cases of Morocco and Egypt, such off-take agreements are already in place. Ammonia itself may eventually develop into a fuel for the shipping and land freight transportation sectors.

If Algeria opts to develop a green hydrogen sector, there is no model for shipping hydrogen through its natural gas pipelines that is commercially feasible given present technologies. Even shipping a blend of 20 percent green hydrogen and 80 percent natural gas through undersea pipelines is of questionable utility both economically and on the basis of the climate change mitigation. In the case of the latter, the 20–80 blend would be at most 6 percent green, not 20 percent, and may not reduce CO_2 emissions at all if a fossil fuel is used to power the additional compression required. Algeria would be well served by reviving its domestic fertilizer production sector through green ammonia production and Algeria's foreign partners concerned with climate change mitigation should incentivize policymakers in Algiers to move in this direction. Similarly for Tunisia, which has no significant hydrocarbon reserves but is a pipeline transit state from Algeria to Italy, green ammonia production would be one of the best ways to jump start the development of its green hydrogen sector. Given the much smaller size of Tunisia's population and therefore its need for green ammonia for domestic fertilizer production, Tunisia could relatively easily develop a green ammonia export sector. Given their successful experiences, Morocco and Egypt themselves have an opportunity to engage Tunisia in developing its green hydrogen sector, promoting the needed expansion of economic cooperation among North Africa nations themselves.

Although green hydrogen production requires relatively little water as an input, water scarcity in each of the four countries is a challenge, although not an insurmountable one. With each of the four nations of North Africa needing to increase its water desalination capacity, there will be a demand competition between green hydrogen and desalination for power generation from renewable energy sources. Morocco and Egypt have shown that private sector partnerships and joint ventures will play an important role in the development of green hydrogen production and in the expansion of solar and wind power generation capacity it requires. The region's international partners can play a useful role by facilitating such private sector partnerships and joint ventures. Ultimately, effective governance by each nation to carry out the required measures to develop the necessary infrastructure will determine the success of the efforts to develop green hydrogen production in North Africa.

Bibliography

'Algeria's Expensive Water Problem.' Stratfor, January 20, 2016. https://worldview.stratfor.com/article/algerias-expensive-water-problem; 'Aquastat.' Food and Agricultural Organization of the United Nations.

'Algeria Average Precipitation.' Trading Economics, n.d. https://tradingeconomics.com/algeria/precipitation.

'Algeria: A Desert Nation Fighting to Maintain Water Supplies.' Stratfor, January 20, 2016. https://worldview.stratfor.com/article/algeria-desert-nation-fighting-maintain-water-supplies.

Ali Habib and Moustefa Ouki. 'Egypt's Low Carbon Hydrogen Development Prospects.' Oxford Institute for Energy Studies, November 2021. https://

a9w7k6q9.stackpathcdn.com/wpcms/wp-content/uploads/2021/11/
Egypts-Low-Carbon-Hydrogen-Development-Prospects-ET04.pdf.

'Ammonia production worldwide in 2021, by country.' Statista, January 2022.
https://www.statista.com/statistics/1266244/global-ammonia-production-
by-country/.

Andrew James Schunke, German Alberto Hernandez Hererra, Lokesh Padhye,
and Terri-Ann Berry, 'Energy Recovery in SWRO Desalination: Current
Status and New Possibilities.' Frontiers, April 3, 2020. https://www.frontiersin.
org/articles/10.3389/frsc.2020.00009/full.

'Benban Solar Park.' NS Energy, n.d. https://www.nsenergybusiness.com/
projects/benban-solar-park.

Christina Brooks, 'Germany leads pack of countries pouring finance into
hydrogen.' IHS Markit, March 24, 2022. https://cleanenergynews.ihsmarkit.
com/research-analysis/germany-tops-table-of-states-pouring-finance-into-
hydrogen.html.

Deutsche Gesellschaft fur Internationale Zusammenarbeit (GIZ) GmbH, 'Study
on the Opportunities of "Power-to-X" in Tunisia'. GIZ. https://energypedia.
info/images/0/0c/Potential_Study_PtX_in_Tunisia_2021.pdf.

EcoConServ Environmental Solutions, 'Benban 1.8GW PV Solar Park Final
Report.' New and Renewable Energy Authority, February 2016. https://www.
eib.org/attachments/registers/65771943.pdf.

'Egypt 6th in world in urea production, produces 7.8M tons of nitrogen
fertilizers.' Egypt Today, December 28, 2021. https://www.egypttoday.com/
Article/3/111326/Egypt-6th-in-world-in-urea-production-produces-7-
8M#:~:text=CAIRO%20%2D%2028%20December%202021%3A%20
Egypt,production%20with%206.7%20million%20tons.

'Egypt cooperates with Belgian "DEME" to start producing, exporting green
hydrogen.' Egypt Today, March 4, 2021. https://www.egypttoday.com/
Article/3/99297/Egypt-cooperates-with-Belgian-DEME-to-start-producing-
exporting-green.

'Egypt to launch $40bn hydrogen strategy before June 2022.' Energy and
Utilities, January 31, 2022. https://energy-utilities.com/egypt-to-launch-
40bn-hydrogen-strategy-before-news116149.html.

Egypt Today staff, 'Egypt eliminates power outages, exports the surplus.' Egypt
Today, December 27, 2021. https://www.egypttoday.com/Article/3/111287/
Egypt-eliminates-power-outages-exports-the-surplus#:~:text=CAIRO%20
%2D%2027%20December%202021%3A%20Egypt's,capacity%20of%20
the%20High%20Dam.

Embassy of Algeria to Croatia, 'Hydrogen Production: Algeria in a Position to
Play Leading Regional Role.' Embassy of Algeria in Croatia. https://www.
ambalgzagreb.com/hydrogen-production-algeria-in-position-to-play-
leading-regional-role/.

European Commission, 'A Hydrogen strategy for a climate-neutral Europe.'
European Commission, July 8, 2020. https://ec.europa.eu/energy/sites/ener/
files/hydrogen_strategy.pdf.

European Training Foundation. 'Summary Note – The future of skills: A case study of the agri-food sector in Morocco.' Europen Training Foundation, 2021. https://www.etf.europa.eu/en/publications-and-resources/publications/future-skills-case-study-agri-food-sector-morocco.

Federal Ministry for Economic Affairs and Energy, 'The National Hydrogen Strategy.' Federal Republic of Germany, June 2020. https://www.bmwk.de/Redaktion/EN/Publikationen/Energie/the-national-hydrogen-strategy.pdf?__blob=publicationFile&v=6; MAP, 'Morocco, Germany Sign Green Hydrogen Cooperation Agreement.' Kingdom of Morocco. June 10, 2020. https://www.maroc.ma/en/news/morocco-germany-sign-green-hydrogen-cooperation-agreement.

Federal Ministry of Economic Cooperation and Development, 'Promoting Renewable Energies, Launching an Energy Transition.' BMZ. https://www.bmz.de/en/countries/tunisia/core-area-responsibility-for-our-planet-climate-and-energy-100138#:~:text=%22Green%22%20hydrogen&text=In%20December%202020%2C%20the%20BMZ,pilot%20projects%20in%20that%20field.

'Fitch Revises Outlook on OCP to Stable; Affirms at "BB+".' Fitch Ratings, October 28, 2020. https://www.fitchratings.com/research/corporate-finance/fitch-revises-outlook-on-ocp-to-stable-affirms-at-bb-28-10-2020.

German-Algerian Energy Partnership. 'Étude Exploratoire sur le Potentiel du Power-to-X (Hydrogène Vert) pour l'Algérie.' German-Algerian Energy Partnership. https://www.energypartnership-algeria.org/fileadmin/user_upload/algeria/21_12_07_Hydrog%C3%A8ne_vert_en_Alg%C3%A9rie_-_Rapport_PE.pdf.

German-Algerian Energy Partnership, 'The German-Algerian Energy Partnership.' The German-Algerian Energy Partnership. https://www.energypartnership-algeria.org/home/.

'German foreign minister visits Morocco after diplomatic row.' Deutsche Welle, August 25, 2022. https://www.dw.com/en/german-foreign-minister-visits-morocco-after-diplomatic-row/a-62923298.

GIEWS – Global Information and Early Warning System, 'Country Profile – Tunisia.' Food and Agriculture Organization of the United Nations, July 27, 2022. https://www.fao.org/giews/countrybrief/country.jsp?code=TUN.

IEA, 'Ammonia Technology Roadmap towards more sustainable nitrogen fertilizer production.' International Energy Agency, 2021. https://iea.blob.core.windows.net/assets/6ee41bb9-8e81-4b64-8701-2acc064ff6e4/AmmoniaTechnologyRoadmap.pdf.

Ines Magoum, 'Algeria: 4 Desalination Plants to be Reactivated between June and August 2021.' Afrik 21, June 18, 2021. https://www.afrik21.africa/en/algeria-4-desalination-plants-to-be-reactivated-between-june-and-august-2021/; Ines Magoum, 'Algeria: Three Seawater Desalination Plants to be Constructed Soon.' Afrik 21, May 12, 2020. https://www.afrik21.africa/en/algeria-three-seawater-desalination-plants-to-be-constructed-

soon/#:~:text=In%20Algeria%2C%2011%20seawater%20desalination,of%20
drinking%20water%20consumed%20nationally.

IRENA, 'Energy Profile – Algeria.' International Renewable Energy Agency,
August 24, 2022. https://www.irena.org/IRENADocuments/Statistical_
Profiles/Africa/Algeria_Africa_RE_SP.pdf

James Burgess, 'Blue hydrogen 20% worse for GHG emissions than natural gas
in heating: study.' S&P Global, August 12, 2021. https://www.spglobal.com/
commodityinsights/en/market-insights/latest-news/natural-gas/081221-
blue-hydrogen-20-worse-for-ghg-emissions-than-natural-gas-in-heating-
study.

Jean Marie Takouleu, 'Egypt: Belgium's Deme signs with the authorities for green
hydrogen studies.' Afrik 21, March 8, 2021. https://www.afrik21.africa/en/
egypt-belgiums-deme-signs-with-the-authorities-for-green-hydrogen-
studies/.

Julie Chaudier, 'Will Hydrogen fuel Morocco's industrial projects of the future?'
The Africa Report, September 6, 2021. https://www.theafricareport.
com/124184/will-hydrogen-fuel-moroccos-industrial-projects-of-the-future/.

Julien Wagner, 'Morocco's OCP – A big, green mining machine.' The Africa
Report. March 7, 2019. https://www.theafricareport.com/413/mining-a-big-
green-mining-machine/.

Lahcen Mokena, 'Morocco's King Launches "Green Generation 2020–2030".'
Asharq Al-Awsat, February 15, 2020. https://english.aawsat.com/home/
article/2132676/moroccos-king-launches-green-generation-2020-2030.

Layli Foroudi, 'Thirsty crops, leaky infrastructure drive Tunisia's water crisis.'
Reuters. November 1, 2019. https://www.reuters.com/article/us-tunisia-
water-land-feature-trfn-idUSKBN1XB2X.1

role="initials">M. Garside, 'Phosphate rock reserves worldwide in 2021. by
country.' Statista, March 15, 2022. https://www.statista.com/statistics/681747/
phosphate-rock-reserves-by-country/.

MAP, 'Head of Government: 2020–2050 National Water Plan, Roadmap to Face
Challenges for Next 30 Years.' Kingdom of Morocco, December 25, 2019.
https://www.maroc.ma/en/news/head-government-2020-2050-national-
water-plan-roadmap-face-challenges-next-30-years.

Michael Barnard, 'CLEAN POWER: Paul Martin Talks H2 Science Coalition &
More Problems With Hydrogen.' Clean Technica. March 1, 2022. https://
cleantechnica.com/2022/03/01/paul-martin-talks-h2-science-coalition-
more-problems-with-hydrogen/.

Michaël Tanchum, 'Egypt's Prospects as an Energy Export Hub Across Three
Continents.' Istituto per gli Studi di Politica Internazionale (ISPI), September
24 2020. https://www.ispionline.it/en/pubblicazione/egypts-prospects-
energy-export-hub-across-three-continents-27408.

Michaël Tanchum, 'Morocco – a top fertiliser producer – could hold a key to the
world's food supply.' The Conversation – Africa, July 10, 2022. https://
theconversation.com/morocco-a-top-fertiliser-producer-could-hold-a-key-
to-the-worlds-food-supply-180797.

Michaël Tanchum, 'Europe–Africa Connectivity Outlook 2021: Post-Covid-19 Challenges and Strategic Opportunities.' Istituto Affari Internaionazionale (IAI), May 20, 2021. https://www.iai.it/sites/default/files/iaip2120.pdf.

Mohammed Abou Zaid, 'Egypt to Open its First Green Hydrogen Plant in November 2022.' Arab News, December 16, 2021. https://www.arabnews.com/node/1987996/business-economy.

Nibal Zgheib, 'EBRD assesses low-carbon hydrogen in Egypt.' European Bank for Reconstruction and Development. March 7, 2022. https://www.ebrd.com/news/2022/ebrd-assesses-lowcarbon-hydrogen-in-egypt.html.

Nicholas Nhede, 'Egypt's largest wind energy farm is now operational.' Smart Energy International, November 5, 2019. https://www.smart-energy.com/renewable-energy/egypts-largest-wind-energy-farm-is-now-operational/.

Nicola Warwick, Paul Griffiths, James Keeble, Alexander Archibald, John Pyle, and Keith Shine. 'Atmospheric implications of increased Hydrogen use.' Government of the United Kingdom. April 2022. https://assets.publishing.service.gov.uk/government/uploads/system/uploads/attachment_data/file/1067144/atmospheric-implications-of-increased-hydrogen-use.pdf.

OCP, 'Sustainability Report 2020.' OCP, August 2021. https://ocpsiteprodsa.blob.core.windows.net/media/2021-08/OCP-Sustainability_report_2020-GRI_certified.pdf.

OCP, 'Sustainability Report 2020.' OCP; OCP, 'Industrial operations,' OCP, n.d., https://www.ocpgroup.ma/industrial-operations.

Oliver Ristau, 'Solar power from the desert.' KfW, October 27, 2021. https://www.kfw.de/stories/environment/renewable-energy/solarstrom-aus-der-wueste/.

Paul Martin, 'CLEAN POWER: Is Hydrogen The Best Option To Replace Natural Gas In The Home? Looking At The Numbers.' Clean Technica, December 14, 2020. https://cleantechnica.com/2020/12/14/can-hydrogen-replace-natural-gas-looking-at-the-numbers/.

Press Release, 'Eni signs an agreement to produce hydrogen in Egypt.' Eni, July 8, 2021. https://www.eni.com/en-IT/media/press-release/2021/07/cs-eni-firma-accordo-produzione-idrogeno-egitto.html.

Press Release, 'New agreement reached by SONATRACH and Eni to accelerate the development of gas projects and decarbonization via green hydrogen.' Eni, May 26, 2022. https://www.eni.com/en-IT/media/press-release/2022/05/new-agreement-eni-sonatrach-gas-development-green-hydrogen-draghi-tebboune.html.

Press Release, 'Scatec partners with Fertiglobe and the Sovereign Fund of Egypt to develop green hydrogen as feedstock for ammonia production in Egypt.' Scatec, October 14, 2021. https://scatec.com/2021/10/14/scatec-partners-with-fertiglobe-and-the-sovereign-fund-of-egypt-to-develop-green-hydrogen-as-feedstock-for-ammonia-production-in-egypt/.

Press Release, 'Scatec's Green Hydrogen Consortium in Egypt selects Plug Power for delivery of 100 MW Electrolyser.' Scatec, November 24, 2021. https://scatec.com/2021/11/24/scatecs-green-hydrogen-consortium-in-egypt-selects-plug-power-for-delivery-of-100-mw-electrolyser/.

Press Release, 'Siemens Energy supports Egypt to develop Green Hydrogen Industry.' Siemens Energy, August 24, 2021. https://press.siemens-energy. com/mea/en/pressrelease/siemens-energy-supports-egypt-develop-green-hydrogen-industry.

Rebecca R. Beswick, Alexandra M. Oliveira, and Yushan Yan, 'Does the Green Hydrogen Economy Have a Water Problem?' *CS Energy Letters* 6 (9): 3167–3169. https://pubs.acs.org/doi/10.1021/acsenergylett.1c01375.

Renewable Centre for Renewable Energy and Energy Efficiency, 'New MOU Signed for the Establishment of a Tunisian-German Green Hydrogen Alliance (Power-to-X).' Renewable Centre for Renewable Energy and Energy Efficiency. https://www.rcreee.org/news/new-mou-signed-establishment-tunisian-german-green-hydrogen-alliance-power-x.

Reuters Staff, 'Desertec shareholders jump ship as solar project folds.' Reuters, October 14, 2014. https://www.reuters.com/article/germany-desertec/desertec-shareholders-jump-ship-as-solar-project-folds-idUSL6N0S535V20141014.

Rianne, 'UM6P and Proton Ventures sign an agreement for the construction of the Green Ammonia Pilot in Jorf Lasfar.' Proton Ventures, July 25, 2021. https://protonventures.com/press-release/um6p-and-proton-ventures-sign-an-agreement-for-the-construction-of-the-green-ammonia-pilot-in-jorf-lasfar/.

Ron Sterk, 'High fertilizer prices, tight supplies may adversely affect 2022 acreage.' FoodBusinessNews, December 12, 2021. https://www. foodbusinessnews.net/articles/20163-high-fertilizer-prices-tight-supplies-may-adversely-affect-2022-acreage.

Russ Quin. 'DTN Retail Fertilizer Trends.' Progressive Farmer, September 22, 2021. https://www.dtnpf.com/agriculture/web/ag/crops/article/2021/09/22/dap-fertilizer-tops-700-per-ton-time#:~:text=DAP%20prices%20increased%201%25%20to,the%20second%20week%20of%20Dec.

Ruth Sharpe, 'Morocco outlines plans for new green ammonia project.' Argus Media, July 20, 2021. https://www.argusmedia.com/en/news/2235820-morocco-outlines-plans-for-new-green-ammonia-project.

Samar Samir. 'Drought Fears Grow as Nile Talks Run On.' Egypt Today, October 3, 2020. https://www.egypttoday.com/Article/15/92628/Drought-Fears-Grow-as-Nile-Talks-Run-On.

'Standard Fertilizers.' OCP, n.d. https://www.ocpgroup.ma/standard-fertilizers.

'Statistical Review of World Energy 2021 | 70th edition.' BP, July 2021. https://www.bp.com/content/dam/bp/business-sites/en/global/corporate/pdfs/energy-economics/statistical-review/bp-stats-review-2021-full-report.pdf.

TAP, 'Water stock in dams down to 722.8 million cubic meters.' Agence Tunisie Afrique Presse, September 17, 2021. https://www.tap.info.tn/en/Portal-Economy/14394669-water-reserves-of.

Trevor Brown, 'OCP's Green Ammonia pilot plant, and the African Institute.' Ammonia Energy Association, August 17, 2018. https://www. ammoniaenergy.org/articles/ocps-green-ammonia-pilot-plant-and-the-african-institute-for-solar-ammonia/.

Tunur, 'Tunisia Germany PtX Dialogue 30th June 2021: Green Hydrogen and Ammonia Opportunities in Tunisia.' Tunur. https://www.tunur.tn/wp-content/uploads/2021/06/TuNur-PtX-Dialogue-VF2.pdf.

Vanessa Szakal, 'Under the Tunisian Sun: Expanding Solar Energy Production for Auto Consumption and Export.' Nawaat, August 22, 2014. https://nawaat.org/2014/08/22/under-the-tunisian-sun-expanding-solar-energy-production-for-autoconsumption-and-export/#:~:text=%C2%ABThe%20DESERTEC%20Foundation%20is%20endorsing,model%2Dfor%2Dthe%2Drest.

Will de Freitas, 'Could the Sahara turn Africa into a solar superpower?' World Economic Forum, January 17, 2020. https://www.weforum.org/agenda/2020/01/solar-panels-sahara-desert-renewable-energy/.

World Bank, 'Middle East and North Africa.' Global Solar Atlas, October 23, 2019. https://globalsolaratlas.info/download/middle-east-and-north-africa.

World Bank, 'Algeria MPO.' World Bank, April 2022. https://thedocs.worldbank.org/en/doc/65cf93926fdb3ea23b72f277fc249a72-0500042021/related/mpo-dza.pdf.

World Bank, 'Egypt – Climate Risk Profile.' World Bank, 2020. https://climateknowledgeportal.worldbank.org/sites/default/files/2021-04/15723-WB_Egypt%20Country%20Profile-WEB-2_0.pdf.

World Bank, 'Fertilizer Consumption – Kilograms per Hectare of Arable Land.' World Bank. https://data.worldbank.org/indicator/AG.CON.FERT.ZS.

World Bank, 'Fertilizer Consumption (% of fertilizer production) – Algeria.' World Bank. https://data.worldbank.org/indicator/AG.CON.FERT.PT.ZS?end=2018&locations=DZ&start=1961&view=chart.

Xinhua, 'Algeria, China sign pacts ahead of 6-bln-USD mega phosphate project.' Xinhua, November 27, 2018. http://www.xinhuanet.com/english/2018-11/27/c_137633212.htm.

Yahya Benabdellah, 'Le projet pilote de production d'ammoniac vert ouvre de grandes perspectives pour le Maroc.' Medias24, September 4, 2022. https://medias24.com/2022/09/04/le-projet-pilote-de-production-dammoniac-vert-ouvre-de-grandes-perspectives-pour-le-maroc/.

PART THREE

CASE STUDIES IN THE ENERGY TRANSITION

8 QATAR'S LNG INDUSTRY IN THE AGE OF HYDROCARBON MARKETS: INSTABILITY AND ENERGY TRANSITION

Nikolay Kozhanov

Abstract

This chapter examines the challenges Qatar, as one of the leading LNG producers, faces from the aftermath of US shale revolution, ongoing global energy transition, the COVID-19 pandemic, and negative economic fallouts of Russia's war in Ukraine. The study will argue that the evolution of market fundamentals under the influence of these factors seriously affected Doha's interests as an LNG producer and forced Qatar and other natural gas producers of the Gulf to fight for their place in the market. The key research question of this chapter is about the depth of impact of the above-mentioned market changes on Qatar's natural gas sector and the geopolitics of Qatar's LNG exports.

Introduction

The high oil and LNG prices in 2021–2022 allowed the Qatari leadership not only to significantly increase the volume of budget earnings, but also to better understand the ongoing processes of market changes and confirm that Qatari development strategies are probably adequate to respond to the challenges posed by the global energy transition. As the analysis of the existing literature shows, not all researchers and policymakers understand the complexity of the nature of the fourth energy transition and the problems it poses for consumers and producers of traditional energy resources.

Many researchers simplify the situation and define the energy transition as a grand replacement of hydrocarbon resources in the energy sector with renewable energy sources.[1] Such a definition overemphasizes the environmental factor of the energy transition and can create a false feeling that the replacement of hydrocarbons with renewable energy sources is the main goal of the energy transition. Thus, some experts argue that the 'energy transition is [about] reducing our ecological footprints – we should stop wasting materials (food, water, etc.) and quit polluting the environment.'[2]

The definition of the energy transition given by the International Renewable Energy Agency (IRENA) somewhat improves the situation by saying that energy transition is 'a pathway toward transformation of the global energy sector from fossil-based to zero-carbon by the second half of this century. At its heart is the need to reduce energy-related CO_2 emissions to limit climate change.'[3] In other words, the use of renewable energy sources is only part of the energy transition, which is a complex combination of the processes of global transformation of energy systems, including the processes of decarbonization, energy efficiency improvement, digitalization, and reforming regulatory systems of energy trade (including through decentralization). However, this definition is also not complete.

In considering the fourth energy transition only as a response to the challenges posed by climate change, researchers miss the most important thing: this response not only affects all elements of the global energy system (production, transportation, and consumption), but also implies a global restructuring of society and the world economy based on the principle of sustainable development. This principle is a distinctive feature that distinguishes the current energy transition from all previous transformations of the energy market, such as the transition from the use of coal to the use of oil, during which the imperative was to increase energy efficiency and accelerate economic growth. The impact of the fourth energy transition on the development of the world economy and society may be even more profound than were previous transitions. According to Mills, the current energy transition 'is not simply the introduction of new technologies, but also involves the changes in markets, institutions and regulations that allow or are induced by technological changes.'[4]

The global scale of the upcoming changes inevitably affects the interests of hydrocarbon producing resources. According to researchers, in the medium- and long-term, adaptation to a new energy order will require Gulf Cooperation Council (GCC) oil and gas producers to:

- restructure their economies and revise their social contracts to withstand a decline in demand and prices for oil and gas resources;
- ensure the survival of their oil and gas industries;
- rebuild their energy systems for a lower carbon future; and
- cope with the growth of competition in traditional (Asian markets).[5]

Qatar is not an exception, given the key role hydrocarbons have played in its socioeconomic development and foreign policy.

The 'Saudi Arabia of gas'

The export of natural gas is centrally important for Qatar's economy. By 2022, natural gas represented Qatar's main and dominant export item. As of 2021, its trade was worth $53.4 billion (61 percent of the country's total exports, see Figure 8.1).[6] From 2016 to 2019, hydrocarbons exports (including oil) provided 55 percent of annual public revenues. Considering also the government's dividends from QatarEnergy,[7] this figure rises to approximately 82 percent.[8] The revenues generated from natural gas exports are the main source of funding for the development and diversification of the country's economy and provide Doha with the necessary financial reserves to address economic challenges.

Due to these revenues, Qatar is able to maintain a social contract that is typical for rentier states. The ruling elite of a country effectively buys the loyalty of its citizens, and can impose certain restrictions on political life, in exchange for expansive wealth transfers and social welfare spending. A high standard of living is ensured through the provision and

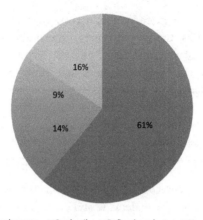

16%

9%

14%

61%

■ Natural gas, LPG, Condensates ■ Crude oil ■ Refined products ■ Non-hydrocarbon products

Figure 8.1 The structure of Qatar's exports, 2022 *Source:* Middle East Economic Survey.

distribution of direct and indirect subsidies. This expensive social contract between Qatari state and society is funded by oil and gas revenues.

The rentier social contract has drawbacks. It encourages the excessive domestic consumption of energy resources. This is an issue for most GCC states' budgets, as it limits the hydrocarbon resources available for export.[9] However, Qatar's small population, significant volumes of gas production, and the relatively unstable and slow pace of development of a petrochemical industry have allowed the Gulf state to avoid feeling major effects of internal consumption of natural gas on its export volume. Despite the fact that the domestic consumption of natural gas in the country almost doubled during the last decade, Doha natural gas export volumes were not significantly impacted. In fact, Qatar has maximized its foreign trade incomes even while maintaining the highest per capita energy consumption in the Middle East (see Figure 8.2).[10] Moreover, in August 2021 – April 2022, the consumption of the natural gas in Qatar was lower than in the previous years. Presumably, the substantial role in this was played by the speeded development of renewables and efficiency of energy consumption in the country.[11] Thus, in mid-2022 Qatar launched the Al Kharsaah solar PV plant, its first large-scale industrial solar project with the initial production capacity of 400MW (subsequently it will reach 800MW).[12]

In the eyes of the world, Qatar is distinguished from other Arab energy producers by the fact that it primarily exports natural gas, rather than oil. The emirate has the third largest natural gas reserves in the world after

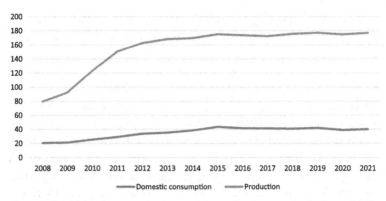

Figure 8.2 Natural gas production and domestic consumption in Qatar, 2008–2021 (bln cubic meters) *Source:* BP.

Russia and Iran,[13] and, as of 2022, was competing with the US for the title of the largest LNG exporter in the world.[14] Other GCC states do not have such significant export potential for natural gas, and oil is the main source of their income.[15] On the one hand, this adds to Qatar's uniqueness, forcing external players to consider it separately from other Gulf monarchies and see it as an actor whose importance for global gas markets is comparable with that of Saudi Arabia's for the global oil trade, leading some researchers to call Qatar the 'Saudi Arabia of gas.'[16] This comparison, although somewhat strained, reflects the essence: Qatar has compensated for its relative insignificance as an oil supplier by increasing its importance as a gas market player, which, from a geopolitical point of view, equates its weight with that of the Kingdom of Saudi Arabia (KSA). From an economic point of view, there is also a certain similarity between the two states in their ability to influence the situation in their respective markets. However, Qatar affects the market not by changing the volume of supply (i.e. it is not playing the role of 'swing producer' as Saudi Arabia does), but by changing the directions of exports (primarily between Europe and Asia) as needed to balance markets.[17] On the other hand, due to the secondary importance of oil incomes for its budget, Qatar is much less interested in coordinating its actions with the KSA and Organization of Petroleum Exporting Countries (OPEC) in the oil market like other Gulf monarchies, although it remains dependent on fluctuations in oil prices through long-term LNG export contracts that are bound to crude prices. This relative distance from oil prices led to the country's withdrawal from OPEC in 2018.

By now, it is generally accepted that Qatar's foreign policy is based on the principle of independence from its regional neighbors and on its ability to have strong political relations with players outside of the region.[18] In in the mid-1990s, the creation of LNG production capacities became a turning point in the history of the country – revenues from LNG exports ensured the financial wealth and, therefore, political independence of the country. Qatar's exit from the foreign policy guardianship of Saudi Arabia began when Khalifa bin Hamad Al-Thani (1995–2013) came to power as the new emir and accelerated the development of LNG capacities; exports began in 1997 and the new emir had the foresight to see them as the basis for the country's future independence.[19] Doha's attempts to influence regional developments during and shortly after the 2011 Arab Spring coincided with the moment when Qatar finally felt confident it could generate the necessary income to fund a more activist foreign policy. Moreover, Doha was seen to moderate its regional ambitions in 2014–2015, when oil and gas markets began to experience low prices under the pressure of changing fundamentals.

Natural gas and exported LNG not only allowed for Qatar's independent foreign policy, they also shaped the nature of the tools used for its conduct. Qatar's hydrocarbon export revenues are actively directed by the state to the needs of its soft power, which includes humanitarian diplomacy, promotion of Qatar as a brand, organization of sporting events, politically oriented investments, and direct financial injections into existing or potential partners of Qatar. The latter approach is often called 'checkbook diplomacy' by researchers.[20] It would be difficult to implement this policy without relying on gas revenues. The Qatar Investment Authority (QIA), established in 2005, helps Qatar to transform its hydrocarbon income into influence. By 2019, the QIA invested

in major European firms such as Porsche with 10%, Volkswagen Group, Siemens, Deutsche Bank, London Stock Exchange with 24%, Barclays and Harrods, Total, GDF Suez, France Telekom, and a 10% share in OMX, the Nordic Stock Exchange in Stockholm, are among Qatari investments along with several others in New York and Washington. A substantial stake of Qatar's investments is made in the Middle East as foreign aid in many countries like Libya, Tunisia, Morocco, Sudan, Eritrea, Indonesia which are crucial for development projects in infrastructure, health, energy and communication. Foreign investments have provided Qatar with substantial gravity in foreign policy, diplomacy, regional influence, and in branding Qatar.'[21]

In terms of the energy transition, natural gas also gives Doha a number of important advantages over the oil-producing giants of the Gulf. LNG and natural gas are considered as cleaner fuels, in terms of CO_2 emissions, compared to oil and can serve as a 'bridge fuel' while the world economy is transitioning to the mass use of renewable energy sources. In other words, natural gas is likely to remain widely used longer than oil will be as the energy transition proceeds. This is a controversial position, but Qatar is actively building its marketing company around it, branding LNG as one of the important elements of energy transition. Qatar has announced an ambitious program to reduce greenhouse gas (GHG) emissions during the production and transportation of natural gas.[22] Doha touts LNG as a pillar of the energy transition, when, in reality, a successful energy transition will harm the interests of both oil and gas producers. This branding effort is intended to ensure the survival (and prosperity) of Qatar throughout a global energy transformation. Qatar's other advantages going into an energy transition include the low cost of LNG production that is supported by revenues from associated petrochemical production; its advantageous geographical position on the map of Eurasia; its possession of its own fleet of LNG tankers; and substantial price and time flexibility with regard to contract terms offered to potential buyers.

However, the energy transition period will not be completely cloudless for Qatar. The country, like other energy producers, will inevitably face a number of challenges. The situation is aggravated by the fact that, in addition to changing energy consumption patterns that imply a greater role of renewables in the global economy, there are a number of other factors that significantly complicate the situation in the hydrocarbon markets and forecasting its development. The most obvious factor is Russia's invasion of Ukraine.

Putin's war in Ukraine and the interests of Qatar

Putin's invasion of Ukraine significantly impacted energy security in the Gulf region. In terms of its external dimension, the military conflict sharply focused the international community on security of energy supply. Western countries suddenly saw Gulf oil and gas producers as potential replacements for Russia at the European energy market and beyond. Russia's war in Ukraine presented the Gulf with a challenge, but also a rare opportunity.

High oil and gas prices, boosted by the Russian aggression against Ukraine, not only replenished Qatari coffers, emptied by the COVID-19 pandemic, they also positively affected Doha's macroeconomic growth indicators. The movement away from Russia as an energy supplier also encouraged service firms and international oil companies (IOCs) to reconsider their presence in the Gulf region, pushing them toward more active interactions with the local NOCs. Russia's withdrawal also provides opportunities in Europe for the regional gas producers. As demonstrated by Qatar's negotiations with European governments in mid-2022, Doha has seized upon the current crisis to negotiate a better position for itself in the market as it does not want to play the role of a fire brigade, which is called for a short time to deal with an emergency. However, this does not negate Qatar's interest in the European market in the long run, particularly if it could secure more favorable conditions, greater export capacities, and sustained demand (with specific emphasis on the long-term contracts). This may be what Qatari officials are suggesting when they say that ensuring European energy security goes beyond the Russian-Ukrainian conflict.[23]

Qatar's motivation is simple. Having almost no available (i.e. uncontracted) LNG volumes for export now, Doha may face an excess of them in the coming five years. Qatar anticipates not only a significant increase in production, from the current 77 to 127 million tons per year by 2027, but also the coming expiration of a number of supply contracts and the commissioning of the U.S. located Golden Pass natural gas liquefaction plant owned by QatarEnergy jointly with Exxon, in 2024–2025. Doha is already actively concluding new contracts with Asian consumers to ensure future demand on its gas, but they are not yet enough to cover Qatar's entire future volumes of LNG. Doha would also like to acquire extra leverages of political influence over the European countries. Thus, declaring itself as one of the guarantors of British energy security or promising gas to Germany, Doha is definitely strengthening its ties with these countries.

Given Qatar's preference to guarantee demand for its gas for years to come, the EU may soon get a chance to access more of the emirate's LNG.

Doha prefers to diversify supplies and is very flexible in its pricing policy (enabled by low-cost production), and the EU can get contracts on favorable terms – with one 'but.' Qatar believes that it is in a stronger negotiating position and will be able to sell its gas in any case. The above-mentioned fact that Qatar has not yet contracted all future volumes does motivate its leadership to look beyond Asia as a consumer market, but this does not mean that the Asian market ceases to be the main and desired target for Qatar's gas. The twenty-seven year long contract signed by Qatar and China in November 2022 on the supply of 4 million tons of LNG a year only proved to Doha that it simply needs more time and efforts to strengthen its already impressive positions in Asia.[24] Meanwhile, Europe is considered as plan B (if some LNG volumes somehow fail to find its place in Asia), with limited time and volume opportunities for Qatar's gas. Moreover, it is possible to assume that when discussing its gas supplies to Europe, Qatar keeps in mind not its own gas, but LNG to be produced at the Golden Pass facility. Consequently, Doha believes that it can demand more favorable conditions to increase its presence in the European market.

Doha put forward three key demands to the EU, which in many ways contradict the current philosophy of the European gas market.[25] Firstly, Qatar has asked that the EU prohibit the resale of supplied LNG outside Europe, to avoid it coming into competition with Doha's supplies to Asia or elsewhere. Secondly, Brussels is expected to close the investigations against Qatar's market policies in Europe started in 2018. Thirdly, Doha insists on trading on contractual principles, and not on the principles of spot trading. Regardless of what the EU chooses, Doha, at least, will not lose. If Europe agrees, Qatar will contract part of its LNG production capacity for the long-run and present the agreement as a negotiating achievement. If not, Doha may use the failure of negotiations as an excuse to Washington why Qatar could not help the Europeans. Events in the coming months may have a decisive, long-term impact on European energy security and Qatar's global LNG exports strategy.[26]

So far, Qatar's approach to negotiations with the Europeans has proved effective. The months since the beginning of the Russian invasion of Ukraine have shown that in Europe there is a queue of those who want to get access to Qatari gas. In this vein, the contract signed by Qatar in November 2022 with Germany for the purchase of 2 million tons of LNG for fifteen years (starting 2026) can be considered a serious achievement of Doha. Despite the fact that the volume of supplies itself is relatively small, the signing of the contract is a psychological victory for Qatar over supporters of energy transition in Europe, who previously considered it impractical to sign long-term gas supply contracts due to European hopes for an early transition to renewable energy sources. Doha was able to insist on the duration of the contract twice as long as Germany were rumored to be initially ready for.[27]

The impact of the Ukrainian crisis on the domestic energy and economic security of the Gulf states is not as positive as in the case of the external dimension. On the one hand, the rising importance of the Gulf adds extra importance to the issue of the hard security of Gulf oil infrastructure (although some forces in the region could exploit this dynamic for their own goals). On the other hand, the unwillingness of the Gulf producers to cooperate with consumers to slow down or reverse the growth of oil prices will lead consumers to alternative responses. This could result in a search for alternative suppliers outside of the Gulf.

The Gulf countries' economies have different levels of tolerance toward the negative outfalls of the war such as rising fuel prices, high inflation rates, and the growing cost of inputs. Yet, even the least vulnerable economies, such as that of Qatar, started to feel the negative pressure of rising fuel prices and energy costs. The high oil incomes also slow down the growth of the non-oil sector of the Gulf economies and reduce short-term incentives to implement diversification programs. In the long run, this impact will only be felt more deeply, potentially leading Gulf players to reconsider their market strategies.

Yet, the Russian war against Ukraine is not the only factor that sets out the backdrop for the ongoing energy transition. Qatar is still managing the fallouts of the shale revolution and COVID-19 pandemic.

The shale revolution and its implications for Qatar LNG

The roots of the gas market transformations that began in the late 2000s and hit the regional markets by the mid-2010s are connected to two factors: the impact of the U.S. shale revolution on the global hydrocarbon market and the beginning of the global energy transition to non-carbon fuels.[28] The shale revolution impacted both global oil and global gas markets. With the shale revolution, the United States not only became the largest producer and exporter of hydrocarbons, but also stimulated the emergence of new market players in other countries. Additionally, the rapidly developing U.S. LNG industry fueled by shale gas motivated even conventional gas producers, such as Russia, to increase their LNG production capacities. This inevitably led to the market oversupply and intensification of rivalry among the key players.

Given that Qatar's long-term LNG contract prices are bound to the fluctuation of oil prices, Doha was also sensitive to the changes in the oil market. Driven by the above-mentioned factors, the growth rates in global oil supply have been steadily surpassing growth in oil demand since 2011, causing the markets' oversupply in recent years. Due to the specifics of shale oil production, neither the 2014–2016 price war waged by the KSA nor subsequent OPEC+ efforts to regulate the market through the reduction of oil output could remove these extra barrels of supply. At the beginning of the pandemic, the global oil market was in this position of oversupply. In 2020, before the onset of COVID-19, supply was forecasted to surpass demand by 2 million barrels per day (bpd), making a fall in oil prices inevitable (although COVID-19 greatly amplified the scale). In other words, the market oversupply that created alternatives to the Gulf suppliers and made theories about the 'uniqueness' of hydrocarbons irrelevant to oil price formation emerged long before the coronavirus. The Arab monarchies have never fully recovered from the 2014–2016 fall in oil prices – the first in in history – caused by the flood of U.S. shale oil output. After 2014, growth rates in the GCC dropped significantly, occasionally demonstrating negative values, and the oil and gas incomes of the key players never fully recovered (see Table 8.1 and Figure 8.3).

The increased competition GCC producers faced was also a result of the ways the shale revolution changed hydrocarbon trade flows. The United States has ceased to be an importing market, becoming a competing exporter and diverting a significant portion of global hydrocarbon exports to Asia, also the main consumer market for GCC oil and gas producers. At the same time, the high sensitivity of shale oil production to oil prices shortened the duration of global oil price cycles and changed their amplitude: given the ability of shale oil producers to quickly increase output if encouraged by the positive market dynamics, oil prices are unable to rise very high or for very long, forcing the GCC countries to forget about the era of ultra-high incomes.

As a result, Qatar was caught in the grip of low prices and growing competition for markets. During the 2015–2020 period, Qatar felt

Table 8.1 *Real GDP growth of GCC member countries 2012–2022 (%)*

	2012	2013	2014	2015	2016	2017	2018	2019	2020	2021	2022[29]
Saudi Arabia	5.4	2.7	3.7	4.1	1.7	-0.7	2.4	0.3	-4.1	3.2	7.7
UAE	4.5	5.1	4.3	5.1	3.1	0.5	1.7	1.3	-6.1	2.3	4.2
Qatar	4.7	4.4	4	3.7	2.1	1.6	1.5	0.1	-2.7	1.5	3.4
Oman	9.1	5.1	1.4	4.7	4.9	0.3	1.8	0.5	-2.8	2	5.6
Kuwait	6.6	1.2	0.5	0.6	2.9	-4.7	1.2	0.7	-8.9	1.3	8.2
Bahrain	3.7	5.4	4.4	2.9	3.5	3.8	2	1.8	-4.9	2.2	3.3

Source: International Monetary Fund (IMF).

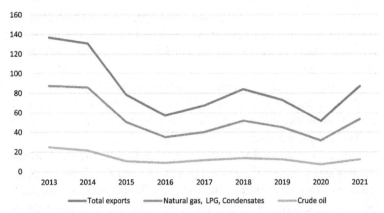

Figure 8.3 Qatar's export revenues, 2013–2021 (USD, bln) *Source:* Ingram, 'Qatar Export Revenues Surge Above $12bn'.

growing competition from the United States and Australia in its key Asian destination for the LNG exports (see Figure 8.4). However, this was not the only unpleasant consequence of the market changes.

Over the past fifteen years, there have been significant changes in the structure of LNG market leaders. If in 2010 the list of main LNG exporters included Qatar, Indonesia, Malaysia, Australia, and Nigeria, by 2019 the market leaders were distributed as follows: Qatar, Australia, the United States, Russia, and Malaysia. Qatar and Australia competed fiercely for their export opportunities, passing the title of top LNG exporter back and forth throughout 2019 and 2020.[30] This change was very significant for Qatar.

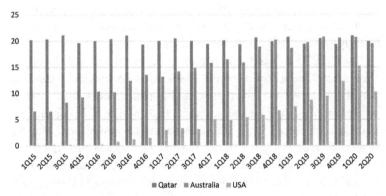

Figure 8.4 LNG exports by Qatar, Australia, and the USA to Asia in 2015–2020 (mln tons). *Source:* Zweiri and Al Qawasmi, *Contemporary Qatar*.

Doha is no longer competing with predominantly developing countries, as in 2010. Now, its main competitors are major political and economic leaders, including the United States – which has traditionally played the role of GCC security guarantor and whose companies are actively present in the emirate's economy, including its gas sector. In the 2000s, America was seen as an LNG importer and as market potential. Doha is inevitably forced to consider the potential political costs of the new field of competition.

The active development of LNG industries globally has made natural gas available to almost the entire world. Players must be flexible not only when signing new contracts, but also must flexibly balance their trade between long-term and spot deliveries. The growing geographical availability of LNG forces its producers to compete with pipeline suppliers. LNG prices are increasingly responding to market signals from the main centers of consumption, which means that sellers are increasingly becoming the price-accepting party. For decades, oil and gas markets were relatively dominated by producers (although the degree and nature of this dominance has been uneven for the last seventy years). Since the early-2010s, the market balance has been gradually shifting in favor of buyers. The shale oil revolution reduced the importance of hydrocarbons as a 'unique' resource, giving consumers the ability to choose among suppliers offering the cheapest price.

Qatar and other GCC countries were thrust into the position of needing to ensure their own sustainable access to markets, thus guaranteeing the adequate development of their own economies. As was mentioned before, the Ukrainian crisis has partially distorted this picture by raising the importance of suppliers. Yet, this situation is largely 'artificial,' driven by a fluid political situation. In the long run, price power is likely to return to the hands of consumers.

The COVID-19 pandemic that hit the region in 2020 only amplified the impact of those existing trends. The slowdown of the global economic activity deepened the oversupply of the hydrocarbons that, in turn, accelerated the fall of oil and gas prices in 2020. The global oil and gas glut, in turn, forced GCC countries to wage a severe price war for hydrocarbon market share. During the first six month of 2020, Qatar and Oman failed to offer competitive prices for their LNG supplies to the shrinking South Korean market. As a result, the volume of their exports fell by 24 percent and 10.5 percent respectively as compared with the same period of 2019. At the same time, Australia, the United States,

Indonesia, Malaysia, and Russia managed to raise their supplies to South Korea.[31] In Taiwan, Doha played differently. It managed to offer appealing prices and increased its export volumes in spite of the negative market conditions. Yet, its main competitors (Russia, the United States, and Indonesia) also managed to raise their exports at the expense of other players, making the gap between them and Qatar smaller.[32] The struggle within the GCC also escalated. Qatar's plans to increase the volume of LNG supplies and get involved in a price war for gas sales with the United States, Australia, and Russia may cause Oman to question whether its products can find a place in foreign markets.[33]

During the first year of the COVID-19 pandemic, the macroeconomic indicators of Qatar deteriorated significantly amid lower revenues caused by the plunge in oil prices and total war for market shares. The fall in oil and gas revenues accompanied by the need to support non-oil sectors hit by the global lockdown triggered a significant budget deficit.[34] Given the dominant role of government institutions in financing the country's economic development, reduction in hydrocarbon revenues inevitably slowed down the implementation of the key development programs. The pandemic also slowed down the development of the GCC oil and gas sector. National oil companies (NOCs), including QatarEnergy, were forced to revise their budgets and cut expenditures for 2020–2021.[35]

Yet, it appears unlikely that the end of the pandemic crisis and Putin's war in Ukraine will lead to a return to the pre-COVID-19 situation, when the problem of Gulf energy security was solely related to the stability of consumers' access to regional hydrocarbons. In the long run, the world is more likely to see relatively low oil prices, frequent market fluctuations, limited potential for growth in oil demand, and intense competition. Under these circumstances, the old rules will not work effectively, and the GCC countries should focus less on fighting the consequences of COVID-19 itself, and more on curbing the negative consequences of fundamental changes in energy markets, whose damaging impact on Arab exporters, including Qatar, was only worsened by the pandemic.

And yet, neither the COVID-19 pandemic nor the shale revolution should be considered an exceptional evil for Qatar and other producers of hydrocarbons from among the Gulf countries. The trials that fell to their lot allowed them to develop a certain behavior strategy that should help them prepare for the energy transition. In the case of Qatar, these measures included:

1 *Maximization of market share.* Doha's response to these challenges was to pursue a market strategy based on the principle of accelerated monetization of available natural resources in order to invest received revenues in the diversification of its own economy. On May 24, 2020, Minister of Energy and QatarEnergy's Chief Executive Officer Saad Al-Kaabi stated that his country not only does not intend to reduce gas exports to the market in order to maintain high prices for liquefied gas, but also considers it necessary to significantly increase production capacity, even if this will lead to a further glut of the market. Al-Kaabi argued that Doha is the most cost-effective gas producer in the world and can cope with market shocks. He added that many other manufacturers will be forced to curtail production due to low prices.[36] In other words, Doha declared its readiness to wage a price war against its opponents. Qatar has been preparing for this scenario for years. In 2017, the country lifted a moratorium on further development of the Northern Dome gas field, and since then has constantly revised its development plans to encourage additional production. QatarEnergy originally planned to increase its liquefaction capacity from 77 million tons per year to 100 million tons per year, but this figure was later increased. Currently, Qatar plans to reach 110 million tons per year output by 2025 and 126 million tons per year by 2027.[37]

2 *Improving the efficiency of the NOC business model.* The need to exist in new conditions forced the Qatari leadership to reconsider the role and place of the country's leading company – QatarEnergy – in the country's economy. In addition to strengthening the management vertical by merging it with other companies (primarily Qatargas), there was also a qualitative change in its role. If early on QatarEnergy acted as a locomotive for the creation of Qatar's economic infrastructure by co-investing various projects not always related to the energy sector, then its exit from non-core assets carried out in the 2010s allowed the company to be more focused on building the Qatari gas empire.

3 *Active interaction with traditional consumers in Asia* to ensure their long-term loyalty as consumers of oil and gas of the Persian Gulf countries, through active political contacts and investments in their petrochemical production. In 2020, the historical hike in

the volumes of Qatar LNG exported to China was determined by the entry into force of two new long-term contracts.[38]

4   *Active foreign investments in the extractive and processing sectors,* including investments in competitors (such as the U.S. shale industry).

5   *Investments in renewable and green energy.*

The strategy Qatar developed of dealing with its direct competitors represents an interesting case. Qatari leadership has clearly indicated its readiness to enter into a price war with competitors both in the LNG market and with those players who prefer pipeline gas exports. However, readiness for confrontation is only one element of the Qatari strategy. Qatar, according to Al-Tamimi, prefers to 'buy competitors' through the policy of active overseas investments in upstream and downstream sectors, including investments in rivals such as the U.S. shale industry.[39] Since the mid-2010s, Qatar actively expanded into the oil and gas sectors of Africa, Latin America, Asia, the EU, and the United States. The logic of the Qatari leadership is quite simple: through investments in various hydrocarbon producers, including its direct competitors, Qatar hedges risks by gaining access to alternative sources of income and also makes its competitors less interested in confrontation.

The American direction is particularly important for Doha. The United States is one of the main guarantors of the security of the Arab country, and competition with Washington for natural gas markets is highly undesirable for Doha. For this reason, Doha tries to focus on cooperation with the United States through mutual economic penetration. Over the years, American business, primarily represented by ExxonMobil, became the largest foreign participant in the development of Qatar's gas industry, and it will probably play a key role in to the current expansion of Qatar's production capacities. For example, ExxonMobil has a 10–30 percent share in twelve of Qatar's fourteen liquefied gas trains. It also helped Doha build a supply chain to Europe. While Doha has its own fleet of gas carriers, ExxonMobil is the largest co-owner of two LNG terminals in Italy and the UK, which are used by Qatar to unload consignments. The Adriatic LNG, with a capacity of 8 billion cubic meters per year, was purposely built to receive Qatari LNG.[40] This model of cooperation was later used by Qatar when, in 2021–2022, it was determining which foreign investors would participate in the development of its LNG production expansion. The preference was given to the Western companies that possessed a developed network of customers, in order to ensure demand on the new volumes of Qatari LNG.[41]

Meeting the Brave New World

So far, the Gulf Cooperation Council (GCC) hydrocarbon producers have received clear evidence that the era of oil and gas is far from over. The current crisis was the result of mistakes in assessments regarding the prospects of energy transition, as well as the speed of oil demand growth and global economic recovery. This has allowed Qatar and other hydrocarbon producers in the Gulf to argue that a hasty rejection of hydrocarbons is dangerous. They are right insofar that the energy transition will be a long and difficult process, aggravated by possible economic shocks if artificially accelerated.[42] The protracted period of energy transition also means the delayed onset of peak oil demand and allow time for hydrocarbon-producing countries to prepare for the moment when oil demand will decrease.[43] The new sustainable energy industry will need time to develop necessary infrastructure for production, transportation, storage, and marketing as well as solutions related to production costs (which are still quite high), global geographical availability of renewable energy, and emissions and environmental standards for clean energy technologies. Meanwhile, traditional fuels will remain in demand. Moreover, the rejection of oil and gas as feedstock for the petrochemical sector looks even more problematic than the rejection of the use of hydrocarbons for the production of transport fuels and electricity.

The energy transition is unlikely to entail a complete rejection of the use of hydrocarbons in favor of sustainable eco-friendly energy sources. Instead, at least at the initial stage, the energy transition will be more focused on how to increase the 'environmental friendliness' of traditional oil and gas extraction and processing. There is, in fact, no unanimity among experts on the long-term prospects of oil market. On the one hand, there are serious concerns that if further underinvested the oil sector could fail to meet existing demand.[44] On the other hand, the market might occasionally be oversupplied, encouraging greater competition among players.[45] Interestingly, the oversupply can be caused by both the slow-down in demand growth and by underinvestment. Thus, there is always a threat that excessive oil prices caused by the initial underinvestment of the oil sector can subsequently draw extra funds into the development of its production capacities creating, at a certain stage, disproportionate volumes of supplies.

In this regard, two more trends that emerged during the current crisis may be important for the Gulf oil and gas producers. First, there is a clear change in the market behavior of one of the main rivals of traditional oil production – shale producers. U.S. shale producers are abandoning their previously adopted principle of 'pumping as much as you can as fast as you can' in favor of a more restrained growth in production. This makes it possible to slow the onset of market oversaturation in 2022.[46] Second, the struggle for cost reduction will remain one of the main market trends determining hydrocarbon producers' survival. This trend is very well understood in the Gulf, and, as was mentioned before, Qatar is building its core strategy around the principle of the low-cost production.

In formulating strategies to develop the gas sector in this environment, Qatari leadership demonstrate greater order and calm than their Western counterparts. Qatar has maintained its focus on maximizing its production potential and strengthening the competitive advantages of its LNG sector. Qatar has built its development plans on two main principles. First, Doha believes that it still has time to adapt to the global energy transition agenda. Thus, while adopting plans on the development of the 'green economy,' Qatar is not in a hurry to implement them, focusing first on investing in the extraction of its natural gas resources. Second, Qatar sees the course to dominate the key hydrocarbon markets as long-term and unchangeable, and nothing should affect its implementation even and especially under the new conditions. In other words, Qatar plans to play the game for as long as oil and gas production can bring in income, even if markets are oversupplied and increasingly competitive.

Qatar is not, however, ignoring the energy transition. On the contrary, within the last two years Doha has substantially increased the pace of the implementation of its green agenda. From 2020 through 2022, the Qatari authorities formulated clear sustainability and green energy development goals for the government and the private sector. Moreover, compared to previous attempts to 'go green,' Doha made more substantial moves toward implementation, perhaps in an effort to shake any appearance of lagging behind Saudi Arabia and the UAE in the use of green technologies. QatarEnergy is not an exception. In 2021, it launched a new sustainability strategy (updated in March 2022) responding to the challenges of an energy transition and positing the company to remain a global energy leader. The document refers to the Qatar National Vision 2030, the United Nation's Sustainable Development Goals (SDGs) and Paris Agreement, while recognizing climate change mitigation as one of QatarEnergy's key priorities. The strategy itself is based on the principle of four 'Cs':

1 *Consolidation* of QatarEnergy's leading position in supplying LNG across the globe by increasing production to 126 million tons per annum by 2027, thus helping the world to replace high GHG-emitting energy sources such as oil and coal.

2 *Curbing* of emissions from the company's operations by flare reduction and energy efficiency improvements to drive down methane emissions.

3 *Creation* of low carbon energy by generating from 2 to 4 gigawatts of solar energy by 2030.

4 *Compensation* for residual emissions through the development of carbon capture and sequestration technology and its use at QatarEnergy facilities (the goal is to capture 7 to 9 million tons per year by 2030).[47]

In practical terms, Qatar sees the energy transition not only as a challenge, but an opportunity if approached correctly. First, it is approaching the transition as an opportunity to further diversify its economy and create new sources of income. In 2026, QatarEnergy plans to launch one of the world's largest blue ammonia production plants, with the output capacity of 1.2 million tons a year. This will not only bring Qatar onto the list of the main blue ammonia producers in the world but also allow Doha to catch up with Saudi Arabia and the UAE in a race for leadership in this new area.[48]

Second, renewables help Qatar manage the domestic consumption of gas resources and ensure that the energy sector and LNG production become more environmentally friendly. In 2022, Qatar declared it plans to launch in 2024 two solar plants in Mesaieed and Ras Lafan industrial areas, with a total production capacity of 875MW respectively. Both of them are to serve QatarEnergy, with the goal of reducing the company's GHG footprint.[49]

Third, in some cases, demonstrative support of energy transition ideas is also a convenient marketing move. In 2021, Qatar Petroleum noisily changed its name to QatarEnergy. The renaming became part of a public relations campaign to promote natural gas as a fuel that can be used during the global transition from the current 'dirty' fuels to the eco-friendly energy sources. At the same time, the trajectory of the company's development has changed little: the main plan of Doha remains to increase gas production in order to ensure its leadership in this market.

The 'energy transition agenda' in Qatar, for now, does not imply the replacement of the hydrocarbon sector with sustainable energy. Instead, it sees the new industry as a complement that allows both the diversification of the Qatari economy and the means of making LNG industries eco-friendly. As written by oil market analyst Tsvetana Paraskova, 'renewable energy could replace more and more fossil fuels in power generation and transportation, but these are not the only industries using oil and gas. From medicines to cosmetics, clothing, and technology, the world will still need oil' and gas.[50] This is well understood in Qatar. Like all GCC countries, it continues to implement its traditional plans for diversification, but with one amendment: a greater focus on the 'greening' of harmful industries by increasing the use of renewable energy sources and reducing the volume of emissions released by hydrocarbons production. In this regard, QatarEnergy is investing in carbon capture and storage (CCS) technology that is meant to reduce the carbon intensity of Qatar's LNG production and help the country reach its goal of cutting CO_2 emissions by 2030.[51] According to the QatarEnergy's sustainability strategy, by 2030 the company expects to:

- decrease its GHG emissions from LNG and upstream facilities by 25% and 15% respectively;
- capture 7–9 million tons of CO_2 a year;
- decrease methane leaks along the gas value chain;
- build renewable energy facilities with a generating capacity of 4GW; and
- stop routine gas flaring.

Additionally, by 2035, QatarEnergy plans to:

- reach 35% and 25% reduction in GHG emissions by the LNG and upstream facilities respectively;
- increase the CO_2 capturing capacity from 9 to 11 million tons a year; and

- generate more than 5GW of electricity from sustainable energy resources.[52]

The current crisis has shown that the future of the GCC countries and their oil and gas sector will not be without challenges. One of the main dynamics to manage will be the growing tensions in global energy markets, with elevated competition internationally and between the Gulf countries as well. The GCC hydrocarbon exporters will not be able to avoid competition with each other even as they attempt to diversify their economies, given similar directions for their exports, visions of sources to fund economic development, and ambitions regarding the markets of new energy resources.

However, the bigger challenge for the GCC countries will be managing growing tensions with hydrocarbon consumers. As the energy transition progresses and markets see frequent oversupply, demand rather than supply will play an increasingly important role in determining the dynamics of oil and gas prices.[53] Moreover, an attempt by producers to exert pressure on price changes by regulating production volumes will cause an increasingly sharp reaction from consumers. Under these circumstances, maintaining good relations with traditional energy consumers will become increasingly important for Qatar as a supplier, requiring more flexibility when signing long-term contracts and, potentially, moves to encourage 'demand growth' through investment in consumption infrastructure of oil and gas recipient countries.

The current energy market environment clearly highlights the urgency for Qatar to develop and implement a strategy to prepare for the energy transition era. Qatar's strategy thus far prioritizes maximizing LNG output and the preparing for increasing market competition as well as possible pressure from consumers. Money received from gas production will be used to ensure the further restructuring of the Qatari economy and develop renewable energy sources and carbon capture. However, in the long run, hydrocarbon production will remain the backbone of the Qatari economic model. Doha's aim is to shape its development plans so as to guarantee the longest possible profitability of the traditional gas sector. The success factors in this quest will probably be the low cost of LNG production, the reduction of harmful emissions from traditional industries, and the maintenance of the necessary level of investment in the gas sector and the new energy sources.

Conclusion

Since Qatar began exporting LNG in 1997, the quest for market supremacy has been vital for Doha's economic survival and political independence. Natural gas has never been just an export commodity for Qatar, but an enabler for the social and economic model. The threats posed by the transformation of the gas market to Qatari economic and political interests thus necessarily provoke a response. Doha's response was to maximize market share (and even to enter a price war). However, this approach is inevitably associated with the costs of competition with rivals, leading Qatar to hedge its risks with attempts to build long-term cooperation with consumers and producers of LNG.

On the consumer side, cooperation is prompted by the open question of who is going to buy the additional volumes of LNG that Qatar is set to produce by 2027. Doha must be more flexible with the terms of future long-term contracts in this environment. QatarEnergy is also developing its capacities to quickly react to price fluctuation by being able to direct more LNG exports toward more profitable spot and short-term markets.

Interaction with direct competitors also remains the important part of Qatar's strategy regarding producers, and it is largely determined by Qatar's status as a small state. Although Doha indicated its readiness to enter into a price war with LNG and pipeline players, it intends to fight only in extreme cases. Instead, Doha tries to 'buy competitors' through active foreign investment in oil, gas, and petrochemical industries of its rivals, including but not limited to the U.S. shale industry. Since the mid-2010s, Qatar has been expanding its presence in the oil and gas sector of Africa, Latin America, Asia, the EU, Russia, and the United States. The logic of the Qatari leadership is quite simple. By investing in various hydrocarbon producers, including its direct competitors, Qatar hedges risks by gaining access to alternative sources of income, and also makes its competitors less interested in confrontation and more likely to collaborate.

Meanwhile, it is still to be seen how the global energy transition affects Qatar's economy and LNG sector. Initial concerns that the support QatarEnergy has shown for the energy transition and sustainable development is just a convenient marketing move might fail the test of time. In 2021 and 2022 the company set the number of concrete development goals whose timely implementation may help QatarEnergy keep up with the main trends of the sustainable and green energy development. However, at least for now, the majority of these moves are aimed to strengthen the country's position in the regional LNG markets, rather than by real ecological concerns. All in all, QatarEnergy's response to the energy transition is based on the following four principles: (1) branding QatarEnergy as a company supporting the energy transition; (2) marketing LNG as a green fuel; (3) supporting the company's 'marketing' and 'branding' campaigns with practical steps aimed at the decrease of the company's negative ecological footprint; and (4) testing new low-carbon methods of energy production and transportation, including blue ammonia.

Bibliography

Ackerman, Wayne, 'Qatar and Global LNG: Potential Pivot from Asia to Europe.' Middle East Institute, February 22, 2022. https://www.mei.edu/publications/qatar-and-global-lng-potential-pivot-asia-europe.

Al-Tamimi, Nasser, *Navigating Uncertainty: Qatar Response to the Global Gas Boom* (Qatar: Doha Brookings Center, 2015).

Azhar, Saeed, 'Aramco to Cut Capital Spending Over Coronavirus; 2019 Profits Plunge.' Reuters, March 15, 2020. https://www.reuters.com/article/us-saudi-aramco-results/aramco-to-cut-capital-spending-over-coronavirus-2019-profits-plunge-idUSKBN21208C.

Bousso, Ron, 'Qatar Petroleum to Slash Spending by 30%.' Reuters, May 21, 2020. https://www.reuters.com/article/us-qp-spending/qatar-petroleum-to-slash-spending-by-30-ceo-idUSKBN22X2HA.

BP, *BP Statistical Review of World Energy, 2021* (London: British Petroleum, 2022).

Byrne, Megan, 'QatarEnergy and Conoco Phillips Sign Deal to Supply Germany with LNG.' Middle East Economic Survey, December 2, 2022. https://www.mees.com/2022/12/2/corporate/qatarenergy-and-conocophillips-sign-deal-to-supply-germany-with-lng/d5bb0170-7248-11ed-8440-7d1c9ee4b388.

Byrne, Megan, 'QatarEnergy Awards Contract for Two New Solar Plants.' Middle East Economic Survey, August 22, 2022. https://www.mees.com/2022/8/26/power-water/qatarenergy-awards-contract-for-two-new-solar-plants/25b5c950-2532-11ed-8c2e-335c44bd78ff.

Byrne, Megan, 'Qatar's Al Kharsaah Solar PV Plant Poised For Startup.' Middle East Economic Survey, April 8, 2022. https://www.mees.com/2022/4/8/power-water/qatars-al-kharsaah-solar-pv-plant-poised-for-startup/ed9e46c0-b736-11ec-920f-8d82a9909eba.

Byrne, Megan, 'Qatar Joins Solar Revolution with Al Kharsaah Start Up.' Middle East Economic Survey, July 29, 2022. https://www.mees.com/2022/7/29/power-water/qatar-joins-solar-revolution-with-al-kharsaah-start-up/95332d30-0f36-11ed-952a-2d7246524700.

Çavuşoğlu, Esra, 'From Rise to Crisis: The Qatari Leadership.' *Turkish Journal of Middle Eastern Studies* 1(7), 2020.

Chapa, Sergio, 'Qatar Reclaims Crown from the U.S. as World's Top LNG Exporter.' Bloomberg, May 2, 2022. https://www.bloomberg.com/news/articles/2022-05-02/qatar-reclaims-crown-from-u-s-as-world-s-top-lng-exporter.

'Climate Change Mitigation,' QatarEnergy, 2022. https://www.qatarenergy.qa/en/Sustainability/Pages/ClimateChangeMitigation.aspx.

Cochrane, Paul, 'Supertanker State: How Qatar is Gambling its Future on Global Gas Dominance. The Middle East Eye, July 2, 2020. https://www.middleeasteye.net/news/qatar-gas-lng-market-oil-prices-dominance.

Cockayne, James, 'Qatar and Oman Cash in as Asian LNG Buyers See Record Import Bill Even as Volumes Slump.' Middle East Economic Survey, July 29, 2022. https://www.mees.com/2022/7/29/opec/qatar-oman-cash-in-as-asian-lng-buyers-see-record-import-bill-even-as-volumes-slump/c51248c0-0f33-11ed-ba1e-31f3c9f8b155.

'Energy Transition: Definition and Solution,' METGroup, 29 July 2021. https://group.met.com/en/media/energy-insight/energy-transition.

GIIGNL, *Annual Report, 2020* (Paris: International Group of Liquified Natural Gas Importers, 2020).

Ingram, Jamie, 'Bahrain Advances Development of Huge Unconventional Reserves,' Middle East Economic Survey, May 29, 2020. https://www.mees.com/2020/5/29/oil-gas/bahrain-advances-development-of-huge-unconventional-reserves/88152130-a1ae-11ea-b099-934732bc3e53.

Ingram, Jamie, 'Kuwait Risks Exhausting Financial Reserves.' Middle East Economic Survey, May 15, 2020. https://www.mees.com/2020/5/15/news-in-brief/kuwait-risks-exhausting-financial-reserves/be312a90-96bf-11ea-9894-7d512e4a1b26.

Ingram, Jamie, 'Qatar Brings Major Players into LNG Expansion.' Middle East Economic Survey, June 24, 2022. https://www.mees.com/2022/6/24/corporate/qatar-brings-major-players-into-lng-expansion/ccc547a0-f3b6-11ec-b3ef-f9e8b796d0a2.

Ingram, Jamie, 'QatarEnergy Revenues Surge to Seven Year High.' Middle East Economic Survey, February 4, 2022. https://www.mees.com/2022/2/4/geopolitical-risk/qatar-export-revenues-surge-to-seven-year-high/f7845460-85d0-11ec-993b-910a64378c83.

Ingram, Jamie, 'Qatar 2018 Revenue Surge Finances Renewed Checkbook Diplomacy.' Middle East Economic Survey, February 1, 2019. https://www.mees.com/2019/2/1/geopolitical-risk/qatar-2018-revenue-surge-finances-renewed-checkbook-diplomacy/d72716c0-2635-11e9-a597-add92238b8b2.

Ingram, Jamie, 'Qatar Retakes Position as No1 Global LNG Partner.' Middle East Economic Survey, July 24, 2020. https://www.mees.com/2020/7/24/opec/qatar-retakes-position-as-no1-global-lng-exporter/31ce03f0-cdb1-11ea-af39-a55bdce6554b.

Ingram, Jamie, 'Qatar Launches "World's Largest" Blue Ammonia Project.' Middle East Economic Survey, September 2, 2022. https://www.mees.

com/2022/9/2/refining-petrochemicals/qatar-launches-worlds-largest-blue-ammonia-project/dcc199b0-2ab0-11ed-a8a5-913ffd3e63d0.

Ingram, Jamie, 'Qatar Export Revenues Surge Above $12bn.' Middle East Economic Survey, September 2, 2022, https://www.mees.com/2022/9/2/economics-finance/qatar-export-revenues-surge-above-12bn/4fod3570-2ab3-11ed-957d-895883ee6164.

IRENA, Energy Transition, IRENA, 2020. https://www.irena.org/energytransition#:⊠:text=The%20energy%20transition%20is%20a,emissions%20to%20limit%20climate%20change.

King, Llewellyn, 'Qatar Sees Green Role for LNG as World Gasps for More Energy.' Forbes, December 4, 2021. https://www.forbes.com/sites/llewellynking/2021/12/04/qatar-sees-green-role-for-lng-as-world-gasps-for-more-energy/?sh=4aff7066601c.

McKinsey, 'Global Oil Supply-and-demand Outlook to 2040.' Energy Insights, February 2021. https://www.mckinsey.com/industries/oil-and-gas/our-insights/global-oil-supply-and-demand-outlook-to-2040.

MEES, 'Korea 1H20 LNG Imports: Qatar Volumes Fall 24% as Australia Closes Gap to Top Supplier.' Middle East Economic Survey, July 17, 2020. https://www.mees.com/2020/7/17/selected-data/korea-1h20-lng-imports-qatar-volumes-fall-24-as-australia-closes-gap-to-top-supplier/445bcf20-c836-11ea-a60c-c59137220e53.

MEES, 'Taiwan 1H20 LNG Imports Qatar Volumes Rise 11% in 1H2020 but Share Down Marginally as Taiwan Diversifies Suppliers.' Middle East Economic Survey, July 17, 2020. https://www.mees.com/2020/7/17/selected-data/taiwan-1h20-lng-imports-qatar-volumes-rise-11-in-1h-2020-but-share-down-marginally-as-taiwan-diversifies-suppliers/55605ad0-c836-11ea-a79c-c757fd9b17ad.

Mills, Andrew, and El Dahan, Maha, 'Qatar Seals 27-year LNG Deal with China as Competition Heats up.' Reuters, November 21, 2022. https://www.reuters.com/business/energy/qatarenergy-signs-27-year-lng-deal-with-chinas-sinopec-2022-11-21/

Mills, Robin, 'A Fine Balance: The Geopolitics of the Global Energy Transition in the Middle East,' in M. Hafner and S. Tagliapietra (eds), The Geopolitics of the Global Energy Transition (Singapore: Springer, 2020), p. 116.

Mirzoev, Tokhir and Ling Zhu (eds), The Future of Oil and Fiscal Sustainability in the GCC Region (Washington: International Monetary Fund, 2020).

Paraskova, Tsvetana 'An Undisputable Truth: The World Still Needs Oil And Gas.' OilPrice, November 16, 2021. https://oilprice.com/Energy/Energy-General/An-Undisputable-Truth-The-World-Still-Needs-Oil-And-Gas.html.

Planning and Statistics Authority of Qatar, Qatar Economic Outlook, 2020–2022 (Doha: Planning and Statistic Authority of Qatar, 2019).

Podymov, Andrey, 'Gazoviy Katar [Qatar of Gas].' Voyennoye Obozreniye, June 3, 2020. https://topwar.ru/171776-gazovyj-katar-sovsem-ne-chert-iz-tabakerki.html.

Qarjouli, Asmahan, 'Qatar says it cannot fill Europe's gas supply alone amid Russia-Ukraine tensions.' DohaNews, February 2, 2022. https://dohanews.co/

qatar-says-it-cannot-fill-europes-gas-supply-alone-amid-russia-ukraine-tensions/.

'QatarEnergy Launches Updated Sustainability Strategy, Reiterates to Produce Clean Energy.' Qatar Tribune, March 8, 2022. https://www.qatar-tribune.com/article/230723/BUSINESS/QatarEnergy-launches-updated-sustainability-strategy-reiterates-to-produce-clean-energy.

Rystad Energy, 'Breakeven Price For New Oil Projects Drops In 2021.' OilPrice, November 17, 2021. https://oilprice.com/Energy/Crude-Oil/Breakeven-Price-For-New-Oil-Projects-Drops-In-2021.html.

Slav, Irina, 'Demand uncertainty could keep oil from breaking $100 – Oil & Gas Middle East.' Oil and Gas Middle East, November 18, 2021. https://www.oilandgasmiddleeast.com/news/demand-uncertainty-could-keep-oil-from-breaking-100.

'What is Energy Transition?', S&P Global, 24 February 2020. https://www.spglobal.com/en/research-insights/articles/what-is-energy-transition#:X:text=Energy%20transition%20refers%20to%20the,well%20as%20lithium%2Dion%20batteries.

Widdershoven, Cyril. 'The Energy Transition Will Be Impossible Without Fossil Fuels.' OilPrice, November 18, 2021. https://oilprice.com/Energy/Energy-General/The-Energy-Transition-Will-Be-Impossible-Without-Fossil-Fuels.html.

Zaremba, Haley, 'The Real Reason Big Oil Is Refusing To Boost Production.' OilPrice, November 18, 2021. https://oilprice.com/Energy/Energy-General/The-Real-Reason-Big-Oil-Is-Refusing-To-Boost-Production.html.

Zhdannikov, Dmitry, 'Qatar seeks EU guarantees emergency gas stays within EU.' Reuters, January 31, 2022. https://www.reuters.com/business/energy/exclusive-qatar-seeks-eu-guarantees-emergency-gas-stays-within-eu-source-2022-01-31/.

Zweiri, Mahjoob, and Farah Al Qawasmi, *Contemporary Qatar: Examining State and Society* (Singapore: Springer, 2021).

9 RENEWABLE ENERGY DIPLOMACY: THE GULF STATES IN THE CAUCASUS AND CENTRAL ASIA

Li-Chen Sim

Abstract

The global energy system is undergoing a transition away from a near-complete dependence on fossil fuels toward a greater reliance on low carbon and renewable energy sources. This chapter examines the foreign policy dimension of the energy transition by focusing on the activities of Gulf energy developers in the Caucasus and Central Asia (CCA). Section one provides a brief overview of Gulf power companies in solar and wind energy projects in the CCA. Sections two, three, and four assess the extent to which geopolitics, social license considerations, and profits respectively, motivate Gulf engagement. Section five concludes with the suggestion that the commercial rationale offers the most persuasive argument overall with regard to Gulf-CCA relations in renewable energy.

Introduction

The global energy system is undergoing a transition away from a near-complete dependence on fossil fuels toward a greater reliance on low carbon and renewable energy sources.[1] The process will be accompanied by increased electrification and digitalization across all sectors as well as decentralization and diversification of energy supply. Part of this agenda will be played out domestically in the adoption of enabling policies through command-and-control approaches and market-based instruments; at the same time, changes in the conduct of foreign relations will also occur at the bilateral, regional, and global scales.

This chapter focuses on the latter dimension of the energy transition to examine the drivers of renewable energy diplomacy of the Gulf states vis-à-vis the Caucasus and Central Asia (CCA). The region comprises three countries in the Caucasus – Georgia, Armenia, and Azerbaijan – and five in Central Asia – Kazakhstan, Kyrgyzstan, Tajikistan, Turkmenistan, and Uzbekistan. Though heterogenous, the CCA was selected as a case study for several reasons that will be developed subsequently: it boasts better than average wind and solar resources for renewable energy, demand for energy is increasing in contrast to countries in Europe, it has been identified as a target market by Gulf power developers, and there is a lack of published research on the Gulf's renewable energy diplomacy in CCA relative to other developing countries or sub-regions in the Middle East.

The chapter proceeds as follows. Section one provides a brief overview of Gulf participation in solar and wind energy projects in the CCA. Sections two, three, and four assess the extent to which geopolitics, social-environmental considerations, and profits, respectively, motivate the behavior of Gulf engagement in the CCA's renewable energy sector. Section five concludes with the suggestion that the commercial rationale offers the most persuasive argument, at least for the medium-term with regard to Gulf-CCA relations in renewable energy. Space constraints limit the discussion of renewable energy to wind, solar, and hydropower projects that augment the generating capacity of power plants; it excludes related processes essential to the uptake of renewable energy projects such as upgrading power transmission lines, reducing energy subsidies, improving energy efficiency, or building energy storage systems.

Gulf participation in renewable energy projects in CCA

The participation of the Gulf states in the deployment of renewable energy projects in the CCA has several features. First, the presence of the

Gulf states is spearheaded by 'national champions', namely ACWA Power (Saudi Arabia) and Masdar (Abu Dhabi), and to a smaller extent Nebras Power (Qatar). ACWA was founded by private Saudi investors in 2004 to explore opportunities offered by the restructuring of the Saudi electricity sector, whereby power generation and water desalination would be opened up to companies from the private sector. Its success caught the attention of the kingdom's sovereign wealth fund (SWF), the Public Investment Fund (PIF), which purchased a minority stake in 2013; today, that stake has increased to 50 percent. In contrast, Masdar and Nebras were created as fully state-owned entities, although their mandates are distinct. As its full name suggests, Masdar was specifically created in 2006 as a 'future energy company' to develop renewables; it is owned by three Abu Dhabi entities, namely the Mubadala SWF (its original owner), water and utilities company Taqa, and Abu Dhabi National Oil Company (ADNOC). As for Nebras, its mandate is to function as the overseas arm of the Qatar Water and Electricity Company, which remains its sole shareholder following the exit of Qatar's SWF in January 2022. Consequently, unlike ACWA or Masdar, Nebras has no domestic assets. Being the newest of the three entities, it is also the smallest with an asset portfolio of 6.5 gigawatts (GW) compared to Masdar's 23GW or ACWA's 42GW.

As corporate enterprises selected or created by their respective governments to represent a national effort to be internationally competitive, these three companies are typically granted privileged access to finance or policies to favor their growth. A case in point is ACWA Power's May 2021 framework agreement with PIF that gives the former the right to develop projects associated with 70 percent of the Kingdom's renewable energy targets. It is little wonder that the company self-identifies as a 'proud Saudi national champion and an ambassador for Vision 2030'.[2] The symbiotic relationship with the state is also advantageous since it translates into lower borrowing costs for the national champion; this correlation was cited by Fitch and Moody's in their first ever credit rating of Masdar.[3] Masdar's new partnership with Abu Dhabi's Taqa and ADNOC has facilitated its growth as a power developer since its renewable portfolio was doubled overnight from 10GW to 23GW in 2022, with ambitions to raise this to over 50GW by 2030. Masdar's stature as a government-related entity has also benefitted its revenue stream: with rent from tenants at Masdar City comprising the second of its two income streams (the first being returns from clean energy projects), the fact that the top five tenants representing 75 percent of the net leasable are mostly fellow government entities, including the UAE Space Agency and Emirates Nuclear Energy Company, is helpful to Masdar's bottom line.[4]

Second, Uzbekistan is currently the focus of attention from the UAE and Saudi Arabia (Table 9.1). Doha's Nebras Power, a much smaller and newer energy champion, has expressed interest in investing in Azerbaijan's renewable energy sector but has yet to make concrete commitments, unlike in Ukraine where it acquired stakes in six existing solar plants.[5]

Third, companies from the Gulf have entered the CCA market through directly negotiated bilateral agreements and successful bids at competitive auctions. Thanks to their global brand recognition, ACWA and Masdar have been courted by CCA state entities eager for foreign investors to demonstrate confidence in their economies. For instance, following the signing of the country's first foreign investment agreement to develop wind power in Azerbaijan, its minister of energy noted that 'after ACWA Power, other companies from Saudi Arabia will follow suit and will invest in Azerbaijan.'[6] Likewise, Masdar's solar plants in Azerbaijan are expected to 'attract other investors to new projects' according to the same minister.[7]

Fourth, Gulf participation in the CCA's renewable energy sector is taking place alongside, rather than at the expense of, investment in fossil-fuel power projects. For instance, ACWA and Nebras are participants in Uzbekistan's Sirdarya 1 and Sirdarya 2 respectively, to develop combined-cycle gas turbine (CCGT) power plants that will consume far less natural gas than the existing and ageing fleet of simple-cycle power plants. This is because, as pointed out by Nebras' chairman, CCGT technology is perceived as 'sustainable' and 'integral' to the increasing shares of intermittent solar and wind energy within the power mix in many countries.[8] In this regard, CCGT plants help to decarbonize and free up Uzbek gas for higher value uses such as exports.

Finally, augmenting the Gulf's presence in the CCA are smaller, privately-owned power developers such as Fotowatio, a subsidiary of Saudi Arabia's Abdul Jamal Latif conglomerate, and Dubai-based Phanes. They have leveraged their prior experience in developing markets in Africa and the Middle East to break into the CCA. AMEA Power, a peer from Dubai, has attempted to make inroads but has thus far not been successful. The fact that the CCA has many sparsely populated areas suffering from intermittent power outages should augur well for smaller

Table 9.1 *List of Gulf RE greenfield projects in South Caucasus and Central Asia**

Project name	Location	Type/capacity	Developer	Agreement type	Status
Navoi	Uzbekistan	Solar, 100MW	Masdar	Auction	Awarded 2018
					Completed in 2021
Zarafshan	Uzbekistan	Wind, 500 MW	Masdar	Bilateral	Awarded 2020
					Completion 2024
Jizzakh	Uzbekistan	Solar, 220MW	Mascar	Auction	Awarded 2021
					Completion 2024
Samarkand	Uzbekistan	Solar, 220MW	Mascar	Auction	Awarded 2021
					Completion 2024
Sherabad	Uzbekistan	Solar, 457MW	Mascar	Auction	Awarded 2021
					Completion 2024
Bash	Uzbekistan	Wind, 500MW	ACWA	Bilateral	Awarded 2021
					Completion 2024

(continued)

Table 9.1 *Continued*

Project name	Location	Type/capacity	Developer	Agreement type	Status
Nukus	Uzbekistan	Wind, 100MW	ACWA	Auction	Awarded 2021
					Completion 2024
Dzhankeldy	Uzbekistan	Wind, 500MW	ACWA	Bilateral	Awarded 2021
					Completion in 2024
Nurata	Uzbekistan	Solar, 200MW	Phanes (UAE)	Bilateral	Awarded 2021
					No details on completion date
Garadagh	Azerbaijan	Solar, 230MW	Masdar	Bilateral	Awarded Jan 2020
					Completion end 2023
Absheron-Khizi	Azerbaijan	Wind, 240MW	ACWA	Bilateral	Awarded December 2020
					Completion end 2023
Ayg-1	Armenia	Solar, 200MW	Masdar	Auction	Awarded 2021
					Completion by end 2023

Masrik-1	Armenia	Solar, 55MW	Fotowatio (KSA)	Auction	Awarded 2018, financial close 2021, completion 2024
Akhali Samgori Solar Power Plant	Georgia	Solar, 100MW	Masdar	Bilateral	Awarded 2021
					No details on completion date

* Includes announced, ongoing, and completed projects.

Source: Author's compilation.

scale, decentralized renewable power facilities that fall within the purview of these privately-owned Gulf developers. In this regard, they complement the utility-scale power provided by the Gulf's national energy champions.

Geopolitical considerations

Much of the extant literature on GCC–Central Asia relations highlights the centrality of geopolitical considerations.[9] For the Gulf states, these relate to addressing the influence of Iran and Turkey in Central Asia and neighboring regions since Iran and Turkey constitute primary security threats for rulers in the Gulf.[10] Influential observers of Gulf affairs have noted, for instance, that 'the Gulf states' national security concerns mainly center on the threat of Iran, both directly to their interests and territorial integrity, and, more broadly, to the spread of Iranian hegemony.'[11]

Iran's role in the Tajik civil war in the 1990s was a source of early concern for GCC states, as was its support for the Islamic Renaissance Party of Tajikistan.[12] In the past few years, there has been an uptick in Iranian outreach to Central Asia, including high level visits, donations of coronavirus-related medical supplies to Kyrgyzstan in 2020, and the establishment of a joint Iranian-Tajik defence committee in 2021 to manage the rise in terrorist attacks by Daesh groups in Afghanistan. As a result, a Saudi-based, Iran-focused think tank warned that Central Asian states were evolving from being 'Iran-weary to Iran-friendly.'[13] Iran has also touted its willingness to facilitate access by these landlocked states to the sea and to its overland links to Asia and Europe.

As for Turkey, its 'soft' cultural-linguistic links to the people of Central Asia and its education outreach complement its 'hard' infrastructure power as an alternative, non-Russian, transport and energy corridor in Eurasia. A case in point was Ankara's declaration in 2021 that it was ready to support the export of Turkmen gas to Europe via a series of gas pipelines running through Turkey that comprise the Southern Gas Corridor. Turkish companies such as Cengiz Enerji and Aksa Enerji have also won contracts to build new gas-fired power plants to replace inefficient and ageing ones in Uzbekistan.

Somewhat less publicly discussed but no less significant is the extent to which intra-Gulf geopolitical competition shapes domestic initiatives and foreign policy behavior. This is because the Gulf constitutes a 'regional security complex' whereby existential threats are perceived to emanate from within, instead of external to, the region.[14] In this connection, intra-Gulf rivalry in terms of free zones, banking, airlines, talent attraction, and sports offer an economic platform to showcase regional prowess and contribute to regime stability.[15] Climate diplomacy has likewise become an instrument of one-upmanship among Gulf states. In a thinly veiled reference to the UAE's announcement of a net zero target by 2050, the first by a Gulf state, Qatar's energy minister noted that many politicians were just 'throwing it out there without a plan' and that a similar pledge by Qatar 'would be very sexy' but 'not the right thing.'[16] The wider Middle East, Africa, and the East Mediterranean already play host to the more interventionist foreign policies – and competing interests – of some Gulf states.[17] In Jordan for example, ACWA and Nebras control 40 percent and 14 percent, respectively, of the country's total installed power capacity, while Masdar's projects there account for 18 percent of installed renewable energy capacity. Gulf energy champions therefore 'augment the already sizeable contribution of their state sponsors to foreign direct investment, remittances, financial aid, and humanitarian assistance,' giving these states considerable influence over their respective relationship with Jordan, widely seen as a linchpin state in the Middle East.[18]

The point here is that the entry of national energy champions into the CCA's renewable energy sector may constitute an attempt to deploy statecraft to minimize geopolitical gains by Iran, Turkey, or rival Arab Gulf states in the region. This is because the Gulf state is a significant (in the case of ACWA) or sole stakeholder in these corporations, as highlighted earlier. Even more noteworthy is the fact that the creation of Nebras in 2014 coincided with the intra-Gulf crisis over Qatar that year and was arguably an attempt to use clean energy diplomacy to emerge from the shadow of Saudi Arabia's traditional regional influence. After all, Qatar's development of liquefied natural gas (LNG) in the 1980s–1990s was similarly premised, while newly independent UAE leveraged its joint ventures with foreign oil companies in the 1970s in its territorial disputes with neighboring Gulf states.[19]

The use of state-owned power developers to facilitate geopolitical aims is particularly relevant in the South Caucasus. Turkey's long-standing political and economic support for Azerbaijan against Armenia was augmented most recently during the Karabakh war in 2020. Drones and training supplied by the Turkish military resulted in a victory by Azerbaijan, which reclaimed some territories that had been lost earlier to

Armenia. Alarmed by Turkey's strategic gains in the South Caucasus on top of those in Syria and the East Mediterranean, the UAE and Saudi Arabia responded by intensifying political, security, and economic cooperation with Greece and Cyprus.[20]

The UAE has also deployed parastatals to engage economically with the South Caucasian states to counter Turkey's influence. In mid-2019, Masdar signed a memorandum of understanding (MoU) with the Armenian National Interests Fund (ANIF) to explore renewable energy projects in the Caucasian state. This crystallized into tangible gains when Masdar won the tender to develop Armenia's Ayg-1 solar plant two years later. Around the same time, Sharjah-based Air Arabia agreed to create Arna, Armenia's national airline, in a joint venture also with ANIF. Additionally, in March 2022, Masdar signed a MoU with the Azeri government to study renewable energy investment in the recently 'liberated' areas of Karabakh and East Zanzagur. Although these designated 'green energy zones' do have good solar and wind potential, the MoU also exemplifies Abu Dhabi's use of economic statecraft – through a state-owned company like Masdar – to curry favor with Azerbaijan and, consequently, to dilute Turkey's influence in Azerbaijan.[21]

Compared to Kazakhstan and Uzbekistan in Central Asia, the South Caucasus offers an inferior commercial proposition for power developers in terms of technical renewable power potential, size of electricity market, and the scale of transmission and distribution losses as noted in the next section. For these reasons, Masdar's forays into the South Caucasus were more likely motivated by the geopolitical aims of its state backer than attractive business opportunities *per se*. This is hardly unprecedented: Masdar has supported the wider strategic aims of its state patron in the UAE–Pacific Partnership Fund, backed by the UAE's Ministry of Foreign Affairs and International Cooperation and Abu Dhabi's Fund for Development, in delivering renewable energy capacity and developing local expertise to maintain such projects. This perspective aligns with a deep literature on the foreign policy role of state-owned corporations.[377]

Geopolitics, however, is an unconvincing lens with which to view Gulf investment in renewable power projects in Central Asia. First, the region does not appear to be a strategic prize for maritime-based powers like the Gulf states since every state in the CCA with the exception of Georgia is landlocked; Uzbekistan is double-landlocked while Kazakhstan is the world's largest landlocked country. Research demonstrating that landlocked developing countries grow an average of 1.5 percent per year slower than countries that are not landlocked due to higher transportation costs – which are a consequence of multiple border crossings, bribery, logistics, cartels – reduce the propensity to trade and with it, the attractiveness of CCA as a market or re-export hub for Eurasia.[23]

Second, Central Asia is well-endowed with a wide variety of critical minerals essential for clean energy production, exploitation of which can ease predicted global supply shortages that may retard plans to scale up adoption of renewable power in the Gulf states.[24] However, only Saudi Arabia has a viable manufacturing sector that is potentially interested in Central Asia as a source of critical minerals for solar and wind components. Bin Omairah's solar panel plant in Tabuk, which began production in 2021, will have a capacity of 1.2GW when fully operational. A Germany company, KACO, is also producing solar inverters in the Kingdom. By comparison, plans to manufacture panels in Duqm, Oman, or polysilicon in Doha, Qatar, seem to have fallen by the wayside. In the UAE, Ducab Metal Business, a subsidiary of state-owned Ducab, produces solar-grade and other high voltage cables in the only copper mill in the country; copper, the primary raw material, is sourced from India and Oman but not presently Central Asia. The geopolitics of critical minerals in Central Asia therefore appears to be less of a priority for Gulf states than for China, the United States, or Japan.[25]

Third, recent Gulf attempts at a détente with Iran and Turkey ahead of a perceived U.S. disengagement from the Middle East cast doubts about the sustainability of geopolitics as a driver of Gulf outreach toward the CCA states.[26] Assuming that the UAE has been recalibrating its foreign policy since 2021 by replacing robust military intervention and proxy politics with dialogue and economic diplomacy, the new approach should benefit energy champions like Masdar. Moreover, a post-JCPOA Iran is likely to be laser-focused on domestic economic reconstruction and recovery after years of sanctions. It is therefore unlikely to prioritize projecting its power into Central Asia even if Russia is distracted by the war in Ukraine. As for Turkey, regaining financial stability in terms of currency, banking, and sovereign debt ahead of the centenary of the founding of the republic in 2023 may constrain further provocative behavior in the South Caucasus. In any case, both Iran and Turkey would have to contend with other actors such as China, Russia, the European Union, India, and international financial institutions keen to maintain or enlarge their respective footprints in the region.[27]

Social license to operate

The activities of Gulf power developers in the CCA are shaped, but not driven, by considerations of a 'social license to operate' or SLO. Defined as 'the level of acceptance or approval continually granted to an organization's operations or project by local community and other stakeholders,' a SLO implies an informal and dynamic bargain between a corporation and multiple social groups or communities impacted by its activities typically in the extraction of natural resources.[28] In the 1990s, Chevron appeared to have lost its SLO when indigenous groups and activists sued the company for toxic dumping in the Ecuadorian Amazon. A SLO is distinct from the formal, legal licence that is granted by a public body to a private company, such as an air pollution permit granted by the U.S. Environment Protection Agency in order for Shell to begin drilling in the Arctic.

The major Gulf power developers are aware of the need to receive and sustain some level of SLO as underlined by references to how they are aligned with various UN Sustainable Development Goals (SDGs) or by demonstrating commitments to corporate social responsibility in their corporate brochures and annual reports.[29] In the CCA, Gulf power developers have pursued a SLO by incorporating environmental, social, and governance (ESG) criteria in renewable power projects. For instance, Uzbeks comprised most of the workers in the construction and maintenance phases of Masdar's Nur Navoi solar plant.[30] The company also designed workforce camps that were in line with guidance from international financial institutions (IFIs) funding the project.[31] In ACWA's case, in line with its ESG commitment to reduce the carbon emission intensity of its portfolio of assets by 50 percent by 2030 with the aim of achieving net-zero by the year 2050, it has refrained from proceeding with developing new coal-fired power plants in CAA and elsewhere.[32] In Uzbekistan, it met with local stakeholders of the Bash wind farm to address their concerns prior to executing construction.[33]

Nevertheless, ESG commitment in CCA sometimes falls short. For example, Masdar's April 2022 MoU with Kyrgyzstan to develop up to 1GW of carbon-free energy through solar and hydropower projects is less sustainable than it appears. Hydropower already accounts for 92 percent of Kyrgyzstan's power generation and additional capacity could worsen the already high rate of water depletion in the region. The latter, caused by inefficient irrigation practices and shrinking glaciers that feed the rivers, may cause water conflicts between upstream countries in Central Asia (Kyrgyzstan and Tajikistan) and its downstream neighbors to be re-ignited.[34]

The December 2021 strategic bilateral agreement between Kazakhstan's sovereign wealth fund, Samruk-Kazyna, and UAE's state-owned companies, according to which the latter would explore greenfield investments of up to 2GW of wind and 2GW of solar projects, is another case in point. This attempt to jump start the UAE's hitherto absence in Kazakhstan's renewable energy sector was abruptly abrogated following a sudden power transition in the country when the chairman of Samruk-Kazyna was purged in January 2022. As the son-in-law of former President Nurusultan Nazarbayev, he was said to wield control over 90 percent of Kazakhstan's economy through the fund and to be involved in corrupt practices; he had previously been sacked as head of the said fund in 2011.[35] The agreement has since been recalled by the Kazakh parliament, possibly over criticisms that it had not preceded by competitive bidding.[36] The UAE may claim the agreement was an unintended victim of 'de-Nazarbayevization' under the new Kazakh administration; after all, Total Eren's wind project with the fund announced around the same time has not come under scrutiny. However, it is equally arguable that more attention should have been paid to governance criteria under ESG, particularly since Samruk-Kazyna has long been flagged for its lack of transparency.

Gulf power developers appear to have monetized the value of an SLO so that it becomes part of their commercial considerations of operating in the CCA. Given that banks, IFIs, insurers, and credit ratings agencies take into account ESG scores, a SLO is valuable to the extent it lowers borrowing costs and facilitates access to a wider pool of sources for project finance.[37] This is particularly significant for Nebras and ACWA, because their group portfolios include power and water assets that run on fossil fuel energy; higher ESG scores in renewable projects in CCA can therefore offset the lower scores typically associated with fossil fuel assets. By comparison, obtaining and maintaining a SLO has less value outside of financial considerations because ESG *per se* is a low priority for most non-state domestic stakeholders in the CCA region, as a result of limited voice in policy-making in authoritarian states.[38]

An SLO for Gulf national energy champions is also valuable to their state patrons who can leverage on green credentials for national goals. These include increasing the soft power and prestige of Gulf states as

Table 9.2 *Real GDP growth in MENA: oil exporters versus oil importers*

	2017	2018	2019	2020	2021	2022 (proj)
MENA oil exporters (%)	1.2	0.1	1.1	−4.4	6.8	5.4
MENA oil importers (%)	3.5	3.8	3.3	−0.8	3.1	4.0
OPEC average oil price (in US$)	52.51	69.78	64.04	41.47	69.72	97.7

Sources: IMF 2020, IMF 2022, Statista 2022.

exemplified through Qatar's hosting of the UN's Conference of the Parties (COP 18) in 2012 – and indeed, the UAE's hosting of the 2023 edition of the conference – or the UAE serving as headquarters for the International Renewable Energy Agency. They also facilitate what critics have referred to as 'greenwashing', namely attempts to legitimize plans to increase production of oil and gas even though the energy sector, accounting for almost three-quarters of global greenhouse gas emissions, plays a significant role in global climate change.[39] Saudi Aramco, for example, has targeted an increase of oil production by one million to 13 million barrels of oil per day (mbpd) by 2027, ADNOC has brought forward plans to raise production capacity from 4.2mbpd to 5mbpd to 2027 from 2030, while Qatar intends to augment its liquefied natural gas production by 2027 to 126 million tons from 77 million tons currently. Despite diversification, hydrocarbon prices, output, and revenues continue to drive economic growth in the Gulf. As implied in Table 9.2, MENA oil exporters have tended to grow more slowly than importers during years when the oil price is less than $70 per barrel because this is below their average fiscal breakeven price; the inverse relationship is observed when oil prices rise to or above $70.

Commercial rationale

More often than not, a variety of commercial considerations underline the behavior of Gulf power developers in the renewable energy sector of the CCA. These include pull factors from CCA such as wind and solar resource potential, electricity demand growth that outstrips current installed capacity, general investment climate, renewable energy-related regulations, announced and delivered renewable energy capacity additions, and availability of credit for renewable energy projects.

Uzbekistan is a useful starting point for a CCA-wide analysis of the nuances of these commercial considerations. Thanks to reforms introduced since late 2016 following the death of its Soviet-era leader, the country has thrown off decades of isolation as underlined by robust growth rates and higher levels of foreign direct investment, with *The Economist* declaring it to be the most improved country in 2019.[40] According to the World Bank's Worldwide Governance Indicators, Uzbekistan has made great strides in dealing with control over corruption, regulatory quality, and rule of law between 2010 and 2019, though it still trails its CCA peers, Kazakhstan and Azerbaijan.[41] Uzbekistan's *Doing Business* ranking rose from 141 to 76 between 2015 and 2019; Kazakhstan (from 77 to 28) and Azerbaijan (from 80 to 25) also recorded improvements.[42] Likewise, Fitch assigned the latter two higher credit ratings than Uzbekistan.[43] These assessments are not surprising: as major oil exporters keen to diversify away from Russian-controlled export routes, Kazakhstan and Azerbaijan were incentivized to undertake market-oriented reforms during the 1990s and early 2000s to attract desperately needed foreign investment.

Looking more narrowly at renewable energy, it is clear that within the CCA, Uzbekistan has the second-best solar energy potential, bested only by Turkmenistan (ESMAP 2020); the latter is largely irrelevant to foreign investors since it is one of the most closed countries in the world. Uzbekistan has excellent wind resources in certain regions but lags most of its CCA peers overall (UNDP 2014). In terms of renewable power regulation, Kazakhstan, Armenia, and, to a lesser extent, Uzbekistan lead the CCA.[44]

With by far the region's largest population of 34.2 million, accounting for just over 37 percent of the CCA's population, and the region's second largest electricity market by installed capacity at 16,000MW, compared to half that in Azerbaijan, Uzbekistan is an attractive proposition.[45] Moreover, it has ambitions to grow its renewable energy sector, with ACWA anticipating a compound annual growth rate of 15 percent between 2017 and 2030 versus 11 percent in Azerbaijan between 2018 and 2025.[46] This is in line with the assessment by 'Climatescope' that

Uzbekistan offers more opportunities in the power sector than any other CCA country.[47] By contrast, Kyrgyzstan and Tajikistan are hobbled by a perfect storm of small electricity markets of 4,300MW and 6,000MW respectively, the seasonal nature of its largely hydropower-based power grid, which makes reliable year-round supply of power challenging for power developers, weak regulatory and investment climates, and corruption levels consistent with 20 percent of the worst performing countries in the world.[48]

Power transmission and distribution losses in Uzbekistan are acceptable at 9 percent. This is just above the global average (8 percent) but better than in Azerbaijan (14 percent) and Armenia (12 percent); the comparable figure is 7 percent in Kazakhstan and a hefty 24 percent in Kyrgyzstan.[49] As the historical distribution center of the Soviet-era electrical grid linking south Kazakhstan and the other Central Asian states through sophisticated transmission lines that crossed its territory, Uzbekistan's withdrawal from the Central Asian Power System (CAPS) in 2009 due to intra-regional disputes cut off Tajikistan completely from the grid, left the grid without its largest supplier (51 percent) of electricity, and resulted in frequent seasonal shortages in Kyrgyzstan.[50] Rejoining CAPS has increased the renewable energy attractiveness of Uzbekistan as a regional supplier not just to Central Asia but also to Afghanistan and through future linkages between CAPS and South Asian power grids.

Unlike their regional peers, Uzbekistan and Kazakhstan have leveraged the expertise and financial largesse offered by IFIs to quickly develop their renewable energy sectors. Uzbekistan was the fifth country, and the only non-African one, to join the World Bank's Scaling Solar program in 2019. By using the program's all-inclusive package of transaction structuring advice, standardized project documents, risk management products, co-financing with the private sector, and insurance by World Bank Group institutions, Uzbekistan has organized and awarded competitive tenders to procure solar photovoltaic power. The cachet of the World Bank also helped to de-risk and crowd-in private sector participation in Uzbekistan, which is arguably less-resourced and less-known than other borrowers. Masdar, for example, was awarded the Navoi, Jizzakh, and Samarkand solar projects through this program. Kazakhstan was in fact the region's earliest adopter of international auctions, a market-based competitive mechanism to drive down the price of installed capacity for renewable energy, which replaced the previous top-down mechanism of a feed-in-tariff system. With advice from the

U.S. Agency for International Development, it organized the first of many auctions in 2018, a year before Uzbekistan.

ACWA and Masdar have been particularly successful in Uzbekistan, as noted earlier. By contrast, they are absent from Kazakhstan's renewable energy development, which has been dominated by international oil and gas companies that acquired early stakes in developing the country's hydrocarbon resources, as well as by Chinese companies, thanks to Almaty's centrality to China's massive Belt and Road Initiative. For instance, investors from Europe account for at least 20 percent of renewable energy projects by installed capacity between 2011 and 2020, while the share for China is 13 percent.[51] The first-mover advantage has therefore been significant for Saudi Arabia and the UAE in emerging developing markets like Uzbekistan.

Complementing the improving investment climate for renewable energy projects in parts of the CCA is the focus on profitability and overseas expansion among Gulf national energy champions and their state patrons. A recent study found that renewable power generated significantly higher total returns over the last ten years, at 422.7 percent against 59 percent for fossil fuels; the former also boasted comparatively lower costs of capital and lower volatility revenue volatility.[52] All of this is good news for Gulf states with ambitious plans to diversify away from hydrocarbon revenues to reduce fiscal volatility associated with such revenues while growing non-oil economic sectors for sustainable development in the near future (Tsai 2018, Sim 2020).[53]

For instance, Qatar Water and Electricity Water Company expects Nebras, through its 'profitable returns' on overseas power and water assets, to generate 40 percent of the group's profit by 2030.[54] Nebras has not indicated prioritizing CCA but given that its recent investments in Ukraine may suffer, it may consider opportunities in the region. In the case of ACWA, it has a long-term strategy to greatly increase the share of renewable energy in its total portfolio gross capacity from 35 percent today to 66 percent by 2030 and 95 percent by 2050.[55] With an estimated 23 percent of market share for power generation in Uzbekistan and with the country accounting for 10 percent of ACWA's gross power capacity – the third largest share outside its home market of Saudi Arabia – Uzbekistan is clearly a priority.[56] As for Masdar, it appears to have secured a privileged relationship to develop renewable energy in Armenia. The tender document for its Ayg-1 solar plant contained an unusual clause whereby Masdar would be given an opportunity to undercut the lowest bid tariff received by a third party.[57] Following presumably lower bids from Russian and Chinese companies, Masdar lowered its original offer of $0.0299 per kilowatt hour to $0.0290 and was duly awarded the project. Consequently, Masdar has ongoing projects in all three South Caucasian states and in Uzbekistan at the end of 2022.

For all the potential offered by renewable energy in the CCA and the success thus far enjoyed by leading Gulf power developers, it remains difficult to see how income from renewable power projects in general can come close to replacing hydrocarbon-derived revenues.[58] Consider that in 2020 Germany earned $3 billion as the largest electricity exporter in the world, albeit just over half of this was from power stations running on non-renewable sources of energy.[59] This was the equivalent of just 11 days worth of oil exports from Saudi Arabia, assuming an average OPEC oil price of $41.50 in 2020 and exports of 7 million barrels per day.

It is also unclear, as previously highlighted, the extent to which the manufacturing sector in the Gulf states can piggyback on solar and wind power plants developed by Gulf-based power developers to intensify economic diversification in the Gulf. The sourcing of renewable power components is highly price sensitive, making it hard to compete with high-volume and high-efficiency panel manufacturers like Jinko Solar, a global leader. Moreover, as noted earlier, ACWA and Masdar are committed to source materials and labor from CCA and other countries where they operate, as part of their ESG practices that facilitate access to renewable energy funding from IFIs.

Conclusion

This chapter has argued that the activities of Gulf national energy champions in the CCA's renewable sector are largely commercially motivated. Even where geopolitics may take precedence, such as for Masdar in Armenia, this does not mean there are zero commercial gains, even if the returns on investment may be less than optimum. The success of these companies and their state sponsors in the CCA remains to be seen since only one of these projects is actually in operation at the time of writing.

With four Gulf states – UAE, Saudi Arabia, Qatar, and Kuwait – among the world's top twenty owners of state capital investments outside of their home country and with more countries looking to create national champions in light of the risks of de-globalization and supply chain issues, it is worth considering the merits of state capitalism.[60] On the one hand, there has long been concerns about the drawbacks of state ownership including corruption, financial losses, distorted markets, and economic diversification. A recent paper, for example, finds that firms in the Middle East and North Africa where the state is a significant shareholder have larger sales and assets than those in the private sector; however, the former are less profitable and less productive, and suffer from lower growth rates in the long run.[61] On the other hand, there are well-run state-owned entities in the Gulf and elsewhere, and there is empirical evidence that state-owned enterprises generally tend to do well in environmental protection, although firms in resource rich countries underperform their peers.[62] Cognizant of best practices that include separating management and ownership roles, ACWA pointedly highlights that '[s]hareholders have forgone their operational involvement and have taken reliance in ACWA Power's management reporting and governance structures.'[63] This, of course, does not void their strategic and financial influence.

In the end, given the continued reliance of Gulf states on state-controlled or state-owned companies, the more relevant issues for renewable energy diplomacy by Gulf states are as follows. First, whether the new breed of Gulf entities funded by sovereign wealth funds such as ACWA and Masdar will be more successful than the more traditional state-owned companies like Nebras. Second, whether national champions like ACWA where the state is a co-investor with private domestic capital will outperform fully state-owned peers like Masdar and Nebras.

Bibliography

Aalto, Pami Kullervo, Heino Nyyssönen, Matti Kojo, and Pallavi Pal (2017), 'Russian nuclear energy diplomacy in Finland and Hungary.' *Eurasian Geography and Economics* 58 (4): 386–417.
ACWA (2021), *ACWA Power Annual Report 2020*. Riyadh: ACWA Power.
ACWA (2021), ACWA Power Highlights.
ACWA (2021), *ACWA Power Prospectus*. Riyadh: ACWA Power.
ACWA (2021), 'ACWA Power: Business Update Presentation.' Riyadh: ACWA Power.
ACWA (2022), *ACWA Power FY2021 Financial Results: Earnings Call Presentation*. Riyadh: ACWA Power.
AECOM (2021), *Environmental and Social Impact Assessment: 100 MW Solar PV Plant by Navoi in Uzbekistan*. Edinburgh: AECOM.

Al-Sulami, Mohammed (2021), 'Arab world should respond to Iran's Central Asia outreach'. Arab News, December 6, 2021. https://www.arabnews.com/node/1981891.

Al-Sulayman, Faris (2021), *Rethinking State Capitalism in the Gulf States: Insights from the China-focused Literature*. Riyadh: King Faisal Center for Research and Islamic Studies.

Alexander, Kristian, and Giorgio Cafiero (2020), *The UAE's Growing Role in Central Asia: Geopolitical Inroads to Challenge Turkey and Iran*. Ljubljana: International Institute for Middle East and Balkan Studies.

Arvis, Jean-François, Gael Raballand, and Jean-François Marteau (2007), *The Cost of Being Landlocked: Logistics Costs and Supply Chain Reliability*. Washington, D.C.: The World Bank. https://openknowledge.worldbank.org/handle/10986/7420.

Azertag (2022), 'Qatari Nebras Power company keen on cooperation with Azerbaijan in construction of wind power plants in Lachin and Kalbajar districts'. Azertag, February 21, 2022. https://azertag.az/en/xeber/Qatari_Nebras_Power_company_keen_on_cooperation_with_Azerbaijan_in_construction_of_wind_power_plants_in_Lachin_and_Kalbajar_districts-2022854. Accessed May 5, 2022.

Babic, Milan, Javier Garcia-Bernardo and Eelke M. Heemskerk (2020), 'The rise of transnational state capital: state-led foreign investment in the 21st century'. *Review of International Political Economy* 27 (3): 433–475.

Balmaceda, Margarita M. (2008), *Energy Dependency, Politics and Corruption in the Former Soviet Union: Russia's Power, Oligarchs' Profits, and Ukraine's Missing Energy Policy, 1995–2006*. London: Routledge.

Bank/ESMAP, W. (2020). *Regulatory Indicators for Sustainable Energy 2020*. Washington, D.C.: World Bank/ESMAP.

Berdikeeva, Saltanat (2020), 'Saudi Arabia's Growing Influence in Central Asia.' Inside Arabia, April 10, 2020. https://insidearabia.com/saudi-arabias-growing-influence-in-central-asia/.

Bianco, Cinzia (2020), 'The GCC Monarchies: Perceptions of the Iranian Threat amid Shifting Geopolitics.' *The International Spectator* 55 (2): 92–107.

Bianco, Cinzia (2020), 'Gulf Monarchies and the Eastern Mediterranean: Growing Ambitions.' European Council on Foreign Relations. https://ecfr.eu/special/eastern_med/gcc.

BloombergNEF (2021), 'Climatescope,' Bloomberg.

Braw, Elisabeth (2021), 'The West Needs Champions.' Foreign Policy, March 4, 2021. https://foreignpolicy.com/2021/03/04/the-west-needs-champions/.

Buzan, Barry (1982), *People, States & Fear: The National Security Problem in International Relations*. Chapel Hill: The University of North Carolina Press.

5 Capitals (2022), 'Uzbekistan: ACWA Power Bash Wind Project.' 5 Capitals Environmental and Management Consulting.

Clemons, Steve (2019), 'Time for America to support its own national champions?' *The Hill*, July 9, 2019. https://thehill.com/opinion/finance/452213-time-for-america-to-support-its-own-national-champions/.

Cluster Evaluation: Solar Power Operations (2022), London, European Bank for
 Reconstruction and Development, 101. https://www.ebrd.com/documents/
 comms-and-bis/cluster-evaluation-solar-power-operations.pdf.
Cook, Steven, and Hussein Ibish (2017), *Turkey and the GCC: Cooperation Amid
 Diverging Interests*. Washington, D.C.: The Arab Gulf States Institute in
 Washington. https://agsiw.org/wp-content/uploads/2017/02/GCCTurkey_
 ONLINE-2.pdf. 8.
Dadlani, Disha (2020), 'ACWA Power inks three deals for Azerbaijan IPP.'
 Construction Week Middle East, December 30, 2020. https://www.
 constructionweekonline.com/projects-tenders/269838-acwa-power-inks-
 deals-for-azerbaijan-ipp. Accessed May 5, 2022.
Dalbaeva, Alina (2018), 'End the Weaponisation of Water in Central Asia.'
 International Crisis Group, March 15, 2018. https://www.crisisgroup.org/
 europe-central-asia/central-asia/kazakhstan/end-weaponisation-water-
 central-asia.
Davidson, Christopher M. (2005), *The United Arab Emirates: A Study in Survival*.
 Boulder: Lynne Reiner. https://www.rienner.com/title/The_United_Arab_
 Emirates_A_Study_in_Survival.
EIU (2020), 'Sports investments reignite Gulf rivalries,' Economist Intelligence.
ESMAP (2020), *Global Photovoltaic Power Potential by Country*. Washington,
 D.C.: World Bank.
European Bank for Reconstruction and Development (2022), 'Cluster
 Evaluation: Solar Power Operations (2022).' https://www.ebrd.com/
 documents/comms-and-bis/cluster-evaluation-solar-power-operations.pdf.
Fawn, Rick (2021), '"Not here for geopolitical interests or games": the EU's 2019
 strategy and the regional and inter-regional competition for Central Asia.'
 Central Asian Survey, August 17, 2021. https://www.tandfonline.com/doi/full
 /10.1080/02634937.2021.1951662.
Fitch (2021), 'Fitch Publishes Abu Dhabi Future Energy Company PJSC'A+'
 IDRs; Outlook Stable.' Paris, Fitch Ratings.
Fitch (2022), Fitch Ratings.
Foxman, Simone (2021), 'Qatar Criticizes Nations for Making Vague Net-Zero
 Pledges.' Bloomberg, October 11, 2021. https://www.bloomberg.com/news/
 articles/2021-10-11/qatar-criticizes-nations-making-net-zero-pledges-
 without-a-plan.
Francisco, Ellennor (2014), *Petroleum Politics: China and its National Oil
 Companies*. Paris: SciencesPo, September 2014. https://www.sciencespo.fr/
 ceri/fr/content/dossiersduceri/petroleum-politics-china-and-its-national-
 oil-companies.
Gartner (2021), *The ESG Imperative: 7 Factors for Finance Leaders to Consider*.
 London: Gartner.
Gause, Gregory (2010), *The International Relations of the Persian Gulf*.
 Cambridge, Cambridge University Press.
GTR (2021), 'ESG in the Middle East: moving from government priority to
 standard practice.' Global Trade Review. https://www.gtreview.com/

supplements/gtr-mena-2021/esg-middle-east-moving-government-priority-standard-practice/.

Gulf News (2022), 'Abu Dhabi's ADQ to pump 4b euros into Greece's economy.' Gulf News, May 9, 2022. https://gulfnews.com/business/abu-dhabis-adq-to-pump-4b-euros-into-greeces-economy-1.1652116728664.

Guzansky, Yoel, and Gallia Lindenstrauss (2021), 'The Growing Alignment Between the Gulf and the Eastern Mediterranean.' Middle East Institute, May 25, 2021. https://www.mei.edu/publications/growing-alignment-between-gulf-and-eastern-mediterranean.

Hashimoto, Kohei, Jareer Elaas, and Stacy Eller (2004), 'Liquefied Natural Gas from Qatar: The Qatargas Project.' Stanford, James A Baker III Institute for Public Policy of Rice University, May 26, 2004. https://www.bakerinstitute.org/research/liquefied-natural-gas-from-qatar-the-qatargas-project.

Hsu, Po-Hsuan, Hao Liang and Pedro Matos (2020), *Leviathan Inc. and Corporate Environmental Engagement*. ECGI Working Paper Series in Finance. Brussels: European Corporate Governance Institute.

ICG (2019), 'Intra-Gulf competition in Africa's Horn: Lessening the Impact.' Brussels, International Crisis Group, September 19, 2019. https://www.crisisgroup.org/middle-east-north-africa/gulf-and-arabian-peninsula/206-intra-gulf-competition-africas-horn-lessening-impact.

IEA/CCFI (2020), *Energy Investing Exploring Risk and Return in the Capital Markets*. London: International Energy Agency and the Centre for Climate Finance & Investment at Imperial College Business School.

Ikromov, Shavkat (2020), 'Mosque Diplomacy in Central Asia: Geopolitics Beginning with the Mihrab.' Voices on Central Asia, December 16, 2020. https://voicesoncentralasia.org/mosque-diplomacy-in-central-asia-geopolitics-beginning-with-the-mihrab/.

IMF (2020), *Statistical Appendix for Regional Economic Outlook: Middle East and Central Asia*. Washington, D.C.: International Monetary Fund.

IMF (2022), 'Fostering Private Sector Led Growth in MENA: A New Role for the State' (prepared for Annual Meeting of Arab Finance Deputies), Washington, D.C., International Monetary Fund.

IMF (2022), *Statistical Appendix for Regional Economic Outlook: Middle East and Central Asia*. Washington, D.C.: International Monetary Fund.

IRENA (2021), *Statistical Profiles*. Abu Dhabi: International Renewable Energy Agency.

Kalantzakos, Sophia (2020), 'The Race for Critical Minerals in an Era of Geopolitical Realignments.' *The International Spectator* 55 (3): 1–16. https://www.tandfonline.com/doi/full/10.1080/03932729.2020.1786926.

Karasik, Theodore (2020), 'Saudi Support of Cyprus Key as Tempers Flare in Mediterranean.' Arab News, January 23, 2020. https://www.arabnews.com/node/1617236.

Kavalski, Emilian (2012), *Central Asia and the Rise of Normative Powers*. London: Bloomsbury Press.

Kazantsev, Andrei, Svetlana Medvedeva, and Ivan Safranchuk (2021), 'Between Russia and China: Central Asia in Greater Eurasia.' *Journal of Eurasian*

Studies 12(1): 57–71. https://journals.sagepub.com/doi/
full/10.1177/1879366521998242.

Kumar, Nirmalya and Jan-Benedict E. M. Steenkamp (2016), 'Emerging nations
need national champions, and national champions need strong support from
the state.' *Asian Management Insights* 3. https://ink.library.smu.edu.sg/
ami/16/.

MacKellar, Landis, Andreas Wörgötter and Julia Wörz (2002), 'Economic
Growth of Landlocked Countries,' in *Ökonomie in Theorie Und Praxis*,
G. Chaloupek, A. Guger, E. Nowotny, and G. Schwödiauer (eds). Berlin,
Springer: 213–226.

Masdar (2022), *Annual Sustainability Report 2021*. Abu Dhabi: Masdar.

Maziad, Marwa and Jake Sotiriadis (2020), 'Turkey's Dangerous New Exports:
Pan-Islamist, Neo-Ottoman Visions and Regional Instability.' Middle East
Institute. https://www.mei.edu/publications/turkeys-dangerous-new-
exports-pan-islamist-neo-ottoman-visions-and-regional

Minenergy (2019), Concept Note for ensuring electricity supply in Uzbekistan
in 2020–2030. Tashkent, Ministry of Energy of the Republic of Uzbekistan.

Mogielnicki, Robert (2021), *A Political Economy of Free Zones in Gulf Arab
States*. London: Palgrave.

Mouraviev, Nikolai (2021), 'Renewable energy in Kazakhstan: Challenges to
policy and governance.' *Energy Policy* 149.

MTAD (2020), 'Announcement on pre-qualification process for utility-scale
solar photovoltaic Ayg-1 project in Armenia.' Yerevan, Armenia Renewable
Resources and Energy Efficiency Fund, Ministry of Territorial
Administration & Infrastructure.

Nebras (2021), Pioneering Future Energy.

Nebras Power (2021), *Annual Report 2020*. Doha: Nebras Power.

Nebras Power (2021), *Annual Report 2020*. Doha: Nebras Power.

Orange, Richard (2010), 'WikiLeaks: Kazakh billionaire who bought Duke of
York's home has "avarice for large bribes".' *The Telegraph*, December 1, 2010.
https://www.telegraph.co.uk/news/worldnews/wikileaks/8170767/
WikiLeaks-Kazakh-billionaire-who-bought-Duke-of-Yorks-home-has-
avarice-for-large-bribes.html.

Peyrouse, Sebastien, (2009). 'The Central Asian power grid in danger?' The
Central Asia-Caucasus Analyst.

Peyrouse, Sebastien, and Sadykzhan Ibraimov (2010), 'Iran's Central Asia
Temptations.' Current Trends in Islamist Ideology 9: 87–101.

PwC (2021), *Renewable Energy Market in Kazakhstan: Potential, Challenges, and
Prospects*. Almaty: PricewaterhouseCoopers.

Qatar Tribune (2019), 'QEWC aims to generate 40% profit from Nebras Power:
MD.' Qatar Tribune.

Rahman, Fareed, (2021). 'Masdar signs deal to develop $200m solar project in
Azerbaijan.' *The National*, April 7, 2021. https://www.thenationalnews.com/
business/energy/masdar-signs-deal-to-develop-200m-solar-project-in-
azerbaijan-1.1198934. Accessed May 5, 2022.

REN21 (2022), *Renewables 2022 Global Status Report*. Paris: REN21 Secretariat.

Reed, Ed (2021), 'Saipem teams up with Aramco for new national champion.' Energy Voice, September 21, 2021. https://www.energyvoice.com/oilandgas/middle-east/351209/saipem-aramco-epc-champion/.

Reuters (2022), 'Kazakh govt recalls bill on $6 bln UAE energy deal from parliament.' Reuters, January 12, 2022. https://www.reuters.com/business/energy/kazakh-govt-recalls-bill-6-bln-uae-energy-deal-parliament-2022-01-12/.

Ritchie, Hannah, and Matt Roser (2020), 'Emissions by sector.' ourworldindata.org.

Saouli, Adham, ed. (2020), *Unfulfilled Aspirations: Middle Power Politics in the Middle East.* Oxford: Oxford University Press. https://academic.oup.com/book/32019.

Saur Energy (2022), 'The Top 5: Biggest Exporters of Electricity in the World.'

Schuster, Kimberly (2018), *Blue Gold: Water Management is Key to Central Asia's Future.* Washington, D.C.: Center for Strategic & International Studies, October 17, 2018. https://www.csis.org/npfp/blue-gold-water-management-key-central-asias-future.

Shankar, A. (2020), 'Time to create global industrial champions.' The Hindu, December 6, 2020. https://www.thehindubusinessline.com/opinion/time-to-create-global-industrial-champions/article33264186.ece.

Sim, Li-Chen (2020), 'Low-carbon energy in the Gulf: Upending the rentier state?' *Energy Research & Social Science* 70.

Sim, Li-Chen (2022), 'Renewable Power Policies in the Arab Gulf States.' Middle East Institute, February 8, 2022. https://www.mei.edu/publications/renewable-power-policies-arab-gulf-states.

Solargis (2020), 'Global Solar Atlas 2.0: Azerbaijan.' World Bank/ESMAP.

Statista (2022), 'Average annual OPEC crude oil price from 1960 to 2022.' Statista. https://www.statista.com/statistics/262858/change-in-opec-crude-oil-prices-since-1960.

Tavsan, Sinan (2021), Middle East players move to detente as U.S. turns focus on China. Nikkei Asia, December 1, 2021. https://asia.nikkei.com/Politics/International-relations/Indo-Pacific/Middle-East-players-move-to-detente-as-U.S.-turns-focus-on-China.

The Economist (2019), 'Which nation improved the most in 2019?' *The Economist.* https://www.economist.com/leaders/2019/12/21/which-nation-improved-the-most-in-2019.

Thomson, Ian and Robert G. Boutilier (2011), 'Social license to operate,' in *SME Mining Engineering Handbook*, ed. P. Darling. Littleton, Colorado: Society for Mining, Metallurgy and Exploration.

TI (2021), *Corruption Perceptions Index.* Berlin: Transparency International.

Tsai, I-Tsung (2018), 'Political economy of energy policy reforms in the Gulf Cooperation Council: Implications of paradigm change in the rentier social contract.' *Energy Research & Social Science* 41: 89–96.

UNDP (2014), *UNDP Europe and Central Asia: Renewable Energy Snapshots.* New York: United Nations Development Program.

Vakulchuk, Roman and Indra Overland (2021), 'Central Asia is a missing link in analyses of critical materials for the global clean energy transition.' *One Earth* 4 (2): 1678–1692. https://www.sciencedirect.com/science/article/pii/S2590332221006606.

Wastnidge, Edward (2020), *Central Asia and the Iran-Saudi rivalry.* POMEPS Studies 38: Washington D.C. The Project on Middle East Political Science. https://pomeps.org/central-asia-and-the-iran-saudi-rivalry.

World Bank (2014), *Electric Power Transmission and Distribution Losses (% of output).* Washington D.C.: World Bank.

World Bank (2015), *Doing Business 2015.* Washington, D.C.: World Bank.

World Bank (2019), *Doing Business 2019.* Washington, D.C.: World Bank.

World Bank (2021), 'The Worldwide Governance Indicators,' World Bank.

Young, Michael (2022), 'Big Diplomatic Moves Show a Middle East Bracing for an Iran Nuclear Deal.' *The National*, March 30, 2022. https://www.thenationalnews.com/opinion/comment/2022/03/30/a-new-approach-among-arab-states-in-the-backdrop-of-a-likely-nuclear-deal/.

Ziadah, Rafeef (2017), 'Constructing a logistics space: Perspectives from the Gulf Cooperation Council.' *Environment and Planning D: Society and Space* 36 (4): 666–682. https://journals.sagepub.com/doi/10.1177/0263775817742916.

CONCLUSION

Karen E. Young

There are many ways to conceptualize the challenges ahead to meet clean energy demand and electrification globally. The first challenge is one of access and equity between wealthy and poorer countries. The second is one of impact. It is among developing economies and those within the Middle East that we expect to see some of the biggest impacts of climate change in rising temperatures, water resource stress, changes in sea levels, and new conditions that affect fisheries as well as tourism as key economic diversification goals. Across MENA, the very options of diversification away from oil and gas production are also those sectors facing threats from climate change. The region is highly-impacted by climate change and it is also under-resourced in terms of access to finance and technology to adapt to changes and reduce its use of carbon-based energy sources. In many places within the region, governments will be stressed to replace the revenues from carbon-based energy exports. What the region needs is access to decarbonization technologies for its existing oil and gas production, and avenues of diversification for new opportunities of clean energy production at home. That will mean electrification, powered by clean energy. Solar and wind resources are good, but existing power infrastructure is disparate and cost structures are often highly-subsidized by states, making the case for building new power production a stress to fiscal policy and out of reach for many governments with poor credit access. The third challenge is the management of external shocks and navigating an energy transition while seeking a broader economic development agenda.

Anticipating changes in the global economy and how finance for an energy transition might be available in very spotty and unequal ways requires a wide disciplinary and technical lens. For this reason, our compilation here is intentionally diverse in approach. We regret it is also limited in geographical scope within the region in its coverage of cases, though we see the breadth of issues as a key effort. The Program on Economics and Energy at the Middle East Institute is one effort to gather scholars and invite research and analysis from a variety of sources and methods of inquiry. This first effort is meant to be a starting point, not a definitive assessment of the field.

We find the Gulf oil and gas producers have already internalized the process of an impending energy transition, meaning a diminishing demand for their most important export revenue sources, and a domestic transformation in labor markets, new capital needs, and a revision of the role of the state in the economy. The global energy transition we encounter today is similar in scope. The price surge of 2022–2023 creates an opportunity for Gulf states to manage existing debt, to make investment decisions on renewable power sectors and net-zero targets, and to double down on liberalization measures. It is also a moment to think about how dominant Gulf producers might reshape the political economy of the wider region to align to their needs, and to reposition their relationship with the United States.

We can expect three trends to define the near term in MENA energy politics:

1   Oil and gas producers will become more disaggregated within the region, in terms of their access to capital, fiscal space for social support, and ability to direct hydrocarbon revenues to invest in domestic climate goals like renewable power production and a diversified economy. The wealthier ones will be called upon to seed a (green) development transition in the weaker ones. The regional political dynamics will change, with a growing role for the dominant Gulf Arab states: Saudi Arabia, the UAE, and Qatar.

2   Gas markets will boost the importance and international profile of producers in the eastern Mediterranean and shift the intra-regional dynamics among producers and their regional investor partners. For Israel, this has security partnership implications as well. For Europe and the United States, competition, innovation, and investment cycles will reshape how the West sees the Middle East and how the gas producers within MENA engage with each other. It may be gas, more than oil, that defines how U.S. foreign policy sees the Middle East in future security and economic partnerships.

3 The aid, investment, and development agenda of the Middle East will become more global in its reach and outlook, driven by the Gulf states and their individual transformations as they seek new markets for their energy products (oil and gas, but also hydrogen and petrochemicals). This has broad implications for the MENA region, but also for Africa and South Asia. Pan-Arab support is less of a guide to aid and investment decisions in economic statecraft with a greater emphasis on return on investment and market sustainability.

The windfall of wealth in Saudi Arabia from the upswing in oil prices from 2022–2023 will be transformational domestically and could reposition the country in the region and beyond. Higher oil production and positive non-hydrocarbon activity are expected to deliver the fastest GDP growth since 2011. The key question will be what the Saudi government decides to do with these proceeds, and whether domestic growth and investment is prioritized over regional financial intervention. Shaping that regional intervention to further the shared goals of providing low- and zero-carbon energy production should be a security and economic priority for U.S. foreign policy. Regional economic development policy, aid to countries in financial crisis and instability will be linked to volatility of the energy transition – with clear opportunities for economic statecraft from the Gulf states.

Twice a year, the World Bank issues macroeconomic updates across its regional coverage. The Middle East North Africa regional economic update for April 2023 is one that may herald a sharp divide, both within the region, in terms of its mixed economic trajectory and expected obstacles to human capital development, and more globally, as a cleavage between energy exporters and importers (Young 2023). The report makes a number of findings on the detrimental long-term effects on human capital development of even temporary economic shocks of inflation and food insecurity. We might expect that more regular shocks, in energy and food prices, whether driven by conflict (as in the case of Russia's invasion of Ukraine) or by climate change, will be a persistent feature of the decades ahead. The second point of division is trickier, as those countries with energy abundance through hydrocarbon exports are not all alike. Those with restricted monetary policies, namely the Gulf states with currency pegs to the U.S. dollar, have weathered the current inflationary environment more easily than most developing oil exporters in the

MENA region. The report signals that as we think about the geopolitics of the energy transition, there are important regional political dimensions and trends of disaggregation for the Middle East, affecting the macroeconomic stability of the places that produce much of our global supply of oil and gas.

The energy transition is expected to proceed with significant swings in hydrocarbon pricing, as our demand for oil may be more persistent than investment and readiness of supply. Those swings can be inflationary, and difficult to predict, especially when combined with political limitations to energy supply, as we have seen in both the sanctions against Russian oil in the West and the implementation of price caps on its sale to the rest of the world. Energy and food pricing are closely linked, in the production of fertilizer, in transport, and often in the simultaneous geographical scarcity (or synergy, in the case of Russia) of both agricultural production and domestic energy production. In the MENA region, there are several countries that are significant importers of both food and fuel, and this correlates in some to a particular vulnerability to exchange rate volatility. Egypt and Tunisia are examples. Conflict states are especially vulnerable when their usual domestic food and energy production is damaged by war (as we see in Yemen), or by government dysfunction (as we see in Lebanon). And while global agricultural commodity prices as well as oil and gas prices have fallen from their mid-2022 highs, it is now the after-effects of low growth, high borrowing costs, and currency depreciation that makes headlines and especially food price inflation so persistent in much of the Middle East and North Africa.

Price shocks, as such, can have long-term developmental consequences. The World Bank's MENA economic update spends considerable time and complex modeling to try and specify exactly how food price inflation is linked to detrimental effects in children's learning and physical growth or stunting, and can have intergenerational effects. In a region where children and young people are the dominant proportion of the population, such a finding in a period of weakening post-pandemic economic recovery can be damning.

The report estimates that as many as 200,000–285,000 newborns may have been at risk of stunting in the developing countries in the Middle East and North Africa due to rising food prices since the war in Ukraine. About 8 million children in the MENA region are forecast to be in food insecurity situations in 2023. Food insecurity in the Middle East did not originate with the war in Ukraine, but the current lower growth, higher borrowing cost environment puts additional pressure on government spending and fiscal priorities for interventions. The MENA region is disaggregating between oil importers and exporters in access to capital and abilities to balance demands of both monetary and fiscal policy. There is some relationship between inflation and debt, at least in the ability to manage debt service priced in foreign currency, usually U.S. dollars.

As the Bank describes:

> Depreciations vis-à-vis the US dollar that led to higher levels of inflation occurred mainly in oil-importing countries such as Egypt, Morocco, and Tunisia. Their current accounts were hit by increases in the prices of food products and oil, most of which are imported. In these economies, this hit coincided with high levels of debt and worsening global financial conditions … One possibility is that countries with higher levels of debt find it more difficult to destine resources to lean against currency pressures, which would increase the likelihood of experiencing larger depreciations and inflating prices of imported goods in domestic currency (World Bank 2023: 11).

There are certainly points of intervention for governments, international financial institutions and aid organizations to consider, including cash transfers and support for maternal nutrition and care to counter-act the risk of food insecurity for children. And we should be cautious about deterministic readings of youth potential based on nutrition and in utero effects alone; there are clearly many opportunities, as well as structural and environmental barriers to human capital across the region, as there are globally. No one is destined to fail. But the current macroeconomic environment in MENA, combined with expected volatility in both energy and food prices due to our energy transition and climate change, means that a generation of children and their families will have to deal with these ups and downs in their household economic planning.

What we can expect across MENA developing oil importers and exporters, as well as in the wealthier GCC exporters, is a shared slow-down in economic growth this year. The World Bank estimates that following the MENA regional average acceleration from 2.3 percent in 2021 to 4.4 percent real GDP per capita growth in 2022, there is likely to be a sharp decline to 1.6 percent for 2023 and just 1.7 percent growth in

2024. Even in the GCC, where per capital GDP grew 5.5 percent in 2022, growth is expected to decelerate to 1.8 percent in 2023. For developing oil exporters (such as Iraq), the slowdown is expected to be less than 1 percent growth in 2023. So even as oil prices remain buoyant, supported by OPEC+ production cuts in April 2023, the wages of oil do not necessarily translate to automatic growth in the current global economic environment, even in the best positioned oil exporting countries of the MENA region. For those states in the region with more difficult inflationary and currency pressures, they will face debt management challenges and they are likely to seek financial assistance, in aid and investment, from the Gulf.

Most importantly, the economic outlook for the Middle East and North Africa depends on a number of external factors, including future oil and gas markets, climate change and environmental shocks, the intra-regional politics of aid and investment, combined with access to finance and intervention from international financial institutions. Opportunities for protecting human capital development, through enabling food security and access to good nutrition, is just one piece of a set of development policy challenges. The recent experience of the Middle East and North Africa region tells us a lot about the connections and risks between food and energy security, and intra-regional variation in vulnerability to external shocks. This book, as a collection of diverse chapters and areas of investigation, is just one effort to contribute to the policy challenges ahead.

Reference

World Bank (2023). The World Bank (Bank for Reconstruction and Development), 'Altered Destinies: The Long Term Effects of Rising Food Prices and Food Insecurity in the Middle East and North Africa.' MENA Economic Update (April 2023), Washington, D.C.
Young, Karen (2023). "Middle East and Africa: Slowing Growth and Rising Food Prices Present Human Capital Challenges," Center for Global Energy Policy, Columbia University, April 2023, https://www.energypolicy.columbia.edu/ middle-east-and-africa-slowing-growth-and-rising-food-prices-present-human-capital-challenges/.

NOTES

1 A LOOK BACK AT 2020: GCC COVID-19 RESPONSE, REFORMS, ENERGY TRANSITION CONCERNS AND MICRO-COMPETITIVENESS

1 $41.8 per barrel based on averaging monthly EIA Brent FOB Europe prices. Brent is a benchmark used to price most of the globally traded crude oil. The price had downward pressure at the beginning of the year due to disagreement between OPEC+ leading members Russia and Saudi Arabia prompting the latter to flood the market with supply as demand began declining due to COVID-19 (Raval, Sheppard, and Brower 2020).

2 Fiscal reliance if considering the sum of all six members' oil revenues as part of the GCC's total budget incomes is lower than the 70 percent average at around 56 percent. See Annex.

3 Fiscal oil breakeven prices estimate the oil price at which state budgets are balanced, leading to neither a surplus nor a deficit. Brent oil prices are used for this paper as all GCC nations are largely oil producers and exporters, except for Qatar where natural gas is the main export commodity, although still tied to oil prices. Fiscal breakeven prices were calculated by author from final fiscal government data provided by official sources.

4 When socioeconomic troubles in the island nation led in 2011 to protests, GCC governments pledged a ten-year, $10 billion aid package to Manama. This may explain the impetus for additional spending in 2012 rising by 14.3 percent above the year prior and is perhaps fuelled by aid from Saudi Arabia and other GCC states.

5 The two $5 billion five-year loans by the National Bank of Abu Dhabi (NBAD) and Al-Hilal Bank in addition to the other $10 billion in bonds to the central bank were due in 2014 and Dubai agreed to a five-year rollover at 1 percent interest rate (Reuters Staff 2014). COVID-19 coincided with payment, so both Emirates agreed to merge assets and companies (Barbuscia, Azhar, and Barbaglia 2020).

6 This partially was the basis for the establishment of Sovereign Wealth Funds (SWFs) as well.

7 On February 24, 2022, Russian armed forces entered Eastern Ukraine which resulted in a humanitarian and energy crisis in Europe. Global crude oil, natural gas, and food prices surged as a result to unprecedented levels (UN Staff 2022).

8 Ammonia is a chemical compound made of three parts hydrogen and one part nitrogen; hence it has the advantage of the ability to carry high hydrogen concentration based on its molecular structure. The compound is envisioned to become a carrier for hydrogen as a fuel source. However, releasing hydrogen from ammonia is an energy intensive process. Also, ammonia is toxic which complicates its transport in comparison to crude oil and natural gas (Thomas and Parks 2006).

9 The package targeted Saudi citizens at private sector companies at up to SAR 9,000 ($2,400) per month for a period of three months and at a total ceiling of $2.39 billion (Arabian Business Staff 2020).

10 Re-named Saudi Central Bank by royal decree in November 2020 (Trade Arabia 2020).

11 Oman's Al Raffd Fund is designed to provide guidance, market research, financing for SMEs and youth entrepreneurship (UN ESCWA 2022). The fund is small and is estimated to have $18 million of assets according to the SWF Institute (SWFI Staff 2022).

12 Long reigning and iconic figure Sultan Qaboos bin Said Al Said passed away two months prior to the pandemic on January 10, 2020 and his cousin Sultan Haitham bin Tariq Al Said ascended to the throne a day after. As Minister of Culture, the new Sultan had overseen formulating Oman's economic diversification strategy 'Oman Vision 2040' in what is seen as preparation for tackling the nation's economic woes. In the aftermath of the pandemic, Sultan Haitham ordered a 10 percent cut in government spending and established a committee to oversee the country's response to the pandemic (Sievers 2020).

13 Sukuk is an Islamic financing certificate similar to a bond but is compliant with Sharia law. Since interest is prohibited in Islam, the certificate is backed by the issuer through a tangible asset where the investors gain direct partial ownership. Bonds are a pre-agreed interest-bearing obligation to be paid back by the issuer at a certain date. But in the case of Sukuk, the investors receive a variable return that depends on the appreciation of the asset itself (Ganti 2022).

14 See country allocation percentages in Figure 1.12.

15 Since the Aramco IPO, Abu Dhabi listed the drilling unit of its National Oil Company (NOC) Adnoc (di Paola and Alloway 2018) which attracted $34 billion in interest. This was followed by Dubai's water and power utility Dewa which drew $86 billion in orders for a $6.1 billion offering. Aramco is planning to list its marketing arm while Abu Dhabi wants to list 10 percent of a petrochemical joint-venture grouping Adnoc with Austrian chemicals giant Borealis (Fioretti and di Paola 2022). In addition to raising funds for the state, the IPOs allow bringing funds to oil and gas assets struggling to draw finances in the age of ESG and sustainable energy investment.

16 The IPOs could also be seen as generating rent from an existing asset. Even, another aspect of governments raiding NOC coffers for social and political purposes (Losman 2010b). The Aramco IPO could also be considered as an equivalent of oil-prepayment when oil producing governments receive payment in advance for oil to be produced in the future (Fattouh, Heidug, and Zakkour 2021).

17 While an exhaustive list does not exist for all the seven Emirates, it is understood that the law excludes strategic industries and operating companies that deal with the country's natural resources.

18 Zakat is an obligatory charity payment to be made by Muslims on their surplus wealth including savings and financial assets at the rate of 2.5 percent in a lunar year (Liberto 2021).

19 The crisis began in June 2017 when Saudi Arabia, the UAE, and Bahrain supported by Egypt severed their diplomatic relations with Qatar. While the four parties coined the crisis a boycott, Doha preferred calling it a blockade. Contentious issues were building for years. Amongst them was the role of Qatari government funded Al Jazeera Media Network, claimed support for the Muslim Brotherhood, and close relations with Iran and Turkey.

2 THE FUTURE OF GULF NOC–IOC PARTNERSHIPS

1 Valérie Marcel and John V. Mitchell, *Oil Titans: National Oil Companies in the Middle East* (London: Chatham House [u.a.], 2006).

2 'Pavilion Unveils GHG Methodology for LNG with Qatar, Chevron,' Energy Intelligence, November 17, 2021, https://www.energyintel.com/0000017d-2cf8-dd20-af7f-2dfdf6160000.

3 'Everything at Once: Transformation of Abu Dhabi's Oil Policy,' Arab Gulf States Institute in Washington, April 15, 2021, https://agsiw.org/everything-at-once-transformation-of-abu-dhabis-oil-policy/.

4 'ADNOC Looking for Partners for ADMA-OPCO Offshore Oil Concession,' Offshore Energy, August 7, 2017, https://www.offshore-energy.biz/adnoc-looking-for-partners-for-adma-opco-offshore-oil-concession/.

5 'ADNOC Announces Plans to Consolidate ADMA-OPCO and ZADCO,' accessed April 7, 2022, https://www.adnoc.ae:443/en/news-and-media/press-releases/2016/adnoc-announces-plans-to-consolidate-adma-opco-and-zadco.

6 'UPDATE 1-BP Strikes Deal for 10 Percent Stake in Abu Dhabi's ADCO Concession,' Reuters, December 17, 2016, sec. Oil Report, https://www.reuters.com/article/energy-emirates-adnoc-bp-idUSL5N1EC0AB.

7 'Our History in Qatar | ExxonMobil Qatar,' ExxonMobil, accessed April 7, 2022, https://www.exxonmobil.com.qa:443/en-QA/Company/Who-we-are/Our-history-in-Qatar.

8 'Qatar Petroleum Taking over Offshore Oil Field from Oxy,' Offshore Energy, October 15, 2018, https://www.offshore-energy.biz/qatar-petroleum-taking-over-offshore-oil-field-from-oxy/.

9 'Al-Shaheen,' North Oil Company, accessed March 31, 2022, https://noc.qa/al-shaheen.html.

10 Katie McQue, 'Qatar to Takeover Qatargas 1 LNG Trains as IOCs Exit,' March 30, 2021, https://www.spglobal.com/commodity-insights/en/market-insights/latest-news/natural-gas/033021-qatar-to-takeover-qatargas-1-lng-trains-as-iocs-exit.

11 'QP Doubles Down on Expansion,' Energy Intelligence, July 6, 2021, https://www.energyintel.com/0000017b-a7dd-de4c-a17b-e7df9e460000.

12 'Exxon Wraps Up Glaucus Appraisal Well,' Energy Intelligence, March 23, 2022, https://www.energyintel.com/0000017f-b2fb-ddab-a1ff-bfffb3340000.

13 'About Golden Pass | Golden Pass LNG,' accessed April 5, 2022, https://www.goldenpasslng.com/about/about-golden-pass.

14 Ellen R. Wald, *Saudi, Inc: The Arabian Kingdom's Pursuit of Profit and Power*, First Pegasus Books edition (New York: Pegasus Books, 2018).

15 Ibid.

16 'Exxon Wraps Up Glaucus Appraisal Well,' Energy Intelligence, March 23, 2022, https://www.energyintel.com/0000017f-b2fb-ddab-a1ff-bfffb3340000.

17 'ADNOC Refining,' accessed April 6, 2022, https://www.adnoc.ae:443/en/adnoc-refining; 'Refining,' accessed April 6, 2022, https://www.qatarenergy.qa/en/WhatWeDo/Pages/Refining.aspx; 'Qatargas – Operations,' accessed April 6, 2022, https://www.qatargas.com/english/operations/laffan-refinery.

18 'SATORP: An Exceptional Partnership,' TotalEnergies.Com, accessed March 28, 2022, https://totalenergies.com/energy-expertise/projects/refining-petrochemical-platform/satorp.

19 'Saudi Aramco Completes Acquisition of Shell's Share of the SASREF Refining Joint Venture,' accessed March 28, 2022, https://www.shell.com/media/news-and-media-releases/2019/saudi-aramco-completes-acquisition-of-shells-share-of-the-sasref-refining-joint-venture.html.

20 'Fujian Refining and Petrochemical Company Ltd.,' accessed March 29, 2022, https://china.aramco.com/en/creating-value/products/refining-and-chemicals/fujian-refining-and-petrochemical-company-ltd.

21 'Motiva Enterprises' Co-Owners to Split U.S. Refineries on May 1: Sources,' Reuters, March 7, 2017, sec. Commodities, https://www.reuters.com/article/us-refineries-motiva-split-idUSKBN16E05B.

22 '3-06-17 Affiliates of Saudi Aramco and Shell Achieve Significant Milestone,' Motiva, accessed March 29, 2022, https://motiva.com/media/in-the-news/3-06-17-affiliates-of-saudi-aramco-and-shell-achieve-significant-milestone.

23 ArgaamPlus, 'Saudi Aramco's Motiva Takes over Flint Hills' Texas Chemical Plant,' ArgaamPlus, accessed March 29, 2022, https://www.argaam.com/en/article/articledetail/id/1328338.

24 'PRefChem At a Glance | PRefChem,' accessed April 6, 2022, https://prefchem.com/prefchem-at-a-glance.

25 Dania Saadi, 'ADNOC Awards Occidental Concession amid Plans to Hit 5 Mil b/d Output,' December 9, 2020, https://www.spglobal.com/commodity-insights/en/market-insights/latest-news/natural-gas/120920-adnoc-awards-occidental-concession-amid-plans-to-hit-5-mil-bd-output; 'Who We Are,' accessed April 2, 2022, https://www.adnoc.ae:443/en/adnoc-sour-gas/about-us/who-we-are.

26 'ADNOC and GE to Develop Decarbonization Roadmap for Power Generation in ADNOC's Downstream and Industry Operations,' accessed April 2, 2022, https://www.adnoc.ae:443/en/news-and-media/press-releases/2021/adnoc-and-ge-to-develop-decarbonization-roadmap-for-power-generation.

27 'Oxy Expands CCS Ambitions Abroad,' Energy Intelligence, October 7, 2021, https://www.energyintel.com/0000017c-5be5-d779-ad7e-dfed0d260000.

28 'Oxy Low Carbon Ventures, Together with Macquarie, Deliver World's First Shipment of Carbon-Neutral Oil,' accessed April 3, 2022, https://www.oxy.com/news/news-releases/oxy-low-carbon-ventures-together-with-macquarie-deliver-worlds-first-shipment-of-carbon-neutral-oil/.

29 'Everything at Once'; 'Historic Milestone for ADNOC as New Trading Arm Begins Derivatives Trading,' accessed April 6, 2022, https://www.adnoc.ae:443/en/news-and-media/press-releases/2020/historic-milestone-for-adnoc-as-new-trading-arm-begins-derivatives-trading.

30 Dania Saadi, 'Murban Futures Contract Opens at $63.43/b as Trading of ADNOC's Flagship Crude Begins,' March 28, 2021, https://www.spglobal.com/commodity-insights/en/market-insights/latest-news/oil/032821-murban-futures-contract-opens-at-6343b-as-trading-of-adnocs-flagship-crude-begins.

31 'ADNOC, Bp and Masdar Agree to Expand UAE-UK New Energy Partnership,' accessed April 3, 2022, https://www.adnoc.ae:443/en/news-and-media/press-releases/2021/adnoc-bp-and-masdar-agree-to-expand-uae-uk-new-energy-partnership.

32 'Qatar LNG Partner Selection Slips,' Energy Intelligence, February 4, 2022, https://www.energyintel.com/0000017e-c69d-d21f-a3fe-cedf78750000.

33 'Germany in Talks With Qatar for LNG Supplies,' Energy Intelligence, March 21, 2022, https://www.energyintel.com/0000017f-ae77-de65-afff-efff8bc60002.

34 'Al Kharsaah, a Pioneering Solar Power Plant in Qatar,' TotalEnergies.com, accessed April 8, 2022, https://totalenergies.com/projects/renewables-electricity/al-kharsaah-pioneering-solar-power-plant-qatar.

35 'Chevron Phillips Chemical and Qatar Petroleum Announce Plans to Jointly Develop U.S. Gulf Coast Petrochemical Project,' Chevron Phillips Chemical, accessed March 31, 2022, https://www.cpchem.com/media-events/news/news-release/chevron-phillips-chemical-and-qatar-petroleum-announce-plans-jointly.

36 Mark Landler, 'Trump Takes Credit for Saudi Move Against Qatar, a U.S. Military Partner,' The New York Times, June 6, 2017, sec. World, https://www.nytimes.com/2017/06/06/world/middleeast/trump-qatar-saudi-arabia.html.

37 'Qatar Buys U.S. F-15s Days After Trump Says Country Funds Terrorism,' accessed March 31, 2022, https://www.nbcnews.com/news/world/qatar-buys-12b-u-s-jets-days-after-trump-says-n772691.

38 'Aramco JV to Develop Major Refinery and Petrochemical Complex in China,' accessed March 29, 2022, https://www.aramco.com/en/news-media/news/2022/aramco-jv-to-develop-major-refinery-and-petrochemical-complex-in-china.

39 'Aramco Starts to Pivot From Focus on Defense,' Energy Intelligence, January 14, 2022, https://www.energyintel.com/0000017e-5867-dd1c-ab7f-fe6777420000.

40 'Aramco and ADNOC: Playing the Long Game,' Arab Gulf States Institute in Washington, June 12, 2019, https://agsiw.org/aramco-and-adnoc-playing-the-long-game/; 'Reliance, Aramco Call off $15 Billion Deal Amid Valuation Differences, Sources Say | Investing News | US News,' accessed April 8, 2022, https://money.usnews.com/investing/news/articles/2021-11-25/reliance-aramco-call-off-15-billion-deal-amid-valuation-differences-sources-say.

41 'Reliance Backs Saudi Aramco Chairman as Independent Director | Reuters,' accessed April 8, 2022, https://www.reuters.com/business/energy/reliance-backs-saudi-aramco-chairman-independent-director-2021-09-29/.

3 MECHANISMS TO FINANCE CLIMATE INVESTMENTS IN THE MIDDLE EAST AND NORTH AFRICA

1 Bogmans, Christian, Lama Kiyasseh, Akito Matsumoto, and Andreas Pescatori, Energy, Efficiency Gains and Economic Development: When Will Global Energy Demand Saturate? International Monetary Fund. November 20, 2020. https://www.imf.org/en/Publications/WP/Issues/2020/11/20/Energy-Efficiency-Gains-and-Economic-Development-When-Will-Global-Energy-Demand-Saturate-49889.

2 ICMA Sustainability Bond Guidelines (SBG) define a sustainability bond as a bond where the proceeds will be exclusively applied to finance or refinance a combination of green and social projects.

3 UN Department of Economic and Social Affairs: Sustainable Development. 'Do you know all 17 SDGs?' https://sdgs.un.org/goals. Accessed April 15, 2022.

4 Bloomberg New Energy Finance, Bloomberg L.P.

5 Refinitiv

6 'Second Party Opinion on Etihad Airways' Sustainability-Linked Financing Framework.' Vigeo Eiris, October 2020. https://www.etihadaviationgroup. com/content/dam/eag/corporate/etihadaviation/en-ae/desktop2/ sustainability/20201020_SLB_SPO_Etihad_VF.pdf. Accessed 15 April, 2022.

7 IRENA, 2020, *Renewable Energy Finance: Sovereign Guarantees*. Renewable Energy Finance Brief 01. International Renwable Energy Agency, Abu Dhabi. January 2020. https://www.irena.org/-/media/Files/IRENA/Agency/ Publication/2020/Jan/IRENA_RE_Sovereign_guarantees_2020.pdf. Accessed April 15, 2022.

8 'Official Export Credit Agencies – Organismes de credit à l'exportation.' OECD. https://www.oecd.org/trade/topics/export-credits/documents/ links-of-official-export-credit-agencies.pdf. Accessed April 15, 2022.

9 'Sukuk.' Corporate Finance Institute. February 12, 2022. https:// corporatefinanceinstitute.com/resources/knowledge/trading-investing/ sukuk/. Accessed April 15, 2022.

10 'Global Sukuk Issuance Likely to Rise at Slow Pace in 2023 amid Volatilities,' Fitch Ratings: Credit Ratings & Analysis for Financial Markets, January 11, 2023. https://www.refinitiv.com/en/resources/special-report/green-sustainability-sukuk-2022-financing-future. Accessed January 21, 2023.

11 Mardi, Marina, Mohamed Rozani Mohamed Osman, and Ahmad Hafiz Abdul Aziz. *Pioneering the Green Sukuk: Three Years On*. World Bank Group: Inclusive Growth and Sustainable Finance Hub in Malaysia. October 2020. https://openknowledge.worldbank.org/bitstream/handle/10986/34569/ Pioneering-the-Green-Sukuk-Three-Years-On. pdf?sequence=1&isAllowed=y. Accessed April 15, 2022.

12 'What You Need to Know About Concessional Finance for Climate Action.' World Bank Group. September 16, 2021. https://www.worldbank.org/en/ news/feature/2021/09/16/what-you-need-to-know-about-concessional-finance-for-climate-action. Accessed April 15, 2022.

13 Watson, Charlene, Liane Schalatek, and Aurélien Evéquoz. 'Climate Finance Regional Briefing: Middle East and North Africa,' Feb 2022. https:// climatefundsupdate.org/wp-content/uploads/2022/03/CFF9-MENA_2021. pdf. Accessed January 20, 2023.

14 'Middle East and North Africa Region.' Climate Investment Funds. https:// www.climateinvestmentfunds.org/country/middle-east-and-north-africa-region. Accessed April 15, 2022.

15 'Rystad: 2022 global energy spending to reach $2 trillion.' *Oil & Gas Journal*, April 7, 2022. https://www.ogj.com/general-interest/economics-markets/article/14270733/rystad-2022-global-energy-spending-to-reach-2-trillion. Accessed April 15, 2022.

16 The IMF defines physical risks as those which can 'materialize directly, through their exposures to corporations, households, and countries that experience climate shocks, or indirectly, through the effects of climate change on the wider economy and feedback effects within the financial system. Exposures manifest themselves through increased default risk of loan portfolios or lower values of assets.' It defines transition risks as those which 'materialize on the asset side of financial institutions, which could incur losses on exposure to firms with business models not built around the economics of low carbon emissions.'

17 Participants in a repurchase agreement include central banks, money market funds, corporate treasurers, pension funds, asset managers, insurance companies, banks, hedge funds, and sovereign wealth funds.

4 POLITICAL PRIORITIES AND ECONOMIC REALITIES: FINANCING THE RENEWABLE ENERGY TRANSITION IN SAUDI ARABIA AND OMAN

1 APICORP Energy Research, 2018. *Saudi Energy Price Reform Getting Serious*. APICORP Energy Research. Dammam, Saudi Arabia: Arab Petroleum Investments Corporation.

2 Joint Research Centre (European Commission), 2019. *Fossil CO2 and GHG emissions of all world countries: 2019 report*. Luxembourg: Publications Office of the European Union. https://op.europa.eu/en/publication-detail/-/publication/9d09ccd1-e0dd-11e9-9c4e-01aa75ed71a1/language-en. Accessed April 5, 2022.

3 Vohra, Anchal, 2021. *The Middle East Is Becoming Literally Uninhabitable*. Foreign Policy. https://foreignpolicy.com/2021/08/24/the-middle-east-is-becoming-literally-uninhabitable/. Accessed April 5, 2022.

4 APICORP Energy Research, 2018.

5 Benali, Leila R., Ramy Al-Ashmawy, and Shatila Suhail, 2021. *MENA Energy Investment Outlook 2021–2025*. Dammam, Saudi Arabia: Arab Petroleum Investment Corporation, p. 38.

6 Implementation Support and Follow-up Unit, 2020. *Annual Report 2019: Towards a Diversified and Sustainable Economy*. Muscat, Oman:

Implementation Support and Follow-up Unit, p.176. https://isfu.gov.om/ISFU-ANNUALREPORT(2019)-Eng.pdf. Accessed April 5, 2022.

7   *National Industrial Development and Logistics Program*. Saudi Arabia. https://www.vision2030.gov.sa/v2030/vrps/nidlp/. Accessed April 5, 2022

8   IRENA, 2016. *Renewable Energy in the Arab Region. Overview of Developments*. Abu Dhabi: International Renewable Energy Agency.

9   'The Law for the Regulation and Privatisation of the Electricity and Related Water Sector.' Oman.

10 APSR, 2021. 'Product Application for Sahim 2.' Muscat, Oman: Authority for Public Services Regulation. https://apsr.om/en/product-application-for-sahim2. Accessed April 5, 2022.

11 Nama Group, 2021. *Annual Report 2020*. Muscat Oman: Nama Group. https://www.nama.om/media/1443/ng-annual-report-2020-english-opt-11.pdf. Accessed April 5, 2022.

12 Prabhu, Conrad, 2021. 'Oman Puts MEDC Privatisation on Hold Pending Review of New Options.' *Oman Observer*. https://www.omanobserver.om/article/1124085/business/energy/oman-puts-medc-privatisation-on-hold-pending-review-of-new-options. Accessed January 25, 2023.

13 Oman Observer, 2021. 'Privatisation of Muscat utility planned by year-end.' https://www.omanobserver.om/article/1100736/business/privatisation-of-muscat-utility-planned-by-year-end. Accessed April 5, 2022.

14 Royal Decree 52/2019 Promulgating the Public Private Partnership Law, Oman.

15 Royal Decree 50/2019 Promulgating the Foreign Capital Investment Law, Oman.

16 PricewaterhouseCoopers, 2021. *Oman: Incentives announced by the Government as part of Oman Vision 2040*. Muscat, Oman: PricewaterhouseCoopers. https://www.pwc.com/m1/en/tax/documents/2021/oman-incentives-announced-by-the-government-as-part-of-oman-vision-2040.pdf. Accessed April 5, 2022.

17 Nama Group, 2021.

18 Al-Badi, Hammam, 2022. 'Oman's OETC Invests $166mln in New Power Networks.' Zawya. https://www.zawya.com/en/projects/utilities/omans-oetc-invests-166mln-in-new-power-networks-bpckp7gl. Accessed January 25, 2023.

19 Reuters, 2022. 'Oman launches first Middle East electricity spot market.' https://www.reuters.com/world/middle-east/oman-launches-first-electricity-spot-market-middle-east-2022-01-26/. Accessed April 5, 2022.

20 OPWP, 2019. *7-Year Statement: 2019–2025*. Muscat, Oman: Oman Power and Water Procurement Co. (SAOC). https://omanpwp.om/PDF/7%20Year%20Statement%202019-2025%20New.pdf. Accessed April 5, 2022.

21 Private Sector Participation Law, Saudi Arabia.

22 Mygov.sa. 2021. *Labor and Employment.* https://www.my.gov.sa/wps/portal/snp/aboutksa/employment#header2_2. Accessed April 5, 2022.

23 Invest Saudi, 2021. *Incentives for Investors.* https://www.investsaudi.sa/en/investor/incentives. Accessed April 5, 2022.

24 APICORP Energy Research, 2018.

25 APICORP Energy Research, 2018.

26 Oq.com. 2022. *Methanol | OQ.* https://oq.com/en/products/intermediates/methanol. Accessed April 5, 2022.

27 Oman News Agency, 2023, 'OQ celebrates opening of $463 million ammonia plant in Salalah.' https://timesofoman.com/article/125541-oq-celebrates-opening-of-463-million-ammonia-plant-in-salalah accessed January 25, 2023.

28 Marubeni, 2021. 'Marubeni Signs Joint Development Agreement for Green Hydrogen & Green Ammonia Production Infrastructure in Oman.' https://www.marubeni.com/en/news/2021/info/00016.html. Accessed April 5, 2022.

29 'Marubeni-led consortium's Green Ammonia project in Oman launch likely in Q1 2028,' 2022: Zawya: https://www.zawya.com/en/projects/industry/marubeni-led-consortiums-green-ammonia-project-in-oman-launch-likely-in-q1-2028-report-siqoiz1a. Accessed January 25, 2023.

30 Oman Investment Authority, 2021. 'As Saudi Crown Prince Visits Oman OIA Companies sign MOUs with their Saudi Counterparts.' https://www.oia.gov.om/Index.php?r=en%2Fsite%2Fnewsview&nid=as-saudi-crown-prince-visits-oman-oia-companies-sign-mous-with-their-saudi-counterparts&csrt=5608872309545054218. Accessed April 5, 2022. Saadi, Dania, 2021, 'Saudi Arabia's ACWA Power, Oman's OQ to study hydrogen project in Dhofar.' Spglobal.com. https://www.spglobal.com/commodity-insights/en/market-insights/latest-news/energy-transition/120821-saudi-arabias-acwa-power-omans-oq-to-study-hydrogen-project-in-dhofar. Accessed April 5, 2022.

31 DEME Group, 2020. 'Kick-off of the Hyport Duqm Green Hydrogen Project.' https://www.deme-group.com/news/kick-hyportr-duqm-green-hydrogen-project. Accessed April 5, 2022.

32 Prabhu, Conrad, 2021. 'Hyport Duqm project eyes 1m mtpa of green ammonia at full capacity.' Oman Observer. https://www.omanobserver.om/article/1111712/business/energy/hyport-duqm-project-eyes-1m-mtpa-of-green-ammonia-at-full-capacity. Accessed April 5, 2022.

33 InterContinental Energy, 2021. 'Green fuels mega project set to make Oman world leader in green hydrogen and green ammonia.' https://intercontinentalenergy.com/documents/ICE-Announcement-20210511.pdf. Accessed April 5, 2022.

34 InterContinental Energy, 2021.

35 Special Economic Zone at Duqm, 2021. 'Duqm, a global centre for green hydrogen production.' https://www.duqm.gov.om/upload/files/Duqm_Magazine25_Greenhydrogen_EN.pdf. Accessed April 5, 2022.

36 Acwapower.com. 2020. *ACWA POWER | Ibri 2 PV IPP*. https://www.acwapower.com/en/projects/ibri-2-pv-ipp/. Accessed April 5, 2022.

37 Almeenaprojects.com, 2020. 'Oman have commissioned 100MW Amin Solar PV Plant.' https://almeenaprojects.com/oman-have-commissioned-100mw-amin-solar-pv-plant/. Accessed April 5, 2022.

38 International Trade Administration, 2020. *Oman's Renewable Energy Projects*. https://www.trade.gov/market-intelligence/omans-renewable-energy-projects. Accessed April 5, 2022.

39 AIIB, 2020. *Ibri II 500MW Solar PV Independent Power Plant Project*. Available at: https://www.aiib.org/en/projects/details/2020/approved/_download/Oman/PSI-Oman-Ibri-II-500MW-Solar-PV-Independent-Power-Plant-Project_March-16-2020.pdf. Accessed April 5, 2022.

40 Fulton, Jonathan, 2019. *China's Gulf Investments Reveal Regional Strategy*. Arab Gulf States Institute in Washington. https://agsiw.org/chinas-gulf-investments-reveal-regional-strategy/. Accessed April 5, 2022.

41 APSR, 2021. 'Product Application for Sahim 2.' Muscat, Oman: Authority for Public Services Regulation. https://apsr.om/en/product-application-for-sahim2. Accessed April 5, 2022.

42 HSBC Oman, 2021. 'HSBC Green Loan.' https://www.hsbc.co.om/loans/products/green/. Accessed April 5, 2022.

43 National Bank of Oman, 2021. *Sustainability Report 2020*. Muscat, Oman: National Bank of Oman. https://www.nbo.om/en/Documents/Annual%20Reports/NBO_Sustainability%20report_English_for%20web.pdf. Accessed April 5, 2022.

44 Abdel-Baky, Mahmoud, and Mahairi Main Garcia, 2021. *Renewable Energy Laws and Regulations Saudi Arabia 2022*. International Comparative Legal Guides International Business Reports. https://iclg.com/practice-areas/renewable-energy-laws-and-regulations/saudi-arabia. Accessed April 5, 2022.

45 Saudi Exim Bank, 2021. *Vision and Mission*. https://saudiexim.gov.sa/en/About/Pages/Vision.aspx. Accessed April 5, 2022.

46 KACST Impact. 2019. *KACST Impact – Smart Energy*. https://kacstimpact.kacst.edu.sa/perspective/45/smart-energy. Accessed April 5, 2022.

47 SEC, 2021. *SEC Annual Report 2020*. Riyadh, Saudi Arabia: Saudi Electricity Company. https://www.se.com.sa/en-us/Lists/AnnualReports/Attachments/22/Annual%20Report-EN-2020.pdf. Accessed April 5, 2022.

48 APICORP Energy Research, 2018.

49 Azhar, Saeed, 2020. 'Saudi Electricity to convert $45 billion in government liabilities into perpetual instrument.' Reuters. https://www.reuters.com/article/saudi-electrcity-debt-int-idUSKBN27W0V0. Accessed April 5, 2022.

50 SEC, 2020. 'Saudi Electricity Company Signs an Agreement with the Government, represented by the Ministry of Finance, to Reclassify its Net

Government Liabilities.' Riyadh, Saudi Arabi: Saudi Electricity Company. https://www.se.com.sa/en-us/invshareholder/Pages/Financial_Agreement. aspx. Accessed April 5, 2022.

51 SEC, 2021. '"Saudi Electricity" announces its financial results for Q2 and first half of 2021.' https://www.se.com.sa/en-us/Pages/newsdetails. aspx?NId=1070. Accessed April 5, 2022.

52 ACWA Power, 2021. *Annual Report 2020*. Riyadh, Saudi Arabia: ACWA Power. Available at: https://acwapower.com/media/341298/acwa-annual-report-2020-en-single-pages.pdf. Accessed April 6, 2022.

53 Power Technology. 2019. *Dumat Al Jandal Wind Farm*. https://www. power-technology.com/projects/dumat-al-jandal-wind-farm/. Accessed April 5, 2022.

54 Oomen, Anup, 2022. 'Saudi's SPPC, ACWA Power ink power purchase agreement for $450mn Ar Rass solar PV project in Saudi Arabia.' Arabian Business. https://www.arabianbusiness.com/industries/energy/saudis-sppc-acwa-power-ink-power-purchase-agreement-for-450mn-ar-rass-solar-pv-project-in-saudi-arabia. Accessed April 5, 2022.

55 Nsenergybusiness.com, 2021. *Sudair PV Solar Power Plant*. https://www. nsenergybusiness.com/projects/sudair-solar-power-plant/. Accessed April 5, 2022.

56 ACWA Power, 2022. *PIF subsidiary* 'Badeel and ACWA Power to develop the MENA region's largest solar energy plant in Saudi Arabia: ACWA Power.' https://www.acwapower.com/news/pif-subsidiary-badeel-and-acwa-power-to-develop-the-mena-regions-largest-solar-energy-plant-in-saudi-arabia/. Accessed January 25, 2023.

57 During the research there have been some indications that ACWA Power has been given preferential treatment in Saudi Arabia during REPDO's competitive tendering process. For example, Masdar's bid for the Sakaka solar power plant was disqualified, with the stated reason being that the technology Masdar proposed – bifacial modules – was unproven. However, the lack of similar cases makes drawing any conclusions difficult. Furthermore, a clear trend that showed ACWA was given preferential treatment would likely have a chilling effect on investments in Saudi Arabia's renewable energy sector, undermining long-term growth.

58 SIDF, 2021. *Annual Report 2020*. Riyadh, Saudi Arabia: Saudi Industrial Development Fund. https://www.sidf.gov.sa/en/AboutSIDF/Pages/AnnualReport.aspx. Accessed April 5, 2022.

59 ACWA Power, 2021. 'ACWA Power announces financial close for 1500 MW Sudair Solar plant and Aramco joining the consortium under PIF renewables program.' https://www.acwapower.com/news/acwa-power-announces-financial-close-for-1500-mw-sudair-solar-plant-and-aramco-joining-the-consortium-under-pif-renewables-program/. Accessed April 5, 2022.

60 Saba, Yousef and Saeed Azhar, 2021. 'Saudi Red Sea project secures $3.8 billion "green" loan for new hotels.' Reuters. https://www.reuters.com/article/saudi-redsea-loans-idUSL4N2MK1MM. Accessed April 5, 2022.

61 SNB, 2021. *SNB Sustainable Finance Framework*. Riyadh, Saudi Arabia: Saudi National Bank. https://www.alahli.com/en-us/Investor_Relation/Documents/SNB-Sustainable-Finance-Framework-15-11-2021-v2.pdf. Accessed April 5, 2022.

62 SABB, 2021. 'SABB Green deposit account.' https://www.sabb.com/en/everyday-banking/accounts/green-deposits/. Accessed April 5, 2022.

63 Saudi Investment Bank, 2019. *Credit Policy Guide – Lending Policy*. Riyadh, Saudi Arabia: Saudi Investment Bank. https://www.saib.com.sa/sites/default/files/2019-09/cpg-en.pdf. Accessed April 5, 2022.

64 Al-Rajhi Bank, 2021. *Al-Rajhi Bank ESG Report 2020*. Riyadh, Saudi Arabia: Al-Rajhi Bank. https://www.alrajhibank.com.sa/ir/esg_report/esg_report.html. Accessed April 5, 2022.

65 Embassy of the People's Republic of China in the United States of America, 2022. 'Wang Yi Holds Telephone Talks with Minister of Foreign Affairs and International Cooperation Sheikh Abdullah bin Zayed Al Nahyan of the UAE.' http://www.china-embassy.org/eng/zgyw/202201/t20220114_10495618.htm. Accessed April 5, 2022.

66 Rapoza, Kenneth, 2021. 'How China's Solar Industry Is Set Up To Be The New Green OPEC.' Forbes. https://www.forbes.com/sites/kenrapoza/2021/03/14/how-chinas-solar-industry-is-set-up-to-be-the-new-green-opec/?sh=688bd3c31446. Accessed April 5, 2022.

67 Invest Saudi, 2020. *Wadi Aldawasir Solar PV 120 MW*. Riyadh, Saudi Arabia: Invest Saudi. https://investsaudi.sa/medias/ew-e-inv-opp-scorecard-wadi-aldawasir-solar-pv-120-mw.pdf?context=bWFzdGVyfHBvcnRhbC1tZWRpYXwzNDI5ODV8YXBwbGljYXRpb24vcGRmfHBvcnRhbC1tZWRpYS9oNGUvaDkzLzg4NTUyyMjA4NzkzOTAucGRmfGEzYTExZDQ1ZjMwMzg5OTNmZDc2YmE0MDkxMjc2NGZjNDdiYjQ5MDFjOTlMDUzMWU3TTjZGFmYzQxMmYxZTTU. Accessed April 5, 2022.

68 'National Industrial Development and Logistics Program,' Saudi Arabia.

69 ACWA Power, 2021. *Annual Report 2020*. Riyadh, Saudi Arabia: ACWA Power. Available at: https://acwapower.com/media/341298/acwa-annual-report-2020-en-single-pages.pdf. Accessed April 6, 2022.

70 Saudi Green Initiative/Middle East Green Initiative, 2021. Middle East Green Initiative Summit Communiqué. https://www.saudigreeninitiative.org/pr/MGI_Communique_26Oct_EN.pdf. Accessed April 5, 2022.

71 Saudi Green Initiative, 2021. 'The Saudi Green Initiative aims to improve quality of life.' https://www.saudigreeninitiative.org/about-saudi-green-initiative/. Accessed April 5, 2022.

5 THE POLITICAL DIMENSIONS OF ENERGY TRANSITION IN MENA: A CHANGING LANDSCAPE AT THE NATIONAL, REGIONAL, AND GLOBAL LEVELS

1 Nader Kabbani and Nejla Ben Mimoun, 'Economic Diversification in the Gulf: Time to redouble efforts,' Brookings Institution, January 31, 2021, https://www.brookings.edu/research/economic-diversification-in-the-gulf-time-to-redouble-efforts/.

2 'Energy mix,' Our World in Data, accessed April 2023, https://ourworldindata.org/energy-mix.

3 'Economic Diversification in Oil-Exporting Arab Countries,' International Monetary Fund, April 29, 2016, https://www.imf.org/en/Publications/Policy-Papers/Issues/2016/12/31/Economic-Diversification-in-Oil-Exporting-Arab-Countries-PP5038.

4 Kabbani and Mimoun, 2021.

5 Jean-Eric Aubert and Jean-Louis Reiffers, 'Knowledge Economies in the Middle East and North Africa: Toward New Development Strategies,' World Bank Series, World Bank Group, 2003, https://digitallibrary.un.org/record/542993?ln=en.

6 'OPEC Share of World Crude Oil Reserves,' OPEC Annual Statistical Bulletin 2022, https://www.opec.org/opec_web/en/data_graphs/330.htm.

7 Arathy Somasekhar, 'US poised to become net exporter of crude oil in 2023,' Reuters, December 19, 2022, https://www.reuters.com/business/energy/us-poised-become-net-exporter-crude-oil-2023-2022-12-19/.

8 Zainab Fattah, 'UAE Joined China, India in Abstaining on UN Ukraine Vote,' Bloomberg News, February 26, 2022, https://www.bloomberg.com/news/articles/2022-02-26/uae-abstained-in-un-vote-on-ukraine-to-put-emphasis-on-diplomacy?leadSource=uverify%20wall.

9 'The UN Resolution on Ukraine: How Did the Middle East Vote?,' Washington Institute for Near East Policy, March 2, 2022, https://www.washingtoninstitute.org/policy-analysis/un-resolution-ukraine-how-did-middle-east-vote.

10 'Europe facing peak oil,' The Greens in the European Parliament, 2012, https://www.greens-efa.eu/legacy/fileadmin/dam/Documents/Publications/Energy/Fossil_fuels/PIC%20petrolier_EN_lowres.pdf.

11 'China surpassed the United States as the world's largest crude oil importer in 2017,' US Energy Information Administration, December 21, 2018, https://www.eia.gov/todayinenergy/detail.php?id=37821.

12 'China Global Investment Tracker', American Enterprise Institute, 2022, https://www.aei.org/china-global-investment-tracker/.

13 'China-Arab States Cooperation Forum Holds the 17th Senior Officials' Meeting and the 6th Senior Official Level Strategic Political Dialogue', Ministry of Foreign Affairs of the People's Republic of China, June 23, 2021, https://www.fmprc.gov.cn/eng/wjbxw/202106/t20210624_9134414.html; Forum on China-Africa Cooperation, accessed April 2023, http://www.focac. org.cn/eng/; 'Shanghai Cooperation Organization', UN Political and Peacebuilding Affairs, accessed April 2023, https://dppa.un.org/en/shanghai-cooperation-organization; Anchal Vohra, 'Xi Jinping Has Transformed China's Middle East Policy', Foreign Policy, February 1, 2022, https://foreignpolicy.com/2022/02/01/xi-jinping-has-transformed-chinas-middle-east-policy/.

6 THE NEXT BIG THING IN MENA POWER – GRIDS AND ENERGY STORAGE

1 International Energy Agency (2021), *World Energy Outlook 2021*, Paris: IEA.

2 Data compiled by author.

3 Data compiled by author.

4 International Energy Agency (2021), *Electricity Market Report: January 2021*, Paris: IEA.

5 Data compiled by author.

6 World Resources Institute (2015), *Ranking the World's Most Water Stressed Countries in 2040*.

7 World Bank Group (2018), *Beyond Scarcity: Water Security in the Middle East and North Africa*, Washington D.C.: World Bank.

8 Geothermal energy consists of the production of electricity through the heat of the planet's sub-surface and is considered baseload power generation.

9 Data compiled from International Renewable Energy Agency (2022), *Renewable Energy Statistics 2022*, Abu Dhabi: IRENA.

10 Ibid.

11 Arab Petroleum Investments Corporation (2022), *MENA Energy Investments 2022–2026*, Dammam: APICORP.

12 International Renewable Energy Agency (2019), 'Five Reasons why Countries in the Region are Turning to Renewables', IRENA, October 20, 2019. Available online: https://www.irena.org/newsroom/articles/2019/Oct/Five-Reasons-Why-Countries-in-the-Arabian-Gulf-are-Turning-to-Renewables.

13 National Academy of Engineering and National Research Council (2010), *The Power of Renewables: Opportunities and Challenges for China and the United States*, Washington, D.C.: The National Academies Press.

14 Bellini, E. (2019), 'Jordan suspends renewables auctions, new licenses for projects over 1 MW', *PV Magazine*, January 28, 2019. Available online: http://surl.li/blkfz.

15 Data compiled by author.

16 Ibid.

17 Sedaoui, R. (2022), 'Energy and the Economy in the Middle East and North Africa,' in M. Hafner and G. Luciani (eds), *The Palgrave Handbook of International Energy Economics*, 667–691, Cham: Palgrave Macmillan.

18 Al-Wesabi et al. (2022), 'A review of Yemen's current energy situation, challenges, strategies, and prospects for using renewable energy systems,' *Environmental Science and Pollution Research*, 53907–53933.

19 Inertia refers to the energy stored in large rotating generators giving the ability to retain rotation. A power network with low inertia is subject to blackouts; General Electric (2021), *Pathways to Faster Decarbonization in the GCC's Power Sector*.

20 Arab Petroleum Investments Corporation (2022), *MENA Energy Investments 2022–2026*, Dammam: APICORP.

21 Arab Petroleum Investments Corporation (2021), *Leveraging Energy Storage Systems in MENA*, Dammam: APICORP.

22 Al-Aqeel, T., and S. Hasan (2020), 'Energy Exchanges on the GCCIA Interconnector,' King Abdullah Petroleum Studies and Research Center.

23 Gianfranco C. (2009), 'Electricity Market Evolution in Europe,' *Scientific Bulletin of the Electrical Engineering Faculty*.

24 Arab Petroleum Investments Corporation (2021), *Leveraging Energy Storage Systems in MENA*, Dammam: APICORP.

25 Ibid.

26 Arab Petroleum Investments Corporation (2021), *Leveraging Energy Storage Systems in MENA*, Dammam: APICORP.

7 GREEN HYDROGEN PRODUCTION IN NORTH AFRICA: CHALLENGES AND OPPORTUNITIES

1 European Commission, 'A hydrogen strategy for a climate-neutral Europe.' European Commission, July 8, 2020. https://ec.europa.eu/energy/sites/ener/files/hydrogen_strategy.pdf.

2   Christina Brooks, 'Germany leads pack of countries pouring finance into hydrogen.' IHS Markit, March 24, 2022. https://cleanenergynews.ihsmarkit.com/research-analysis/germany-tops-table-of-states-pouring-finance-into-hydrogen.html.

3   World Bank, 'Middle East and North Africa.' Global Solar Atlas, October 23, 2019. https://globalsolaratlas.info/download/middle-east-and-north-africa.

4   Ibid.

5   https://worldbank-atlas.s3.amazonaws.com/download/Germany/Germany_DNI_mid-size-map_156x220mm-300dpi_v20191205.png?AWSAccessKeyI d=ASIAS2HACIWTKLQ3FB42&Expires=1661085091&Signature=SJYa C%2FCrLawiZ4wl7CxLO1gGMlY%3D&x-amz-security-token=IQoJb3Jp Z2luX2VjEOT%2F%2F%2F%2F%2F%2F%2F%2F%2FwEaCWV1LX dlc3QtMSJHMEUCIGt4MqvO7Se7A%2BYe5AklZkJTkkvJP41uTjg2b476 LE88AiEA1XD9ooKOrCtEs4FXIraiLkg3WdtLwTEqiaDHCeezCkIq1QM IXRAEGgwxOTM3NDM0MzkyNzAiDMXvAIN4qs2p9r7JgiqyAyEoGm DMeUzVtNWhkg16y9HpL0niV%2F0%2FDGKM8m49jT1r4F1VmiEQ sam0E6RK2ZCDfbOAT7GwGrn4%2FJBwdmhLfCPWh%2FJ5zsHZKGffg AvzSSsh%2F9HiBDtJyyvgj4l5%2FL6aeaNO%2FafPWq0mw8uoQeJ9z%2 Bn%2Bjkrd80wLkkLugkFKoP%2FO5jzo26OMmPlKcVqYd5%2FIacyYhN 7Eendt1JZu4quzPQUlrAXzF82BAXi4zNCIJQAA6BEgpRRvxTlXVGV nrvy5Mmu4PKOTH5gPuPXXfJij8FjkKGSauXgVBkbOkBmeVNXCPQv 8PRIpDM5b2uhoaBkTc1O7rwtlckDTLPPvyXQm%2Bo06O6z3ACUkRv kiFlnpF61A0jvVnvMDsz3Y0nHLA1PgMGsCloBQXC26J8nMRciVuNoq ctMf3gXdHAfFUgYoGboh%2BhgnkJHjxoURTWpM%2BoAGdf2jHtZx7 DzvAd%2BB7B9282gN1mA0hKpJP1ZlDlLS8jQGwPM4Q9yPRfzCenPfC jKY3HN71Z6nhDLqkBXNhlXJQ%2FnW3Vd6B9NcLbdakRmSTFhOSK 77gbOoYvKmOvpYRTEQWjW%2FMLi%2BiJgGOp4BiiJRYadMGa4Z6 mB0VjadCCuJ4lawKjdht8q%2BkO%2Fq9MEwX6R7hu9H9azTx5IgwPnIc GDHIQT5PifgCN2v9FFtCE9Y3EO4otH0TlaZmDhkISqDicFg1%2B%2B% 2BuPiGZbiOETRWCUZlQg%2BtUV3Zc1Qfx%2BVln48YbSOX%2BlUheJC jAj6RX52sJAlRCGIR35s1mwGmLji9Oy8cDoquC%2FPPfSbR%2FzSw%3D.

6   Will de Freitas, 'Could the Sahara turn Africa into a solar superpower?' World Economic Forum. January 17, 2020. https://www.weforum.org/agenda/2020/01/solar-panels-sahara-desert-renewable-energy/.

7   For an example of wind power in the region, see the discussion on Egypt's advances in wind power in Michaël Tanchum, 'Egypt's Prospects as an Energy Export Hub Across Three Continents,' Istituto per gli Studi di Politica Internazionale (ISPI), September 24, 2020. https://www.ispionline.it/en/pubblicazione/egypts-prospects-energy-export-hub-across-three-continents-27408.

8   Reuters Staff, 'Desertec shareholders jump ship as solar project folds.' Reuters, October 14, 2014. https://www.reuters.com/article/germany-desertec/desertec-shareholders-jump-ship-as-solar-project-folds-idUSL6N0S535V20141014.

9 'Statistical Review of World Energy 2021 | 70th edition.' BP, July 2021. https://www.bp.com/content/dam/bp/business-sites/en/global/corporate/pdfs/energy-economics/statistical-review/bp-stats-review-2021-full-report.pdf.

10 EcoConServ Environmental Solutions, 'Benban 1.8GW PV Solar Park Final Report.' New and Renewable Energy Authority, February 2016. https://www.eib.org/attachments/registers/65771943.pdf.

11 'Benban Solar Park.' NS Energy, n.d. https://www.nsenergybusiness.com/projects/benban-solar-park.

12 Nicholas Nhede, 'Egypt's largest wind energy farm is now operational.' Smart Energy International, November 5, 2019. https://www.smart-energy.com/renewable-energy/egypts-largest-wind-energy-farm-is-now-operational/.

13 Egypt Today staff. 'Egypt eliminates power outages, exports the surplus.' Egypt Today. December 27, 2021. https://www.egypttoday.com/Article/3/111287/Egypt-eliminates-power-outages-exports-the-surplus#:~:text=CAIRO%20%2D%2027%20December%202021%3A%20Egypt's,capacity%20of%20the%20High%20Dam.

14 IEA, 'Ammonia Technology Roadmap towards more sustainable nitrogen fertilizer production.' International Energy Agency, 2021. https://iea.blob.core.windows.net/assets/6ee41bb9-8e81-4b64-8701-2acc064ff6e4/AmmoniaTechnologyRoadmap.pdf.

15 Michaël Tanchum, 'Morocco – a top fertiliser producer – could hold a key to the world's food supply.' The Conversation – Africa, July 10, 2022. https://theconversation.com/morocco-a-top-fertiliser-producer-could-hold-a-key-to-the-worlds-food-supply-180797.

16 M. Garside, 'Phosphate rock reserves worldwide in 2021, by country.' Statista, March 15, 2022. https://www.statista.com/statistics/681747/phosphate-rock-reserves-by-country/.

17 OCP, 'Sustainability Report 2020.' OCP, August 2021. https://ocpsiteprodsa.blob.core.windows.net/media/2021-08/OCP-Sustainability_report_2020-GRI_certified.pdf.

18 'Fitch Revises Outlook on OCP to Stable; Affirms at "BB+".' Fitch Ratings, October 28, 2020. https://www.fitchratings.com/research/corporate-finance/fitch-revises-outlook-on-ocp-to-stable-affirms-at-bb-28-10-2020.

19 'Standard Fertilizers.' OCP, n.d. https://www.ocpgroup.ma/standard-fertilizers.

20 Ron Sterk, 'High fertilizer prices, tight supplies may adversely affect 2022 acreage.' FoodBusinessNews, December 12, 2021. https://www.foodbusinessnews.net/articles/20163-high-fertilizer-prices-tight-supplies-may-adversely-affect-2022-acreage.

21 Ibid.

22 Russ Quin, 'DTN Retail Fertilizer Trends.' Progressive Farmer, September 22, 2021. https://www.dtnpf.com/agriculture/web/ag/crops/article/2021/09/22/

dap-fertilizer-tops-700-per-ton-time#:~:text=DAP%20prices%20
increased%201%25%20to,the%20second%20week%20of%20Dec.

23 Julie Chaudier, 'Will Hydrogen fuel Morocco's industrial projects of the future?' The Africa Report, September 6, 2021. https://www.theafricareport.com/124184/will-hydrogen-fuel-moroccos-industrial-projects-of-the-future/.

24 Trevor Brown, 'OCP's Green Ammonia pilot plant, and the African Institute.' Ammonia Energy Association, August 17, 2018. https://www.ammoniaenergy.org/articles/ocps-green-ammonia-pilot-plant-and-the-african-institute-for-solar-ammonia/.

25 OCP, 'Sustainability Report 2020.' OCP, August 2021.

26 Ibid.

27 Federal Ministry for Economic Affairs and Energy, 'The National Hydrogen Strategy.' Federal Republic of Germany, June 2020. https://www.bmwk.de/Redaktion/EN/Publikationen/Energie/the-national-hydrogen-strategy.pdf?__blob=publicationFile&v=6; MAP, 'Morocco, Germany Sign Green Hydrogen Cooperation Agreement.' Kingdom of Morocco, June 10, 2020. https://www.maroc.ma/en/news/morocco-germany-sign-green-hydrogen-cooperation-agreement.

28 Julie Chaudier, 'Will Hydrogen fuel Morocco's industrial projects of the future?' The Africa Report, September 6, 2021.

29 Oliver Ristau, 'Solar power from the desert.' KfW, October 27, 2021. https://www.kfw.de/stories/environment/renewable-energy/solarstrom-aus-der-wueste/.

30 'German foreign minister visits Morocco after diplomatic row.' Deutsche Welle, August 25, 2022. https://www.dw.com/en/german-foreign-minister-visits-morocco-after-diplomatic-row/a-62923298.

31 Ruth Sharpe, 'Morocco outlines plans for new green ammonia project.' Argus Media, July 20, 2021. https://www.argusmedia.com/en/news/2235820-morocco-outlines-plans-for-new-green-ammonia-project.

32 Yahya Benabdellah, 'Le projet pilote de production d'ammoniac vert ouvre de grandes perspectives pour le Maroc.' Medias24, September 4, 2022. https://medias24.com/2022/09/04/le-projet-pilote-de-production-dammoniac-vert-ouvre-de-grandes-perspectives-pour-le-maroc/.

33 Rianne, 'UM6P and Proton Ventures sign an agreement for the construction of the Green Ammonia Pilot in Jorf Lasfar.' Proton Ventures, July 25, 2021. https://protonventures.com/press-release/um6p-and-proton-ventures-sign-an-agreement-for-the-construction-of-the-green-ammonia-pilot-in-jorf-lasfar/.

34 Rebecca R. Beswick, Alexandra M. Oliveira, and Yushan Yan, 'Does the Green Hydrogen Economy Have a Water Problem?' *CS Energy Letters* 6 (9): 3167–3169. https://pubs.acs.org/doi/10.1021/acsenergylett.1c01375.

35 Julien Wagner, 'Morocco's OCP – A big, green mining machine.' The Africa Report, March 7, 2019. https://www.theafricareport.com/413/mining-a-big-green-mining-machine/.

36 OCP, 'Sustainability Report 2020.' OCP; OCP, 'Industrial operations, OCP, n.d. https://www.ocpgroup.ma/industrial-operations.

37 European Training Foundation, 'Summary Note – The future of skills: A case study of the agri-food sector in Morocco.' Europen Training Foundation, 2021. https://www.etf.europa.eu/en/publications-and-resources/publications/future-skills-case-study-agri-food-sector-morocco.

38 Lahcen Mokena, 'Morocco's King Launches "Green Generation 2020–2030."' Asharq Al-Awsat, February 15, 2020. https://english.aawsat.com/home/article/2132676/moroccos-king-launches-green-generation-2020-2030.

39 MAP, 'Head of Government: 2020–2050 National Water Plan, Roadmap to Face Challenges for Next 30 years.' Kingdom of Morocco, December 25, 2019. https://www.maroc.ma/en/news/head-government-2020-2050-national-water-plan-roadmap-face-challenges-next-30-years.

40 Andrew James Schunke, German Alberto Hernandez Hererra, Lokesh Padhye, Terri-Ann Berry, 'Energy Recovery in SWRO Desalination: Current Status and New Possibilities.' Frontiers, April 3, 2020. https://www.frontiersin.org/articles/10.3389/frsc.2020.00009/full.

41 'Ammonia production worldwide in 2021, by country.' Statista, January 2022. https://www.statista.com/statistics/1266244/global-ammonia-production-by-country/.

42 'Egypt to launch $40bn hydrogen strategy before June 2022.' Energy and Utilities, January 31, 2022. https://energy-utilities.com/egypt-to-launch-40bn-hydrogen-strategy-before-news116149.html.

43 Nibal Zgheib, 'EBRD assesses low-carbon hydrogen in Egypt.' European Bank for Reconstruction and Development, March 7, 2022. https://www.ebrd.com/news/2022/ebrd-assesses-lowcarbon-hydrogen-in-egypt.html.

44 'Egypt cooperates with Belgian "DEME" to start producing, exporting green hydrogen.' Egypt Today, March 4, 2021. https://www.egypttoday.com/Article/3/99297/Egypt-cooperates-with-Belgian-DEME-to-start-producing-exporting-green.

45 Jean Marie Takouleu, 'Egypt: Belgium's Deme signs with the authorities for green hydrogen studies.' Afrik 21, March 8, 2021. https://www.afrik21.africa/en/egypt-belgiums-deme-signs-with-the-authorities-for-green-hydrogen-studies/.

46 World Bank, 'Egypt – Climate Risk Profile.' World Bank, 2020. https://climateknowledgeportal.worldbank.org/sites/default/files/2021-04/15723-WB_Egypt%20Country%20Profile-WEB-2_0.pdf.

47 Samar Samir, 'Drought Fears Grow as Nile Talks Run On.' Egypt Today, October 3, 2020. https://www.egypttoday.com/Article/15/92628/Drought-Fears-Grow-as-Nile-Talks-Run-On.

48 Ibid.

49 Ali Habib and Moustefa Ouki, 'Egypt's Low Carbon Hydrogen Development Prospects.' Oxford Institute for Energy Studies, November 2021. https://

a9w7k6q9.stackpathcdn.com/wpcms/wp-content/uploads/2021/11/
Egypts-Low-Carbon-Hydrogen-Development-Prospects-ET04.pdf.

50 Press Release, 'Scatec's Green Hydrogen Consortium in Egypt selects Plug Power for delivery of 100 MW Electrolyser.' Scatec., November 24, 2021. https://scatec.com/2021/11/24/scatecs-green-hydrogen-consortium-in-egypt-selects-plug-power-for-delivery-of-100-mw-electrolyser/.

51 Ibid.; Mohammed Abou Zaid, 'Egypt to Open its First Green Hydrogen Plant in November 2022.' Arab News, December 16, 2021. https://www.arabnews.com/node/1987996/business-economy.

52 Press Release, 'Scatec partners with Fertiglobe and the Sovereign Fund of Egypt to develop green hydrogen as feedstock for ammonia production in Egypt.' Scatec, October 14, 2021. https://scatec.com/2021/10/14/scatec-partners-with-fertiglobe-and-the-sovereign-fund-of-egypt-to-develop-green-hydrogen-as-feedstock-for-ammonia-production-in-egypt/.

53 Press Release, 'Siemens Energy supports Egypt to develop Green Hydrogen Industry.' Siemens Energy, August 24, 2021. https://press.siemens-energy.com/mea/en/pressrelease/siemens-energy-supports-egypt-develop-green-hydrogen-industry.

54 Ibid.

55 Ali Habib and Moustefa Ouki, 'Egypt's Low Carbon Hydrogen Development Prospects.' Oxford Institute for Energy Studies, November 2021.

56 Press Release, 'Eni signs an agreement to produce hydrogen in Egypt.' Eni, July 8, 2021. https://www.eni.com/en-IT/media/press-release/2021/07/cs-eni-firma-accordo-produzione-idrogeno-egitto.html.

57 'Egypt 6th in world in urea production, produces 7.8M tons of nitrogen fertilizers.' Egypt Today, December 28, 2021. https://www.egypttoday.com/Article/3/111326/Egypt-6th-in-world-in-urea-production-produces-7-8M#:~:text=CAIRO%20%2D%2028%20December%202021%3A%20Egypt,production%20with%206.7%20million%20tons.

58 IRENA, 'Energy Profile – Algeria.' International Renewable Energy Agency, August 24, 2022. https://www.irena.org/IRENADocuments/Statistical_Profiles/Africa/Algeria_Africa_RE_SP.pdf

59 World Bank, 'Algeria MPO.' World Bank, April 2022. https://thedocs.worldbank.org/en/doc/65cf93926fdb3ea23b72f277fc249a72-0500042021/related/mpo-dza.pdf.

60 Michaël Tanchum, 'Europe–Africa Connectivity Outlook 2021: Post-Covid-19 Challenges and Strategic Opportunities.' Istituto Affari Internaionazionale (IAI), May 20, 2021. https://www.iai.it/sites/default/files/iaip2120.pdf.

61 Michael Barnard, 'CLEAN POWER: Paul Martin Talks H2 Science Coalition & More Problems With Hydrogen.' Clean Technica, March 1, 2022. https://cleantechnica.com/2022/03/01/paul-martin-talks-h2-science-coalition-more-problems-with-hydrogen/.

62 James Burgess, 'Blue hydrogen 20% worse for GHG emissions than natural gas in heating: study.' S&P Global, August 12, 2021. https://www.spglobal.com/commodityinsights/en/market-insights/latest-news/natural-gas/081221-blue-hydrogen-20-worse-for-ghg-emissions-than-natural-gas-in-heating-study.

63 Nicola Warwick, Paul Griffiths, James Keeble, Alexander Archibald, John Pyle, and Keith Shine, 'Atmospheric implications of increased Hydrogen use.' Government of the United Kingdom. April 2022. https://assets.publishing.service.gov.uk/government/uploads/system/uploads/attachment_data/file/1067144/atmospheric-implications-of-increased-hydrogen-use.pdf.

64 Paul Martin, 'CLEAN POWER: Is Hydrogen The Best Option To Replace Natural Gas In The Home? Looking At The Numbers.' Clean Technica, December 14, 2020. https://cleantechnica.com/2020/12/14/can-hydrogen-replace-natural-gas-looking-at-the-numbers/.

65 Ibid.

66 German-Algerian Energy Partnership, 'The German-Algerian Energy Partnership.' The German-Algerian Energy Partnership. https://www.energypartnership-algeria.org/home/.

67 German-Algerian Energy Partnership, 'Étude Exploratoire sur le Potentiel du Power-to-X (Hydrogène Vert) pour l'Algérie.' German-Algerian Energy Partnership. https://www.energypartnership-algeria.org/fileadmin/user_upload/algeria/21_12_07_Hydrog%C3%A8ne_vert_en_Alg%C3%A9rie_-_Rapport_PE.pdf.

68 Ibid.

69 Ibid.

70 Ibid.

71 Embassy of Algeria to Croatia, 'Hydrogen Production: Algeria in a Position to Play Leading Regional Role.' Embassy of Algeria in Croatia. https://www.ambalgzagreb.com/hydrogen-production-algeria-in-position-to-play-leading-regional-role/.

72 Press Release, 'New agreement reached by SONATRACH and Eni to accelerate the development of gas projects and decarbonization via green hydrogen.' Eni, May 26, 2022. https://www.eni.com/en-IT/media/press-release/2022/05/new-agreement-eni-sonatrach-gas-development-green-hydrogen-draghi-tebboune.html.

73 James Burgess, 'Blue hydrogen 20% worse for GHG emissions than natural gas in heating: study.' S&P Global.

74 World Bank, 'Fertilizer Consumption (% of fertilizer production) – Algeria.' World Bank. https://data.worldbank.org/indicator/AG.CON.FERT.PT.ZS?end=2018&locations=DZ&start=1961&view=chart.

75 World Bank, 'Fertilizer Consumption – Kilograms per Hectare of Arable Land.' World Bank. https://data.worldbank.org/indicator/AG.CON.FERT.ZS.

76 Xinhua. 'Algeria, China sign pacts ahead of 6-bln-USD mega phosphate project.' Xinhua, November 27, 2018. http://www.xinhuanet.com/english/2018-11/27/c_137633212.htm.

77 'Algeria's Expensive Water Problem.' Stratfor, January 20, 2016. https://worldview.stratfor.com/article/algerias-expensive-water-problem; 'Aquastat.' Food and Agricultural Organization of the United Nations.

78 'Algeria: A Desert Nation Fighting to Maintain Water Supplies.' Stratfor, January 20, 2016. https://worldview.stratfor.com/article/algeria-desert-nation-fighting-maintain-water-supplies.

79 'Algeria Average Precipitation.' Trading Economics, n.d. https://tradingeconomics.com/algeria/precipitation.

80 Ines Magoum, 'Algeria: 4 Desalination Plants to be Reactivated between June and August 2021.' Afrik 21, June 18, 2021. https://www.afrik21.africa/en/algeria-4-desalination-plants-to-be-reactivated-between-june-and-august-2021/; Ines Magoum, 'Algeria: Three Seawater Desalination Plants to be Constructed Soon.' Afrik 21, May 12, 2020. https://www.afrik21.africa/en/algeria-three-seawater-desalination-plants-to-be-constructed-soon/#:~:text=In%20Algeria%2C%2011%20seawater%20desalination,of%20drinking%20water%20consumed%20nationally.

81 Vanessa Szakal, 'Under the Tunisian Sun: Expanding Solar Energy Production for Auto Consumption and Export.' Nawaat, August 22, 2014. https://nawaat.org/2014/08/22/under-the-tunisian-sun-expanding-solar-energy-production-for-autoconsumption-and-export/#:~:text=%C2%ABThe%20DESERTEC%20Foundation%20is%20endorsing,model%2Dfor%2Dthe%2Drest.

82 Ibid.

83 Federal Ministry of Economic Cooperation and Development, 'Promoting Renewable Energies, Launching an Energy Transition.' BMZ. https://www.bmz.de/en/countries/tunisia/core-area-responsibility-for-our-planet-climate-and-energy-100138#:~:text=%22Green%22%20hydrogen&text=In%20December%202020%2C%20the%20BMZ,pilot%20projects%20in%20that%20field.

84 Renewable Centre for Renewable Energy and Energy Efficiency, 'New MOU Signed for the Establishment of a Tunisian-German Green Hydrogen Alliance (Power-to-X).' Renewable Centre for Renewable Energy and Energy Efficiency. https://www.rcreee.org/news/new-mou-signed-establishment-tunisian-german-green-hydrogen-alliance-power-x.

85 Tunur, 'Tunisia Germany PtX Dialogue 30th June 2021: Green Hydrogen and Ammonia Opportunities in Tunisia.' Tunur. https://www.tunur.tn/wp-content/uploads/2021/06/TuNur-PtX-Dialogue-VF2.pdf.

86 Deutsche Gesellschaft fur Internationale Zusammenarbeit (GIZ) GmbH, 'Study on the Opportunities of "Power-to-X" in Tunisia.' GIZ. https://energypedia.info/images/0/0c/Potential_Study_PtX_in_Tunisia_2021.pdf.

87 GIEWS – Global Information and Early Warning System, 'Country Profile – Tunisia.' Food and Agriculture Organization of the United Nations, July 27, 2022. https://www.fao.org/giews/countrybrief/country.jsp?code=TUN.

88 Layli Foroudi, 'Thirsty crops, leaky infrastructure drive Tunisia's water crisis.' Reuters, November 1, 2019. https://www.reuters.com/article/us-tunisia-water-land-feature-trfn-idUSKBN1XB2X.1

89 Ibid.

90 TAP, 'Water stock in dams down to 722.8 million cubic meters.' Agence Tunisie Afrique Presse, September 17, 2021. https://www.tap.info.tn/en/Portal-Economy/14394669-water-reserves-of.

8 QATAR'S LNG INDUSTRY IN THE AGE OF HYDROCARBON MARKETS INSTABILITY AND ENERGY TRANSITION

1 'What is Energy Transition?' S&P Global, 24 February 2020. https://www.spglobal.com/en/research-insights/articles/what-is-energy-transition#:~:text=Energy%20transition%20refers%20to%20the,well%20as%20lithium%2Dion%20batteries.

2 'Energy Transition: Definition and Solution,' MET Group, 29 July 2021. https://group.met.com/en/media/energy-insight/energy-transition

3 IRENA, Energy Transition, IRENA, 2020. https://www.irena.org/energytransition#:~:text=The%20energy%20transition%20is%20a,emissions%20to%20limit%20climate%20change.

4 Mills, Robin, 'A Fine Balance: The Geopolitics of the Global Energy Transition in the Middle East,' in M. Hafner and S. Tagliapietra (ed), The Geopolitics of the Global Energy Transition (Singapore: Springer, 2020). 116.

5 Ibid.

6 Ingram, Jamie, 'QatarEnergy Revenues Surge to Seven Year High,' Middle East Economic Survey, February 4, 2022. https://www.mees.com/2022/2/4/geopolitical-risk/qatar-export-revenues-surge-to-seven-year-high/f7845460-85d0-11ec-993b-910a64378c83.

7 Before October 2021, the official name of QatarEnergy was Qatar Petroleum. However, to avoid unnecessary confusion, this chapter uses the current name of the company.

8 Planning and Statistics Authority of Qatar, Qatar Economic Outlook. 2020–2022. (Doha: Planning and Statistic Authority of Qatar, 2019).

9 Mirzoev, Tokhir, and Ling Zhu (eds), *The Future of Oil and Fiscal Sustainability in the GCC Region* (Washington: International Monetary Fund, 2020).

10 In terms of per capita energy consumption, Qatar is almost twice as high as the United Arab Emirates, Kuwait, and KSA, which ranked second, third, and fourth in the region in 2018 (BP, *BP Statistical Review of World Energy, 2019*, London: British Petroleum, 2020, pp. 8, 12).

11 Byrne, Megan, 'Qatar Joins Solar Revolution with Al Kharsaah Start Up,' Middle East Economic Survey, July 29, 2022. https://www.mees.com/2022/7/29/power-water/qatar-joins-solar-revolution-with-al-kharsaah-start-up/95332d30-0f36-11ed-952a-2d7246524700.

12 Ibid.

13 BP, *BP Statistical Review of World Energy, 2019* (London: British Petroleum, 2020), pp. 12, 90.

14 Ackerman, Wayne, 'Qatar and Global LNG: Potential Pivot from Asia to Europe,' Middle East Institute, February 22, 2022. https://www.mei.edu/publications/qatar-and-global-lng-potential-pivot-asia-europe; Chapa, Sergio, 'Qatar Reclaims Crown from the U.S. as World's Top LNG Exporter,' Bloomberg, May 2, 2022. https://www.bloomberg.com/news/articles/2022-05-02/qatar-reclaims-crown-from-u-s-as-world-s-top-lng-exporter.

15 Ingram, Jamie, 'Qatar Retakes Position as No1 Global LNG Partner.' *The Middle East Economic Survey.* July 24, 2020. https://www.mees.com/2020/7/24/opec/qatar-retakes-position-as-no1-global-lng-exporter/31ce03f0-cdb1-11ea-af39-a55bdce6554b.

16 Cochrane, Paul, 'Supertanker State: How Qatar is Gambling its Future on Global Gas Dominance.' *The Middle East Eye*, July 2, 2020. https://www.middleeasteye.net/news/qatar-gas-lng-market-oil-prices-dominance.

17 Swing producer/swing supplier is a supplier with large spare producing capacities that can affect the situation at the markets through the change in commodity supply. See: https://www.arcenergyinstitute.com/defining-the-swing-producer/.

18 Çavuşoğlu, Esra, 'From Rise to Crisis: The Qatari Leadership.' *Turkish Journal of Middle Eastern Studies* 1(7), 2020: 86.

19 Ibid., 85.

20 Ingram, Jamie, 'Qatar 2018 Revenue Surge Finances Renewed Checkbook Diplomacy.' *Middle East Economic Survey*, February 1, 2019. https://www.mees.com/2019/2/1/geopolitical-risk/qatar-2018-revenue-surge-finances-renewed-checkbook-diplomacy/d72716c0-2635-11e9-a597-add92238b8b2.

21 Çavuşoğlu, 'From Rise to Crisis: The Qatari Leadership,' 90.

22 King, Llewellyn, 'Qatar Sees Green Role for LNG as World Gasps for More Energy.' *Forbes*, December 4, 2021. https://www.forbes.com/sites/

llewellynking/2021/12/04/qatar-sees-green-role-for-lng-as-world-gasps-for-more-energy/?sh=4aff7066601c.

23 Qarjouli, Asmahan, 'Qatar says it cannot fill Europe's gas supply alone amid Russia-Ukraine tensions.' DohaNews, February 2, 2022. https://dohanews.co/qatar-says-it-cannot-fill-europes-gas-supply-alone-amid-russia-ukraine-tensions/.

24 Mills, Andrew, and El Dahan, Maha, 'Qatar Seals 27-year LNG Deal with China as Competition Heats up.' Reuters, November 21, 2022. https://www.reuters.com/business/energy/qatarenergy-signs-27-year-lng-deal-with-chinas-sinopec-2022-11-21/.

25 Zhdannikov, Dmitry, 'Qatar seeks EU guarantees emergency gas stays within EU.' *Reuters,* January 31, 2022. https://www.reuters.com/business/energy/exclusive-qatar-seeks-eu-guarantees-emergency-gas-stays-within-eu-source-2022-01-31/.

26 Ibid.

27 Byrne, Megan, 'QatarEnergy and Conoco Phillips Sign Deal to Supply Germany with LNG.' Middle East Economic Survey, December 2, 2022. https://www.mees.com/2022/12/2/corporate/qatarenergy-and-conocophillips-sign-deal-to-supply-germany-with-lng/d5bb0170-7248-11ed-8440-7d1c9ee4b388.

28 The U.S. shale revolution is a term marking the beginning of the active use of the combination of hydraulic fracturing, horizonal mining, and seismic technologies that allowed the United States to substantially increase the production of shale oil and gas in the late 2000s and 2010s, subsequently turning the country into one of the world's largest producers and exporters of hydrocarbons.

29 IMF assessments.

30 Cochrane, Paul, 'Supertanker State: How Qatar is Gambling its Future on Global Gas Dominance.' *The Middle East Eye,* July 2, 2020. https://www.middleeasteye.net/news/qatar-gas-lng-market-oil-prices-dominance.

31 MEES, 'Korea 1H20 LNG Imports: Qatar Volumes Fall 24% as Australia Closes Gap to Top Supplier.' *The Middle East Economic Survey,* July 17, 2020. https://www.mees.com/2020/7/17/selected-data/korea-1h20-lng-imports-qatar-volumes-fall-24-as-australia-closes-gap-to-top-supplier/445bcf20-c836-11ea-a60c-c59137220e53.

32 MEES, 'Taiwan 1H20 LNG Imports: Qatar Volumes Rise 11% in 1H2020 but Share Down Marginally as Taiwan Diversifies Suppliers.' *The Middle East Economic Survey,* July 17, 2020. https://www.mees.com/2020/7/17/selected-data/taiwan-1h20-lng-imports-qatar-volumes-rise-11-in-1h-2020-but-share-down-marginally-as-taiwan-diversifies-suppliers/55605ad0-c836-11ea-a79c-c757fd9b17ad.

33 Ingram, Jamie, 'Bahrain Advances Development of Huge Unconventional Reserves.' *The Middle East Economic Survey,* May 29, 2020. https://www.mees.

com/2020/5/29/oil-gas/bahrain-advances-development-of-huge-unconventional-reserves/88152130-a1ae-11ea-b099-934732bc3e53.

34 Ingram, Jamie, 'Kuwait Risks Exhausting Financial Reserves.' *The Middle East Economic Survey*, May 15, 2020. https://www.mees.com/2020/5/15/news-in-brief/kuwait-risks-exhausting-financial-reserves/be312a90-96bf-11ea-9894-7d512e4a1b26.

35 Azhar, Saeed, 'Aramco to Cut Capital Spending Over Coronavirus; 2019 Profits Plunge.' *Reuters*, March 15, 2020. https://www.reuters.com/article/us-saudi-aramco-results/aramco-to-cut-capital-spending-over-coronavirus-2019-profits-plunge-idUSKBN21208C; Bousso, Ron, 'Qatar Petroleum to Slash Spending by 30%.' *Reuters*, May 21, 2020. https://www.reuters.com/article/us-qp-spending/qatar-petroleum-to-slash-spending-by-30-ceo-idUSKBN22X2HA.

36 Podymov, Andrey, 'Gazoviy Katar [Qatar of Gas].' *Voyennoye Obozreniye*, June 3, 2020. https://topwar.ru/171776-gazovyj-katar-sovsem-ne-chert-iz-tabakerki.html.

37 Ackerman, Wayne, 'Qatar and Global LNG: Potential Pivot from Asia to Europe.' Middle East Institute, February 22, 2022. https://www.mei.edu/publications/qatar-and-global-lng-potential-pivot-asia-europe.

38 Cockayne, James, 'Qatar and Oman Cash in as Asian LNG Buyers See Record Import Bill Even as Volumes Slump.' Middle East Economic Survey, July 29, 2022. https://www.mees.com/2022/7/29/opec/qatar-oman-cash-in-as-asian-lng-buyers-see-record-import-bill-even-as-volumes-slump/c51248c0-0f33-11ed-ba1e-31f3c9f8b155.

39 Al-Tamimi, Nasser, *Navigating Uncertainty: Qatar Response to the Global Gas Boom* (Qatar: Doha Brookings Center, 2015).

40 GIIGNL, *Annual Report, 2020* (Paris: International Group of Liquified Natural Gas Importers, 2020).

41 Ingram, Jamie, 'Qatar Brings Major Players into LNG Expansion.' Middle East Economic Survey, June 24, 2022. https://www.mees.com/2022/6/24/corporate/qatar-brings-major-players-into-lng-expansion/ccc547a0-f3b6-11ec-b3ef-f9e8b796d0a2.

42 Slav, Irina, 'Demand uncertainty could keep oil from breaking $100 – Oil & Gas Middle East.' *Oil and Gas Middle East*, November 18, 2021. https://www.oilandgasmiddleeast.com/news/demand-uncertainty-could-keep-oil-from-breaking-100; Widdershoven, Cyril, 'The Energy Transition Will Be Impossible Without Fossil Fuels.' *OilPrice*, November 18, 2021. https://oilprice.com/Energy/Energy-General/The-Energy-Transition-Will-Be-Impossible-Without-Fossil-Fuels.html.

43 Widdershoven, Cyril, 'The Energy Transition Will Be Impossible Without Fossil Fuels.'

44 McKinsey, 'Global Oil Supply-and-demand Outlook to 2040,' *Energy Insights*, February 2021. https://www.mckinsey.com/industries/oil-and-gas/our-insights/global-oil-supply-and-demand-outlook-to-2040.

45 Rystad Energy, 'Breakeven Price For New Oil Projects Drops In 2021.' *OilPrice*, November 17, 2021. https://oilprice.com/Energy/Crude-Oil/ Breakeven-Price-For-New-Oil-Projects-Drops-In-2021.html.

46 Zaremba, Haley, 'The Real Reason Big Oil Is Refusing To Boost Production.' OilPrice, November 18, 2021. https://oilprice.com/Energy/Energy-General/ The-Real-Reason-Big-Oil-Is-Refusing-To-Boost-Production.html.

47 'Climate Change Mitigation.' QatarEnergy, 2022. https://www.qatarenergy.qa/ en/Sustainability/Pages/ClimateChangeMitigation.aspx.

48 Ingram, Jamie, 'Qatar Launches "World's Largest" Blue Ammonia Project', Middle East Economic Survey, September 2, 2022. https://www.mees. com/2022/9/2/refining-petrochemicals/qatar-launches-worlds-largest-blue- ammonia-project/dcc199b0-2ab0-11ed-a8a5-913ffd3e63d0.

49 Byrne, Megan, 'QatarEnergy Awards Contract for Two New Solar Plants.' Middle East Economic Survey, August 22, 2022. https://www.mees. com/2022/8/26/power-water/qatarenergy-awards-contract-for-two-new- solar-plants/25b5c950-2532-11ed-8c2e-335c44bd78ff.

50 Paraskova, Tsvetana, 'An Undisputable Truth: The World Still Needs Oil And Gas.' *OilPrice,* November 16, 2021. https://oilprice.com/Energy/ Energy-General/An-Undisputable-Truth-The-World-Still-Needs-Oil- And-Gas.html.

51 Byrne, Megan, 'Qatar's Al Kharsaah Solar PV Plant Poised For Startup.' Middle East Economic Survey, April 8, 2022. https://www.mees. com/2022/4/8/power-water/qatars-al-kharsaah-solar-pv-plant-poised-for- startup/ed9e46c0-b736-11ec-920f-8d82a9909eba.

52 'QatarEnergy Launches Updated Sustainability Strategy, Reiterates to Produce Clean Energy.' Qatar Tribune, March 8, 2022. https://www.qatar- tribune.com/article/230723/BUSINESS/QatarEnergy-launches-updated- sustainability-strategy-reiterates-to-produce-clean-energy.

53 Rystad Energy, 'Breakeven Price For New Oil Projects Drops In 2021.' *OilPrice*, November 17, 2021. https://oilprice.com/Energy/Crude-Oil/ Breakeven-Price-For-New-Oil-Projects-Drops-In-2021.html.

9 RENEWABLE ENERGY DIPLOMACY: THE GULF STATES IN THE CAUCASUS AND CENTRAL ASIA

1 *Renewables 2022 Global Status Report* (2022). REN21. Paris: REN21 Secretariat, 37, 44.

2 ACWA (2021), *ACWA Power Annual Report 2020*. Riyadh: ACWA Power.

3   Fitch (2021), 'Fitch Publishes Abu Dhabi Future Energy Company PJSC'A+'
    IDRs; Outlook Stable.' Paris, Fitch Ratings.

4   Fitch (2021).

5   Azertag (2022), 'Qatari Nebras Power company keen on cooperation with
    Azerbaijan in construction of wind power plants in Lachin and Kalbajar
    districts.' Azertag, February 21, 2022. https://azertag.az/en/xeber/Qatari_
    Nebras_Power_company_keen_on_cooperation_with_Azerbaijan_in_
    construction_of_wind_power_plants_in_Lachin_and_Kalbajar_
    districts-2022854. Accessed May 5, 2022.

6   Dadlani, Disha (2020), 'ACWA Power inks three deals for Azerbaijan IPP.'
    Construction Week Middle East, December 30, 2020. https://www.
    constructionweekonline.com/projects-tenders/269838-acwa-power-inks-
    deals-for-azerbaijan-ipp. Accessed May 5, 2022.

7   Rahman, Fareed (2021), 'Masdar signs deal to develop $200m solar project in
    Azerbaijan.' *The National*, April 7, 2021. https://www.thenationalnews.com/
    business/energy/masdar-signs-deal-to-develop-200m-solar-project-in-
    azerbaijan-1.1198934. Accessed May 5, 2022.

8   Nebras (2021), Pioneering Future Energy. Nebras. 9.

9   Alexander, Kristian, and Giorgio Cafiero (2020), *The UAE's Growing Role in
    Central Asia: Geopolitical Inroads to Challenge Turkey and Iran.* Ljubljana:
    International Institute for Middle East and Balkan Studies; Berdikeeva,
    Saltanat (2020), 'Saudi Arabia's Growing Influence in Central Asia.' Inside
    Arabia, April 10, 2020. https://insidearabia.com/saudi-arabias-growing-
    influence-in-central-asia/; Ikromov, Shavkat (2020), 'Mosque Diplomacy in
    Central Asia: Geopolitics Beginning with the Mihrab.' Voices on Central Asia,
    December 16, 2020. https://voicesoncentralasia.org/mosque-diplomacy-in-
    central-asia-geopolitics-beginning-with-the-mihrab/; Wastnidge, Edward
    (2020), *Central Asia and the Iran-Saudi rivalry.* Washington DC, POMEPS
    Studies 38: The Project on Middle East Political Science. https://pomeps.org/
    central-asia-and-the-iran-saudi-rivalry.

10 Bianco, Cinzia (2020), 'The GCC Monarchies: Perceptions of the Iranian
    Threat amid Shifting Geopolitics.' *The International Spectator* 55 (2): 92=107;
    Maziad, Marwa, and Jake Sotiriadis (2020), 'Turkey's Dangerous New
    Exports: Pan-Islamist, Neo-Ottoman Visions and Regional Instability.'
    Middle East Institute. https://www.mei.edu/publications/turkeys-dangerous-
    new-exports-pan-islamist-neo-ottoman-visions-and-regional.

11 Cook, Steven, and Hussein Ibish (2017). *Turkey and the GCC: Cooperation
    Amid Diverging Interests.* Washington D.C.: The Arab Gulf States Institute in
    Washington. https://agsiw.org/wp-content/uploads/2017/02/GCCTurkey_
    ONLINE-2.pdf. 8.

12 Peyrouse, Sebastien, and Sadykzhan Ibraimov (2010), 'Iran's Central Asia
    Temptations.' *Current Trends in Islamist Ideology* 9: 87–101.

13 Al-Sulami, Mohammed (2021), 'Arab world should respond to Iran's Central Asia outreach.' Arab News, December 6, 2021. https://www.arabnews.com/node/1981891.

14 Buzan, Barry (1982), *People, States & Fear: The National Security Problem in International Relations*. Chapel Hill: The University of North Carolina Press; Gause, Gregory (2010), *The International Relations of the Persian Gulf*. Cambridge: Cambridge University Press.

15 Ziadah, Rafeef (2017), 'Constructing a logistics space: Perspectives from the Gulf Cooperation Council.' Environment and Planning D: Society and Space 36 (4): 666–682. https://journals.sagepub.com/doi/10.1177/0263775817742916; Mogielnicki, Robert (2021), *A Political Economy of Free Zones in Gulf Arab States*. London: Palgrave.

16 Cited by Foxman, Simone (2021), 'Qatar Criticizes Nations for Making Vague Net-Zero Pledges.' Bloomberg, October 11, 2021. https://www.bloomberg.com/news/articles/2021-10-11/qatar-criticizes-nations-making-net-zero-pledges-without-a-plan.

17 ICG (2019), 'Intra-Gulf competition in Africa's Horn: Lessening the Impact.' Brussels, International Crisis Group, September 19, 2019. https://www.crisisgroup.org/middle-east-north-africa/gulf-and-arabian-peninsula/206-intra-gulf-competition-africas-horn-lessening-impact; Bianco, Cinzia (2020), 'Gulf Monarchies and the Eastern Mediterranean: Growing Ambitions.' European Council on Foreign Relations. https://ecfr.eu/special/eastern_med/gcc; Saouli, Adham, ed. (2020), *Unfulfilled Aspirations: Middle Power Politics in the Middle East*. Oxford: Oxford University Press. https://academic.oup.com/book/32019.

18 Sim, Li-Chen (2022), 'Renewable Power Policies in the Arab Gulf States.' Middle East Institute, February 8, 2022. https://www.mei.edu/publications/renewable-power-policies-arab-gulf-states.

19 Hashimoto, Kohei, Jareer Elaas, and Stacy Eller (2004), 'Liquefied Natural Gas from Qatar: The Qatargas Project.' Stanford, James A Baker III Institute for Public Policy of Rice University, May 26, 2004. https://www.bakerinstitute.org/research/liquefied-natural-gas-from-qatar-the-qatargas-project; Davidson, Christopher M. (2005), *The United Arab Emirates: A Study in Survival*. Boulder: Lynne Reiner. https://www.rienner.com/title/The_United_Arab_Emirates_A_Study_in_Survival.

20 Karasik, Theodore (2020), 'Saudi Support of Cyprus Key as Tempers Flare in Mediterranean.' Arab News, January 23, 2020. https://www.arabnews.com/node/1617236; Guzansky, Yoel, and Gallia Lindenstrauss (2021), 'The Growing Alignment Between the Gulf and the Eastern Mediterranean.' Middle East Institute, May 25, 2021. https://www.mei.edu/publications/growing-alignment-between-gulf-and-eastern-mediterranean; Gulf News (2022), 'Abu Dhabi's ADQ to pump 4b euros into Greece's economy. Gulf News, May 9, 2022. https://gulfnews.com/business/abu-dhabis-adq-to-pump-4b-euros-into-greeces-economy-1.1652116728664.

21 Solargis (2020), 'Global Solar Atlas 2.0: Azerbaijan.' World Bank/ESMAP.

```

**22** Balmaceda, Margarita M. (2008), *Energy Dependency, Politics and Corruption in the Former Soviet Union: Russia's Power, Oligarchs' Profits, and Ukraine's Missing Energy Policy, 1995–2006*. London; Routledge; Francisco, Ellennor (2014), *Petroleum Politics: China and its National Oil Companies*. Paris: SciencesPo, September 2014. https://www.sciencespo.fr/ceri/fr/content/dossiersduceri/petroleum-politics-china-and-its-national-oil-companies; Aalto, Pami Kullervo, Heino Nyyssönen, Matti Kojo, and Pallavi Pal (2017). 'Russian nuclear energy diplomacy in Finland and Hungary.' *Eurasian Geography and Economics*, 58 (4): 386–417; Babic, Milan, Javier Garcia-Bernardo and Eelke M. Heemskerk (2020), 'The rise of transnational state capital: state-led foreign investment in the 21st century.' *Review of International Political Economy* 27 (3): 433–475.

**23** MacKellar, Landis, Andreas Wörgötter and Julia Wörz (2002), 'Economic Growth of Landlocked Countries,' in *Ökonomie in Theorie Und Praxis*, G. Chaloupek, A. Guger, E. Nowotny, and G. Schwödiauer (eds). Berlin, Springer: 213–226; Arvis, Jean-François, Gael Raballand, and Jean-François Marteau (2007), *The Cost of Being Landlocked: Logistics Costs and Supply Chain Reliability*. Washington, D.C.: The World Bank. https://openknowledge.worldbank.org/handle/10986/7420.

**24** Vakulchuk, Roman, and Indra Overland (2021), 'Central Asia is a missing link in analyses of critical materials for the global clean energy transition.' *One Earth* 4 (2): 1678–1692. https://www.sciencedirect.com/science/article/pii/S2590332221006606.

**25** Kalantzakos, Sophia (2020), 'The Race for Critical Minerals in an Era of Geopolitical Realignments.' *The International Spectator* 55 (3): 1–16. https://www.tandfonline.com/doi/full/10.1080/03932729.2020.1786926; Vakulchuk and Overland (2021).

**26** Tavsan, Sinan (2021), 'Middle East players move to detente as U.S. turns focus on China.' *Nikkei Asia*, December 1, 2021. https://asia.nikkei.com/Politics/International-relations/Indo-Pacific/Middle-East-players-move-to-detente-as-U.S.-turns-focus-on-China; Young, Michael (2022), 'Big Diplomatic Moves Show a Middle East Bracing for an Iran Nuclear Deal.' *The National*, March 30, 2022. https://www.thenationalnews.com/opinion/comment/2022/03/30/a-new-approach-among-arab-states-in-the-backdrop-of-a-likely-nuclear-deal/.

**27** Kavalski, Emilian (2012), *Central Asia and the Rise of Normative Powers*. London, Bloomsbury Press; Fawn, Rick (2021), '"Not here for geopolitical interests or games": the EU's 2019 strategy and the regional and inter-regional competition for Central Asia.' *Central Asian Survey*, August 17, 2021. https://www.tandfonline.com/doi/full/10.1080/02634937.2021.1951662; Kazantsev, Andrei, Svetlana Medvedeva, and Ivan Safranchuk (2021), 'Between Russia and China: Central Asia in Greater Eurasia.' *Journal of Eurasian Studies* 12 (1): 57–71. https://journals.sagepub.com/doi/full/10.1177/1879366521998242.
```

28 Thomson, Ian, and Robert G. Boutilier (2011), 'Social license to operate,' in *SME Mining Engineering Handbook*, ed. P. Darling. Littleton, Colorado: Society for Mining, Metallurgy and Exploration.

29 ACWA (2021), *ACWA Power Annual Report 2020*. Riyadh: ACWA Power, 70; Nebras Power (2021), *Annual Report 2020*. Doha: Nebras Power, 54–63; Masdar (2022), *Annual Sustainability Report 2021*. Abu Dhabi: Masdar, 23.

30 *Cluster Evaluation: Solar Power Operations (2022)*, London, European Bank for Reconstruction and Development. 101. https://www.ebrd.com/documents/comms-and-bis/cluster-evaluation-solar-power-operations.pdf.

31 AECOM (2021), *Environmental and Social Impact Assessment: 100 MW Solar PV Plant by Navoi in Uzbekistan*. Edinburgh: AECOM, 206.

32 ACWA (2021), *ACWA Power Annual Report 2020* 70.

33 5 Capitals (2022), 'Uzbekistan: ACWA Power Bash Wind Project,' 5 Capitals Environmental and Management Consulting.

34 Dalbaeva, Alina (2018), 'End the Weaponisation of Water in Central Asia.' International Crisis Group, March 15, 2018. https://www.crisisgroup.org/europe-central-asia/central-asia/kazakhstan/end-weaponisation-water-central-asia; Schuster, Kimberly (2018), *Blue Gold: Water Management is Key to Central Asia's Future*. Washington, D.C.: Center for Strategic & International Studies, October 17, 2018. https://www.csis.org/npfp/blue-gold-water-management-key-central-asias-future.

35 Orange, Richard (2010), 'WikiLeaks: Kazakh billionaire who bought Duke of York's home has "avarice for large bribes".' *The Telegraph*, December 1, 2010. https://www.telegraph.co.uk/news/worldnews/wikileaks/8170767/WikiLeaks-Kazakh-billionaire-who-bought-Duke-of-Yorks-home-has-avarice-for-large-bribes.html.

36 Reuters (2022), 'Kazakh govt recalls bill on $6 bln UAE energy deal from parliament.' Reuters, January 12, 2022. https://www.reuters.com/business/energy/kazakh-govt-recalls-bill-6-bln-uae-energy-deal-parliament-2022-01-12/.

37 Gartner (2021), *The ESG Imperative: 7 Factors for Finance Leaders to Consider*. London: Gartner; GTR (2021), 'ESG in the Middle East: moving from government priority to standard practice.' Global Trade Review. https://www.gtreview.com/supplements/gtr-mena-2021/esg-middle-east-moving-government-priority-standard-practice/.

38 Mouraviev, Nikolai (2021), 'Renewable energy in Kazakhstan: Challenges to policy and governance.' *Energy Policy* 149; World Bank (2021), 'The Worldwide Governance Indicators,' World Bank.

39 Ritchie, Hannah, and Matt Roser (2020), 'Emissions by sector.' ourworldindata.org.

40 The Economist, (2019), 'Which nation improved the most in 2019?' *The Economist*. https://www.economist.com/leaders/2019/12/21/which-nation-improved-the-most-in-2019.

41 World Bank (2021), 'The Worldwide Governance Indicators,' World Bank.

42 World Bank (2015), *Doing Business 2015*. Washington. D.C.: World Bank; World Bank (2019), *Doing Business 2019*. Washington, D.C.: World Bank.

43 Fitch (2022), Fitch Ratings.

44 ESMAP (2020), *Global Photovoltaic Power Potential by Country*. Washington D.C.: World Bank; BloombergNEF (2021), 'Climatescope,' Bloomberg.

45 IRENA (2021), *Statistical Profiles*. Abu Dhabi: International Renewable Energy Agency.

46 Minenergy (2019), 'Concept Note for ensuring electricity supply in Uzbekistan in 2020–2030,' Tashkent, Ministry of Energy of the Republic of Uzbekistan; ACWA (2021), *ACWA Power Annual Report 2020*. Riyadh: ACWA Power.

47 BloombergNEF (2021). 'Climatescope,' Bloomberg.

48 IRENA (2021), *Statistical Profiles*. Abu Dhabi: International Renewable Energy Agency; TI (2021), *Corruption Perceptions Index*. Berlin: Transparency International.

49 World Bank (2014), *Electric Power Transmission and Distribution Losses (% of output)*. Washington, D.C.: World Bank.

50 Peyrouse, Sebastien (2009), 'The Central Asian power grid in danger?' The Central Asia-Caucasus Analyst.

51 PwC (2021), *Renewable Energy Market in Kazakhstan: Potential, Challenges, and Prospects*. Almaty: PricewaterhouseCoopers, 22.

52 IEA/CCFI (2020), *Energy Investing Exploring Risk and Return in the Capital Markets*. London: International Energy Agency and the Centre for Climate Finance & Investment at Imperial College Business School.

53 Tsai, I-Tsung (2018), 'Political economy of energy policy reforms in the Gulf Cooperation Council: Implications of paradigm change in the rentier social contract.' *Energy Research & Social Science* 41: 89–96.

54 Qatar Tribune (2019), 'QEWC aims to generate 40% profit from Nebras Power: MD.' Qatar Tribune.

55 ACWA (2022), *ACWA Power FY2021 Financial Results: Earnings Call Presentation.* Riyadh: ACWA Power, 2, 6.

56 ACWA (2021), ACWA Power Highlights.

57 MTAD (2020), 'Announcement on pre-qualification process for utility-scale solar photovoltaic Ayg-1 project in Armenia.' Yerevan, Armenia Renewable Resources and Energy Efficiency Fund, Ministry of Territorial Administration & Infrastructure.

58 Sim, Li-Chen (2020), 'Low-carbon energy in the Gulf: Upending the rentier state?' *Energy Research & Social Science* 70; Al-Sulayman, Faris (2021), *Rethinking State Capitalism in the Gulf States: Insights from the China-focused Literature*. Riyadh: King Faisal Center for Research and Islamic Studies.

59 Saur Energy (2022), 'The Top 5: Biggest Exporters of Electricity in the World,' Saur Energy.

60 Babic, Garcia-Bernardo and Heemskerk (2020), 14; Kumar, Nirmalya, and Jan-Benedict E. M. Steenkamp (2016), 'Emerging nations need national champions, and national champions need strong support from the state.' *Asian Management Insights* 3. https://ink.library.smu.edu.sg/ami/16/; Clemons, Steve (2019), 'Time for America to support its own national champions?' *The Hill*, July 9, 2019. https://thehill.com/opinion/ finance/452213-time-for-america-to-support-its-own-national-champions/. Braw, Elisabeth (2021), 'The West Needs Champions.' *Foreign Policy*, March 4, 2021. https://foreignpolicy.com/2021/03/04/the-west-needs-champions/; Reed, Ed (2021), 'Saipem teams up with Aramco for new national champion.' *Energy Voice*, September 21, 2021. https://www.energyvoice.com/oilandgas/ middle-east/351209/saipem-aramco-epc-champion/.

61 IMF (2022), 'Fostering Private Sector Led Growth in MENA: A New Role for the State' (prepared for Annual Meeting of Arab Finance Deputies), Washington, D.C., International Monetary Fund.

62 Hsu, Po-Hsuan, Hao Liang and Pedro Matos (2020), *Leviathan Inc. and Corporate Environmental Engagement*. ECGI Working Paper Series in Finance. Brussels: European Corporate Governance Institute.

63 ACWA (2021). ACWA Power Highlights.

INDEX

Abdulaziz bin Salman Al Saud
      (Prince, Saudi Arabia) 18
ACWA Power (Saudi Arabia)
      in CCA 240, 241f–242f, 249–250,
            253
      founding of 239
      in MENA 103f, 104f, 105f
      in Oman 134, 135
      PIF, partnership with 96, 127,
            137–138, 140–141, 239
      preferential treatment 280 n.57
ADNOC (Abu Dhabi National Oil
      Company UAE)
      blue ammonia exports 21
      oil production 72, 81, 250
      partnerships NOC-IOC, 65–66,
            67–68, 75–78
Africa, North, *see* North Africa
agricultural industry, *see* fertilizer
      production
Algeria
      China's role in 195
      debt profile 114f
      green hydrogen industry 184,
            193–196, 198–199
      hydrocarbon dependence 91f
      power supply 172, 193
Al-Ula summit (GCC) 37
ammonia, definition 270 n.8
      see also blue ammonia; green
            ammonia
Aramco, *see* Saudi Aramco
Armenia 242f, 243f, 246, 252, 253
Azerbaijan 240, 242f, 246, 251, 252

Baerbock, Annalena 189
Bahrain

bonds and Sukuk 30f, 98f
      COVID response 24, 27, 29
      fiscal and economic data 11f, 12f,
            56f–58f, 91f, 114f
      fossil fuel reserve levels 9f, 147
      GDP trends 28f, 220f
      revenues and spending 9f, 13f, 15,
            23f, 33f, 269 n.4
      tax laws 32–33, 35
banks
      COVID, response to 19, 24, 25–26
      energy financing role 113–115,
            135, 138–139
batteries 176, 177, 185
Belt and Road Initiative (BRI, China)
            134, 139, 156, 253
blended finance (BF) 88, 102, 108,
            108f
blockchains 116–117
Bloomberg projections 16
blue ammonia, 20–21, 228
blue finance 88, 97, 100
blue hydrogen 76, 185, 193, 195
bonds and Sukuk
      definitions 96, 270 n.13, 275 n.2
      economic recovery 27, 29–31
      green and blue assets 96–100
      green bond growth 92–94
      issuances 27, 30f, 31
      sustainability bond issuances
            93f–94f, 98f–99f
Brent oil prices 11, 14–16, 16f,
            54f–63f, 269 n.1

capital markets 88, 92, 93f–94f,
      96–102, 116
      see also climate investments

carbon markets 116–117
CCA (Caucasus and Central Asia)
  energy markets in 250–255
  geopolitics and GCC 244–247,
    254–255
  renewable energy projects
    238–240, 241f–243f, 244
  social license to operate 248–250
CCE (circular carbon economy) 10,
  20–21, 140
CCGT (combined-cycle gas turbine)
  power plants 240
CCS (carbon capture and storage) 76,
  229
CCUS (carbon capture, utilization,
  and storage) 10, 20, 21
Central Asia, see CCA (Caucasus and
  Central Asia)
Central Asian Power System (CAPS)
  252
China
  BRI 156, 253
  energy imports 37–38, 155
  GCC, relations with 139–140
  Oman and 128, 134
  Qatar and 78, 217, 224–225
  role in MENA 103f, 155, 156–158,
    195
  Saudi Arabia and 73, 75, 137
  solar cell manufacturing 140
China-GCC Free Trade Area (FTA)
  139
circular carbon economy (CCE) 10,
  20–21, 140
Clean Technology Fund (CTF) 108,
  109f, 110f
climate change
  energy demands and 17–20,
    166–167
  financial impacts 114–115
  local solutions and DNS 116–117
  as threat multiplier 101f
climate investments 95–102, 111–120
  see also finance structures
combined-cycle gas turbine (CCGT)
  power plants 240

commodity prices 10–11, 111–112,
  112f, 266
concessional finance 102
COP27 (U.N. Framework
  Convention on Climate
  Change) 87–88, 191
COVID-19 pandemic (2020)
  fiscal response 27–31
  GCC fiscal response 8–10, 11,
    21–27
  GCC tax and labor reforms 32–37
  impact on GCC's total GDP 22
  impacts on oil and gas
    investments 111–112
  LNG market, impacts on 222–223
  see also oil price shock (2020)

decarbonization, see economic
  diversification; energy
  transition
demand growth, energy 18–19,
  165–167, 226–227, 230, 251
demand shock, see oil price shock
  (2020)
Development Agenda 2030
  (international) 151–152
development finance institutions
  (DFIs) 87, 102–103, 108f
diversification, see economic
  diversification; energy
  transition
DNS (debt-for-nature swaps) 88,
  116–118
  see also climate investments

economic diversification
  challenges 159–160
  drivers for 126–127, 152
  impacts of 11–13, 150–151
  political aspects 147–150
  power grid interconnectivity
    173–174
  trends in 151–153
Egypt
  China's role in 156
  climate finance 104f, 110f, 111

debt profile 114f
green hydrogen industry 183, 184,
    191–193
natural gas industry 186–187
power grid interconnectivity 172,
    173
Eight Country Interconnection
    (EIJLLPST) 172
electric vehicles 167
electricity demand, *see* demand
    growth, energy; power grid
    capacity
electricity grid, *see* power grid
    capacity
energy crisis (1973-1974) 148–149
energy markets
    carbon markets 116–117
    COVID's effects on 222–223, 264
    demand projections 17–20, 18f,
        90, 147, 226–227
    foreign ownership 131–132
    geopolitical factors 148–150,
        244–247, 254–255, 264–265
    grid interconnections and
        172–173, 174
    market structure 8, 9f, 89–90,
        151–153, 209–211, 226–231
    oil importers *vs.* exporters 250,
        250f
    oil prices and 31, 266, 267–268
    security as driver 17, 168, 179
    shale producers' strategy 227
    see also energy transition; shale
        revolution (U.S.)
energy storage systems (ESS)
    175–179
    see also power grid capacity
energy transition
    carbon credits and blockchain 117
    challenges 113–115, 159–160,
        165–167, 263–264
    country commitments 168–169
    definition 210
    drivers for 125–127, 168, 180, 186
    finance mechanisms 87–89,
        111–113

GCC partnerships 74–75, 82,
    237–238
global trends 167–169
governance structures 115,
    141–142
political aspects 19, 147–150,
    153–158, 244–247, 264–268
political economy 139–141
privatization 127–129, 130–131
public sector 2, 92–94, 95–96
risk reduction 150–153
EOR (enhanced oil recovery) 20, 195
ESG (environmental, social, and
    governance) metrics 88, 90, 92,
    116, 248–249
ESS (energy storage systems)
    175–179
    see also power grid capacity
Eurasia, *see* Caucasus and Central
    Asia (CCA)
European countries
    Algerian partnership 194–195
    Egyptian partnership 191–193
    Qatar and LNG 78, 214–215,
        216–218
European Union (E.U.) 19–20, 174,
    183–184
Export Credit Agencies (ECAs)
    95–96

fertilizer production
    Algeria's industry 195–196,
        198–199
    green ammonia 187–191
    Morocco's industry 187–188,
        190–191
    in North Africa 184, 187, 198
    Tunisia's industry 197
finance structures
    blended finance 88, 102, 108, 108f
    climate funds 108–111
    concessional finance 102
    corporate *vs.* project finance 100,
        102
    DNS 116–118
    donors and grants 102

ESG-based repo 116
governance of 115
investments, bilateral and
multilateral 102–111
public sector 111–113
sustainable finance 88–89, 90–94,
139
targeted funds 119–120
taxation 8, 21, 32–37, 131, 132
financial crisis (2009) 15
fiscal breakeven oil prices
Brent vs. 14–16, 16f, 54f–63f
definition 269 n.3
economic impacts 250
hydrocarbon dependence 91f
fossil fuels
demand projections 17–20, 18f,
90, 226–227
offshore resources 69–70
reserves and sustainability
147–148
as stranded assets 114–115
fuel switching, see energy transition;
power mix

G20 (Group of Twenty) 20
Gaza and West Bank, debt profile
114f
GCC, see Gulf Cooperation Council
(GCC)
GCCIA (Gulf Cooperation Council
Interconnection Authority)
172
geopolitics
access to resources 153–154, 247
energy policies and 148–150,
159–160, 264–265
ESS deployment drivers and
limitations 177–178
of GCC-CCA relations 244–247,
254–255
political power structures
153–156
Saudi Arabia-Iran 157–158
Georgia 243f
geothermal energy 168

German National Hydrogen Strategy
188–189
Germany 133, 183–184, 189
gray hydrogen 185, 188
green ammonia 133–134, 184,
187–191
green hydrogen
Algeria and 194–195
Egypt and 191–193
Morocco and 188–189
production sector development
183–184, 198–199
transport of 187, 197
Tunisia and 196–198
UAE and 115f, 133
uses for 184–187
water scarcity and 190, 192, 196,
197
Green Morocco Plan (Plan Maroc
Vert, PMV) 190
greenwashing 97
Gulf Cooperation Council (GCC)
CCA, projects in 238–244,
249–250
CCA, rivalry in 244–246
China, relations with
139–140
COVID response 21–27
debt 27–31, 30f
development and diversification
strategies 1–2, 20–21, 141–142,
151–152
drivers for diversification 17–20,
125–127, 218
economic data 7–8, 9f, 11–13,
28f–29f, 54f–63f, 220f
economic diversification 8, 10,
151–153
energy markets 219, 221–223
fiscal policies 32–40
foreign investment in 32–35,
37–40
government spending 8, 13f,
16f, 23f
grid interconnectivity 172
gross official reserves 23f

hydrocarbon industry 10–17, 11f, 12f, 269 n.2
nationalism 17
partnerships, international 19–20, 65–67, 74–75
Gulf Crisis (Qatar-Bahrain Rift, 2017) 26, 37, 245, 271 n.19

Hawaii (U.S.), renewable energy model 179
Hollub, Vicki 76
hydrocarbons
    demand projections 17–20, 18f, 90, 226–227
    exports of 12f, 89–90, 91f, 193–194
    GDP and GCC reliance on 11–13, 269 n.2
    indicators, economic 9f
    revenues 11f, 12f
    as stranded assets 114–115
hydrogen
    blue hydrogen 76, 185, 193, 195
    gray hydrogen 185, 188
    see also green hydrogen
hydropower 168, 248–249, 252

ICMA (International Capital Market Association) 97, 275 n.2
IEA (International Energy Agency) 18, 93f–94f
independent power producers (IPPs) 97f, 132
inflation
    impacts on policy 19, 27, 218
    macroeconomics of 265–268
    role of public sector 111–112
initial public offerings (IPOs) 31, 271 n.16
international oil companies (IOCs) 65–67, 74–75, 82
IPOs (initial public offerings) 31, 270 n.15, 271 n.16
IPPs (independent power producers) 97f, 132

Iran
    in CCA 244, 245
    debt profile 114f
    détente with Turkey 247
    hydrocarbon dependence 91f
    Saudi Arabia and 157–158
Iraq 91f, 114f, 155, 170–173
Islamic Development Bank (IsDB) 120f
Islamic-compliant bonds, see bonds and Sukuk

Al-Jadaan, Mohammed 33
Japan 20–21, 77, 105f, 106f, 133
Jordan
    China's role in 156
    debt profile 114f
    energy transition 107f, 166, 168–169
    grid interconnectivity 172, 173

Al Kaabi, Saad 81, 224
Kafala System (GCC) 35
Karabakh War (2020) 245–246
Kazakhstan 249
Khalifa bin Hamad Al Thani (Emir, Qatar) 214
Kuwait
    COVID response 25
    debt 27, 29, 30f, 114f
    economic data 9f, 28f, 54f–55f, 220f
    energy policy 168
    gross official reserves 23f
    hydrocarbons and 11f, 12f, 91f
    power grid capacity 172
    revenues and spending 13, 13f, 23f
    tax laws 32, 35
Kyrgyzstan 244, 248–249

labor markets 32–37
Lebanon 114f, 170, 172
Libya 91f, 172
LNG (liquefied natural gas) 12–13, 19, 78, 218–226, 228

Maghreb Countries Interconnection 172

Malaysia 74, 221

Masdar (Abu Dhabi, UAE)
  growth as power developer 239–240
  renewable projects in CCA 241f–243f, 246, 248, 253–254
  renewable projects in MENA 105f, 107f, 115, 140, 141
  restructuring 77

MENA Blue (World Bank) 100

Middle East Green Initiative 140

Mohammad bin Salman Al Saud (Crown Prince, Saudi Arabia) 31, 33, 36, 131

Morocco
  climate finance recipient 106f, 110f, 111
  debt profile 114f
  energy strategy 168–169, 183, 184, 186, 188–189
  green ammonia and 187–191
  power grid 172, 177

national oil companies (NOCs) 65–67, 74–75, 82
  see also ADNOC (Abu Dhabi National Oil Company, UAE); QatarEnergy (QE); Saudi Aramco

natural gas 69, 188, 215, 218–226, 240
  see also LNG (liquefied natural gas)

Nebras Power (Qatar) 134, 140–141, 239–240, 249–250

NEOM (Saudi Arabia) 2, 21, 39, 117f, 133

net-zero initiatives 2, 18, 20, 117, 245

North Africa
  CTF interventions in 110f
  energy strategy 183–184
  green hydrogen sector development 184–187, 198–199

partnership, Europe-Egypt 191–193
partnership, Europe-Morocco 188–189

oil embargo (1973-1974) 148–149

oil industry, see energy markets; EOR (enhanced oil recovery)

oil price downturn (2014)
  fiscal response 31
  impacts of 90, 112f, 125–126, 134
  prices leading up to 14–16
  tax reforms 32

oil price shock (2020)
  energy markets and 226–227
  GCC fiscal response 8–10
  OPEC response to 14–15
  price surge 19, 209–210, 264
  Saudi-Russian relations and 269 n.1
  see also COVID-19 pandemic (2020)

oil shock (1973-1974) 148–149

Oman
  China's role in 128, 134
  COVID response 26, 27, 270 n.11
  debt 29–31, 30f, 114f
  drivers for diversification 126–127
  economic data 9f, 28f, 60f–61f, 220f
  energy policy 127–130, 133–135, 141–142
  finance structures 13f, 35, 132–135
  fiscal policy 23f, 132–135
  fossil fuel reserves 147
  grid infrastructure 129–130, 133
  hydrocarbons and 11f, 12f, 91f
  solar energy projects 128, 134, 135

OPEC (Organization of Petroleum Exporting Countries) 14–15, 148–149

OPEC+ agreement (2016) 16, 39

Palestine 172
Paris Agreement (2015) 17

Petrochemicals, *see* hydrocarbons
PIF (Public Investment Fund, Saudi
    Arabia)
    ACWA, partnership with 96, 127,
        137–138, 140–141, 239
    diversification projects 31, 36
    green bond sales 94f
pipelines
    challenges 187, 193–194, 197–198
    geopolitics 244
Plan Maroc Vert (Green Morocco
    Plan, PMV) 190
power grid capacity
    demand increase 166–167,
        179–180
    diversification challenges 168
    expansion and modernization
        169–171
    inertia and 284 n.19
    interconnectivity 171–174, 252
    rural electrification 129, 171, 175,
        178
    shortages 167, 240, 244
    stability and 165–166, 169–171,
        175–176
    storage systems 175–179
power mix
    CCE approach 10, 20–21, 140
    CCGT approach 240
    renewables portion in 168, 179,
        186
    supply stability 169–171, 175–176,
        180
    see also renewable energy projects,
        non-hydrogen
private sector
    challenges 113–115, 152–153
    climate investments 96–102
    development of 90, 183
public sector 95–96, 111–113
pumped hydro storage (PHS) 176,
    177

Qatar
    COVID response 24–25
    debt 27, 30f, 114f

development strategies 209–211,
    231–232
economic data 9f, 28f, 58f–59f,
    220f
energy market 91f, 212f, 219–222
energy policy 223–230
energy production and
    consumption 212, 213f, 293
    n.10
energy security 70, 215–218
exports, hydrocarbon 12f, 19, 78,
    211–215, 221f, 228
geopolitics and 154, 155
Gulf Crisis 26, 271 n.19
Nebras Power 134, 140–141,
    239–240, 249–250
revenues and spending 11f, 12f,
    13f, 23f
Saudi Arabia, relations with 214
shale revolution, impacts of
    218–226
solar energy projects 228
tax laws 34–35
Qatar Investment Authority (QIA)
    32, 214–215
Qatar Petroleum, *see* QatarEnergy
    (QE)
Qatar-Bahrain Rift (Gulf Crisis,
    2017) 26, 37, 245
QatarEnergy (QE)
    energy transition strategy 224,
        228–229, 232
    oil refining capacity 72
    partnerships, international 65,
        68–72, 78–80
Quincy Pact (Saudi Arabia-U.S.) 153

renewable energy projects, non-
    hydrogen
    GCC in CCA 248–255
    Hawaiian model 179
    MENA's potential 167–168
    trends 237–244
    see also power mix
rent-based economies, *see* energy
    markets

REPowerEU strategy (E.U.) 19
repurchase agreements ("repo") 116,
    276 n.17
rift, *see* Qatar-Bahrain Rift (Gulf
    Crisis, 2017)
risks, physical *vs.* transition 276 n.16
rural electrification 129, 171, 175, 178
Russia-Ukraine war (2022-) 1, 18, 19,
    78, 154-155, 215-218

Salman bin Abdulaziz Al Saud (King,
    Saudi Arabia) 25
Saudi Arabia
    carbon credits 117f
    COVID response 25, 270 n.9
    debt 27, 30f, 114f
    drivers for diversification 126-127
    economic data 9f, 23f, 28f,
        55f-56f, 220f
    energy market 155, 166
    energy project funding 103f-104f,
        105f, 107f
    energy strategy 36, 39, 130-132,
        141-142, 168
    finance structures 135-139
    fiscal policy 94f, 98f-99f, 135-139
    grid capacity 170, 172-173
    hydrocarbons and 11f, 12f, 91f
    National Infrastructure Fund
        119
    NEOM city 2, 21, 39, 117f, 133
    privatization in 136
    Qatar, relations with 214
    rapprochement with Iran 157-158
    revenues and spending 13f, 23f,
        33f, 265
    solar energy projects 96, 97f, 137,
        247
    tax laws 32-33, 34
    U.S., relations with 153-154
Saudi Aramco
    IPO funding 31, 271 n.16
    oil refining capacity 72
    partnerships, international 65,
        72-74, 80-81
    PIF and 31

Saudi Green Initiative (SGI, Saudi
    Arabia) 140-141
Scholz, Olaf 189
shale revolution (U.S.)
    definition 294 n.28
    impacts on GCC 153-154
    impacts on global markets
        218-219
    natural gas market, impacts on
        209, 218-226
    see also energy markets
Shari'a-compliant bonds, *see* bonds
    and Sukuk
social license to operate (SLO) 248,
    249-250
solar photovoltaic (PV) power
    challenges 170
    projects and potential for 126,
        240, 241f-243f, 248
sovereign wealth funds (SWFs) 22,
    269 n.6
Sukuk, *see* bonds and Sukuk
sustainable finance 88-89, 90-94,
    139, *see also* climate
    investments
Syria 172

Tajikistan 244
Tamim bin Hamad Al Thani (Emir,
    Qatar) 80
targeted funds 119-120
    see also climate investments
taxation 8, 21, 32-37, 131, 132
thermal energy 177
Trump, Donald 80
Tunisia 103f, 114f, 172, 196-198
Turkey 156, 172, 244, 245-246, 247
Turkmenistan 244

Ukraine conflict (2022-) 1, 18, 19, 78,
    154-155, 215-218
United Arab Emirates (UAE)
    China's role in 156
    COVID response 22, 24
    debt 30f, 114f
    economic conditions 15, 38f

economic data 9f, 28f, 59f–60f, 220f
economic growth 37–38
energy market 77, 93f–94f, 98f–99f
energy project financing 105f
foreign policy 246, 247
green hydrogen production 115f
gross official reserves 23f
hydrocarbons and 11f, 12f, 91f
partnerships, international 75–78
revenues and spending 23f
spending and revenues 13f, 33f
tax and labor laws 32–34, 35, 271 n.17
see also ADNOC (Abu Dhabi National Oil Company, UAE); Masdar (Abu Dhabi, UAE)
United Nations (U.N.) 87–88, 117, 191
United States (U.S.)
LNG industry 219, 221f
MENA policy 154, 247
Qatar and 80, 225–226
Saudi Arabia and 153–154
see also shale revolution (U.S.)
Uzbekistan
emerging markets in 251–253

IsDB impact investment fund 120f
renewable energy projects 240, 241f–242f
social license to operate 248
Turkey and 244

variable renewable energy (VRE) 169–171, 175–176
see also power grid capacity
Vision 2030 (Egypt) 93f
Vision 2030 (Qatar) 228–230
Vision 2030 (Saudi Arabia) 36, 39, 126, 131
Vision 2040 (Oman) 126, 270 n.12

water scarcity 190, 192, 196, 197
West Bank and Gaza, debt profile 114f
wind power projects
in CCA 241f–242f, 251, 252
challenges for 170
in North Africa 185–186
in Oman 134
World Bank 100, 265–268

Yemen 171, 173

Zakat 34, 271 n.18